Maria's Code

Maria's Code

CYNTHIA ENGELMANN

Copyright © 2023 Cynthia Emgelmann

The moral right of the author has been asserted.

Apart from any fair dealing for the purposes of research or private study, or criticism or review, as permitted under the Copyright, Designs and Patents Act 1988, this publication may only be reproduced, stored or transmitted, in any form or by any means, with the prior permission in writing of the publishers, or in the case of reprographic reproduction in accordance with the terms of licences issued by the Copyright Licensing Agency. Enquiries concerning reproduction outside those terms should be sent to the publishers.

Matador
Unit E2 Airfield Business Park,
Harrison Road, Market Harborough,
Leicestershire. LE16 7UL
Tel: 0116 279 2299
Email: books@troubador.co.uk
Web: www.troubador.co.uk/matador
Twitter: @matadorbooks

ISBN 978 1803135 519

British Library Cataloguing in Publication Data.
A catalogue record for this book is available from the British Library.

Printed and bound by CPI Group (UK) Ltd, Croydon, CR0 4YY
Typeset in 11pt Garamond by Troubador Publishing Ltd, Leicester, UK

Matador is an imprint of Troubador Publishing Ltd

Dedicated to the victims and survivors
of the Hidden Polish Holocaust.

INTRODUCTION

The backdrop to Maria's memoir is a hidden Holocaust.

Poland submitted evidence of war crimes against the Polish nation to the Nuremberg Trials in 1945. It was rejected by Stalin who claimed that it was 'fragmented and unreliable' and he had much to conceal, for he too had persecuted the Poles. Surrounded by the debris of the conflict, the British and Americans ceded to Stalin's demands.

Hence, no Polish witnesses were called to give evidence at the trial and the voice of the nation was effectively silenced. Forty-eight years of Russian occupation followed and the Polish voice remained gagged.

Finally, in 1992, the last of the Russian occupying forces left Polish soil. At last, for the Poles, WWII was over. Emerging from their political isolation, they discovered that the Holocaust of the Jews occupied centre stage, while Poland lurked in the wings, enveloped in a mist of suspicion and whispers of collaboration and betrayal.

It would take time for the Polish nation to sort itself out. Two generations had been born since the end of WWII and those that could remember were grandparents and in their seventies. They had buried their memories deep and were loath to recall the horrors. Archives and libraries, having concealed documents during the occupation, were wary of sharing information. Adjacent regions had little idea about what had happened in the neighbouring area.

By 2021, several quarterly journals were discussing the details of the tragic events in Poland during the WWII period. They describe the Nazi regime of terror that Hitler's plan to reclaim the territories of West Prussia, allocated to Poland by the Treaty of Versailles, imposed on the Polish nation the methodical the ethnic cleansing to create 'lebensraum' (living space) for German settlers and the consequences that followed.

The Molotov Ribbentrop Pact was secret. Signed on 23rd August, 1939, it tied up the loose ends for Hitler's General Plan East, a plan known only to his closest cohorts. Primarily, it broke the non-aggression pact between Russia and Poland that should have lasted until 1943. According to the new agreement, Russia would support the Germans in the suppression of the Poles. Poland itself would be divided with Russia taking the eastern half and Germany, the western. The General Government, a north/south strip in the middle that included Warsaw and Cracow would be reserved for the Poles, with a German Gauleiter in charge. Further, Russia would return to German territory the ethnic Germans that had settled in the Baltic countries and elsewhere within her zone of influence.

The General Plan East is summed up by a speech made by Himmler at a meeting of concentration camp commandants in Posen on 15th March 1940. The report was submitted to the Nuremberg Trial. but buried by Stalin.

"It is essential that all our staff, men and women, should know that our chief and most important aim is to capture all the Polish leaders... so as to render them harmless. You, gentlemen, being in charge of the camps know best how to achieve this. All skilled workers of Polish origin will be utilised in our war industries. Then all Poles will disappear from the world. In the course of this responsible work, you must root out Polishness quickly and within the planned stages... It is essential that the great German people should regard it as its chief task – to destroy all Poles."

In a memorandum to Hitler the following month, Himmler noted "...I hope that we shall succeed in destroying the concept of 'Jew', as there exists the likelihood of a mass resettlement of Jews in Africa or some other colony." The Jews therefore, at that moment in time, were not the focus for extermination.

In 1941, the failure of Italy to procure control over the Suez Canal meant that egress by German transports from the Mediterranean to the east coast of Africa was blocked. It is possible that the dream of resettling the Jews on the African continent faded as fierce fighting ensued along her northern shores making the task of the resettlement of Europe's Jews nigh impossible. By the beginning of 1942, Africa was no longer an option and The Final Solution decision was made.

In the spring of 1939, a list of political 'undesirables' had been compiled in Germany. For Warsaw and the Central Government, it contained approximately 35,000 names of the elite, social leaders and intellectuals. For Posen (Poznań) and the New Reich Territories, the list contained 150,000 names. Not only were the above targeted but also the owners of property, albeit land, industrial, commercial or domestic, all to be arrested and executed immediately. By Christmas, the majority of those whose names were on the list were dead. The term 'political' referred solely to the Poles. Today the use of the term has become less specific.

The persecution had started immediately in the wake of the German rapid advance through Poland. In the small towns and villages, the arrestees named on the political list, were assembled in the central square and executed in public by firing squads. The bodies were then returned to their stunned and grieving families for burial. Thus, the mass grave that provides historical evidence, was avoided.

In a city where such actions would have caused considerable unrest, a different method was employed. There were two major prisons in Posen. Ordinary criminals were held in the civilian gaol. Breaking the curfew, carrying a stick (a weapon) in public or speaking Polish on the street, along with stealing a crust of bread were criminal offences and the prison rapidly became very overcrowded. A guillotine was introduced in June 1940 to resolve the problem. This primitive machine took 1,800 lives. The dismembered head rolled loose in the body bag when returned to its family for burial.

Fort VII became the city slaughterhouse for citizens of Posen whose names appeared on the political list.

At first, prisoners were hanged, ten at a time in the large reception cell and individuals were shot against a wall, having spent the previous night in the small cell opposite, contemplating the blood stains. They were also starved, deprived of water, beaten or worked to death in a series of bizarre 'experiments'. Barely a week after Poland surrendered, one of the bunkers on the roof of the Fort was rigged up as a gas chamber with a generator feeding carbon monoxide through a hole in the front wall. Among the first victims were all the children attending a school for the disabled. It was two hours before their screams subsided and a further half hour before the bunker fell totally silent.

In charge of the gassing facility, was H. Lange, a man who honed his craft in Fort VII. In 1941, he supplied the mobile gas units that followed the German advance into Russia and in 1942, he was consulted about the construction of the Auschwitz gas chambers.

Before the end of September 1939, the evictions started. In the wealthier areas of the city, a knock at the door after curfew, announced the arrival of the SS. Methodically, street by street, Polish families were evicted from their homes.

They were given fifteen minutes to gather essentials enough to fill a small suitcase and obliged to leave all valuables behind except their wedding ring and 20 zloty. They were then escorted to the main railway station to await transport eastwards in cattle trucks. The transports continued daily until May the following year (1940), Polish Jews and Christians travelling together, to Lichtmanstadt (Łódź) on the western border of the General Government. The deportations were only interrupted on 4th-5th January when, during a temperature drop to below -40C, the truck doors were rolled back to reveal that 90% of the cargo had frozen to death en route.

Lichtmanstadt (Lódz) was the last stop before entering the territory of the General Government. Here the arrivals were separated into groups. Men and grown male teenagers were assigned to a concentration camp, providing the slave labour that was the core of the miners and construction workers that built so many of the secret facilities for the German arms industry. None would survive the war as once a project was complete, security demanded that all workers should perish.

Jewish families were accommodated in the Łódź ghetto to await deportation out of Europe to a new homeland, wherever that might be.

Children with blue eyes and blonde hair were selected for the gene pool of the Children's Camp to await adoption by German couples.

The remainder, mothers with small children and the aged, were delivered into the General Government to manage as best they could. The influx of hundreds and thousands of homeless, desperate people into the region soon overwhelmed the efforts of the resident Poles who organised charities that supplied shelter and food.

The daily transports continued and the situation became critical. Even Hans Frank, the Gauleiter for the General Government pleaded with Hitler to call a halt to them. To no avail and it was the Poles themselves that eased the overcrowding, by abandoning their homeland, escaping over the southern border of the General Government and travelling on foot through the mountains of Czechoslovakia to Hungary. By early spring, the trickle had become an exodus of thousands. The journey was arduous and the cold and exhaustion took their toll on the elderly and very young. From Hungary, they continued south.

As the execution of political elite neared its conclusion, Fort VII became the prison for suspected members of the resistance and dissidents in general. They were political prisoners, a term used today that denies their Polish origins!

In April, 1943, the whole operation was moved to the Poggenburg camp near the village of Zabikowo, some 15 km from the city centre.

Introduction

The General Plan East is the backdrop to Maria's memoir and destiny decreed that she should survive to give evidence. The War Reparations Commission estimated that 6 million of her fellow countrymen perished, over half that number being the entire population of Polish Jews. Yet today it us known that 2,250,000 children died in camps and recently, America returned to Germany the files that they retrieved from concentration camps in 1945. There are seventeen million of them, each file holding a record of an individual slave labourer, some Jewish, some Roma, some homosexuals and paedophiles. The vast majority of the files however relate to Political prisoners from Poland, suggesting that the loss of 6,000,000 Polish citizens was a vast under-estimate.

Maria's Code includes two biographical accounts that are intrinsically related to each other. Maria's Story was the primary inspiration for Safari to Poland.

Shortly before she died in 1986, Maria gave the manuscript of her book to the author. After translation from German into English, the text revealed an extraordinary story about a young Polish dancer, her relationship with a German officer and her imprisonment in a camp called Poggenburg. Poggenburg at that time was untraceable, suggesting that the story was a dramatic work of fiction. The manuscript gathered dust for nearly a decade.

The quest to discover the truth behind Maria's story began when Norman Davies informed the author that Poggenburg was the German name for a camp that is now known as Zabikowo. He suggested that further information might be obtained by writing to the Zachodni Institute in Poznań.

Safari to Poland was born. In 1995, the author set out for Poland to meet dr. Marian Woźniak, the archivist at the Instytut Zachodni.

Initially, Maria's story was regarded as fictional by the archivist but gradually, he realised that the work was no fairy tale and that by investigating the leads that Maria gave, several mysteries about the camp were resolved. No prisoner had left such a full account of life in the camp and none had survived in the camp for as long as Maria and her mother. Did they collaborate with the Germans to protect themselves? The evidence available was inconclusive.

It took several applications to different German archives in order to uncover the military role of Maria's German officer. Persistence was rewarded. He turned out to be the crucial factor that made Maria's story possible.

Against the backdrop of the shifting sands of a country emerging from a 45-year occupation by the USSR, Safari to Poland describes a voyage of discovery into the past. Unintentionally, the author found herself part of a movement to collate historical facts about events in Poland that had lain hidden since WWII. In 1995, the pools of information, scattered around Poland were yet to yield the material that had been secreted away from prying eyes. Today, it is possible to find Fort VII and Zabikowo on the Internet and slowly, the Polish story has become less fragmented.

ACKNOWLEDGEMENTS

I am grateful to Norman Davies for firing the starting pistol by suggesting that I contact the Institut Zachodni in Poznań and to the president of the Institute for permitting an unknown westerner to venture into their substantial archive during the 1990s. I owe a great deal to the diligence and enthusiasm of the late dr. Marian Woźniak, and to his colleague Ludwik Misiek, President of the AK Society. I am also indebted to Dorota Latour and her family, the Augustynek family, Jurek Paczke and Ania Michaelska for their hospitality, generosity, encouragement and for their assistance in scaling a huge language barrier. Lisa Waite translated the original manuscript, called 'Liebes, Geliebtes Leben' and Patricia Wood insisted on deciphering and typing the mountain of handwritten notes that had accumulated over the years. And a big thank you to Lene Romann-Aas and Nasrin Zarriasateiny, who both financed my numerous visits to Poland by arranging the horse-riding clinics for me to instruct in Norway.

The contribution of them all is appreciated beyond measure.

Safari to Poland

1

1985

The phone had rung late in the evening. The message conveyed the news that Maria had collapsed and was dying.

"Please visit her. She is asking for you," the voice begged.

Belinda knew that she must agree. She made hasty arrangements to ensure that the children would be collected from school in the afternoon, and set out the following morning for north Buckinghamshire.

The directions to find the clinic proved to be accurate and two and a half hours later, she parked in a tree-lined avenue outside the gates of a low white building that exuded clinical correctness. The blonde receptionist greeted her with a cheerful smile.

"Maria Kurzke? – Ah yes, room sixteen." The smile remained stuck on her face. "Could you take a seat while I enquire whether it is convenient for you to see her?" she said, closing the register firmly.

"Thank you," said Belinda, becoming aware of the pristine order of the bright décor. She elected to sit in the corner of the sofa. A pile of magazines was stacked in front of her but she preferred to retreat into her own thoughts. Maria was dying; the cancer treatment had not worked. One of her technicolour friends was losing her grasp on life. During the ten years that they had known each other, so much had happened.

It had all started when Belinda had answered an advertisement regarding a horse for sale. She had phoned to be told by a foreign-sounding lady, that the owner was out, but if she would be good enough to leave her name and number, she would ring back that evening. The 'owner' did return her call; it was the same voice that had spoken earlier.

"Yes, you may come to try the horse." She was informed. It seemed that the owner of the voice had done some homework and had actually 'vetted'

Belinda. It appeared that her track record was familiar to this stranger and her CV duly approved. It was not normal to check out a customer before a viewing.

She went to see the horse, was knocked to the ground when it kicked her in the midriff, but subsequently bought the animal. She had also met the voice for the first time.

Her initial impression of Maria was that she had the appearance of a 'Smersch' agent. Her hair was dyed jet-black and cut in a shoulder-length pageboy style. The face of the middle-aged woman was puffy, with small grey eyes that seemed to seek and assess every movement in their focus. Belinda had felt naked.

But in that first encounter, they established a rapport. Maria had a certain panache about her that Belinda found intriguing. She also seemed to have a fathomless knowledge and understanding of horses.

Over the years, whenever there was a crisis in her life, Maria would reach for the phone and pour out her troubles to Belinda. One of her beloved horses had been slashed by an unknown person; her groom was threatening to leave; her landlord was pressing for money. There was always a major panic in the air. And then last year, a lump in her shoulder had been diagnosed as cancer. Maria convinced herself that the doctors were wrong and carried her lodestone in her pocket to protect her against such inconveniences. But the doctors had been right and now she was hospitalised in a private clinic. Maria herself was penniless, but she still had supportive friends.

Maria, who was in her mid-sixties, had been born in Poland. Since the day they met, Belinda had always known her as a colourful character. At times, she was belligerent and demanding, at others she seemed exceptionally kind and understanding. She had made few friends and many enemies. She was highly self-opinionated and this tended to easily upset acquaintances. But she was magic with animals, horses in particular. She understood and empathised with them as she would with small children.

Maria had taken Belinda's eight-year-old daughter under her wing and amidst much giggling and laughter, had taught her to vault on to her pony and stand on its back while it cantered around the riding school.

Now it was different. Her horses were gone and Maria herself was dying.

"Mrs White? Please come this way." The nurse had interrupted her reverie. Belinda grabbed her handbag, rose awkwardly to her feet and followed the sturdy figure along the corridor.

"B'linta, thank you for coming." Maria looked a long way from dead. Belinda had imagined finding her lying prone, but she was sitting upright with a broad grin on her face and a cigarette in her right hand.

"Maria you old toad, what are you doing – smoking!!" Belinda squeaked.

"Oh, that – they think I am dying, so I can do what I want. Would you like a drink?" She swept up a half empty bottle of whisky from the bedside table with her free hand and waved it at Belinda.

"You're crazy, woman!" gasped the astonished Belinda. "You're not supposed to do either of those things. How do you get away with it?" Maria's eyes twinkled mischievously.

"I make a nuisance if they take them away," she replied. "Everyone who visits brings me drink, and I only agree that when I smoke, the oxygen bottles are removed. You know, in case I make explosion!"

Belinda recognised that the fight had not abandoned her eccentric friend. She could still impose her will on those about her, even if they were paragons of health.

"Oh Maria, you don't change!" said Belinda and leant over the bed to embrace her sick friend.

Maria barely paused for breath before starting to issue orders. "You remember the little black horse?"

"Yeeees," replied Belinda, recalling the bundle of fury that she had watched one day as it had let rip with all four feet in its anxiety to get to the gate first.

"You must take him," Maria continued.

"Oh?" Belinda's mouth gaped.

"Yes! He has no home, the others are settled but he… he… nobody wants him!" There had still been four horses in the stables when she was taken ill.

"Please B'linta!" she pleaded. Belinda arrived at a decision.

"OK, I'll look after him until things get sorted out," she agreed.

"I'll pay you!" Maria offered.

"Don't worry about it. If it will make you happy, he's welcome for as long as necessary." Privately, Belinda had little faith in Maria's ability to pay anything. The cost of her room with its little ensuite bathroom would provide her with enough headaches for a while.

"And I want you to do a little job for me too."

'What next?' Belinda wondered.

"I need you to fetch some things from the flat before you go today."

Maria had given her several little jobs to do and it was late afternoon before Belinda returned with a package that she had collected along with several other necessities from Maria's flat. Tea was served and Maria unwrapped the brown paper from the parcel. The conversation had wandered in the direction of the Second World War. Maria was telling her something about a time in prison and a Gestapo death sentence.

Belinda began to get a little confused. Surely, if the Gestapo issued a death sentence, you were dead and not able to talk about it forty or so years later.

"B'linta! I want to give you my book. Yes, I have written it – many years ago now. I have tried to get it published after the war, but they said I had to make the sexy bits sexier and it did not happen this way, so I would not change it." Maria had removed a battered folder from the parcel and was offering it to Belinda. Puzzled, Belinda took the gift.

"What's it about?" she had queried, for some reason imagining that it was a summary of Maria's life experience with horses. Somehow, she could not picture Maria sitting still long enough to write a book nor to be logical enough to tell a story from beginning to end without interminable deviations.

"You will see!" answered Maria with one of her all-knowing smirks on her face. "You will see!" Belinda glanced down at the first page. It was neatly typed in double spacing, but the text was not in English.

"It's in German!" exclaimed Belinda. "I can't read German!"

"You know a little and you will manage!" Maria seemed confident that Belinda could and would decipher the text. Belinda was not so sure.

"Why are you giving it to me?" she asked.

"I am not going to live much longer and I need to know that my book is in safe hands. Maybe you will get it published."

Belinda felt doubtful about that too. She knew absolutely nothing about the world of publishing but who was she to deny the wishes of a dying friend.

"There is one thing I must tell you." Maria continued. "I have changed some names, for their protection. But they are all dead now, so if you can find which ones I have changed, you can do what you like with it. And, I have borrowed a small section, but that also really happened. You can make the sexy bits sexier – whatever is necessary."

"I have no idea what you are talking about, Maria, especially the bit about dying. Come and stay for Christmas!" It had been a spur of the moment invitation with no guarantee that the guest would ever see another Christmas.

"Thank you, B'linta. I would like that." Maria had replied, her puffed face dissolving into a warm smile.

As she left the clinic, Belinda encountered the nurse in charge of the ward.

"How ill is Maria Kurzke?" she asked.

"I'm afraid I must tell you that she has only days to live," replied the nurse with a suitable mournful expression.

"Oh," said Belinda, pausing as the image of Maria in her smoke-filled room passed before her eyes. Somehow, she could not see the energy that the woman displayed deteriorating to death in only a few days. The medical fraternity could predict a closure all they liked. The spirit of the patient was still fighting.

"I have a feeling that she is made of tougher boot leather than you think," she said. "She ain't ready to go yet!"

The nurse did not argue. The expression on her face spoke for her. 'You cannot accept what I am saying. It is normal. I have met many people like you before who will not accept the inevitable.

"Maybe," she said. They shook hands and parted.

2

Maria walked out of the hospital the following week and three months later Belinda had fetched her in the car.

"Have you read my book?" were almost the first words that Maria spoke.

"I've translated half of the first chapter," replied Belinda. "But I'm none the wiser yet."

"You will see," said Maria mysteriously. She loved intrigue. It was part and parcel of her nature. Belinda did not press her. There were so many things to arrange before she would be ready for the annual festivities and the subject did not get mentioned again. Neither Belinda nor Maria realised that destiny would indeed interfere and that the subject of the book would in fact never again be mentioned between them.

There was a mad scramble on Christmas Eve to beg, borrow or steal more whisky. Belinda had stocked up with four bottles in preparation for Maria's visit, but a bottle a day seemed to be what was required and that evening, the one remaining bottle was obviously not going to last the three days of the holiday. Rationing was imposed. Two fingers worth first thing in the morning would be left on the draining board; another at lunch time and a third in the evening. Maria protested, but was given the choice of either consuming the supply in one day with nothing thereafter, or drinking her tipple in controlled amounts. She had opted for the latter and Belinda took charge of the bottle. Maria gradually became a more pleasant person over the next three days. She mellowed.

As soon as Christmas was over, Maria decided to go home. Since her illness in September, she had lived with friends. Though no longer living in her own apartment she still indulged in her staple diet of whisky. The abstinence from her daily quota of alcohol had disconcerted her.

The journey back to Oxfordshire took several hours and within minutes of arriving at the farm cottage, Maria had found her reserve supply of 'eau de vie' and filled a tumbler to the brim.

Belinda's last visual memory of Maria was the picture of her leaning on the Aga in the kitchen, and raising the glass to her lips.

Their eyes had met and communicated 'Thank you, but I am home and happy' with an 'I understand' response.

In January, February and March of the New Year, first Belinda's husband caught the flu, followed by each of the children. Belinda herself had one day in bed and as mothers rarely seem to be allowed to convalesce for long, she pottered around for weeks in a semi daze. As soon as everyone was on their feet again, the youngest went down with measles. Three days later, his older sister followed suit. It never seemed to stop and Belinda was unable to find a spare day to get away to see how Maria was getting along.

Then one morning, the phone rang.

"Maria died at six o'clock this morning!" said the voice on the other end of the line.

'Damn' thought Belinda, wishing that she had phoned earlier that week or somehow found the time to visit her terminally ill friend. Now it was too late. She had translated odd pages from the manuscript and discovered that it was not about horses at all. She had also realised that to appreciate the whole story, she would have to employ the services of someone who spoke German fluently. But already, there were questions... which only Maria could have answered.

After the funeral, Belinda found herself helping a mutual friend to sort through a trunk of papers that had belonged to Maria. Most of it consisted of obsolete bills and legal documents referring to debts. There seemed to be no system in the filing, but amongst the muddle, they found some letters and documents written in German. Neither of the women were able to identify what was or what was not important, so anything that could not be identified was stuffed unceremoniously into a plastic bag for checking later. Any photos that came to light (some were fairly ancient) also went into the bag.

Many months later, Belinda received and read the completed translation. The story shook her rigid. It told of such an amazing sequence of events that she could not bring herself to believe that it was not fiction. Such things only happened in James Bond films. Yet if it was true, how much it revealed about a woman who had had so few friends by the end of her life. She had been arrogant, which was understandable if she had belonged to the Polish aristocracy. She had been highly strung with a vivid imagination and it was possible to understand that too, if she really had been on the stage before the war and had signed on with UFA film studios during the war. She had been extremely emotional and could argue with great passion and conviction. This side of her character was reflected in the style of the writing. Belinda could 'hear' Maria talking. Her ability to describe had been so vivid that she could paint a verbal picture very effectively. It was as though she had written a film script rather than a book.

'I wonder...' Belinda thought to herself. 'I wonder if I can find out whether it is true or not. I'll try for the Poggenburg camp first and see if anyone has heard of it.' Nobody had! In fact Belinda found that very little at all was known about wartime Poland except that the inhabitants had a rough time and had fled their country in droves. Over forty years later, the country was still under Soviet control, and information from behind the Iron Curtain was unreliable.

"It's a crazy story and Maria was nutty anyway," Belinda said to herself as she tucked the manuscript away on the highest shelf in the broom cupboard. There it lay, undisturbed, for nearly eight years.

3

1995

In 1989, the political Wall between Western Europe and the USSR dissolved. East Germany became accessible to visitors from the West. It was a further three years before Russia vacated Poland. Belinda's children were now young adults and she had time to take a second serious look at the translation and spend more time searching for facts that might support Maria's story.

Belinda's involvement with horses came to an abrupt closure when her head was squashed by a horse rolling backwards over her. Her balance and sight no longer co-ordinating, she had to find a more sedentary occupation and enrolled for one of the better-known writing courses. Three months into the course, she had reason to knock the dust off the translation of Maria's manuscript. Curiosity took control.

Her initial inquiries were disappointing. Poggenburg could still not be traced. Someone suggested that as it was a German name, perhaps there was a Polish equivalent used today, by which it was better known. Belinda felt a bit stupid. 'Of course' she mused. Hours spent on the telephone proved fruitless and days scouring the history books revealed that knowledge of Poland had not progressed much in the post-war years.

The trail eventually led to Professor Norman Davies in Oxford who suggested that possibly the Zachodni (Western) Institute in Poznań might be able to help. It was there that archives for the Home Army and the resistance were to be found. He also informed her that Poggenburg had been the German name for a camp that was now referred to as Zabikowo.

This was the first glimmer of positive news that Belinda had heard and without delay, she wrote to the Institute, once again casting a line and hoping that a fish, however small, might attach itself to the hook.

The answer arrived two weeks later. Yes, they knew of Poggenburg. They confirmed that it was the German name for Zabikowo, the Gestapo high security prison that had been built during the war, to the south of Poznań. Moreover, they seemed to have some idea of who Maria was! The English in the letter was not easy to comprehend, but there was a suggestion that she had been a member of the AK, whatever that was. Both she and her mother had code names. 'Was her mother a Jewess?' they wanted to know.

Rather than clarify Maria's story, these titbits of information only confused Belinda more. Maria had mentioned only one covert act in her manuscript that had been connected with the resistance and that had led to her arrest. She did not write about any involvement with the mysterious AK. Her mother on the other hand, might well have been very active. Yet Maria did not even give her a name. She was always just 'my mother'.

Despite the shoal of red herrings that seemed to have popped out of the water at the same time, Belinda was relieved to hear that Poggenburg had actually existed. The only other fact that she had previously been able to verify was that in 1942, 2nd March had been a Monday as Maria stated. Now at last, she had found the prison camp. That they had actually heard of Maria was astounding. However, what they knew did not seem to relate to Maria's version. Perhaps it was still all fiction, with an element of fact based on personal experience. Belinda remained sceptical. Letters passed back and forth between England and Poland and Belinda's curiosity increased. It soon became obvious to her that the only way that she was going to get to the bottom of things was to make an excursion to Poland itself. There were, however, one or two major drawbacks.

The language was possibly the biggest problem. Polish had not featured as an 'O' level subject at school and at first this seemed to be an insurmountable obstacle. Getting there and finding accommodation also seemed to cause the travel agency some difficulty, for they had only heard of Warsaw. Poznań lies halfway between Berlin and Warsaw and the British tourist industry did not send their customers to such out of the way places.

"It would be easier if you wanted to go to the jungles of Malaysia, madam," suggested the assistant as she punched her computer keyboard rather viciously. "Where did you say Poznań was?" she asked for the third time.

Even acquiring a few zloty from the bank proved impossible. To complicate matters, Poland had just revalued and had knocked four or five noughts from their currency, so no one was quite sure how much the pound was worth.

In desperation, Belinda bought a return plane ticket to Warsaw. Now she was committed. But as the departure date neared, she began to panic. While she still had not been able to obtain any zloty, she had managed to acquire a phrase book and dictionary. She spent hours on the telephone talking with kind people at the Polish Embassy and anyone who had recently been to Poland and discovered some of the pitfalls to be avoided.

"Do not take a taxi from outside the airport before first agreeing the fare," was one piece of advice. "They will charge a foreigner three times the correct fare otherwise."

"But what is the 'correct fare'?" enquired Belinda.

"Oh… about 6 or 7 zloty from the airport to the main station," was the reply. "… and, you'll most probably have to queue for at least half an hour at the station for a train ticket. You'll find that you have to queue everywhere. And don't give anything to the beggars. They are on the look out for foreigners. I would advise you to take all the labels off your baggage as soon as you get there so that you don't draw attention to where you've just come from. If you do not watch your baggage every second, it will disappear."

"How long will the train journey take?" asked Belinda. "That should take, let's see, about three hours." Belinda was beginning to wonder whether the whole venture was wise. She had tried to find a travelling companion without success. Visions of standing in a queue for hours, surrounded by beggars and handcuffed to her bags, did not seem too appealing. When she got to the ticket kiosk, she then had to buy a ticket and with no Polish on the tip of her tongue, she would be helpless.

"I would also advise you to buy a first-class ticket for the train. Second class is a bit rough by British standards."

"Thank you!" said Belinda to the voice of doom on the other end of the line and as she put down the receiver, she thought to herself, 'Dear Lord, what have I let myself in for?'

"Nothing ventured…! Life's got very ordinary these days. It needs a lift," she said aloud, addressing the refrigerator door.

4

MONDAY 18TH SEPTEMBER 1995

And so it came to pass, that two weeks later, Belinda found herself on a LOT flight to Warsaw. As she settled into her seat, she had the feeling that destiny had taken control. During the last week, doors of opportunity had opened. Coincidence had played its first obvious trick on her causing her to wonder what destiny had in mind.

When she had made enquiries at the Sikorski Institute, the archives for the wartime Polish Government in Exile that can be found in London, it had been suggested that she read works by J. Garlinski. A chance encounter with a friend while out on the weekly shopping duty, had led to a meeting with the renowned expert and author of many books on Poland. The friend had met him while on holiday and knew his telephone number. Even bumping into the friend was an obscure event. It had been several years since they had clapped eyes on each other.

She had made a call to Joseph Garlinski and arranged to meet him in London. The visit was not encouraging. Mr Garlinski had been a prisoner in Auschwitz. He bore the tell-tale tattoo on his arm. He had written many books on the conditions in Poland but he claimed that with time, publishers had started to reject his work on the grounds that there was not enough public interest, especially when the writer was a Catholic Pole rather than Jewish.

"When I am in the USA and they discover that I have a tattoo, they assume immediately that I am Jewish. They seem to think that there were only Jews in Auschwitz – but they were the minority. They are surprised and do not believe me. No one wants to hear the other side of the story," Garlinski explained. "I would advise you not to bother to try to get your friend's story published. You will be disappointed."

Belinda felt very small in his company. Tragedy was written on his face, frustration in the frame of his mouth. Belinda was not deterred, and the interview had strengthened her determination to discover more.

Two days later, she boarded the plane for Warsaw. She had not been able to get hold of any zloty, which she would need on arrival for the taxi and train fares so she would have to make a pit stop at the Bureau de Change in the airport. She hoped the queue would not be too long for she had barely two hours in which to cross Warsaw and catch the train.

A young African, wearing a bright orange fez and tabard, interrupted her reverie.

"Excuse me!" he said politely. "Would it be possible to sit in the empty seat beside you? I feel isolated away from my friends."

Belinda looked across the aisle and could see several rows of orange fezzes.

"Be my guest," she replied, removing her bag from the seat. "I need someone to talk to, so please tell me why you are all dressed in uniform."

"We all come from Kenya and belong to a dancing troupe. We are dancing in Warsaw tonight." The young man was charming and explained to Belinda about the dance company that travelled all over the world. He introduced her to his sister-in-law.

"I am chaperoning her," he said. "My brother was not selected this time." Belinda exchanged nods and smiles with his sister-in-law who sat across the aisle. If this was a taste of things to come, the next week was going to be very interesting, Belinda mused.

When they landed, she mingled with the dancers and queued with them to acquire some zloty from a dour cashier with an expressionless face before moving on to passport control. Two Americans joined them, one tall and serious, the other short and round, very cheerful and dressed as though he had haphazardly snatched up all his clothes at a jumble sale.

"Will you come to watch us tonight?" asked her new African acquaintance.

"I would love to," Belinda replied, "but I'm expected in Poznań tonight." regretting that her planned schedule would not permit a deviation.

By the time she had dragged her luggage into the foyer, everyone had disappeared. Indeed, compared to Heathrow, Warsaw airport was a desert. Most of the signs were incomprehensible. A few had German translations, but very few displayed an English word. After a few minutes, Belinda spotted a tourist sign with an arrow pointing down to a counter, behind which another sombre lady prowled. Ten precious minutes passed before she arrived at the front of the queue.

"Taxi? Train? This way!" and a finger shot over the desk, pointing to the far corner of the vast hall.

'Odd!' thought Belinda, 'I was under the impression that the station was in the centre of the city.'

She smiled, nodded her thanks and picked up her bags to trail over to a new queue. It was getting late and she began to wonder if destiny meant her to catch even the second of the only two trains that were scheduled to leave for Poznań that afternoon.

The woman selling the train tickets spoke not a word of English. Belinda had realised this while waiting. It had taken a full ten minutes, lots of gesticulation, the writing of names on scraps of paper and two telephone calls to settle the requirements of the American gentleman ahead of her. She would surely miss the train at this rate. But fate at this point lent a helping hand.

The young lady behind her was fluently bilingual and also wanting to catch a train. She intervened and five minutes later Belinda had a first-class ticket in her hand, her seat booked and the offer of a lift and all for 37 zloty (£10.) 'Miracles can still happen,' she thought to herself and gratefully accepted the offer. Her saviour cursed the traffic. "I've never known it to be so slow," she complained. The broad avenues were lined with gardens instead of houses.

"To whom do they all belong?" she asked.

"Everyone has the right to a plot," came the answer. "They were originally for vegetables, but they can use them for anything. They often build weekend bungalows in them." Belinda could see the occasional roof peeping out above the trees. Of vegetable plots, there was no sign.

"There's the station," announced the driver.

"Where?" Belinda asked.

"There, ahead of us!"

"What! That 'thing' in the middle of the chaos."

"Yup, impressive isn't it."

"But, where are the trains?"

"All underground."

The car was making its way across an endless succession of junctions, edging towards a building that rose out of the centre of a vast open space. Large hotels lined the edge of the area, but between them and the station was a no-man's-land filled with roads and tramways.

"I don't think that I would like to drive in this city. How on earth do you know which way is which?"

"By experience!" laughed her chauffeur.

At the station, she was escorted to the correct platform before being abandoned. She could only marvel at the generosity of a total stranger. A small Asian boy approached, hand outstretched, his brown eyes wide and pleading. A woman and several more children hovered behind a loaded trolley. She had been warned in the plethora of helpful hints that she had been given that she would encounter beggars and that she should not succumb to their advances on any account as any sign of generosity would attract a mob of supplicants. A female travelling alone would be particularly vulnerable. It gave Belinda an uncomfortable feeling to have to ignore the child, especially when he reached up to gently paw her sleeve, but she did not react and eventually he wandered away.

The platform was depressing, dirty and devoid of colour. Tunnels gaped at either end, lights glowing in the distance. Few people spoke and the lack of sound seemed strange. When the train arrived, two minutes late, there was a sudden rush to climb aboard. This was a feat of athleticism in itself. The step up to the carriage was nearly two foot high. It was not designed for middle-aged travellers with large suitcases.

While the daylight lasted, Belinda gazed out of the window at the flatness of the Polish landscape. 'No wonder the hordes of Europe have galloped this way over the centuries,' she mused, 'there's not a bump the size of a molehill to get in the way.'

The train passed through few towns, only twice slowing for built up areas during the 300-kilometre journey. Houses were small, single storied and unpainted. In the countryside, the landscape was broken by mature woodland, which separated enormous fields that were meticulously divided into long strips each with a diminutive cottage built at one end. The standard stock of each farm was two cows and sometimes a horse grazing on a small fenced piece of ground near the house. She saw only one tractor and came to the conclusion that 'farming' was very much a hand to mouth existence.

When the light faded, Belinda took down her holdall from the luggage rack. A couple of crosswords, a packet of biscuits and ten chapters of a book later, the train started to slow down for Poznań. Belinda prayed that she had understood the fax that had arrived from the Instytut Zachodni only yesterday. It had been in Polish and after two hours toil with the assistance of her dictionary, she had established that someone would be meeting the train and that she was to look out for a red and white armband. If she could not find the red and white armband she would have a problem. She was now a long way from home, surrounded by people with whom she had difficulty communicating, no accommodation and it was getting late. It had been a long day! 'What if he's not here,' she thought, panicking just a little.

But the Gods were doing their duty and through the dirty glass she spotted the flash of colour that she sought.

The train would only hesitate in Poznań. If she failed to get off in time, Berlin was the next stop and the corridor of the carriage suddenly seemed stupidly narrow for manoeuvring luggage. When she finally got to the door, the platform appeared to be miles away. Hampered by a suitcase, the eighteen-inch-step down, followed by a leap across the chasm between the train and platform itself looked formidable. Belinda momentarily wished that she had the jumping ability of a kangaroo.

The platform was crowded with a seething mass of grey people, tea trolleys and baggage. The only colour to be seen on that drab station was the red and white armband (she later discovered that it was a symbol for the AK – the Polish Home Army) that adorned the arm of a kindly faced, elderly gentleman. From the doorway of the carriage, Belinda waved to attract his attention. He noticed her and approached the train.

"Pani White?" he enquired. A wave of relief swept over Belinda as she nodded her head vigorously. The face below her dissolved into a radiant smile of welcome. He stretched out his hand, the palm uppermost and his gesture most gallant. She felt safe. Fortune had not let her down and with every second that ticked by she became more confident.

It was a strange experience for Belinda to find everything slotting so neatly into place. Her relief at seeing the armband was a sign. To her it felt as though something, someone, was paving the way for her. The journey had been so remarkably easy. Where there should have been problems, chance had intervened, and the anticipated problem had evaporated. She had needed company on the plane and an interesting young man had amused her. She had needed money and the exchange cubicle was the only kiosk in the corridor between the plane and the passport control. She had needed a train ticket and help in the translation had appeared seemingly from nowhere, accompanied by the offer of a lift to the station. Belinda was used to small misfortunes disrupting her plans. She had become used to the fact that the obvious, straightforward route could never succeed and it was wise to have alternative options available when plan 'A' went pear shaped. She had taken the precaution of procuring the telephone number of the British Embassy in Warsaw, just in case she had missed the second train and would have need for assistance to find overnight accommodation – plan 'B'. But, for once in her life plan 'A' had worked and had almost taken on a life of its own. It was as though she had a fairy godmother waving a wand and organising the schedule.

Looking down at the proffered hand and the red and white armband, Belinda had a strong suspicion that fate had taken charge, as if she was predestined to be here. The journey to Poznań had been designed by an ethereal being. It was as though destiny had dictated the events during her journey and dictated her safe arrival in Poznań. It was meant to happen.

"May I help you with your suitcase?" The voice was deep and mellow. Belinda blinked. Her thoughts had been miles away.

"Oh, thank you! It is quite heavy," she said and bent down to slide her case to the edge of the step.

"This is fine," said her host and with energy that belied his age, he grabbed the handle of the case and swung it down to the platform. He once again proffered his hand to steady her descent. Belinda was grateful that she had decided to travel in trousers. The hand ensured that she did not break her neck.

She felt like throwing her arms around the stranger standing in front of her. She felt so happy, grateful, surprised and relieved all mixed up together. To add icing to the cake, the gentleman spoke surprisingly good English!

"May I introduce myself," he said, and bowed slightly as he continued. "Ludwik Misiek. I am pleased to meet you."

"Oh Mr Misiek, it is wonderful to meet you," said Belinda in reply, looking up into the man's face, for he was somewhat taller than Belinda.

"How kind of you to wait for the train!"

"This is no problem," said Ludwik, smiling, "but you will have to excuse me. The doctor is waiting at the other end of the train. I will fetch him." He strolled off down the platform taking long easy strides. The train belched steam and started to draw away. At first the retreating crowd swirled about her then started to thin. Belinda shifted from one foot to the other and tried to catch a glimpse of the doctor that she had come all this way to meet. She saw his red and white armband first, flapping up and down at chest height behind the reversing figure of Mr. Misiek. The latter was being driven backwards towards her as though the arm had cyclonic powers. Only when they were some ten yards from where she stood, did Ludwik turn around and Belinda was able to get her first sighting of the doctor. Her immediate impression was that here was the inspiration for the grumpiest of Snow White's dwarves. The mouth turned down at both ends. The lines on the face running vertically into each other, created an expression of miserable pessimism. His arms still gesticulating wildly and hardly pausing for breath in what seemed like a running commentary for Ludwik's benefit, the gnome-like figure dashed forward. The face suddenly transformed into a beatific smile as he took Belinda's hand, bowed low and raised her hand to his lips. The kiss that she felt on the back of her hand was gentle and so reverently placed. She was taken aback by the sincerity of the gesture.

'Thank God someone warned me about that one,' she thought, congratulating herself on yielding her hand without any resistance. The sensation, however, was humbling. It was somehow so very old fashioned, yet created a sense of mutual respect that was a morale-boosting novelty to the British visitor.

The two men took charge of her suitcase and the briefcase that contained the manuscript and dictionary. Freed of her bags, she felt inches taller as she followed them out of the station.

"We take the tram? This is suitable for you?" enquired Ludwik. The doctor had been talking non-stop since they met.

"The doctor, he says that he is so sad that he cannot speak in English, but he says that he hopes that you had a good journey."

"Please tell the doctor that the journey was fantastic and that I am very pleased to meet him at last," Belinda replied.

When they emerged from the station, it was raining; a Welsh-like mist which permeated with a damp clamminess. The road was dimly lit, more like a village high street than the major thoroughfare of a city. Both the doctor and Ludwik unrolled their umbrellas. The doctor presented his to Belinda and the two men sheltered under Ludwik's. They crossed the road. Belinda tottered precariously on the slippery cobbled stones, stepping warily over the tramlines. The pavement was no less hazardous. The flagstones were uneven, the edges abutting at varying angles and height, threatening catastrophe to the unwary pedestrian. Belinda found herself peering down with concentration in order that she did not twist her ankle within minutes of arriving at her destination. If the street lighting had been brighter, it might have helped, but the weather transformed the lamps into glowing orbs, forlorn foggy moons, hanging over the road. She was glad that she wore flat-soled boots and not heeled shoes.

As the odd trio waited in the drizzle for a tram, Belinda began to feel rather lonely.

"Just what are you doing here?" a small voice screamed inside her head. The thought bored holes in her confidence. Where the relief at finding the red and white armband had temporarily injected a positive boost, the greyness and damp discomfort now affected her mood in a negative way. How on earth had she managed to get herself into the predicament in which she now found herself; hundreds of miles from home; in a country where no amount of fragmentary knowledge of the French or the German language were of any use. She had absolutely no idea where she was to spend the night and perhaps the craziest aspect of it all, she was on her own. There was no one to whom she could turn if her luck changed and took a dive. She must have been insane to have even contemplated such a journey into the unknown and for a moment, she felt as though she had been dropped into a time warp. Was she really awake? Or was the whole adventure some ill-conceived nightmare?

Each time a tram rattled to a halt by the pavement edge, her two companions indulged in animated discussion. Heads would shake and the tram, groaning in protest, moved forward into the gloom of the dimly lit street. At last, the head shaking changed to nods and she was invited with gestures to climb up the two tall steps into the stationary tram. 'Not much concession to the ancient or infirm,' she thought as she dropped gratefully into an empty seat.

Thick condensation covered the windows and she was unable to see the street outside, as specks of light hopped from one water droplet to the next. Wiping the window, she peered out, but the rivulets of water distorted the glass. Ludwik, the elder of the two men, tried to point out the buildings of note but the noise of the tram and the unsteadiness of its passage added to the problem of actually being able to see anything through the windows and eventually he gave up and found a seat on the other side of the aisle.

Her two companions did not seem to be too familiar with the protocol of Polish tram travel. They appeared to be uncertain as to how to operate the DIY ticket machine and spent several minutes in animated discussion, debating which way up the ticket should be presented. Belinda took advantage of their preoccupation with practical technicalities and slid into her own world. She could imagine Maria looking down from above, that smug 'know-it-all' expression on her face.

'Right madam,' she thought, addressing her long dead friend. 'You have got me here and I will admit you have been very efficient. But, what next?'

Her thoughts meandered back to her visit to Joseph Garlinski. She had felt so ignorant and foolish in his presence. When discussing the possible validity of Maria's story, he had given a dismissive opinion. He had not heard of a camp called Poggenburg and too many people had written fictional versions of the truth. Belinda had learned little. Listening to Garlinski, it had seemed increasingly more possible that Maria's story had been a wild fiction of her very vivid imagination.

Garlinski had referred to dreadful things. Belinda had sat riveted in her chair, aware of the intolerable sadness and tenseness that welled from the man. His whole body portrayed a dignified tragedy that she found overwhelming. The seed of curiosity had been sown in that heavy atmosphere and had started to thrust out its first shoots. In the following weeks the seedling had flourished.

It was an enquiry at the Slavonic School of Languages that had culminated in a telephone conversation with Professor Norman Davies and the contact she had made with the Zachodni Institute in Poznań.

A hand tugged at her sleeve. Ludwik shouted close to her ear as the tram started to slow, the brakes causing a high-pitched keening sound as metal skidded on metal.

"We get off now."

Belinda, startled out her reverie, took a second to remember where she was before responding with a nod.

This street was brightly lit; a total contrast to the murky thoroughfare by the railway station. Large shops with elaborate window displays lined the broad pavement. Cars and people fought for right of way in the road. Sparks flew from beneath low-slung vehicles as they bounced over the cobbles and across the tramlines. "The sump replacement business must be good here," concluded Belinda as she trotted along in the wake of Ludwik and the doctor.

They turned into a quiet side street. The road narrowed, sloping downhill with small two-storey houses leaning over the pavement. Belinda followed demurely, wondering where the two men were taking her.

Abruptly the alley opened out into a large cobbled square. Old facades, painted in greens, blues and purples vied with each other on all sides. In the centre, a huge cathedral-like building held solemn court.

Belinda gazed about her, astounded at the contrast of her surroundings to the dullness of the station and its street and the narrow lane down which they had just walked. She was no connoisseur of historical architecture, but she could appreciate the variety of form and colour that now surrounded her.

"This is the Stary Rynek – in English – the Old Market," announced Ludwik.

Belinda paused to take in the scene. It was enchanting; quaint and full of character yet at the same time dignified, with a sense of pride in its history.

The two men had strolled on ahead of her, busily chattering. Belinda had to hurry to catch up with them. They were heading for a dimly lit passage that led into the shadows of a jumble of buildings in the centre of the square.

The alley was narrow with few windows and doors. Belinda began to hope that they were arriving at her lodgings. By habit a coffee drinker, she suddenly had the urge to down a huge cup of sweet tea, put her feet up and hibernate for a while, but she was to be disappointed.

They stopped at a low door and the doctor produced a large number of keys from his pocket. The jangle as he selected the key that he wanted would have kept a gaoler happy. Once inside, they were faced with another locked door and there was more jangling before they climbed a rickety staircase to the first floor. Three more locked doors later, the doctor ushered her into his cupboard-sized office. Surely Fort Knox could not have been better secured.

Her host offered her coffee and cognac. Aware that politeness on her part was essential, she accepted, but wished sincerely that after her long, somewhat anxious day, they would take mercy on her.

It was her tendency to fall off the chair with her eyes closed that possibly drew attention to the fact that she was bushed. Belinda did not know or care. She was only relieved when, formalities over, the party was again on the move towards the exit. She fervently hoped that they would not have far to go. This time her prayers were answered.

Her room was on the third floor of the 'Dom Polonii', situated at the corner of the Stary Rynek. The window looked out over the square. The ceiling sloped into the apex of the roof. It was regally furnished with a bench sofa and chairs, a coffee table, a writing desk, an enormous television, twin beds, wardrobes, side tables and chests of drawers. The en-suite bathroom was accessed from the hallway. It was luxurious – and all for the equivalent of five pounds per night! The only disadvantage it had was the height off the ground. There was no lift and the stairs had seemed endless.

After the two men left, Belinda unpacked, bathed, dined on a few biscuits and slid gratefully between the crisp sheets.

Immediately, blissful oblivion engulfed her.

Stary Rynek in Poznań

5

TUESDAY 19TH SEPTEMBER 1995

The following morning dawned bright and clear. Gone was the dreary rain of the previous evening. The windows of her room looked out directly over the Stary Rynek. She noticed the undulating rooftops where age had caused the sagging of the support beams. She could admire the complex plasterwork under the eaves, unaware that all the buildings around the square had been rebuilt in the sixties to replicate those that had been destroyed during the Second World War. The bright morning sunlight sharpened the colour of the stucco figures that adorned the larger buildings in the square, creating a festive carnival atmosphere.

Women were busy with besom brooms, sweeping the pavements, the gutters and cracks between the cobblestones of the road. The place was alive with people. A purposeful bustle filled the square. Belinda gradually became aware that although there was a dull hum in the background, there was not a motor vehicle in sight. Later she was able to confirm that the Stary Rynek was restricted to pedestrians only.

She had almost finished dressing when the telephone on the bedside table burst into aggressive song. Belinda grabbed the receiver.

"Moment," said a woman's voice. A muffled conversation in Polish followed before she heard the welcome voice of Ludwik Misiek.

"You are ready?" he asked.

"Yes, I will be with you in a couple of minutes," replied Belinda.

"You come?" asked Ludwik, puzzlement in his voice. Belinda realised that she must keep her English simple.

"I am coming," she said, paying attention to the speed and articulation of her words.

Grabbing her handbag, she turned the keys in each of the locks of the door to her room, following the instructions that she had been given the previous evening and started down the six flights of stairs.

On the first landing, black and white photographs were displayed in a case on the wall. Ludwik was waiting for her in the foyer so she did not have time to observe more than the general theme of the pictures, that of devastation and chaos.

When she reached the first floor, she passed a smartly dressed young man. They exchanged nods of acknowledgement before she descended to ground level and the sturdy locked door at the bottom of the stair well. Belinda pressed a button and the concierge released the door from the reception desk in the foyer. Freedom. She felt as though she had successfully escaped from a prison.

Ludwik was waiting patiently for her to appear. He greeted her warmly.

"We walk to dr Woźniak," he announced. Belinda obediently followed him into the street outside.

In the centre of the Stary Rynek were a number of buildings. Now that there was daylight, Belinda could see the almshouses squatting beside the town hall with its pillared balcony above the front entrance. Behind them lay the maze of narrow alleys and dr Woźniak's lair.

Ludwik, in his anonymous grey mackintosh strode briskly forward over the uneven cobbles while Belinda negotiated the rough surface with some hesitation. Her bifocals were not conducive to sure footedness in such circumstances. Halfway down the narrow alley, Ludwik stopped. Belinda recognised the door that lead to Woźniak's den. She had been so switched off the previous evening that she had not paid attention to much detail. It was the height of the door that had jarred her memory. Ludwik stabbed at the doorbell button and pushed the door open. It was a pre-arranged signal. At the other end of the short dingy entrance hall was the second door and another button. This time, admittance required voice recognition.

No longer stupefied by a long journey and now fully alert after a sound night's sleep, the claustrophobic proportions of the small reception area seemed to shrink even more as they waited to be admitted

Ludwik Misiek

Dr Marian Woźniak with his wife and daughters, Małgosia and Marta

into the office complex. The security precautions seemed extreme. Both at her lodgings and here at the office, several keys were needed to open a single door. Were intruders in Poland so difficult to keep out?

Dr Woźniak himself came to the door to let them in. They followed him up the staircase to the first floor, every stair complaining noisily and announcing the approach of the visitors. Expressionless faces peered up from typewriting machines as they passed open office doors. The doctor produced his bunch of keys, inserting two of them into different locks in the door before ushering Ludwik and Belinda into the corridor beyond. It required still further key rattling, accompanied by frustrated muttering for the final door to be unlocked. It would appear that even the secretaries needed to be firmly kept away from the innermost sanctum.

The doctor's private office was a glorious den of chaos. Books, files and loose papers were stacked on every horizontal surface. The office itself was barely twelve feet square. Two of the walls were lined with cupboards and a large desk occupied most of the centre of the room.

"Would you like coffee?" asked Ludwik, "and perhaps something to eat?" The idea of both was very welcome to Belinda. Apart from the packet of biscuits, she had not travelled with food supplies, nor had she been able to purchase anything since she arrived in Poland. Dr. Woźniak busied himself with a small coffee-making machine situated on the crowded shelf behind his desk. From a paper bag, he produced a cheese roll.

"Thank you very much," she said. Belinda smiled and bit hungrily into her roll. It tasted good, as did the coffee and she started to feel human again.

As soon as she had eaten, the two men were on their feet and making preparations to move on. She had been given no explanation of the day's schedule and was prepared for anything but expecting nothing. However, when Ludwik mentioned that they were walking to the town council offices to find a car, Belinda was puzzled. Where could they be going that necessitated a car, she wondered. The language barrier seemed incredibly high at that moment. Ludwik was struggling with the translation. His mastery of English was dependant on resurrecting a vocabulary that he had not used in forty years. He coped well for a short period, but his stamina was short lived. Hoping that Ludwik's now halting English would suffice, she turned to him for some explanation of the day's agenda.

"We drive to Fort VII and Zabikowo," Ludwik stated emphatically, continuing, "the Institute does not have car. We borrow from council."

A sight-seeing trip to the prisons was on the menu. Maria had described Fort VII as a bunker system. What would remain after all these years, a cavern perhaps or a dark hole with a rusting gate to keep intruders out? And Poggenburg? Had that been burnt to the ground in January 1945 as Maria had heard rumoured? Was it a deserted spot as described by the woman at the Polish Embassy in London where you could still walk on the bones of the dead? Belinda could barely contain her excitement. Was she to find all the answers so quickly?

They had been walking for what seemed like hours. At last they arrived in a large triangular green space with tall trees along one side that gave shelter to rows of bicycle stands. The middle of the area was packed with parked cars and luxurious five storey apartment blocks, their windows, decorated with flowers and fancy curtains, filled the skyline. Belinda paused for breath. The noise of traffic was behind them and the scene was suddenly so tranquil.

She was not permitted to linger long. Dr Woźniak was consulting his watch and within minutes they were on the move again.

They approached a wide gateway, leading into a courtyard. A boom across the entrance impeded further progress and negotiations with the watchman were necessary before they were permitted to enter.

"This is council office," said Ludwik. "It is a very old monastery. You see there the old chapel." He pointed to the far end of the courtyard. High above their heads, windows with patches of stained glass hinted at the past glories of the chapel. The religious community must have once been powerful to justify a building of such size, thought Belinda.

The main door was locked but after some discussion and rattling of door handles, the doctor found a way in. It seemed very strange to Belinda that the council offices had such obscure methods of access, but the place was deserted. They met not a single soul as they marched along the ground floor corridor with carved stone arches meeting overhead. They climbed a wide stone staircase, the passage of many feet having scooped shallow swathes out of each step. The first-floor landing led to a long gallery, its tall windows overlooking an inner courtyard. On the wall opposite was a row of sturdy unmarked doors.

Dr Woźniak hesitated. Even he seemed perplexed by the complete lack of directional signs. He arrived at a decision and knocked on the nearest door. There was no answer, so he tried the next. This time it was opened and the party was ushered into a large, airy reception room. Coffee was served and the babble of voices filled the air. Belinda found herself introduced to various people. She smiled and shook hands. Conversation was impossible until an angel in the form of a female councillor admitted shyly that she could speak a little English. Belinda felt suddenly immensely relieved and, finding that 'a little' was a very conservative estimate of the woman's ability, soon found that she had an ally.

Belinda needed to laugh and Anna soon demonstrated that she had a sense of humour. There was a muddle over the numbers of coffee cups required, when Belinda watched the expression on Anna's face and started to grin. Their eyes met and an understanding passed between them that needed no words.

"Please will you explain to me just what is going on!" said Belinda, as she settled back into the sofa. Anna had seated herself on the chair beside her. "I am at a loss to know what to expect next." Anna smiled at her.

"First you go to meet the chairman of the council. And afterwards we drive to Fort VII."

"Oh thank you! I was under the impression that was what was scheduled to happen, but I have been totally confused by all the talking and I have the impression that we seemed to have got lost. You said 'we', are you coming to the Fort as well?"

"If this is suitable for you? Yes."

The two women were busy swapping credentials with regard to families and children when it became apparent that the coffee break was over and the door had opened. After more hand shaking and head nodding, the party found themselves back in the long gallery.

Belinda's patience was getting a little frayed. She was not used to conforming to miles of protocol. However, she had no choice and followed the two men to the far end of the gallery, hoping that soon she would be able to escape from the sterile, almost hostile atmosphere of the building. Old that it was, she found the meticulous attention to anonymity, no sign of anyone's name on the office doors or even pictures on the walls, increasingly oppressive. She started to feel hemmed in, trapped like an Alice in Wonderland in a maze from which there was no escape.

The chairman of the council was a cheerful looking man. He kissed the back of Belinda's hand and gestured her towards a seat. The air buzzed with gibberish. 'I wonder who they think I am?' pondered Belinda. 'They seem to be treating me with great respect and I am causing a lot of people a lot of inconvenience.' She was only a farmer's wife with a curiosity to satisfy. 'Go with the flow,' she told herself, 'there is nothing that you can do about it.' More coffee appeared and the discussion continued at full volume until suddenly it was all over. Everyone got up to leave. The chairman pushed a book into Belinda's hand, nodding and smiling.

"For me?" she queried.

"Tak, tak!" This she understood, 'tak' meaning 'yes' and 'nie' meaning 'no' being the sum total of her Polish vocabulary to date. "Thank you!" she said, making a mental note that she ought to discover the polish equivalent as soon as possible. They shook hands. The book, she realised as they all made their way back to the courtyard, was written in Polish.

༄༅༅

A red saloon car awaited them. With the addition of Anna, there were now four in the party plus the driver. It was a tight squeeze for all the passengers. The vehicle belonged to the council and was driven by one of its employees.

"The archive have no money, so the council help us," explained Ludwik. As the tallest with long legs, he occupied the passenger seat beside the driver while the two women and dr Woźniak somehow wedged themselves into the back seat.

They drove for nearly half an hour, towards the outskirts Poznań, before turning off the road into what appeared to be a small park. The car slowed.

"This is Fort VII," announced Ludwik, glancing back over his shoulder.

Belinda peered past the driver's head, through the windscreen. She could see nothing but a line of tall trees.

"To the right," continued Ludwik. "It is the entrance."

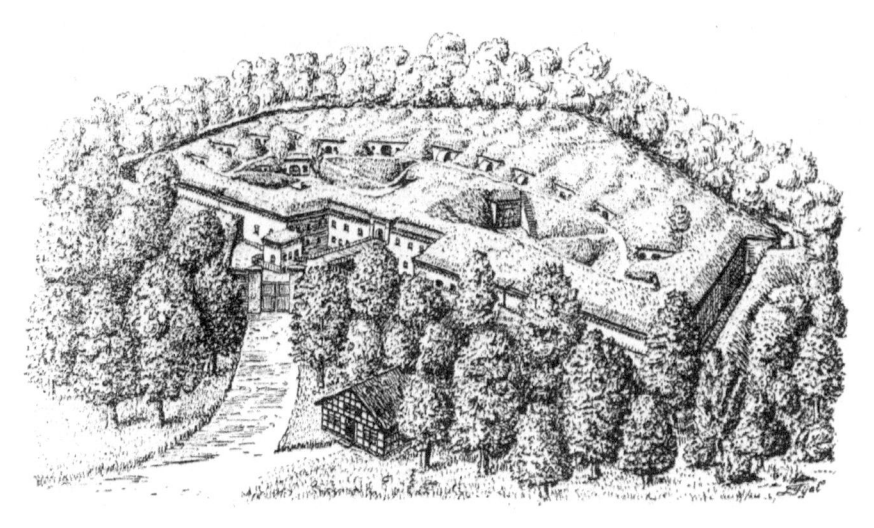

Fort VII

She had to rub the condensation off the window before she saw the grey metal gates with two very solid looking brick pillars on either side. They were closed. 'Is this it?' she wondered. No structure was visible above the gates, only the thick line of trees that stretched into the distance. She made a move to find the door handle, but Anna shook her head.

"We will go a little further and park the car," she said. The car moved forward again and turned right onto the grass verge. There was no trace of a track for vehicles, only a footpath that disappeared into the trees. Finally they stopped and disentangled themselves from the back seat. Belinda looked about her. Even the gate and its pillars were now hidden from view. She concluded that little could remain of the bunkers of the Fort and that they were about to inspect the gate on foot.

But instead of turning towards the gate, her companions set off along the path under the trees. Deciding that this was the mystery tour of all mystery tours, Belinda followed, slipping and sliding on the greasy earth as the track mounted a steep bank.

Nothing could have prepared her for the sight at the top. The Fort lay below her. She reached for her camera. Dr Woźniak looked concerned and stretched out his hand, pointing at the camera case. He barked an instruction at Ludwik. His manner had suddenly become so aggressive he half ran towards her flapping his arms. Belinda cringed and took a step backwards.

FORT VII

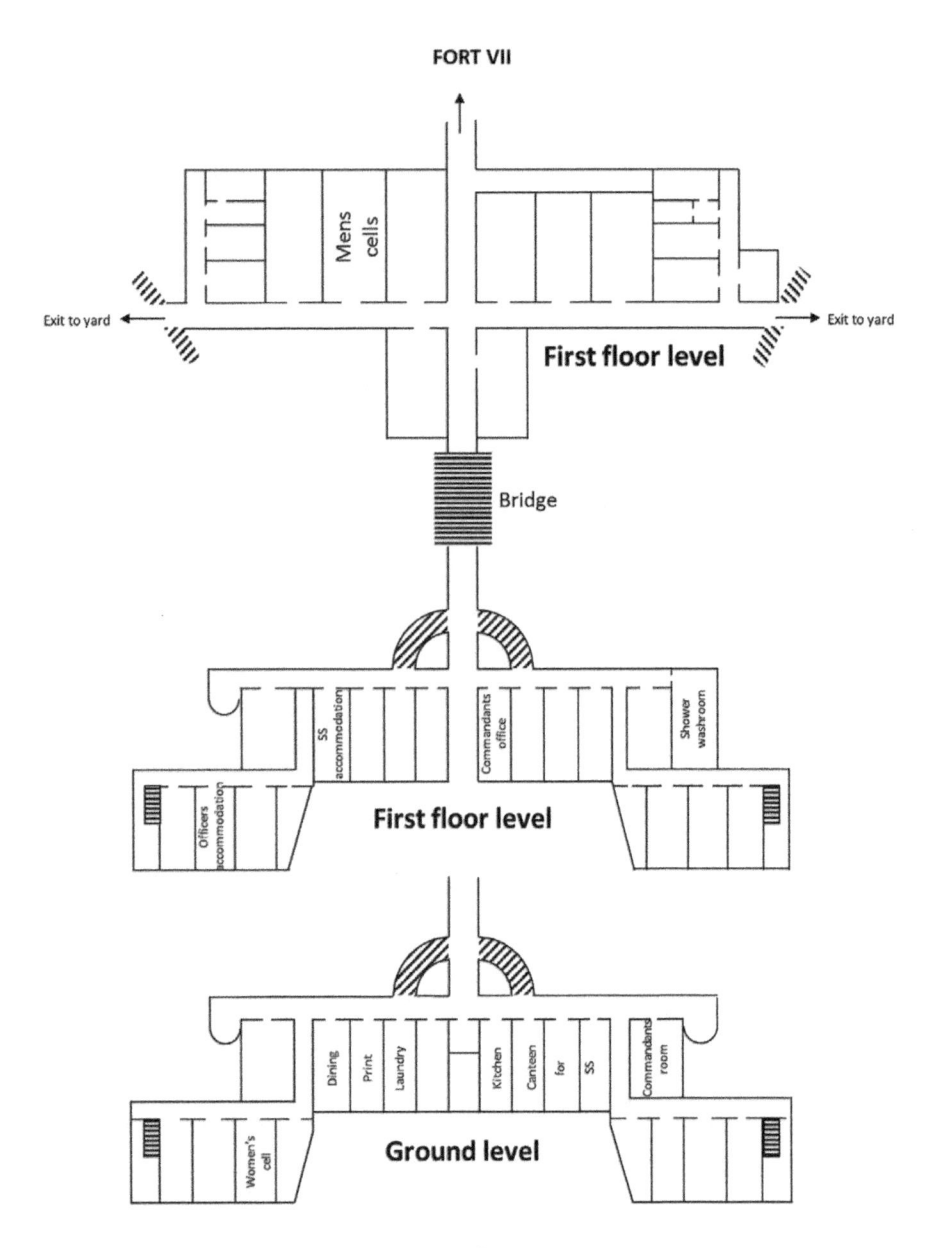

Layout of Fort VII

"No! No!" he was almost shouting. "It is not permitted to take photograph here!" Disappointed, Belinda dropped the camera back into its case. She became aware of raised voices. She seemed to have become the object of a serious discussion, which ceased as abruptly as it had started.

"It is OK," said Ludwik. "In this case, it is possible that you may take photo." Belinda was puzzled. Why the taking of a photograph should first be strictly forbidden but permitted only seconds later mystified her. She quickly took several snaps before they changed their minds again.

Ludwik stood at her shoulder and pointed out interesting features.

"You see the bridge over the gully... and the gate of the entrance into the main bunker?"

The facade of the Fort was built of brick, two storeys high and topped with five to six feet of earth on which grew long grass. The ground line of the wall was symmetrical, with the bridge and entrance in the middle and the walls on either side stretching for some 150 metres. It was not in the least bit derelict and was in fact occupied and in use. Lorries and men could be seen moving about in the broad forecourt.

"We go this way." Ludwik indicated a tired rustic gate that barred the way to a footbridge across the chasm of the wide gully in front of the Fort. As they walked across, he touched her elbow. "See," he said. "There is the cell for the 'Kobiety', how do you say... the ladies... no?"

"You mean the women's cell?" replied Belinda, trying to conceal the excitement in her voice.

"Where?"

Entrance to Fort VII with women's cells in foreground

"On the corner, on the ground floor," came the reply. Belinda stared. Her thoughts traversed the years. This was where Maria had been incarcerated in 1943. It was a chilling sensation to be suddenly so close to the past. This was the hell hole into which the Gestapo had delivered her, unchanged in fifty-five years.

But there was more, much more.

At the other end of the footbridge another gate and a notice board to one side on which the word 'Museum' was proudly displayed. The path descended between earthen banks into a broad pit, the sloping sides of which soared some forty feet to meet the sky. To the left, half way up the slope, could be seen a row of oval shaped metal doors. The opposite bank was broken at its base by irregular openings to passageways and alcoves. Straight ahead were two ominous looking metal doors, through which a London bus could have been driven with ease.

The small party climbed up a path leading to the row of doors. From this vantage point, it was possible to get a clearer view of the complete layout. Ludwik began a grim commentary.

"The big doors lead into the main bunker. Trucks with the prisoners could be driven directly into this section." His hand shot out, pointing at one of the indentations on their right. "This is the place where they shoot prisoners." Following the pointed finger, Belinda could see that one of the alcoves at the base of the opposite bank was brick lined. A single red flower lay on the ground.

"The condemned prisoners were kept in the cell on the left." She could just make out the grill of the cell. It was only two or three yards from the flower and overlooked the site of the executions. The anguish of those waiting to die – the thought was chilling.

"And the stone steps beside the big door – prisoners were forced to climb up and down until they fell with exhaustion. If they did not get up, they were shot immediately." Belinda did not want to hear more. 'What was this place? Who were the prisoners?'

She turned her back on the gruesome reminders of the past only to be faced with more historical horrors. She could not escape. Beside the first oval door was a large plaque inscribed in Polish, German and at the bottom, in English.

'HERE IN OCTOBER 1939
NAZI GERMANY BEGAN
THE MASS EXTERMINATION
OF MENTALLY ILL PEOPLE
BY THE USE OF GASS'

Belinda stared at the words uncomprehendingly. She read them again slowly, allowing time for them to make sense. The doubling of the S in the word gas momentarily distracted her, but then the meaning and the implications started to ferment inside her head.

"But the Germans only started the invasion at the beginning of September and Poland did not surrender until the end of the month," she spluttered. "How could they be organised to do such dreadful things in such a short space of time?"

Plaque outside gas bunker at Fort VII

She was not offered an answer. Ludwik shrugged his shoulders. Dr Woźniak pulled a wry face and rolled his eyes. Anna gazed at her feet.

"They killed forty of them at a time. That is the number of people that they could push into the bunker. They used carbon monoxide gas. It took a long time." Belinda peered into the shadows. She could almost touch the apex of the ceiling and the brick walls curved to the floor. The bunker was cut some twelve feet deep into the bank. It seemed crowded for only four people to stand inside it.

The next three bunkers were lined with wall plaques bearing the names of those who had been executed.

"What does 'lat' mean?" Belinda asked. Each name was followed by the word and a number.

"This means 'age'." replied Ludwik.

"But... then some of them were very old?" she said, studying the lists. "Who were they...? and why were they arrested?"

"They were the important men of the city, the councillors, the teachers, the professors, the lawyers. Anyone who they thought might organise resistance. They were all Polish." Belinda studied the endless list of names. There were hundreds

Gas bunker no. 17 at Fort VII

of them mostly in their thirties, forties and fifties, a few in their eighties and a very few in their teens. Belinda felt numb. The implications were horrendous. There should have been a thousand questions to ask, but the realisation that so many had been executed purely because of their responsible place in society, struck her dumb. She had read that the Poles had been persecuted, but had never understood the full portent of what she had read. Suddenly the reality had come home to her. The Germans had planned this from the beginning. Before the invasion, they knew what they were going to do and had wasted no time putting the plans into action.

Her trip to Poland had taken a serious turn. Her concern to verify Maria's story had suddenly become secondary to the context of the events themselves.

She heard Ludwik's voice at her side. Lost in thought, Belinda physically shuddered as she hardly caught his words let alone understood their meaning.

"They are ready for us in the museum," he was trying to tell her. "It is this way." Belinda looked up into his eyes.

"This place is so sad," she said.

"Tak, it is a terrible place." The expression in his eyes receded into distant memories and for a moment he stood still, his whole body limp.

"Many terrible things happened here," he continued. "Come. This way."

Main cell

Belinda followed him down the slope into the gully and into the entrance of a large bunker, which was dug deep into the hill under the row of gas chambers. It housed the artefacts of the museum. They were very few in number.

The main corridor was lined in brick, arching some twenty feet high over the ten-foot wide passage.

"What was this used for?" asked Belinda.

"This is the corridor to the main cell," replied Ludwik. "Here is the cell." He indicated a vast cavern to the left. "It held 150 prisoners at a time."

Dr Woźniak was talking to one of the museum staff, blocking the view to the end of the main passageway. As Belinda turned to look at what Ludwik was trying to show her, she caught a glimpse of the object beyond them. For a second, she felt as though she was again in a time warp. She could not believe her eyes, or if she dare, surely it could not be relevant to the Second World War.

Guillotine used in criminal prison in Młynska Street

"Is that what I think it is?" she whispered to Ludwik.

"It is the guillotine," he replied as though reading her thoughts.

"But what is it doing here?"

"1,800 people died this way," he added.

Memories of history lessons about the French Revolution flooded into her head. She had always thought that the use of the guillotine had been a particularly macabre and bloody machine.

It would have been quick and very final for the victim, but somehow extraordinarily sadistic for the executioners.

"I can't believe it," said Belinda when at last she managed to find the words. She stared at the vicious tool of death unable to comprehend the magnitude of the crime.

"It was not used in this prison." She heard Ludwik's voice as though from a great distance. "It was used in Młynska, the prison in Poznań for people accused of civil offences," he added.

"For civil offences?" queried Belinda.

"Yes! For people who commit crime of theft for example."

"That carried a death penalty?"

"Yes! If you are hungry and you steal bread, you would be executed." His tone of voice was flat and expressionless.

Belinda became powerfully aware that she had stumbled into a pit of tragedy. She felt embarrassed and guilty of her ignorance. She, a British woman, was naively being drawn into something that was far bigger than anything that she had ever experienced in her sheltered and privileged life. She looked up at the wall, seeing rows of faces, some very young, some old and wrinkled, the faces of dignified, intelligent people. Had they all died in this place? Assuredly, or they would not have earned the right to feature in the portrait gallery.

As she wandered among the rows of show cases in the enormous cell: the lock of hair wound into a small pathetic bracelet, the brick with a name and a date scratched into the surface; the notes written on scraps of paper in an unsteady hand, she began to feel the desperation of the place. The depression that she had started to feel outside was taking a serious hold on her. She felt numb. Whispering voices seemed to be calling out to her, invisible hands stretching towards her. She had to escape. She needed fresh air and sunshine to assure her that the world she knew still existed.

Her companions probably thought her behaviour a little odd, but Belinda did not care as she hurried, almost running out of the cell. Her flight towards the exit of the bunker, was barred by a tall stranger.

It was the curator of the museum and he obviously wished to say something to her. Belinda made an effort to recover her composure and accepted the book that he held out towards her, smiling and nodding her gratitude and frustrated by her ignorance of the illusive Polish word for 'thank you'.

"Thank you, thank you very much!" she said. As she turned to leave, she glanced down at her latest acquisition and almost dropped it. The front cover depicted hands, fingers stretched, desperate and helpless, reaching towards her. She tightened her grip on the book, her knuckles turning white.

'Maria, what are you doing?' she thought. 'You knew... you knew!' In her mind's eye she saw Maria, leaning against the huge fire place in the kitchen of her lodgings in Oxfordshire, the full tumbler of whisky in her hand and that all too familiar expression of smugness on her face; that knowing look which appeared whenever she wanted to be evasive. Belinda had learned to withdraw from further trespass when she saw that look. She recalled the day that Maria, out of the blue, had announced that she had been sentenced to death by the Gestapo. She had mentioned the matter again when she visited her at the clinic. It had been the second time that Maria had made the claim.

On the first occasion, Belinda had attempted to learn more. Curious, she had demanded to know why and, as Maria was sitting there in front of her, very much alive, how come that she had escaped execution? She had wasted her breath. Maria gave her one of her knowing looks and told her, "One day you will understand." Had she planned even then, two years before she discovered that she might be terminally ill, to give the manuscript to Belinda before she died. The whole thing was a mystery to Belinda. She had not been particularly close to the woman at any time yet the manuscript had been delivered into her hands for safekeeping. True, the unpublished book had collected dust in the broom cupboard for years and not until the intervention of a bad riding accident that radically altered her daily routine, had Belinda retrieved it from the shelf. Now it had brought her to Poland.

'Why did she choose to drop it in my lap?'

The question would not go away.

6

The visit to the Fort could well have been sufficient for one day. However, the availability of the council car as free transport had to be exploited to the full. The small party paused for a short lunch break before driving on to Zabikowo, the camp that had superseded Fort VII in 1943 and where Maria had been imprisoned until January 1945. It lay south of Poznań, some 15 kilometres beyond the city limits.

After the horrors of the Fort, Belinda prepared herself. Back home, in England, she had been warned that the camp was now a deserted area, where it was rumoured that you might crush human bones underfoot. It sounded ghoulish. However, she was beginning to realise the enormity of the events that took place here at the very start of the war and suspected that anything was possible.

Maria had written about a camp called Poggenburg. Discovering that the modern name for the place was Zabikowo was one of the big breaks in Belinda's quest to discover the validity of her story. That the site of the camp still existed, was the only solid piece of information that she had confirmed before she left England. She was still, however, uncertain as to what sort of camp it was and why it had been so small and so discretely hidden from public view. There were so many questions she needed to ask which needed explicit answers. Ludwik, bless him, had his limitations as a translator. Although very willing to please, prolonged explanations were obviously a strain for him. The only alternative was for Belinda to observe everything, forget nothing and try to disseminate what she had witnessed at some time in the future.

The car turned off the main highway. They had been passing fewer and fewer houses as they travelled south along a road that would pass as a poor-quality country lane in England. The single storey dwellings had gradually become more and more dilapidated, with large lumps of plaster missing and rotting, unpainted windows draped with tired, grimy curtains.

The driver slowed to a snail's pace, steering from one verge to the other to avoid

Museum for Zabikowo (The Commandant's house)

Water reservoir in Poggenburg Camp (Zabikowo)

the worst of the potholes. Eventually he stopped outside a large, rectangular hut, recently replastered in grey colourless concrete. Except for two small windows set high in the wall, the building was remarkable only for its featureless drabness.

"This is the museum for Zabikowo," announced Anna. There was no indication of what the building contained; no sign or board to attract the passer-by. They entered through the one and only access, a metal door at one end.

Inside, there were displays of the horrors that had been found in the camp. The single room contained a few artefacts and a collection of disturbing photographs; skeletal physiques and despairing faces; pictures of the blackened bodies of the victims who had died when the camp was burned to the ground in January 1945. There were also hundreds of photographs, taken in better times, of people fashionably dressed or in uniform; all doomed to end their days at Zabikowo. The curator was as sombre as his domain.

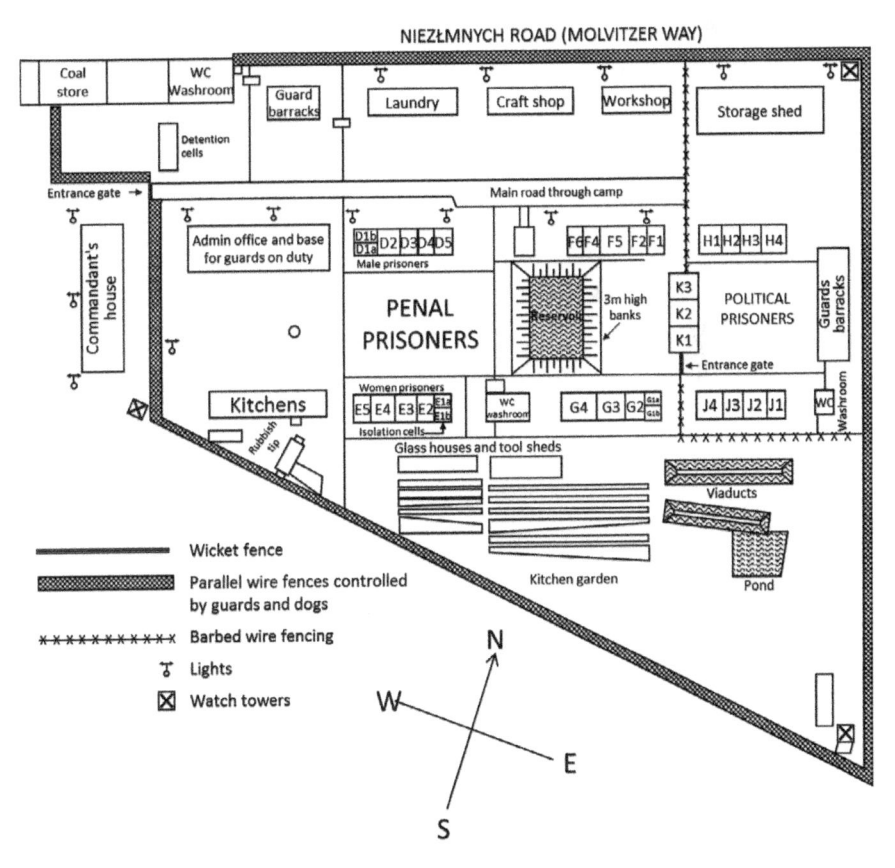

Map of the Poggenburg (Zabikowo) High Security Camp

Belinda could not get out of the place fast enough. She felt stifled, flushing alternating between hot and cold as she waited impatiently for the introductions and discussions demanded by protocol to end.

The museum and its contents were oppressive and as they had arrived in the car, she had observed the wire fence and watch tower further down the road, and was eager to inspect the camp itself.

The site of Żabikowo had been laid out as a memorial park. Iron railings surrounded rows of tall trees that stood guard over the remaining foundations of the huts and barracks of the camp.

The arrangement of the layout seemed strangely familiar to Belinda. Maria's description had not been in great detail, but immediately she was aware that something was amiss with the modern boundary of the park. Further, the area was too exposed. Maria had described it as having been in a pit that was concealed from the road.

"It is too small," she confided to Ludwik. "Was it larger in 1944?"

The question was repeated to dr Woźniak who flapped his arms, wagged his head from side to side and held forth for several minutes in reply. In the end, he shrugged and waved a hand towards the end of the camp area. Belinda caught his drift. She was right, there was more.

"Can we go and have a look?" she asked.

The party set off at a brisk march to the far end of the camp along the gravelled path that dissected the site. Peering through the undergrowth, she saw below her what could have been described as a pit. It was a tangle of weeds. There were signs of demarcation lines, suggesting that the area had been used recently for allotments.

"The Doctor says that the camp was also down there. It was the area for Jews and political prisoners," commented Ludwik. Belinda nodded with satisfaction. The terrain conformed more accurately to her expectations.

"But he say that the women prisoners not in this part," continued Ludwik.

'Odd,' thought Belinda, keeping her own council this time. 'Maria was down there at some time, whatever he says. It is the only way that she would have known what it looked like.' When the time was more opportune, further enquiries would have to be made.

Approaching the hedge, they had passed a high bank on the right.

"What is that?" she asked as she turned.

"This is the reservoir," replied Ludwik. Dr Woźniak burst into voluble action. "The water for the showers, washhouse, latrines – not for drinking," he continued trying to translate and listen at the same time.

"Can we go up to see?" enquired their inquisitive pupil.

The bank was steep and very slippery, but the climb, assisted by the occasional grab at a tuft of grass was well worthwhile. The reservoir was a medium sized swimming pool, a path six foot wide running around the edge. It was possibly eight feet deep with internal walls that sloped from the bottom to the rim at a forty-five-degree angle. There was no visible means by which the water entered or left the pool.

"How did it work?" asked Belinda.

"The prisoners worked a pump by walking around the pool, dragging heavy wooden poles." said Ludwik after the obligatory pause for discussion in Polish with dr Woźniak.

The explanation cleared up a curious observation made by Maria in her book. She had commented rather sarcastically about seeing men carrying beams around the compound in what she saw as senseless labour. What she had not seen from ground level was the reservoir. It was probable that as a female prisoner, she had never climbed the slope and therefore was unaware of what lay on the top of the mound.

"If a prisoner fell exhausted from the work, he would be pushed into the water," continued Ludwik in echo to the doctor's commentary. "You see the shape of the sides, they were slippery and the prisoner could not reach the edge. He could not get out and eventually, he drowned."

For the umpteenth time that day Belinda felt her guts tighten. Each fragment of information hit her afresh as though it was the first. She had been unprepared for a confrontation with stark reality. She felt drowned by it all, feeling the tragedy of the spirits that still lingered.

From her vantage point at the top of the bank, she had a clear view of the sites of the various huts and barracks of the camp. She slithered down the slope and walked back past the memorial. Nearing the gate, she stopped abruptly. A rectangle, smaller than the rest, lay on her right. An engraved stone would have given her a clue had she been able to read Polish, but instinctively, she knew what had stood there in 1944 – the death barrack, where condemned prisoners were held. According to Maria, a red lamp shone outside whenever it was occupied.

The red light was rarely unlit. Here, prisoners had suffered eternal torture. No one emerged alive.

That evening, she sat in her room at the top of the Dom Polonii in a daze. She could not face the idea of food. Instead, she gulped down cup after cup of black coffee. Well into the night, she made notes on what she had seen and heard during the day. There was so much and as her thoughts sifted the information, the implications were endless.

As far as Maria was concerned, Fort VII and Poggenburg were no figment of her imagination. The question as to whether Maria's story was based on fact or fiction had indisputably been answered. The two prisons had been a horrendous reality. However, beyond the fact that the camps had existed lay the questions as to why they existed at all and when Fort VII had come into use.

Belinda had read an account of the Nuremberg trials at which one of the accusations against the prisoners suggested that the 'Holocaust' had been planned before the war started. If the term holocaust referred to the Poles as well as the Jews, Slovaks and gypsies, she had that day seen proof that it had certainly been planned before the invasion of Poland in September 1939 and that the plan had been carried out with bestial ferocity. At Nuremberg, however, she had understood that the 'Holocaust' related to the gas chambers of the extermination camps and the mass slaughter of the Jews. Proof of forethought in that direction was less clear. 'What did happen to the Jews of Poznań?' she wondered. The whole matter required closer investigation.

WEDNESDAY 20TH SEPTEMBER 1995

The following day, Belinda reported to the little office at the centre of the Stary Rynek. Dr Woźniak had busied himself with the antique coffee machine, which competed for space on the small shelf next to the telephone. Conversation was impossible. As she sipped the steaming brew, she took note of the clutter in the room. Books, folders, boxes and loose leaves of paper were stacked in precarious heaps on every horizontal surface. A prehistoric typewriter squatted in the middle of the central desk surrounded by the muddle. An old-fashioned hatstand and three chairs filled what little floor space remained. When the door opened to admit a visitor, a ritual chess game ensued whereby the newcomer was accommodated, by stacking one heap upon another until a chair was free or two square feet of floor space had been cleared.

Ludwik arrived, freshened by a good night's sleep, he was eager to wrestle again with the English language. Belinda, on the other hand was still somewhat overwhelmed by the revelations of the previous day. She had not slept well and she felt that the events unfolding around her had taken on a purpose of their own. She was in a time warp and found it hard to relate to the immediate present. A mere observer, she had become entangled in surreal horror concerning events that had happened over half a century ago.

As the morning progressed, a small heap of paper grew on the desk in front of her. The doctor had unearthed a prehistoric photocopier which had been concealed on a shelf and was making copies of various documents; prison lists; a letter; pages from books; lists of members of the Polish resistance army (Armia Krajowa – AK). Maria and her mother, it seemed, had been fairly notorious. Their names had turned up with surprising regularity.

Already there was a divergence from the story as Maria had told it. They were both members of the resistance. Maria had been code named 'Nana' and her mother, 'Jaga'. What role they played in the AK, however, was impossible to establish. No obvious reference to such activity had been made by Maria in her story and very little was known about 'BLOC', the Berlin based unit to which they were linked.

'Nana', Maria's code name was a stumbling block. Maria had given her stage name as 'Nana Sullivan' and it is doubtful that the same title would have been used as a code name when her identity could be too easily established. She had suggested several times, that her mother may well have had contact with the resistance movement and therefore 'Jaga' as a code name for her was valid. Whether Maria had been involved to the same degree was, in Belinda's mind, questionable.

"Was Maria a Jewess?" Ludwik had asked at one point.

"I don't think so," replied Belinda, racking her brain for any indication in Maria's writings that could give her a clue. She drew a blank.

"No, definitely not," she decided. Dr Woźniak screwed up his face and muttered aloud.

"Dr Woźniak say her mother was identified as Jewess in Poggenburg. He say she have a long nose."

This was a novel turn. What was the significance of a long nose and why should an aquiline feature necessarily identify the owner as Jewish?

"If she had long nose, this enough to make the Germans suspect that she was Jewish," he continued after several minutes translating delay. "She failed the 'Jews Test'," he concluded.

"And what exactly was that?" exclaimed Belinda puzzled. More delay ensued before Ludwik scratched his head and gazed up at the ceiling searching for inspiration.

"The 'Jews Test' was a mask which was placed over the face. If the face fitted certain – how you say – measurements, the person identified as Jewish." It took a moment for the meaning of his explanation to sink in. 'Dear God, how many non-Jews were swept into the net because their facial features conformed to the Nazi idea of a Jewish profile?' she wondered.

"What happened to the Jews in Poznań?" she asked. Ludwik referred to the doctor for enlightenment.

"They were arrested and placed in ghetto near Zabikowo," came the reply. "From there, they were transported to camps in the General Government of Poland sometime in 1942," he concluded.

"And how do you know that Maria's mother was identified as a Jewess in

Poggenburg, or Zabikowo as you call it?" This was a new element in her enquiries, which needed clarifying.

"She is mentioned in a letter that was written by another woman prisoner in the camp," explained Ludwik.

Belinda remembered the photographs, which she had found amongst Maria's papers after she had died. One in particular was a full-face portrait of Maria with her mother. She had brought copies with her, and retrieving her brief case from beneath the desk, she quickly located them.

"Could these help perhaps?" she asked. She passed them over to the doctor. He almost snatched them from her hand. Within seconds, he was crooning with satisfaction. The photos included several of a very glamorous and elaborately dressed young lady, who had posed for the camera in a number of dramatic poses. He came to the one of Maria with her mother.

"Is this Maria with her mother, Antonina?" asked Ludwik.

"I think so," replied Belinda. The doctor let out a gleeful whoop, throwing his arms into the air, his puckered face lit up in satisfaction.

"The doctor say, she has a long nose!" explained Ludwik unnecessarily.

If only all the mysteries had been so simple to solve.

A list of female prisoners in Fort VII was added to the growing heap of papers. It did not include the names of Maria Weychanowna and her mother, Antonina Weychan. It did, however, include all the women arrested following an incident in the village of Mosina.

Maria had not given details of the 'Mosina case'. She had asked questions on the very first night of her imprisonment, discovering the name of the village from which her cell companions had been taken. In her innocence, she had tried to make conversation with them, but suspecting that she might have been a German 'plant', the women refused to enlighten her and she had not discovered the reason for their arrest. An informant in the cell had betrayed her. The following day, she had been brutally beaten by a German officer during an interrogation session. He accused her of questioning the women to gain information for the resistance. There was a German spy in the cell, but it was not Maria. It had been her first bitter lesson in camp discipline.

"Can you tell me about Mosina?" she asked.

"Mosina? Yes, I check with dr Woźniak." Ten minutes later, Ludwik started his explanation. He was tiring. The concentration needed to continually translate into a language that he had not used for so long, was waning. He struggled on manfully.

"In 1942, a virus infection, how you say, a 'bug', was discovered in Warsaw. It was smuggled across the border, between the Wartegau (New Reich Territories) and General Government and delivered to secret destination in Posen. Here it is developed and a quantity produced. The virus was tested in Mosina. Village not far from city. The experiment resulted in the death of two Germans and one cow." Ludvik paused for breath.

"In reprisal, the Germans arrested 124 people who lived in the village. It included 48 women. Some arrested in December 1942 and the rest in January 1943. They were all imprisoned in Fort VII," he concluded.

In March, Maria and her mother had joined them in Cell 17.

The severity of the reprisal seemed excessive as a revenge for two German dead. Perhaps the dead cow was significant, proving that the virus was deadly for more than one animal species. The 'case' must have been considered of great importance. If an instrument of germ warfare were available to the Polish resistance, the implications would have been far reaching. A prolonged investigation followed. Few hostages survived. The fifty women, including Maria Górska, a medical doctor, were interned in Fort VII during the winter of 1942/43 and later moved to Poggenburg.

They either died from malnutrition or illness or were transported eastwards towards the end of 1944, shortly before the camp was evacuated. Many of the children of the arrestees were transported to the Children's Camp in Lichtmanstadt (today known as Łódź) situated to the southwest of Warsaw. The men, husbands, sons and brothers, were either executed immediately or transported to concentration camps outside the Reich Territories of Poland.

Dr Maria Górska's name appeared among a list of prisoners who managed to escape during the evacuation at the end of war. She had made her home in London, where she had died in 1993.

There had been only one doctor in Poggenburg, namely, the prisoner from Mosina. She had to be the doctor friend that had inspired Maria and saved her life on at least two occasions. Sadly Belinda had delayed too long to start her enquiries. A prime witness that would have been able to confirm Maria Weychan's claims was now beyond reach. Of her it was known that while in the camp, she cooperated with the Germans by signing the death certificates of the victims of 'accidental death' syndrome. This was enough for dr Woźniak to disapprove of her. She had collaborated! Belinda felt that it was a harsh attitude to take. As the only medically qualified person in Poggenburg, she was the only person that could legally sign a death certificate. A lifeless corpse was beyond help, so how confirmation of death with a signature could, in the circumstances, be condemned as 'collaboration,' seemed somewhat arbitrary to her. The moment of confrontation passed, but it had made Belinda aware of the thin line that, if crossed, defined a 'traitor'.

The evidence so far was corroborating Maria's story and it would seem that beyond doubt, at least as far as her imprisonment was concerned, her account was fact and not fiction.

There were still many things that needed further investigation. The reasons behind her survival in the camp suggested collaboration of some kind. Why had the Germans not executed her unless she had proven useful to them?

The doctor had not yet seen the complete manuscript. The material that he had produced so far had been in response to direct questions that Belinda had asked in her introductory letters. He had not been able to refer to Maria's account for clues and therefore the material had thus far not been influenced by any pre-knowledge of what needed to be confirmed. He had obviously dug deep to discover many of the personal details that related to Maria, but he expressed, with Ludwik's help, some scepticism about the validity of the complete manuscript. Belinda knew that his attitude was not without foundation. The true identity of most of the characters in her story had been concealed and her ability to dramatise had added a flavour of fantasy, which was hard to relate to everyday existence. Even during the last ten years of her life, Belinda had come to recognise that, if necessary, Maria could have made a Wagnerian drama out of a fly walking up a wall. Belinda had nursed strong doubts about the degree of drama in the text, fearing that the manuscript would be received with derision in Poland as a parody. Having ascertained that a large percentage of the content was based very much on fact, she had revised her opinion. With some confidence, she produced the copy of the original manuscript that she had brought with her.

As she drew the photocopy from her briefcase, the doctor, who had been talking non-stop, suddenly fell silent. She offered him the bound German script. His eyes opened wide. Ludwik asked for confirmation that this was a copy of the German manuscript and the doctor sank down into his chair with a satisfied grunt. He started to read.

More coffee was served heralding the conclusion of the morning conference. Ludwik visibly relaxed and his command of English returned. Buttered rolls appeared and dr Woźniak placed a handsome apple into Belinda's hand.

He smiled at Belinda and waited for Ludwik to translate. "Dr Woźniak say he grow apple in his garden. It is very special Polish apple," explained Ludwik.

"Yabooeck!" said the doctor, pointing to the apple. Belinda appreciated that she was about to learn another essential Polish word.

"Dr Woźniak say it is from his garden in the country," repeated Ludwik in answer to the question written on Belinda's face. "It is a good Polish apple." The doctor hardly seemed to notice the serving of refreshments. His attention was focused entirely on the typed pages in his hand.

The fruit did indeed look tempting. It was large and the colour of a Cox's Orange Pippin. When she bit into it (Ludwik had not been exaggerating) the fruit tasted delicious.

"The doctor has garden in Kórnik, 30 kilometres from Poznań," Ludwik continued chattily. "It have little house for living in weekends and many fruit trees."

Kórnik was also Ludwik's family home, he told her. Now retired, he assisted dr. Woźniak as a volunteer. He lived in an apartment in the suburbs of Poznań with his wife. They had a married daughter and three grandchildren.

As she rose to leave, tucking the sheaf of papers into her briefcase, she asked one last question. "Please, Ludwik, can you help me with the Polish word for 'thank you'?"

"This is easy." Ludwik grinned down at her. He lowered his voice and in a confidential tone continued. "Think you are, how you say, a little 'tipsy' and that you try to say in English 'thank you'. It maybe sound something like 'shenkyoo' and it is the same in Polish if you add ye on the end."

"Now that I should be able to remember," said Belinda. "Shenkuye!" Everyone laughed at her efforts.

They were joined in the afternoon by the doctor's teenage daughter, Małgosia, who shyly offered to relieve Ludwik of his translating responsibilities. She was petite in stature, her movements cautious; dainty, like an inquisitive bird. She teased her grumpy looking parent and he pouted and tutted in response, while obviously bursting with pride of his pretty daughter.

The party abandoned the tiny office. With much jangling of keys, the inner and outer doors were locked by a muttering doctor who tried first one then another key into the numerous keyholes in each door. His personal Fort Knox safely secured, they emerged into the afternoon sun.

"You are going to meet the director of the Zachodni Institute," Małgosia offered as an explanation, as they proceeded towards an ornate and imposing building on one side of the square. "This is the headquarters of the Institute."

Belinda wished that she had been given warning of the appointment. A comb through her hair and a lipstick check would not have gone amiss.

In the event, the director of the Zachodni turned out to be a charming grey-haired gentleman, who babbled incomprehensibly to the doctor while nodding and smiling warmly at Belinda. He proffered assistance in finding Maria's maternal grandparents, surnamed Szymanski and where they had lived.

The visit was short and sweet. Soon the party was retreating down the stone stairs that swept up to the first floor from the vestibule. They emerged once again into the sunshine of the Stary Rynek. The group broke up, the doctor returning to his office, while Ludwik, Małgosia and Belinda set off in search of the high school that featured in Maria's manuscript.

They had tramped for miles in seemingly endless circles. Małgosia was politely tired, Ludwik was gallantly weary and the soles of Belinda's feet burned in complaint. The trio retired to a small coffee shop to recuperate.

Belinda had been busy with her camera, taking photographs of the Marcellinski Boulevard, lined with shops, the largest of which displayed religious books and statues in its show windows. None of the other wide streets surrounding the Stary Rynek boasted such an emporium. In contrast, the shops were small. The range of retailers for haberdashery, groceries, jewellery, china, shoes and newspapers repeated itself every one hundred yards or so.

They had passed the city hospital, a grim building with heavy traffic grumbling past, surrounded by noise, fumes and bustle. Its small windows and dirty walls gave the impression of a prison rather than an institution for restoring health.

The search for the site of the Sacré Coeur School had proven singularly unsuccessful.

After the mental shock of visit to Fort VII and Zabikowo the previous day, her second day in Poznań had been physically exhausting but less of a trial for the nerves. Having bid farewell to her equally weary companions, she ventured into a small grocery store en route back to the Dom Polonii and purchased coffee, milk, fruit, ham and bread in order that, once she had climbed to her crows-nest in the roof, she would not have to torment her feet again for a while.

A long soak in the bath, restored her to some degree of normality. Afterwards, she curled up in front of the enormous television screen. Perhaps watching a dubbed English film with subtitles might help her to hear the lilt of the language and at the same time, understand what was being said by reading the subtitles. The ambitious idea was thwarted by the method used to translate the film. An expressionless voice drowned the English into incomprehensiveness. The second channel available was showing a bloody battle. Russian tanks charged ruthlessly over everything in their path. Ragged Poles ran about in bare feet, gallantly waving tattered flags. The choice was limited and hardly entertaining. Belinda soon opted to hit the hay.

8

THURSDAY 21ST SEPTEMBER 1995

The rendezvous in dr Woźniak's office was scheduled for a civilised hour and there was no need to hurtle out of bed at sunrise. The offices below her room on the third floor were already occupied by the time Belinda descended to the small kitchen to make a cup of coffee. While she was waiting for the kettle to boil, the same young man who she had encountered two days before appeared in the doorway and introduced himself in impeccable English. He worked in the office and was occupied with the promotion of Poland's tourist industry, Belinda learned. He was very interested in the reason for her visit to Poznań and they chatted for several minutes.

By ten o'clock, Belinda was back in the now familiar muddle of the doctor's office. Ludwik had read a quarter of Maria's manuscript overnight and had much to discuss with dr Woźniak. They had been working on the snippets that Belinda had mentioned in her letters. Now they had the original meat of the text to chew over and digest.

The first point that dr Woźniak picked up on concerned the school that Maria mentioned in her opening chapter. He proclaimed emphatically that there was no such place within the area that Maria described, but that he would make enquiries. Belinda began to suspect that the doctor was sceptical about the accuracy of Maria's pre-war lifestyle. Ludwik explained to her that too many survivors had been found to distort the facts in their memoirs and at this stage, neither of them were certain that the manuscript contained true fact or was a fiction based on fact.

Letters from witnesses showed, as well as the prison lists that Maria had been in Poggenburg. It was also fact that the women from Mosina had been in Fort VII and Poggenburg. But documentary confirmation of Maria's imprisonment in Fort VII was missing along with many other details. If the boarding school that she described as lying north of Posen had not existed, serious doubt was cast on what followed. According to her story, Maria persuaded her mother to allow her to take up a stage career. In January 1939, she was dancing solo in the café clubs of Warsaw. She met and fell in love with Herbert Kurzke, the son of a woman that her mother had known at school when she lived in Bochum, Germany. September 1st, war with Germany was announced. Herbert disappeared. Maria made her way back to Posen. Herbert reappeared wearing a German uniform. The story went on but with the school missing, the roots were severed.

As for meeting the women from Mosina, it was possible that Maria had gleaned the story from the prisoners when she met them in Poggenburg. That for the moment was dr Woźniak's argument.

Before leaving home, Belinda had scoured maps, attempting to locate the village of Mosina. The name had sounded more Italian than Polish. Not finding it, she had doubted its existence. Mosina did exist and she was disappointed to be told that perhaps the school did not.

The discussions continued during dinner that evening at dr Woźniak's first floor apartment, a ten-minute walk from the Stary Rynek. Belinda was introduced to his family, to his wife, his daughter Małgosia, whom she had met previously, his son (speaking excellent English), his son's wife who was training to be an English teacher and Marta, his youngest daughter. They all made her feel very welcome. More maps of Poznań appeared, old and new, so that comparisons could be made. From the older map, the chain of fortresses could be more easily discerned. Like a long necklace they hung as stones on a chain due south of the citadel that resembled a symmetrically shaped crown to the north of the city centre.

There were twelve of them – Fort I to Fort XII. Some had fallen into ruin and were beyond repair, but besides Fort VII, two had been used during the War to house POWs; the Russians in one, the British in another. Each Fort was a regular half a mile distant from the next with a smaller bunker installation midway between the main forts. From the maps, the citadel appeared to cover a vast area and Belinda expressed an interest to explore it if possible. The proposed excursion was duly 'organised'.

Britain was celebrating the fifty years of peace since the end of WWII in 1945. Dr Woźniak became agitated when this subject arose in the conversation. Poland, the country that caused Britain to declare war on Germany in the first place, had only just emerged from the end of 'the War'. She had been occupied for fifty years when the Russians withdrew in 1989, five years by Germany and forty-five years by the Soviet Union. For the Poles, the war had not ceased in 1945 and the current Western celebrations sounded hollow and meaningless to them.

The resistance movement had not ceased to exist in 1945. It just had a new target. Riots in Poznań in the 50s, 60s and 70s had resulted in bloodshed and heartache with the coffin of repression screwed down tighter each time. Only post the strikes in Gdansk did the smell of freedom become stronger and confidence grow in the possibility that national autonomy was an achievable goal.

Of the Zachodni Institute itself, Belinda was led to understand that it had become effective only during the last six to seven years, but that it was still not taken seriously by its past associates. London, Berlin and Warsaw patronised rather than cooperated with the Institute. Belinda recalled the condescending attitude of the woman at the Polish Embassy in London. Two small pieces of the jigsaw puzzle locked together.

9

FRIDAY 22ND SEPTEMBER 1995

The director of Instytut Zachodni was true to his word. Box files containing records of families and their domiciles had been hauled from the cellar of the Institute and awaited the investigating trio next morning. The square boxes were covered in dust, battered and worn. They contained thousands of brittle zerox records, filed in haphazard alphabetical order.

Ludwik, dr Woźniak and Belinda each took a box, checking them to find those with the 'S' (Szymanski) records. Ten minutes later, they were getting warmer, but as the fragile pieces of paper had not always been returned into their correct order, a careful check of each record had to be made.

There were several moments of excitement when a 'possible' came to light, but as with a cryptic crossword, when the correct piece of paper was found, the answer was obvious. Maria's grandfather, grandmother, her mother, an aunt and four uncles were listed at the same address in 1927. The date of their return to Poland had been recorded and when they moved to a new abode, the records had been updated.

Vertical crosses had been drawn by the names of Maria's grandfather, Jan Szymanski and his eldest son, Alois Szymanski. Dr Woźniak did not seem to be certain what they signified. He thought that it most probably meant that they were confirmed dead.

Comparing the Szymanski record with others in the box, Belinda observed that many names were marked in the same fashion. Did it signify death? She noticed that the marks made on the Szymanski records were subtly different. That beside the name of the uncle was simple and had been drawn only the once. That beside the grandfather's name had been scored heavily several times and with a pressure that had left a marked indentation in the paper. The hand that held the pen had been forceful and final. An intuition told her that the crosses most surely meant death.

She became aware that Ludwik was saying something to her. The words were partially drifting over her head. The scrap of paper with its sign of death had focused her attention so much that her surroundings and company had faded into the background. The vigour with which the cross by Maria's grandfather had been repeatedly penned, caused her to wonder who had held the pen with such passion. If Szymanski senior had been active in encouraging the Scout movement and kept company with Polish Generals as Maria had described, his death would have been welcomed by the German invaders – and he was supposed to have been executed in 1939. Questions started to bubble up out of the mire, tumbling chaotically over each. It was frustrating that the language barrier reduced communication to the speed of a snail crawling backwards.

'Yes, these records had been used by the Germans.' 'Yes, the crosses had been added by them.' 'Yes, the crosses did signify death.' 'Yes, yes, yes... Belinda began to feel revulsion for the aging paper in her hand. It had once been held by other hands, hands belonging to people with evil intent. They had consulted it to locate the houses of blacklisted 'undesirables', sought out their prey and had recorded their success. Key figures had been systematically removed from the Polish society. The files were consulted a second time to identify the streets of the city from where whole families would be removed during the 'ethnic cleansing' from the new Reich Territory of Poles in 1939/40.

This time even larger chunks of the jigsaw puzzle slotted into place. Maria's German fiancé Herbert had informed her mother about which streets would be cleared the following night and Antonina had in turn, warned friends in the area. Arrest and immediate deportation had thus been avoided by some families.

They found refuge with friends instead of remaining at home to receive unwelcome visitors. Return was possible the next day, as the SS would have been busy elsewhere. But how had Herbert come by this information? Maria had not identified his role in the German forces and his information had been accurate until the night when the SS knocked on the door of 5, Piekary Street, the home of her grandparents where she and her mother had sought refuge.

Herbert's role was becoming significant. His records in the German armed forces would have to be traced when she returned to England.

Further consultation with the files revealed Maria's family background. Antonina Szymanska had married Władysław Weychan in 1920. Maria was born in 1922, but her parents divorced in 1924. Later investigations by dr Woźniak revealed the reason for the divorce. Władysław strayed into the arms of his second cousin and a baby was expected! Antonina subsequently made her home in an apartment owned by General Tadeusz Szymanski. They too were distant cousins.

These facts revealed a conundrum.

Maria had portrayed her 'grandfather' in a way that he could be identified as Tadeusz Szymanski, whereas her real grandfather was a retired mining engineer who managed a newsagent in a poorer part of the city. Perhaps Antonina had been 'adopted' by the more affluent side of the family and Maria had grown up under the impression that Tadeusz was her true grandfather. The lifestyle that she described was certainly that of a privileged child.

The problem of identifying the 'grandfather' included the problem of identifying her 'father'. Władysław Weychan had disappeared from the records in 1929. He had sired two children with his cousin, both of whom had died within a year of birth. Maria's 'father' during the 30s was not he.

The research in the files had posed more questions than it had answered. Some could be resolved. Others were lost forever in the dust of time.

By mid-morning, Belinda and her new colleagues were trekking northwards to the citadel. Maps and diagrams had not prepared her for the enormous scale of the place. The main entrance required the visitors to scale a high embankment by climbing a succession of wide steps. A tall column crowned the summit. By the time they reached the top, Belinda's knees were weak. They had climbed nearly 100 stone steps, passed graveyards on the one side and mature trees on the other, the embankment forming a high, steep hill to protect the citadel itself. At the top of the steps, the ground was flat, an area cleared of trees and the size of three football pitches to the right, tarmac paths leading into woodland on the left. There was no sign of a structure that could possibly be a citadel. 'Perhaps, like Fort VII, it is subterranean' Belinda pondered. The area was flat and featureless apart from the forest and stretched far into the distance; no buildings, no ruins; nothing but trees. Belinda was somewhat perplexed as to what to expect. She was not sure quite what she was looking for. The panorama of trees was disappointing.

Wishing that communication was easier, she followed her two escorts as they gesticulated at each other and pointed in opposing directions. They seemed undecided as to which path they should take. Straight ahead was perhaps too obvious. Not knowing what they were talking about, Belinda had only their tone of voice, their body language and facial expression to indicate the theme of the discussion. She had almost lost interest by the time Ludwik announced, "We go this way."

She dogged their footsteps. Soon the path began a slow descent, widening, as it led towards a depression. She could now see, on the far side, a row of several tall brick arches. Each arch framed a large window.

They entered a door under the arch furthest to the right, signed a visitor's book and started to inspect the contents of the little museum within. The items were few. Faded prints with explanations in Polish lined the walls. The artefacts in the display cases were meaningless to her. As in the museums of Fort VII and Zabikowo, she found the grim exhibits very oppressive. Boredom was setting in as she settled on a low wall to muse.

She was not permitted to daydream. Dr Woźniak had the curator in tow, a metal ring of large keys dangling from his hand.

"We go this way," announced Ludwik.

Outside, the curator was wrestling with the lock of a wrought iron gate to one side of the museum entrance. Beyond it, narrow steps led upwards to the turfed roof covering the museum, a stout fence of metal bars defending the area from trespass. The trio climbed the steps and emerged at the top to look down on a collection of wartime lorries and aeroplanes that had been completely hidden by the ridge.

Not being particularly knowledgeable about vehicles or machines that flew, Belinda was at a loss at how to appear interested. The lorries were parked one behind the other and her imagination leapt the years. She was walking along a roadside with the roar of their engines in her ears.

She stared at the large biplane. It looked so unbattered for its age. Unexpectedly, she found common ground with Ludwik.

"We use a machine like this to tow the gliders up into the sky at my club," he said.

"A fifty-year-old plane like that," Belinda said in an incredulous tone.

"Oh yes! It is very, how you say – good. The mechanisms are very simple and easy to repair."

"Do you glide?" asked Belinda.

"Not so much now, but in the past, I obtained the 'Three Cs.'" Ludwik grew perceptibly in height as he announced his achievement.

"Now I know what that is," said Belinda. "My uncle also has the 'Three Cs' for his gliding. You are an expert."

"Your uncle?" Ludwik's eyes sparkled. The number of glider pilots worldwide that acquire the accolade, are few. "His name?"

"Waghorn. Mervyn Waghorn."

"Ah, I do not know this name," Ludwik looked apologetic. "It is not so well known here, the people in the West."

Belinda had flown in a glider only once in her life. She still had vivid recollections of the experience; terrified by the noise made by the wind as the winch pulled the machine into the sky; rapture at the peace that followed when the cable was dropped and the wonderment of the magnificent view. The pilot had been a very good friend of her uncle who had worked for De Haveland in Hatfield and Sydney before becoming the National Gliding Champion in Australia.

Ludwik warmed to his subject when he realised that Belinda had connections with his personal enthusiasm for a sport. At last, a common denominator, a bridge across the divide! In a country that in many ways seemed to be in a time warp, Belinda had encountered a parallel with her own cultural background.

Soon they were trudging back across the wooded space to the outer embankment. They descended by a side route through the graveyards. The graves were grouped according to nationality. They stopped by five gravestones of a British aircrew that had died when their plane crashed near Posen. They were the only British graves. She became aware of the loneliness of dying in a far-flung place, with no family to bury and care for ones remains. That duty had been reverentially undertaken by strangers, who to this day kept their graves tidy. Others, she could see, did not receive such attention.

As they walked south to the Stary Rynek, she learned more about the citadel and the surrounding area. In January/February 1945, during the attack on Posen by the Russians, the northern part of the city had been flattened.

"2,000 Germans lie here," announced dr Woźniak, pointing to a garage forecourt, "and 5,000 Russians there," waving his arm in the direction of a playing field.

"Many, many more soldiers killed," added Ludwik.

The significance of the well-tended graves of the British airmen at the citadel suddenly increased. While their sacrifice was still honoured, the remains of thousands of German and Russian soldiers were sealed unceremoniously under tarmac and concrete.

10

Returning to her lodgings was to experience secure bliss. As the heavy door at the bottom of the stairs thumped shut and the lock clicked, the death and destruction of the morning remained on the other side.

As she made coffee in the little kitchen, she again met the young man who was employed in the office. He too took a cup and described his work regarding tourist promotion and contacting Poles worldwide. So many nationals had been obliged to leave Poland during the war in order to survive and had been unable to return afterwards because the Russians were in occupation. Two generations had been born in exile and only now could they safely return to the land of their forefathers.

It was another new concept for Belinda to digest. England was a part of the British Isles and had enjoyed the benefits of being an island off the main landmass of Europe. The Channel, La Manche or German Sea, but all the same stretch of water depending from which coast one looked at it, was a convenient 'ditch' that had thwarted potential invaders for hundreds of years. The Romans and Vikings had managed to cross it, but so long ago that it was certainly not within living memory. Poland and her people had a history of exploitation by her neighbours and until very recently had been subject to the regime of an overlord who ruled by suppression and fear.

Belinda had understood from Maria's story, that the standard of living between WWI and WWII had been comparable to anywhere else in Europe. The lifestyle and expectations had been utterly destroyed by the German invasion in 1939 and only now, after fifty years, was Poland emerging from an enforced hibernation that had left it in a suspended animation.

Belinda was ignorant. She recalled school lessons in the early 60s, when the question of Poland's recent history had arisen. A girl at the school had been the daughter of Polish émigrés. "It is all too complicated," the teacher had explained, and that was all that she had learned. No explanation was offered. As the subject matter was pronounced to be complicated, perhaps requiring the brain to be engaged to understand the problems, the whole class was unanimously relieved that the subject was dropped and the lesson had moved on to simpler topics.

When she returned home, she would have to start seeking out the material that would fill the chasms in her knowledge.

From her guidebook, Belinda learned that the city of Poznań is situated on the river Warta in the centre of the area of Poland known as Wielkopolska (Greater Poland).

Over a thousand years ago, it had been in the region of Wielkopolska that the Polish state originated. Because of its geographical position, Poznań had been an important centre throughout the turbulent history of Poland, not least in the last century.

In 968, two years after the emergence of Poland as an independent state, Poznań became the chosen settlement for the site of the first bishopric and cathedral, which served thereafter as the necropolis of the kings and princes of the Piast dynasty. The city had received its town charter in 1253 and situated as it was on the junction of several traditional trade routes, it developed rapidly into a major trading centre. Royal patronage meant that majestic buildings are seen in every street of the old town, although most are today converted into centres of culture, museums, art galleries or libraries.

During the last hundred years, the citizens of Poznań have had an extraordinary influence on the fate of Poland. In the nineteenth century, when the region was under Prussian control, the city became the main theatre of patriotic action in the struggle for independence culminating in the Greater Poland Rising in 1918.

The Treaty of Versailles confirmed the victory and after many centuries of often violent history, Poland once again became a united nation.

Most of the northern part of the town had been destroyed at the end of WWII. In January 1945, the German army made a stand against the advancing Russian forces. They occupied the bunkers of the citadel and held Stalin's army at bay for a full month. The fighting was costly for both sides and most of the historic old town was reduced to rubble in the battle.

But once the carnage had been cleared, instead of replacing the expensive old with inexpensive new, the historic buildings of the city were meticulously rebuilt in the 60s and restored to their original glory. Today, the palaces, churches and municipal buildings of the city once again stand as reminders of Poznań's rich heritage.

As she turned the pages of her guidebook, she began to wonder. Poland had only recently emerged from behind the iron curtain, yet all this restoration seemed to have taken place soon after the war. From the pictures that she was looking at, of glittering ornate interiors, no expense or trouble had been spared. The collection of photographs, hanging in the stairwell of her lodgings, depicted roofless terraces, burnt-out facades and heaps of rubble. Now wiser, Belinda would pay them closer attention when next she passed.

SATURDAY 23RD SEPTEMBER 1995

11

For the first time since her arrival, Belinda did not have to be bright eyed and bushy tailed by 7.30 in the morning. All week she had been punctual to the minute for the early appointments with dr Woźniak. The offices below her were also closed for the weekend and she met no one as she crept down the stairs, in a dishevelled state of dress, to the kitchen to make her coffee.

It was a bright sunny day, the sky a shimmering blue as she opened the windows and gazed down on the square below. Already, it was busy with family groups, couples and teenagers crisscrossing the cobblestones and the elderly shuffling along the more even surface of the pavement. Kiosks were being erected in front of the central complex of buildings, the traders bobbing back and forth arranging their wares. A number of coffee houses had annexed their section of the roadway and had erected low platforms on which they had placed tables and chairs for their customers. The striped canopies rippled in the gentle breeze.

Perched on the windowsill, her knees drawn up under her chin, Belinda people-watched for nearly an hour; observing the pixie-like waitresses darting to and fro across the pavement between the coffee house and canopy, the 'major domo' loitering in the doorway issuing instructions, youngsters greeting each other, lingering in groups, then scattering, the lone figure waiting interminably for one who never came. She also noticed the beggars, attracted to the most crowded spots, touching people on the arm, fixing them with a defiant stare and holding out a hand, the palm upturned.

With a sigh, Belinda climbed down from the sill and glared at the mountain of books and papers that littered the coffee table. With time to call her own, she realised that she must do some work to sort out the information that she had harvested in the past four days. Not comprehending even the titles of the books and pamphlets that she had been given, she had to make sure that she marked each to at least denote the source and the occasion. Her notes too, needed attention and she needed to collate them in such a way that they would make sense in the future.

Dr Woźniak had lent her a list of the old German street names for Posen, relating them to the current street names of Poznań today. The list was precious and Belinda had promised to return it within a few weeks. Her memory being so poor and the mundane chaos of home life being so distracting, she decided to explore the list, find the relevant streets and return the document on Monday, before she left Poland.

Her labours were disturbed by the sound of cars hooting in the square. Curious as to the cause of the excitement, Belinda peered out from her eerie to see two cars chasing each other around the centre of the Stary Rynek, scattering unwary pedestrians. The friendly waves from bystanders and the glimpse of white in the rear seat of the car suggested the cause for the invasion of motor vehicles in the pedestrian precinct. It appeared that it was traditional for newlyweds to be driven triumphantly around the town hall accompanied by the orchestral din of a blaring horn. Belinda was to be reconciled to such interruptions every twenty minutes.

Soon after 11 o'clock, the ominous thunder of fire engine bells filled the air causing Belinda to abruptly abandoned her paperwork. From her window, she saw half a dozen engines racing towards the Dom Polonii. For so many to be called out, there must be a disaster nearby. Belinda fleetingly prayed that it was not the pizzeria in the cellar of her lodgings. Her only exit was via the internal stairwell and she would be trapped.

But no, all was well! It was yet another wedding procession on its lap of honour, the engine drivers smartly dressed in uniforms adorned with gold braid. The fire brigade was celebrating.

Belinda spent the afternoon exploring the narrow streets around the Stary Rynek. After getting lost several times in the alleys around the square, she espied a shop window offering amongst the religious books, souvenir guides and maps of the town.

Inside the shop, the books were displayed on inaccessible shelves, requiring the help of an assistant to retrieve them. The middle-aged woman who came forward had the brusque air of an officious schoolteacher. She scowled and shook her head vigorously as soon as she realised that Belinda was English and immediately marched noisily across the shop, her derision of a dissolute western

European expressed by the stolid clump of her footfall. She stopped by the girl minding the till. They swapped places.

The next generation, not only could speak English quite respectably but was as charming as her colleague was brusque.

During the afternoon, a large wooden platform had been erected in the corner of the square nearest to the Dom Polonii. Drums and cymbals were arranged on the pavement side of the dais with a battery of lights facing them from the front of the apron. A small crowd of shoppers gazed open mouthed while their children licked studiously on ice creams as the paraphernalia of a modern pop group was assembled.

When the microphones were tested, Belinda realised with horror that every decibel collected in her room above as though it was a resonance chamber. The closed double windows gave some defence, but the glass rattled with every thump.

As darkness fell, the group started to play in earnest. Their repertoire was not bad but the musical variation was limited and repetitious. A large crowd had gathered in the square. They were motionless, no one attempted to dance or sway to the rhythm. The spectacle of the stage effects, the flashing lights and puffs of smoke seemed to hypnotise them.

She was rescued by the telephone. Dr Woźniak and his daughter Małgosia were downstairs and invited her to join them for coffee. Together, they descended to the peace of the pizzeria in the basement of the building.

Małgosia was a lively slip of a girl in her late teens. She had acquired her knowledge of English behind the school desk but her accent and syntax were remarkable. Her education had been excellent. She lacked only practise and confidence. It was her job to translate for her father out of whose mouth poured a continuous torrent of words.

The conversation turned to the street names of Poznań . Having done some homework on the subject, Belinda was able to contribute to the discussion and even offered some information that dr Woźniak challenged. She resorted to fetching the maps from her room to demonstrate her point before the doctor would agree that she was correct.

It was still 'early' and dr Woźniak decided that it would be appropriate to attempt to find the Szymanski family house in Piekary Street. Thus it was that the odd trio could be found trudging around the bombsites of Poznań at 10 o'clock at night.

Piekary Street lay close to the Stary Rynek at the top of a slight hill. It did not take long to walk the distance. Only half of the apartments were still standing, impressive solid buildings for people with well-lined pockets. Number 5, the address of Maria's grandparents, was gone. A car park filled the plot. Roman Szymanski Street would have led into Piekary Street at right angles between numbers 7 and 8. Dr Woźniak expressed a particular interest in the apartment at No: 8a, it seemed important to him, but Belinda failed to discover the significance. She cursed the language barrier.

On one side of Szymanskiego (the ending of the place name indicating that it had belonged to the Szymanski estate), the five-storey apartments blocks remained though in a poor state of repair. On the other side of the road, only the grass covered foundations of four large buildings could be seen. A corrugated iron fence protected the area, just as she recalled seeing around the London bombsites in the nineteen fifties.

Belinda wanted to know why the site, so close to the centre of Poznań, had not been redeveloped after fifty years. Dr Woźniak was non-committal, muttering that perhaps either the owners could not be traced or city planning indecision and lack of capital could be the reason. He shrugged his shoulders in defeat.

On the lower end of Szymanskiego, the terraced buildings were less grandiose, the facade broken at regular intervals by arches, wide enough for the passage of a vehicle and barred by heavy wooden doors. Dr Woźniak was looking at No: 8, the residence of Halina Szymanska in Posen. He paused and scrutinised the metal plates beside the entrance. The lettering was obscured by chipped paint and defacement. Suddenly, he shot both hands into the air, indicating to Belinda that he had struck gold.

The huge doors, unvarnished and bearing the scars of time, stood ajar. He pushed one open and they entered a dingy passageway with a high ceiling. The ancient paint was flaking away, the plaster crumbling and the ornate mouldings along the top of the walls were covered in a thick layer of black grime.

The tunnel led to the back of the building into a very empty concrete yard, enclosed on the far side by a high brick wall. Not a refuse bin, clothesline or scrap of paper lurked in the corners. Belinda assumed that pre-war, it contained the stabling yard and carriage house that served the more affluent properties at the other end of the street. Today it was a bleak no-mans-land.

Halina's apartment had been on the ground floor, wide wooden steps swept upwards, spiralling out of view. They had been well worn by many feet. The explorers ventured to the door, but decided not to disturb the occupants as it was getting late. The whole place had been neglected; it had not been decorated in many years. In communist times, the doctor explained, nobody cared or took the responsibility.

As they retraced their steps past the corrugated iron fencing, the doctor remarked that this was not the sort of area that one should wander through at night. 'He tells me now!' thought Belinda, wondering whether he was warning her not to repeat the exercise alone.

Shortly before midnight, they were indulging in yet another cup of coffee. Poor Małgosia was flagging. She had needed to concentrate and work hard to stay abreast of her father's chatter. Dr Woźniak was by this time in full flow and was trying to get a number of stories across the language divide. Małgosia was faltering and Belinda gleaned only tempting morsels of the stories. Belinda was aware of her ignorance of the AK, what it stood for and what it aimed to achieve. Whenever it had been mentioned, she had nodded wisely to hide her confusion. One of the stories that sounded very interesting concerned Kastania I and Kastania II, successful Gestapo plots to expose the local AK militia, but a tiring translator obliterated the details. A second story concerned a Polish female prisoner who had satisfied the lust of the cook at Poggenburg. For a few moments, Belinda suspected that she might have been Maria's mother Antonina. The cook was caught, court-martialled and condemned to death by hanging. His crime was sexual misbehaviour with a Pole rather than abuse of a prisoner. The woman was sentenced to death and was sent to an extermination centre.

"Besides," added dr Woźniak. "Antonina would have been too old and scraggy to have been of interest." She would have been forty-seven years old. Belinda protested at his chauvinistic remark. They had all laughed. He was probably right.

12

SUNDAY 24TH SEPTEMBER 1995

The pop group was silent by the time Belinda wearily climbed the stairs to bed. Peering from her window in the morning, she could see people dressed in their Sunday best hurrying across the square to attend Holy Mass. The churches were not obvious. They were not sited grandly in their own space, but were squeezed between ordinary terraced houses. Even the larger churches often shared the same frontage as the rest of the buildings in the street and were defined only by portico steps that led upwards to the entrance. Below her, the tangle of chairs and equipment was a forlorn reminder of the pop session.

She returned to the task of sorting the material that she had collected during the week. With a dictionary to hand, she deciphered the titles of the books that she had been given, despairing at the thought of having to translate the close print of the text. Her Polish vocabulary had expanded now to seven words, 'yes, no, please, thank you, large and many', (tak, nie, prosze, dziékuje, duze and bardzo). It was not going to be very much help.

The doctor and Małgosia returned to her lodgings at noon. They had decided to take Belinda to an exhibition of film posters at the Palace of Culture.

They walked westwards from the Stary Rynek. The Palace proved to be a grim castle built by the Prussians, the grey stonework blackened by pollution. The arched portals swallow them into a stark gullet. The air was dank and the décor lacked decoration or colour of any kind. Shadowy grey steps rose in front of them leading deeper into the bowels of the beast. As they entered the vast, empty hall, they peered around, seeking signs that might indicate the way to the exhibition. Having detected over-discreet arrows pointing upward, they climbed a stairwell between high walls of grey stone.

The display of film posters that the party found on the first floor was extraordinary. It resembled a sea of stands each with sixteen posters hung back to back on eight arms. The place was eerily silent. They were the only visitors.

Belinda started to inspect the nearest exhibits, posters of films that she had never heard of depicted ghoulish figures and exotic fantasy. She was not impressed. She felt that whoever had planned the display, was making a very pointed statement about the decadence of films from the West, while the regimented arrangement of the octagonal stands illustrated the no-nonsense correctness of the East.

Dr Woźniak and Małgosia also seemed somewhat taken aback and after a few minutes Małgosia asked, "Do you like it?"

"To be honest – no. It gives me the creeps," replied Belinda.

"Me too," she said.

"Let's find some coffee in a more cheerful place," suggested Belinda.

"I think my father too think this a good idea."

A minder appeared from a side door. They had been talking in whispers and she was perhaps curious that they had not ventured further to inspect her charges. Dr Woźniak waved at her, wagged his head and the three of them scuttled down the stairs and hurried across the foyer to the street.

The sun was warm after the chill of the palace. They turned right and entered a park where they were immediately confronted by an enormous memorial of two interlinked crosses. Carved into the stone of one, was 1956, and on the other, 1968, 1974, 1976 and 1980.

Belinda hesitated,

"What do the dates mean?"

"This is a memorial for the uprisings against communism in Poznań," explained Małgosia. "Polish people died."

It was another era of Polish history of which Belinda knew absolutely nothing. The revolt in Gdansk in 1981 had caught the attention of the British press as had the rebellion in Czechoslovakia in 1968, but she could recall no reference to bloody uprisings in Poland. Had she been asleep when they were reported, or had the British press ignored them? Once again, she nodded with a noncommittal expression on her face.

Several hundred metres further on, their stroll in the balmy autumn sun took them past a modern memorial in commemoration of the fallen of WWII. A low sweep of concrete formed the roof of a cavern, beneath which, there were lists of names inscribed.

The grotesque posters swam before her mind's eye. Belinda found herself pondering over the inane film industry of her world that pushed the barriers of imagination to the extreme in the guise of entertainment, while the Polish world had at the same time experienced the extremes in reality. Britain suddenly became a very privileged island of safety and sanity.

13

MONDAY 25TH SEPTEMBER 1995

Ludwik strolled into the office that morning with a smug expression on his face.

"I've found it," he announced.

"Found what?" asked Belinda.

"The school near Otorova."

"You haven't!" exclaimed a sceptical Belinda. Ludvik beamed down at her, his satisfaction evident.

"I have," he continued. "It is by a hill. It has turrets. It is occupied by nuns of the Ursulanki."

"Oh, Ludwik! You deserve a medal. That is just how Maria describes it." Belinda could hardly contain her excitement. She wanted to rush out there and then to see for herself.

"It is an old palace in a village called Szamotuli." Having divulged this important information to Belinda, he became aware of the doctors vociferous demands for an explanation of what was under discussion. For a whole week, ever since he had read the first chapter of Maria's story, he had been declaring that the school was a figment of her imagination. According to his reckoning there was no school within ten kilometres of the church that the school attended to sing at Sunday Mass.

"Fikcja, fikcja, (fiction)" he had repeated every time the matter came up. Now he was being told that the school was 'fakt'. He did not like to be contradicted.

Belinda returned to the Dom Poloniito to finish packing. She had decided that she should take a look at Warsaw before returning home and had hoped to catch an early morning train so that she could explore the city before catching the afternoon flight. The Polish transport system had not obliged with an early train. Undeterred, she decided to travel the day before and stay overnight in a hotel. Ludwik, her self-appointed travel agent, had been unable to secure a reasonably priced bed for the night. As a last resort, Belinda approached the young man who worked in the offices on the second floor. Several phone calls later, he too had not succeeded in securing any accommodation.

"I'll try headquarters," he said. "They might be able to help." He again picked up the phone and talked for a few minutes before replacing the receiver.

"They'll phone back in ten minutes," he said. "Can I make you a cup of coffee while we wait?" Belinda was a coffee addict.

"That would be kind of you," she responded, realising as he disappeared out of the door that she should possibly glean some information about the organisation that employed the young man. Soon he was back with a steaming cup of coffee and almost immediately the telephone rang. After a short conversation in a subdued voice, he put down the phone, turned towards Belinda and announced that a room had been reserved. Much relieved, Belinda thanked him and gratefully accepted the scrap of paper on which was written an address. "Show this to the taxi driver. He will know where it is," he said. Her excitement at finding a bed when none seemed to be available made Belinda forget about asking any more questions and she trotted out of the office to collect her luggage.

It was nearly time to leave. Her baggage had become heavier with the added weight of books and papers that she had acquired in Poznań and Belinda wondered how she was going to put the material to good purpose. Most of the printed matter was written in Polish and she had not yet reconciled herself to the possibility that, just when she was beginning to lose agility at sourcing vocabulary in her mother tongue, she must face the problem of acquiring knowledge of a new and very alien language.

Ludwik and dr Woźniak escorted her to the train. They found a near empty first-class compartment, spoke courteously but firmly to a young gentleman in the corner seat to ensure her welfare and exit from the train at Warsaw, expressing concern that Moscow lay beyond if she perchance fell asleep at the critical moment. Belinda was moved by the ceremony, of the leave-taking and the bouquet of roses that Ludwik had presented to her. The treatment that she had received throughout her stay had been respectful in the extreme, quaintly old fashioned at times, but would have been excellent polish for her ego – if only she had one.

As the train squealed into motion, she waved to her new friends, as they slid out of her life. The flat Polish landscape soon disappeared into the greyness of dusk as she sped eastwards deep in thought.

She was gently dozing, when her guardian in the corner of the compartment aroused her. The three-hour train journey had passed in a flash. It was raining as she towed her luggage out of the railway station. The taxis immediately to hand, looked dubious. In the drizzle, she crossed the road to the line of Mercedes parked outside the Marriott hotel. Most cab drivers in Warsaw, she was discovering, had a practical knowledge of English. Belinda showed the driver the slip of paper on which was written the address of her destination. He read the address, looked hard at her then, shrugged his shoulders. Yes, he knew where it was.

As they turned off the main street, the driver commented that he did not know of a hotel at this address.

"They are expecting me," replied Belinda.

The cab stopped in front of a gothic styled building, a line of tall round columns supporting the roof of the portico.

"Are you sure?" the driver enquired, opening his door. None of the windows showed any light and only the glass panes of a small door shone yellow. The door was locked and the driver rang the bell and thumped on the glass. In seconds, a middle-aged woman responded. She opened the door a few inches and words were exchanged while Belinda waited close behind her chauffeur. "Tak, Pani White." The cab driver's mouth sagged open in bafflement.

"So you are expected," he said, as he returned to the car shrugging his shoulders and shaking his head before heaving Belinda's luggage from the boot.

"It is very strange," Belinda heard him mutter in English.

Once inside, she signed a register at a desk in the corner of the entrance hall and was ushered past a large open-plan office into a vast reception area. Apart from the concierge the place was deserted. She could hear the silence. The two women climbed the broad staircase that swept gracefully upwards into darkness. The Polish woman found a light switch and revealed another vast reception area and another flight of stairs leading heavenward to the second floor.

While Belinda caught her breath after the long climb, the concierge became busy with keys. She knew not a word of English but was imaginative with sign language. She showed Belinda into her room, demonstrated how to secure the four locks on the door, where to find light switches and how to find the toilet and shower. The ceiling of the bedroom was as high as the room was long. Simply furnished, the beds were draped in brightly coloured hand knitted blankets, the tall windows draped with thin curtains.

Belinda had consumed neither food nor drink since midday and it was now nearly 8pm.

"Kawe?" she asked. The concierge looked dismayed and started to say something in Polish. Belinda made a sign of incomprehension then inspired, she opened her handbag. With the help of a small dictionary, the kindly concierge invited Belinda to join her downstairs for some coffee that she would gladly share. After taking a quick shower in the Neolithic shower room where the water drained into a huge puddle in the centre of the concrete floor, Belinda descended the regal staircase to the ground floor. She found the concierge in her cubicle engrossed in a war film, twisted bodies and Russian tanks filling the enormous television screen. As they shared a flask of coffee and Belinda nibbled politely on stale shortbread biscuits, the dictionary frequently passed back and forth. Gradually, basic data about family and past times sifted across the language barrier. They were undisturbed and Belinda concluded that they truly were the only two breathing beings in the palatial building.

14

TUESDAY 26TH SEPTEMBER

Daylight streamed through the inadequate curtains early the next morning and Belinda was up and dressed by six thirty. Gazing out of the window, she could see the river Vistula in the distance. She repacked her luggage and manhandled it down the first flight of stairs. In daylight, she could appreciate just how vast the spaces within the building were, how high and ornate the ceilings, the richness of the panelled walls. She crossed the circular landing to explore. Opening the enormous double doors facing the head of the stairs, she found herself in a huge elongated room in the centre of which stood a long table, ornately carved and surrounded by an equally imposing set of chairs. The décor contrasted in every way to her accommodation. One rich and opulent, the other stripped of all unnecessary frills. And who was the bogie man that had to be kept at bay by the numerous locks on the door? Belinda was suitably mystified.

Leaving her baggage with the amiable concierge, Belinda set foot on the street. Turning right, she headed for the city centre to find the cathedral with its five golden orbs. It was early, but the locals were abroad. She almost missed the cathedral, for she had expected it to be set back from the road. Entering the narrow streets leading to the old market square, she had not thought to look directly upwards to locate her target. Maria had described the golden orbs as she had remembered them from the picture in her convent school. She too had missed them when she first arrived in Warsaw in the winter of 1938/39. Falling snow had concealed them then. In 1995, they adorned the restored cathedral, the original building having been reduced to a heap of rubble during the war.

A service was in progress, but the passing visitor was deterred from entering by a disembodied voice, that remonstrated against any interruptions of the mass by casual sightseers. Belinda continued her walk to the old market. An old man hobbled past her as she paused to familiarise herself with her surroundings. From his wicker basket protruded the end of a freshly baked loaf. A handsome cab clattered by, the horse shod with thick, heavily studded shoes that enabled the animal to stay upright on the uneven cobbles. This part of Warsaw was stirring itself, preparing for another day of tourist occupation.

The narrow streets of the old quarter were similar to those surrounding the Stary Rynek in Poznań. Compared to the pompous grandeur of the square in Poznań, this one was quaint, almost intimate and half the size. The low terraced houses that enclosed the area were painted in bright colours, each individual and different from its neighbour, each rebuilt as a replica of what existed before the war. In the apartments overlooking the square, heads could be seen at breakfast tables.

Emerging from the old part of the city, Belinda found herself walking along wide avenues, past imposing hotels and government buildings, solid and seemingly indestructible, the walls still bearing the scars of battle.

Leaving the Vistula and city centre behind her, Belinda turned north and soon became hopelessly lost in a jungle of high-rise apartment blocks. Each street seemed to be the same as the next and the grey blandness of the exteriors made the buildings indistinguishable from each other. She consulted her map, but could not pinpoint her position. The time was ticking by, she should get back to base within the next half hour but the street seemed as deserted as her 'hotel'. Suddenly a small car drove by and pulled over to park. Praying that the driver spoke English, she approached the woman as she locked her vehicle.

"Of course I can help you." she heard in answer to her plea, the English spoken with only a hint of an accent. When shown on the map exactly where they were, Belinda was mildly perturbed. She had covered more ground than she realised and it would be a half hour steady trot across a large park before she would be back near the city centre.

The tourists were emerging as she passed the 'old town'. Several horse drawn carriages waited in a line, the foremost loading its first passengers. A drunk staggered across the pavement, bumping roughly into two young girls. In a flash, an officious woman had pounced on him and was busy wagging her finger and reprimanding him as Belinda hurried past.

To settle her bill for one night's lodging, Belinda was escorted to a small office in an annex towards the rear of the main building. She waited whilst a woman filled out a form in triplicate. Three sombre officials sat behind the desk, saying nothing, doing little except inspecting the forms as they were passed back and forth along the table. Belinda waited. Eventually the silence was broken, she did not understand, but proffered the required amount of zloty. The money was solemnly counted and receipted. The procedure took over ten minutes. The sum involved was approximately ten pounds. It seemed that the Poles had not yet shaken off the yolk of ceremonial officialdom. Time was irrelevant and waiting was part of the game.

Taxi is a universal word and Belinda had no problem communicating her need to the receptionist. Once again, the driver spoke excellent English. He had been driving taxis for twenty-one years and his was (of course) a member of the best taxi association in Warsaw. Belinda enquired of him what he knew of the building that they had just left. The answer slightly bemused her. "This palace! It is the Ministry of Culture" he had replied.

Belinda could only ponder on the sequence of events that had caused her to lodge in a building that had at one time been the centre for intelligence agents.

As she sipped her second cup of coffee in the airport restaurant, she imagined Maria looking down on her. 'Are you happy now?' she thought.

There was no answer, but that could be expected. Maria would have replied with a satisfied grin and a slow nodding of the head. What she had seen and heard during the past week had opened a door into history of which she had been totally unaware; a secret nightmare that challenged the secure, untroubled British culture into which she had been born. Three years after the Russian tide had receded, the 'traditions' of the communist era still lingered. Dr Woźniak had pointed out that Poland had been under occupation for fifty years; five years of Nazi rule followed by forty-five years of communism. Two generations had reached adulthood under oppressive regimes. Society had not yet adjusted to its new freedom. Freedom, a privilege assumed in Britain and still a mystifying gift in Poland.

She had started out on her journey to Poznań with a mixture of dreams in her head. Her purpose had been to discover whether Maria's story was based on fact or whether that too had been a dream. Belinda returned home, knowing that her dream had turned into a nightmare. Maria's story had led her into uncharted waters, a chapter of World War II history that had been concealed at the time and subsequently distorted by political control. She would need time for the tidal wave of information to settle back into proportion. And then...? Destiny might provide an answer.

15

DESTINY TOOK CONTROL

Acting on a whim, Belinda decided to fly to San Francisco to attend the wedding of a friend's son, something that she would have never considered doing before her accident.

Since squashing her skull in 1992, she had been plagued by a number of invisible problems. She appeared normal on the outside, but inside, her world had become fractured and her perceptions distorted. She had smashed her 'internal clocks', those subconscious mechanisms that dictate when food or drink is needed and sleep is necessary. She no longer ever felt hungry, thirsty or tired. She had to remember to eat and to go to bed. If she forgot, which she did frequently, she did not care.

Not caring was the dominant feature that surprised her most. All her life she had been introspective. Suddenly, she was free from her inhibitions, saying and doing things without the restraint of consideration. It was as though her reflex responses escaped without the rubber stamp of conscience. Caution was not in her vocabulary.

On the physical side, the double vision was so bad that identifying the doctor's two fingers on one hand was irrelevant. She could see two arms and on each arm there would be two fingers. Watching the television, she could see two separated screens and focus on either the one on the right hand side or the one on the left. It was a wasted talent for both screens showed the same picture.

The lack of visual constancy meant that her balance was affected and she was in constant danger of toppling. She had invested in spectacles with prisms and although they had helped, they had not eradicated the problem.

The idea of travelling nearly halfway round the world just for a wedding was a mere bagatelle. Travelling alone as she had done the year before to Poland held no fears even if she would have to write the route and address down to remind herself of where she was going.

Unable to obtain a direct flight to San Francisco, she had spent a brief night in the Essex hotel overlooking Lake Michigan in Chicago before flying on early the next morning. On arrival in San Francisco, she had just missed the bus north to Sonoma and boarded a coach to Napa instead with the promise of a taxi to ferry her across the valley to her destination. A cab was waiting when she descended from the bus and the cab driver had quoted her a fare. When his meter reached the forecast amount before he had found the house, it was disconnected, a chivalrous gesture that was much appreciated by his passenger.

The wedding, hosted by her friend's ex-sister-in-law had been a splendid occasion. The garden filled with blue and white flowering plants, provided a perfect setting. Belinda had been designated a large room on the first floor of the main house and had observed most of the ceremony from the large veranda which overlooked the garden, recording the spectacle as though through a camera lens. The following Tuesday, she was scheduled to fly to Las Vegas to visit her cousin.

Belinda White did not leave Sonoma.

On Monday night, she was the last guest to use the bathroom at the top of the stair well. When she came out, the landing light had been switched off and momentarily she lost her bearings in the pitch darkness. In that second, she changed direction. Instead of stepping out across the landing, she stepped off the top of the stairs. She bounced twice as she descended the twenty-one steps. On the first bounce, she landed on her back. She rolled, her legs rattled down the railings of the banisters. She then pitched forward and landed on the top of her head, hearing a sharp cracking sound before losing consciousness.

Belinda no longer existed.

ॐ ॐ ॐ

I woke up on the doormat, just inside the front door. I was aware of what had happened and my initial reaction was anger. What a dumb thing to have done. The noise that I had heard as I hurtled down the stairs caused me to suspect that I may have damaged my neck. I dared not to tempt providence by trying to move. I was in trouble and I would have raised the devil with the moans of despair that echoed around the darkened house. I must have passed out again, for the next thing that I remember was a cupped hand offering a heap of small white pills.

"What are they?" I had asked.

"Arnica!" was the reply. "It will deal with the shock." I munched the pills realising that at the very least my fingers functioned and that therefore my neck was intact. I then enquired of my toes whether they had the inclination to receive orders. They did. Neither my neck nor my back had been damaged. In fact, nothing was broken. Even my spectacles were unscathed.

The incident was a dramatic cure for the shifted plates of my skull. Although I had undergone treatments by a chiropractor in an attempt to manipulate the plates into their correct position, the flattened area at the base of the skull had stubbornly remained flat. Landing on my head with considerable force resulted in the plates of my skull re-jigging themselves. Once again, I had a round head and the pressure had been taken off the area of my brain that had caused major problems with my balance and eyesight. Destiny had taken control of my life yet again. It had required the right staircase, even if it was necessary to travel to the far side of America and it required someone to blind me at the right moment so that I would 'accidentally' dive down the stairs. It is extremely doubtful that I would ever have discovered anyone in the medical fraternity who would have prescribed such a treatment.

I should have killed myself, but in the event, the arnica coped with the shock. Arnica cream applied to the sore areas on my shoulder, elbow and wrists also prevented bruising, confirmed by an area that I missed in the middle of my upper arm, which turned every colour of the rainbow during the following week.

It was a strange twist of fate. Above all, with the passing of 'Belinda', all the peculiarities, which had plagued me for the last four years, also dissolved. Most of the 'internal clocks' kicked back into gear. My return to an even keel was instantaneous. Having decided that all limbs were intact, I had bunny-hopped my legs under me, using just one hand on the mat for support. The co-ordination and balance required for such a feat were back in place. Walking a straight line was no longer a problem.

My hostess was exceedingly perturbed about my health. She assured me that she was insured if complications set in after I left. But, there were no complications. Besides, how do you sue for compensation for a few bruises when the nett result is a cure for the problems that had contributed to the accident in the first place?

Thus, I left behind Belinda on the doormat of my Californian hosts.

Authors note:
The reader is reminded that Maria's Story is printed in the second half of this book. The time frame of her story has been adjusted to correspond with the length of time that Maria and her mother were imprisoned but, in all other respects, the text relates directly to the translation of the original manuscript. The remainder of

'Safari to Poland' constantly refers to incidents and claims within that script and are somewhat confusing without foreknowledge of the evidence that Maria presents. It is therefore recommended that the reader turns to Maria's Story (after Chapter 34) before continuing with the research adventure.

16

Prior to Belinda's involuntary excursion down the stairs, her memory had also been severely damaged. That which happened two days previously was forgotten history. Appointments two days hence confused themselves with those scheduled for three or four days away. Mentally, she would panic as all the dates melted together into a scrambled muddle. She had maintained some sanity by only allowing herself to take each day as an individual item. Knowing the shortcomings of her recall, she had taken the precaution of writing notes each day about what she had seen and learned.

Today, I would think twice, if not several times, that venturing forth into Eastern Europe alone might be inadvisable. In hindsight it was. But in 1995, Belinda seemed to be guided by an invisible hand that paved her way, similar to that which permitted Moses to cross the Dead Sea. It did not seem to matter that communication alone might be difficult between people who did not share a common language.

The language barrier in Poland had been surmountable but frustrating. Explanations were always sketchy to avoid the use of complicated vocabulary. Discussions were frequently ended by dr Woźniak's laconic humour, a grimace, and a shrug of the shoulders. The fragments of information that could be gleaned were sinister, disturbing and not cohesive.

Belinda's trust astounds me now. Then, I was someone else, drifting on the ebb and flow of fortune without questioning the wisdom of such behaviour.

On returning from California, I had immediately remarked on the dilapidated state of my home. The double vision had meant that for several years, only the dirt that accumulated above waist level had been noticed. Stooping to deal with the detritus at a lower level had caused the second cousin to dizziness and this position had only been possible for very short periods. Now I could attack the household chores without my attention wandering or my sense of reality receding. I embarked upon a major 'spring clean'.

While sorting through a drawer of the writing desk, I found a supermarket carrier bag. On investigation, I found that it contained all the papers and photographs that I had retrieved from Maria's trunk in 1986. It had been completely forgotten.

The discovery inspired a fresh enthusiasm to get to the bottom of Maria's story. A week later, the documents that were written in German, had been translated in full, confirming a number of relevant details.

In 1963, Maria and her mother had made a claim against the German Government for compensation. Her mother, Antonina, had argued that she was obliged to wear the Star of David in Poggenburg, erroneously identifying her as a Jewess because of her suspect profile. The property that was confiscated as a result of their arrest had been substantial.

The case had progressed to the High Court in Berlin by 1964. Affidavits in support of Maria's case had been made by Herbert Kurzke, Alfred Weidemann and two women, Vera Novacek and her sister, Pelagia. Unfortunately, that made by Weidemann was missing from the collection, but the statement made by Kurzke, confirming Maria's presence in Berlin and Poggenburg, had survived. There were also two short statements from two sisters that described Maria's condition during her internment in Poggenburg and immediately after her escape in January 1945.

The court decision was the final document relating to the case. The claim was categorically denied on the grounds that no Pole could be as wealthy as was claimed and further, they had not been arrested for being Jewish but as escapees from transportation in 1939.

The main inference that can be drawn from such a conclusion is that no Pole, from the German point of view, could be affluent. Nearly twenty years after the War had finished, was it still legally assumed that all Poles were insignificant and poor in Germany's terms? Who did they assume had held the wealth in Poland – solely the Jews?

A sinister thought had permeated into my head. The only reference that the history books made to the fate of the Poles in 1939, almost always mentioned little except the execution of the intellectuals, the aristocracy and the landowners. Was the Nazi harvest so complete that survivors in these categories were never recognised by Germany? Were they so few in number, that they could be ignored, their very existence denied?

The plastic bag contained more treasures; photographs of 'Nana' and Antonina together; of Herbert soon after his release from a Russian gulag in

1954 and one showing him in the uniform of a German police officer. There was also a photo of his gravestone in Germany, inscribed in English, 'To be or not to be. You have answered this question!' He took his own life in 1974. In a used envelope, I found two small newspaper cuttings announcing Herbert's release from prison. No mention was made of his wartime activities, but both scraps of fragile newsprint made reference to his prowess on the football field. In 1936, he had played for Germany against Everton and distinguished himself by scoring the winning goal. Tall, blonde, handsome and athletic, he had been a national hero – a Nordic type, an Adonis that was so idolised by Hitler and his henchmen.

The visit to Poland in 1995 had opened my eyes. The contents of the plastic bag suddenly added large pieces to the overall picture. However, not all of them slotted easily into the frame.

Among the other papers was a letter from a 'Fred' Weidemann, dated 1947. It had described his holiday away from the film studios and inquired what progress Maria had made with 'our project'. The statement made to the court in 1963 must surely have been made by the same man. Was it possible that he could still be alive and could clarify the substance of 'our project'? It seemed unlikely. It was only a nagging thought that 'our project' might concern the manuscript, but the quest to seek answers to more prominent questions side-lined Weidemann for the moment.

Copies of the various relevant documents were sent to dr Woźniak. At the same time, a request for the service records of Herbert Kurzke was sought from the National Archives in Berlin.

Dr Woźniak seemed delighted with the new information and immediately traced the families of Vera Novacek and Pelagia. He discovered that both women had been in the service of Maria's family. Vera, the older of the two sisters had settled in Maldon, Essex and had died in 1962. Pelagia was still alive and had been thrilled to hear about Maria and her mother. Apparently, during the dark years immediately after the war, her family had received parcels of food from England. 'Anyone would think that Maria was an angel from heaven,' the doctor wrote. He had problems, however, when he interviewed the woman and tried to establish her role in the Szymanski household. 'After forty-five years of communism,' he confided, 'the servant was in charge and the master was the slave!' He learned that she had worked part-time in a newsagent's shop owned by Maria's grandfather, but she would not admit to having been in service. The mosaic of shifting attitudes under political regimes was possibly interfering with memory.

The foray into the German archive was disappointing. An H. Kurtske had been traced in the regular army. He had spent most of the war in Norway as a driver. It did not sound like Maria's Herbert. The question arising from the text of Maria's manuscript remained – what had been the role of the man? What was he doing in Oranienburg in 1941/3? Why had it taken from March to December 1943 for his court-martial to be heard? Who were the 'friends' who could prevent Maria's death sentence from reaching Poggenburg after it had been endorsed by the judge at the court-martial session?

Oranienburg, I learned, had been a centre for police training and intelligence agents. The Abwehr (German Intelligence network) was headed by Admiral Canaris, the friend and saviour of Halina Szymanska, the wife of Poland's pre-war military attaché to Berlin. Szymanski was the maiden name of Maria's mother. Was there a connection? The jigsaw puzzle was becoming complicated and ever more intriguing.

I decided to discover more about the admiral. The Imperial War Museum found a dozen books about the gentleman of which that by Heinz Höhne was selected for further study. I read the whole tome from cover to cover and was left with the impression that Canaris had ducked and dived ahead of Hitler, attempting to soften the effects of military attack with timely warnings to the foe. The author also described how Canaris had met Halina somewhere to the south west of Warsaw in September 1939 and had given her a lift back to Posen and warned her about returning home. On Canaris's advice, Halina had taken refuge with a 'distant relative'.

Maria told a very similar story. In her version, it had been her mother Antonina who had approached a German general 'with epaulettes dancing on his shoulders' and obtained a lift from Warsaw to Posen in his car. Could this be a coincidence? Could two German generals be so considerate to stranded Polish ladies?

The notion that Maria had heard Halina's story and adopted it as her own, was further endorsed by Joseph Garlinski. In his book *The Swiss Corridor* he describes how Admiral Canaris's car very nearly ran Halina down in Posen. Again, Maria described a very similar incident. In her account, the event led to repeated visits to the Szymanski apartment by Herbert, who had witnessed the near accident together with his friend, a 'very jolly' fellow from the Rhineland. Heinz Höhne too provides a clue. He referred to Piekenbrock, promoted to head of Abwehr I in 1941, as a 'jolly Rhinelander'.

Was it possible that Ina, Maria's distant cousin, who resided temporarily in her grandparents' apartment in 1939 was in truth Halina Szymanska, the agent that Canaris installed in Switzerland as a link with the Allies. Coincidence is a nasty convenience. However, if Ina could be identified as Halina, the closeness of the accounts would be explained. The possibility that Maria had heard the story from her relative after the war can be dismissed. The biography was written in 1945/6. Maria had been trapped in Berlin until 1947 while Halina had lived far away in Switzerland. The two women had no opportunity to compare notes when the war ended.

With time I discovered that there were further parallels. Hohne stated that Halina met Canaris several times while she remained in Posen. According to Maria, her cousin, Ina, was pursued by the 'jolly fellow' from the Rhineland. She had been given the impression that the couple were engaging in a clandestine affair, but if the fellow from the Rhineland was Piekenbrock, Halina was in fact being escorted to meetings with Canaris.

It is a known fact that Halina left the country in October 1939 to travel to Switzerland and that it was Canaris who arranged her transport from Poland. Ina, according to Maria, 'left the country on the advice of friends in October 1939'. The similarity of the stories was enough to convince me that Maria's cousin Ina was Halina Szymanska.

At this stage, the situation was like that of building a house of cards. The basement was constructed from a series of theoretical conclusions. If the theory was correct, Herbert as an acquaintance of Piekenbrock became a very significant cog in a puzzle that was rapidly gaining a third dimension.

It became of paramount importance to uncover Herbert's wartime role.

The adventure trip to Poznań had opened the door on a terrible and tragic episode in Poland's history for which I had been blissfully unprepared. I assumed that I was ignorant; that I had not read the right books. During the following months, however, I discovered that the horrors of the camps in Poland had been discussed in depth, but only after the decision on 'The Final Solution' made in 1942. Very little material referred to that area of Poland to the west, the Wartegau, which became Reich territory at the beginning of the war in September 1939. It was as though it disappeared off the world map and became a blank page in English history books.

The development of the slave labour camps, the ethnic cleansing and disappearance of hundreds of thousands of Poles was invariably dismissed in a few sentences. It was difficult to understand why the 'holocaust' excluded a deliberate and sustained attack on the Polish nation.

I started to comb through encyclopaedias and every historical tome that I could lay my hands on, trying to find traces of the events in the Wartegau or New Reich Territories in 1939. I discovered that my first impression was not incorrect. There was very little reference to events in Poland for the first two years of World War II and no mention whatever was made to the ethnic cleansing of the region to create the 'lebensraum' of Hitler's dreams. Dr Woźniak had repeatedly stressed to me that the Polish population of Poznań had been decimated – literally. Of the 272,000 Polish nationals that lived in the city in 1939, only 27,000 remained in 1944. Gradually, I began to understand the significance of what I had been told by my mentor, dr Woźniak. "The borders of the Wartegau were 'hermetically' sealed." Hardly a mouse would have succeeded in passing the new demarcation lines between the area and the General Government, the central region of Poland, let alone a courier with information about the fate of the Polish nationals.

Dr Woźniak had given me a diagram of the routes that radio messages took in order to reach the Western allies. It showed that they were often relayed via Switzerland, Spain or Sweden. While messages were frequently broadcast from Warsaw and elsewhere, nothing came out of the Wartegau.

Post-war, the Russians had taken control of the whole of Poland. Europe was in chaos. The discovery of the concentration camps in Poland had horrified even those who were inured to horror. The camps were built on Polish territory and there was some speculation as to how far the Poles were implicitly responsible by permitting their development. The concentration of world attention on the persecution of the Jews eclipsed the plight of the Polish nation. The Jewish Holocaust has been described many times by survivors, whereas as the years passed, the information that emerged relating to the fate of the Pole was full of contradictions. Historians seem to have some difficulty assessing what really happened in Poland. The information that was available was dislocated, confusing and seemed to lack any logic.

A number of developments resulted from the first visit. A vigorous correspondence with dr Woźniak evolved. He wrote in Polish, I wrote in English. I took two to three days to translate the several pages that he sent me and two dictionaries fell apart from overuse in my efforts to decipher the meaning of his missives, while he took two to three weeks to persuade his daughter or a member of his staff to convert my epistles.

Maria's manuscript proved increasingly interesting. Whereas at first, dr Woźniak had been dismissive of the text as being fictional and lacking in historical importance, with time, it was discovered that much of Maria's claims were indeed possible, unlikely though they seemed at first glance.

Her Russian ballet master was still alive and in business in 1949. Together with his wife, who had performed on stage as a prima ballerina at the opera house in Posen before the war, they continued to teach ballet into the nineteen fifties.

There were few reports about prisoners who had experienced life in Poggenburg. Most of the German records were destroyed when the camp was abandoned in January 1945. During the previous three months, the number of prisoners had been reduced. Daily executions or transport to other concentration camps had almost halved the number, and new arrestees had been sent immediately westward. It is estimated that less than a thousand prisoners remained in January, but as the Russian front approached, it became necessary for the camp to be evacuated.

It was the middle of winter and the temperatures would have been well below freezing. Those prisoners, who were strong enough to walk, were marched into Posen on 15th January, where they were united with the inmates of the city criminal prison in Młynska Street. A column of some two thousand prisoners set out towards Germany. The journey was over three hundred kilometres and few survived. As with other evacuation marches from the concentration camps of Poland, weakness from starvation and inadequate protection from the cold caused many to collapse. Those who could walk no further, were shot as the guards at the rear of the column passed them and the bodies abandoned by the roadside.

The fate of those too weak to leave Poggenburg was discovered by the horrified citizens of Posen three days later. The barracks had been burned to the ground with prisoners locked inside. Seventy-five blackened corpses were found in the ashes of the huts.

Close by, a group of dead Polish prisoners was also discovered in the churchyard. It would seem that they had arrived too late to join the evacuation march and had been executed.

According to Maria, news about the destruction of Poggenburg had filtered through to Berlin by March 1945. As rumour is inclined to do, the reports were exaggerated and the camp was said to have been full of prisoners when it was set on fire. But whether it was 75 or 750 prisoners, the act of murder by the incineration of the victims remains an evil crime.

In another area of the jigsaw puzzle a number of seemingly unrelated pieces were accumulating. Dr Woźniak had found Maria's name on a list of prisoners who had spoken to the German Inspector of Camps, Gerhard Wiebek. The inspector had been gathering evidence against the behaviour of Hans Walter, the Camp Commandant of Poggenburg.

In the spring of 1943, Wiebek had been appointed the Inspector of Camps for the whole of the west of Poland. His brief also included Auschwitz. He lived in Posen and was married to a Polish woman who had been born in the city.

Early in 1943, an edict had emerged from the German capital, stating that all death sentences were to be confirmed by authorities in Berlin before the sentence was carried out. Too many 'accidental deaths' were decimating the labour force.

The Commandant of Poggenburg, Hans Walter, was a charming fellow to his friends and family. His treatment of his prisoners in Poggenburg, however, revealed a terrifyingly sadistic maniac. Initially, Poggenburg was a prison for Poles suspected of resistance activities, who had been arrested by the Gestapo. Interrogations by the Gestapo often left prisoners severely weakened or injured at the commencement of their internment. Many prisoners remained in the camp only during the period before sentencing. If they were condemned to death, they were transported to one of the camps with a gas chamber, either Majdanek or Grosse Rosen. Only those with short 'correctional' sentences served their time in Poggenburg, usually for three months. Thereafter, they were released under strict instructions that they did not reveal to anyone the treatment that they had received. To do so meant instant re-arrest and transportation to eternity.

The gremlin in the system was Walter. He enjoyed tormenting his prisoners and as a result, they very often did not continue to live. Walter had however, a mutual understanding with his Gestapo masters. They cooperated with each other, and 'accidental' deaths were reported as casualties of the interrogations. In his official capacity, Wiebek endeavoured for over a year to find a crack in this convenient relationship. He was aware of the high death rate amongst the prisoners and he suspected Walter of flouting the regulations issued by Berlin, but could acquire no proof.

Dr Woźniak did not know exactly what had caused Wiebek to enter Poggenburg with an armed guard and arrest Commandant Walter along with nineteen of his staff on 4th October 1944. His only clue was that 'he had caused the death of a prisoner without the appropriate piece of paper.' Subsequently, Walter hanged himself. He was found three days later, swinging lifeless in his cell... "A few days earlier than expected," Wiebek had reported. While searching through the statements that had been collected from witnesses who had served a short-term sentence in Poggenburg and later released, dr Woźniak had uncovered more references to Maria and her mother.

Jósefa Jaszmarek was still only fifteen years old when she was interviewed. In the booklet 'Pamietniki Ocalonych' (Memories of Survivors), Jósefa had described Maria's mother, Antonina and Maria.

"In the shed of the camp garden area, was Mrs Wajchan. She was a remarkable person who occupied all her time cultivating the ground. She was respected for whenever she demanded work to be done it was always necessary and a great deal depended on it.

"Mrs Wajchan (I do not know how to spell her name correctly), was often together with her daughter. It was said that she was from German Jewish origins and that in order to protect her daughter, she had signed the volkslist. In Zabikowo, there were also German prisoners. Some were accused of helping Poles and others had committed minor criminal offences... She had her own personal cell, a larger food ration, her own clothes and in winter a woollen coat – green, similar to a military uniform. The capo and the work leaders wore red coats. I remember during my time in Zabikowo that twice, Mrs Wajchan and her daughter wore green coats but most of the time they wore black ones. It was as though the authorities were not able to decide whether to treat her as German or whether she was undeserving of the privileges.

Mrs Wajchan was a tall, strongly built woman, with large black sparkling eyes and a rather prominent aquiline nose... Her daughter was a very beautiful girl (she looked about 20 years old) and worked in the sewing shed. Mrs Wajchan had a powerful voice and a fantastic vocabulary of German swear words. While beating a stick against her chest or any other object, she would scream abuse at the guards. Such behaviour created an impression that she was crude and a bully. I very soon realised that underneath this mask, she had only the purpose of distracting the vigilance of the Germans. For, she held meetings in her shed, which was very close to the guardhouse and Commandant Walter's office. In reality, the Germans controlled us with convictions and cruelty but, Mrs Wajchan took care of us..."

Jósefa was in the prison for only a couple of months. Maria and her mother were held there for almost the entirety of the camp's existence, i.e. May 1943 to January 1945. This caused dr Woźniak some concern. If Antonina had sworn at and threatened the guards as Jósefa described, the mystery as to why her behaviour was tolerated was mystifying. She spoke German perfectly. She had been born and educated in Germany and German was her first language, but that would not have preserved the life of most prisoners in a similar situation. Who or what protected the Weychan women?

I was beginning to understand the role of the Poggenburg/Zabikowo camp. It was in many respects, a 'transit' camp for most prisoners. It was not intended as a long-term prison, rather a place where Poles suspected of involvement with the resistance were held while further investigations were made by the Gestapo stationed in Posen. With few exceptions, most prisoners were transported after sentencing, either to labour camps or for execution in the gas chamber. Poggenburg itself was not a death camp. Execution of the sentence would have initially been delayed so that Maria could appear as a witness at the court martial of her German husband, Herbert Kurzke. The court-martial judge had confirmed her death sentence and sent her back to Poggenburg to await execution.

When reading her book, I had entered a world of fantasy at this point. How could it be possible to avoid execution while a helpless prisoner? Maria described in her writing how, after the trial, she had spent a few happy hours alone with her husband before boarding the train to return to the camp. He had consoled her by telling her that the order would never reach the camp. It read like a romantic interlude that could only end in tragedy. Unless – unless Kurzke was more than he seemed. The court-martial incident threw up several red herrings. It also seemed curious that Herbert's case was delayed nine months before it was heard in the courts of Königsburg. I had two problems with this. The first concerned the timing. In wartime, nine months seems to be an extraordinarily long delay to bring court-martial proceedings against an active serviceman. Unfortunately, the full extent of the accusations that were brought against Kurzke remain obscure and clues were not obtainable from Maria's account. The second itch concerned the place. Königsburg (Kalinin), a city in the northeast corner of Prussia close to the USSR border, seemed a strange place to hold a court martial for someone based in Berlin. Furthermore, Maria's train journey to Königsburg seemed to be no longer than six hours which seemed to me to be a particularly short time for a 800 km distance through bandit country in wartime.

Maria's arrest by the Gestapo in March 1943 had been in the presence of Kurzke. He had accompanied the two women from Berlin to Posen, unaware of the mission that his wife had undertaken for the resistance group in Berlin. Maria had been observed by an old school acquaintance and followed to the house of 'Jan Jankowski', where she had delivered a suitcase full of money and subsequently had been betrayed. The suitcase was found by the Gestapo. But they failed to find either the money nor, at the time, 'Jankowski'.

17

By 1997, I was still more than a little confused. The complex problem of Poland's history had by this time bitten deep and would not go away. Maria's presence in the camps had been confirmed beyond doubt, but there was a nagging question about why she had not been executed.

Her husband, Herbert Kurzke, had not been traced by the German archives and to find his role in the German forces was becoming increasingly important. I made a decision. I would return to Poland and visit the archives in Berlin en route.

Curiosity ruled. As each layer of the onion was stripped away, another more pungent layer was being revealed and as the context of Maria's story was teased open, the vapours of intrigue invited further research into the realms of 'intelligence'.

I was married with three growing children and a partner who tolerated my eccentric whims, but with only the kitchen table to consult and no financial reward for my efforts, the second trip to Poland had to be carefully planned and budgeted.

Sarah, a friend since student days at University College, London, was enlisted to accompany me on the trip. Her daughter had studied Polish at the East European School of Languages and she had acquaintances in Berlin and Poland who were willing to provide beds. I purchased the tickets for the flight and Sarah took care of the accommodation. Little did I realise that the spectre of predestination would again rear its head.

Ludwik had written in March, saying that a series of documentaries was being planned, featuring Posen during the war period. One of the programmes would be based on Maria and if I was agreeable, they would like to include me in the film. He would be grateful if I could confirm that I would be in Poznań during the month of April so that matters could be arranged. All they needed was an interview in Fort VII, which did not sound too stressful. I was game.

The plan to fly to Berlin before taking the train heading for Poznań meant that I could visit the Bundesarchiv and press home some of the questions that I had submitted. Instinct was impelling me to learn more about the Abwehr, of which Admiral Canaris was the chief. The only film to have been made about him was produced by an Alfred Weidenmann in 1954. Coincidences are not pleasant to negotiate, for in print they are too convenient. But, should Alfred Weidemann the scriptwriter (whose letter to Maria, dated 1947, I had discovered in the forgotten plastic bag) ever turn out to be Alfred Weidenmann the film director, the opportunity to see his film at the Film Archive in Berlin was not to be missed. A viewing therefore was booked to be included on the Berlin agenda.

On arrival at Heathrow to check in, I was greeted with a message. Sarah had realised halfway to the airport that she had forgotten her passport. The message warned that she might be a bit late as she had to return home to retrieve it.

I waited by the check-in for the next hour and a half. For some obscure reason, I was unable to leave the ticket at the desk for Sarah to pick up if she arrived in time, yet if I walked through the passport control with the ticket, my friend would not be able to get on the plane even if she did appear.

When the final call for boarding came over the loud speaker and I was about to give up all hope, I spotted Sarah's head, hair flying as she dashed through the hall. I was exhausted with relief. If Sarah had not made it, I had no idea where I would have spent the night. The schedule that we had planned for the next few days would have been ruined.

All was well! Minutes later we boarded the plane to Berlin.

Tegel airport reminded me of Stansted before it had been developed with old, single storey huts accommodating the constant stream of incoming and outgoing passengers. Soon we were in a taxi, driving eastwards to find our lodgings.

The next day we took a train into the city and found the Film Archive in Fehrbelliner Platz, where I had arranged to see the film made in 1954 about Admiral Wilhelm Canaris.

The archive was housed in a forbidding building with an equally forbidding Frau in charge of the reception desk. We were escorted down stately corridors with high ceilings, encountering nobody, before being ushered into a large and very empty lecture room. An enormous television screen filled one corner of the theatre and a copy of the film on video was thrust into Sarah's hand. Our escort gave instructions about how to summon help if necessary and excused herself. As she closed the door behind her, an eerie silence filled the vast room. Sarah and I looked at each other, neither wishing to be the first to break the stillness.

"Wow!" said Sarah eventually, her voice echoing around the room. "This is all very impressive." She spoke in a loud whisper.

I nodded in agreement. "It's all a bit over the top, now you come to mention it," I muttered.

Sarah burst out laughing. 'What's the matter with us? Why are we being so dozey? We can make as much noise as we like. Come on, give us a song'.

The spell was broken and soon we were intent on watching the only film that has ever been made about the enigmatic Admiral Canaris, chief of the German Intelligence during the World War II.

Suspecting that Canaris featured in Maria's story, I was curious to find out whether any of the material had leached into a film that may have been directed by the same man that had helped her with her 'project'. I was to be disappointed. Halina Szymanska was not mentioned. Canaris was portrayed as an amiable, middle-aged 'uncle' who had a tendency to fret and fuss about the dangers that threatened his agents and friends.

He appeared to be a sincere, self-effacing man, clever at keeping in the shadows and able to divert or avoid trouble to protect the integrity of his intelligence service. The historian, Heinz Höhne describes a similar character. Whatever Hitler's next move, Canaris was always two steps ahead of him, negotiating and paving the way, able to foresee major confrontations between conflicting interests so that violent excesses were avoided if at all possible.

Many books have been written about Germany's Abwehr Chief. Some condemn him as a traitor others honour him as a hero. For a long time he was Hitler's confidante. They were friends. In 1943, Hitler lost faith in his Intelligence Service and began to mistrust Canaris. The pendulum of power swung and in 1944, Canaris was under house arrest. Hitler, it is said, still respected and liked the man and it was with regret that he ordered the execution of his 'friend' a few days before the fall of Berlin.

I had formed my own psychological picture of the man. The glimpses of the character that I had identified in Maria's book as Canaris, did not contradict the character that was portrayed by the film. He was a man who would have been shocked by the brutality that he witnessed in September 1939 and although he may previously have been a conforming Nazi party member, the consequences of ethnic cleansing and Nazi attacks on the civilian population during the first months of the invasion of Poland had caused him a massive moral dilemma. If he betrayed Hitler, it would have been during the weeks spent in Posen that the seeds of rebellion were sown. He enlisted Halina, installed her in the safety of

Switzerland and with her help, passed top-secret German information to the British.

Emerging from the Film Archive, we were so busy discussing what we had just seen that we paid little attention to the state of the Platz. Only when we returned to our lodgings, did we learn that while we had been tucked away in the nether regions of the archive, there had been a noisy demonstration of some 3,000 civil servants in the square outside. Our hostess enlightened us regarding the public display of protest.

Berlin was bankrupt. She was an art teacher and had not been paid by the city authorities for three months, neither had many of the civil servants. To alleviate the situation, it had been suggested that the civil servants be reduced in number and redeployed in the provinces. The unions were unhappy with this idea and hence the mass gathering outside the Film Archive that afternoon.

The news puzzled both of us. In Britain we had become used to the idea that the German economy was under control and that roses flourished in the garden. What we had just learned threw a different light on the situation and we started to pose further questions.

Hilka, our hostess, was depressed by the current financial climate in Berlin. She explained that since the wall came down in 1989, money that had flowed into West Berlin from Britain and the USA had dried up. She had appreciated that this would probably happen. The funds intended to support the west part of the city that until recently had been isolated and surrounded by East Germany, had now been diverted into a bottomless financial hole to regenerate the east of the country.

The concept of the pre-1989 isolation of the population of West Berlin suddenly hit home for me. The shabby airport had been their only link to the outside world. A weekend trip into the countryside had been impossible and the only alternative had been to spend time on the lakes and shores of the Wannsee.

The afternoon was spent sightseeing, Hilka offering to give us a guided tour of East Berlin. We emerged from the Ubahn at the Brandenburg Gate, having chugged through many of the stations of the eastern section of the underground without stopping. While the wall had existed pre 1989, all the stations under East Berlin had been blacked out. They still awaited refurbishment. One of them, Oranienburg had been the access for the Sachsenhausen concentration camp during the war, a camp that was well inside the city limits.

East Berlin itself was in the process of amazing redevelopment. While the city authorities in West Berlin were declaring that they had insufficient funds to support their schools, the massive reconstruction of East Berlin was striding ahead. Where the wall had once stood and the area of 'no-man's-land' that had been beyond it, a city of cranes had sprung up. As far as the eye could see, heaps of building materials were dwarfed by the onelegged monsters. Venturing deeper into a maze of featureless architecture, graffiti leapt from every wall. How the artist could reach three floors above the street was food for thought. Compared to the bustle in West Berlin, the streets were deserted. A few facades had received a coat of paint but otherwise, grimy grey predominated. It was a depressing atmosphere and the imposing monolithic museums and municipal buildings on the banks of the river Spree did nothing but add to the sobriety.

We returned through the Brandenburg Gate, where even the Reichstag was obscured by a wall of scaffolding.

Footsore after the long trek, we returned to Hilka's home. After a quick wash and brush up, it took a few minutes to walk to the local Greek restaurant for dinner.

Ernst, Hilka's former husband and their daughter Jana, had already ordered their meal by the time we arrived. He was a victim of moods and suffered spells of deep depression. Among other projects, he managed an 'arty' postcard business. Although in good humour to greet his old friend Sarah, he often lapsed into silence, rejoining the conversation with a remark, the sense or the humour of which was somewhat difficult to gauge. It did not detract from the hilarity of the evening, however, and before the party broke up, Ernst had promised to take Sarah and me to the Wannsee in the morning.

But fate intervened. Ernst took a dive and was forced to consult his doctor. Kind though his offer had been, I nurtured another plot. I had been in touch with the Bundesarchiv in Berlin and my letter of enquiry had yielded little. Perhaps a personal application would be more successful.

Finkenstein Allé did not appear too far away on the map, so after breakfast, Sarah and I set forth on foot to discover where Dr R. held office. Half an hour later, we arrived at the gatehouse of the largest archive in the city, a complex of very austere buildings set back from the road. An American ex-serviceman supplied us with the passes that were needed and pointed us in the right direction. Block 9C proved to be a wooden structure tucked behind the three main mansions and a phone call from the lobby conjured up a rather distraught Dr R.

"What do you want?" he muttered benignly as we climbed the stairs to his office. At first, he did not seem to understand. He did not remember and could find no record of our correspondence on his computer. Copies of the photographs that had been sent to him had vanished. In desperation he diverted us to the charge of a colleague who continued the search. Minutes passed, but just when all channels seemed to have been explored, Dr R burst into the room with the news that he had located the file. We were informed that we should descend to the reading room where we could view certain microfilms and records.

I was looking for details of the cast for 'Die Grosse Freiheit', the film that was completed in 1944 and for which Maria had signed a contract with UFA in March 1942. Though the search yielded nothing, I did learn that the film organisation had been meticulous about the correctness of identity papers. The contract would not have been confirmed until they had all been made available. This explained why Maria, her mother and Herbert Kurzke had taken the risk of returning to Poland in 1943 in order to acquire them when their repeated applications through the normal channels had failed to produce a result.

Herbert's role in the German forces was still a mystery. Enquiries into the Wehrmacht lists had proved disappointing. Hoping that the SS records would be more fruitful, I enquired where the SS lists might be found.

"They are all here," came the reply, for in 1996 the three military archives had been combined and were all now at the Bundesarchiv in Berlin. As yet, they had not been co-ordinated and so it was necessary to search each archive separately. Kurzke's name did not immediately leap onto the screen of his monitor and it might take a bit of time to track him down. Dr R's colleague, however, had become intrigued by the story and promised to do some more digging. I should phone him the following week to find whether he had made any progress.

The glimmer of hope that a large piece of the jigsaw might be found, had made the visit to the archive well worthwhile. Victorious, we returned to base through the leafy suburbs, pausing to admire the lush gardens and houses that lined the route.

By mid-afternoon we had repacked our baggage and were ready to move on. Ernst had recovered from his morning depression and had brought round some of his postcards and his latest catalogues. We realised that German 'humour' was slightly different from the British sense. To us it seemed more dour than comic. As we were exchanging goodbyes, Hilka produced the worn piece of paper that had informed her mother that she was eligible for a widow's pension. For her mother, it had been the first intimation that her husband was no longer alive. He had died in one of Germany's wartime labour camps.

It was a sharp reminder that German civilians and their families had also suffered terrible abuse during the Nazi regime.

We headed back to East Berlin to find the main station for trains heading eastwards. Soon Berlin lay behind us and we were travelling through endless forest. Trees grew close to the track and through the window we saw few signs of habitation. The stations that we passed were grey and neglected. It was not a long journey and by western standards, the first-class tickets had been exceedingly cheap.

As we neared Gorzów, the first stop inside the Polish border, we noticed the queue of traffic on the road running parallel to the railway line. It stretched as far as the eye could see and beyond as the train rattled along the track. We learned later that at weekends, the East Germans flocked to the Polish border to take advantage of the vast open-air markets on the Polish side where they could purchase goods that were not available on their own side of the border! In East Germany, such goods did not exist.

Passports were checked as soon as we descended from the train and Sarah spotted her friend Monika in the waiting crowd. By her side, her small daughter held up a single rose in welcome. The flood of disembarking passengers swept the little girl off her feet and momentarily she was in danger of being trampled. Monica, a delicate, pretty woman instantly evolved into a tigress, leaping to her child's rescue and spitting venom at the careless perpetrators. Once in the street, Monica looked disconcerted. Her car was small and my suitcase was rather large; too large to fit into the minute boot of the vehicle. Fitting three adults, two children and a large suitcase into a mini sized space took some time, but there was a will and a way and soon we were speeding along avenues lined with tall trees. We turned off the highway onto a sand track into the depths of the forest and now Monika had to fight the wheel of the car to prevent it disappearing into the ruts and getting stuck. Some two kilometres later, we ground to a halt in the back yard of a derelict looking stone built farmhouse. Large chunks of plaster were missing from the walls. The guttering was broken and hanging. The end of the roof ridge did not connect to the end gable. Many of the windows were broken or boarded. As we extricated ourselves from the car, a bearded man appeared in the doorway and greeted Sarah warmly. Formal introductions followed. Monica'shusband spoke little English and after a polite nod and handshake he discretely disappeared, while two massive, white, mountain sheepdogs, chained to a shed at the side of the yard, barked incessantly, their long matted coats leaping like the fringes of Chinese dragons.

The single storey farm house was in a very bad state of health. Inside, the half metre thick walls were covered with a plaster that crumbled to the touch.

The farm house

The house had once been the village tavern. Now there was no village and we had seen only two farmhouses as we approached. The large front room that had served as the public bar, was stacked high with newspapers. Panes of glass were missing from the windows and the substitute planks of wood shut out the light. But though the furniture was minimal, the inhabitable parts of the farmhouse were welcoming.

Later that evening, Sarah took me aside. While chatting with her friend Monika, she had been asked about the purpose of my visit to Poznań, the final destination of my second visit to Poland. "There was some reference to film making and that you were the English woman who was expected. Is it possible that they are talking about you?" asked Sarah.

I was more than a little astonished. Certainly, there had been a suggestion that I might participate in a television documentary, but I had been given the impression that it was to be only for a few seconds and hardly important enough to warrant the news spreading one hundred and fifty kilometres down the road. I assured her that I could not possibly be the same person and that there must surely be talking about another English woman.

How naive of me!

18

A few days later, Sarah returned to England and Jurek, Monica's husband, offered to drive me in his car to Poznań. He had business in the city and it would save me from returning to Berlin with Sarah and then catching the fast train back again as I had planned. A cross-country train link route was possible, but not a wise venture for a non-Polish speaking foreigner. I accepted his kind offer gladly.

En route, he collected a friend from Gorzów and I waited in the car for so long that I began to think that I had been abandoned. The two men eventually returned and I was presented with a scroll of paper, the charter of the city. I was a little bewildered by the pomp and ceremony. Who was I supposed to be that I deserved elevation to a 'freeman' of Gorzow?

A discussion ensued. I sat in the rear of the car, trying to resolve the extraordinary coincidences which seemed to be engulfing me. It seemed that I was the English woman 'of importance' who was expected, but how had this sort of information filtered through to a family of strangers living in a rundown farmhouse in the middle of nowhere? How was it possible that the occupants of the only private Polish home in which (through devious circumstances) I had stayed, come to know about a project that should have been totally off their map? The whole matter was both mysterious and definitely rather odd.

Jurek and his friend dropped me off at the Telenova studios, a modern glass building close to a football stadium. It was late and the office staff had left, but I was escorted to a large room and left to await the next chapter of the adventure. Nearly forty-five minutes later, Ludwik collected me in his new car and once again I was installed in the Dom Polonii overlooking the Stary Rynek. It was familiar territory at last and the ruffled feathers settled back into place.

The next morning was spent in dr Woźniak's office. Many more references had been sourced since my first visit eighteen months earlier. It had been revealed that the relatives living at Pickary 5, had all been involved with pre-war intelligence and therefore that Maria had grown up in an environment that nurtured clandestine activity. A number of people called in and the conversation in Polish at times seemed heated. One gentleman was particularly noticeable for his air of smart importance. He spoke at length and in an excited manner, gesticulating continuously. Unable to understand a single word, I studied the expression on his face and his body language. Both were seriously earnest.

Ludwik offered some enlightenment. "He was a prisoner in Poggenburg and will be in the film."

Patiently Ludwik explained the reason for the man's animation. He was to describe an event that demonstrated the bizarre treatment that the commandant of Poggenburg bestowed upon his prisoners. In January 1944, he, together with nine other men and two women had been covered from head to toe in a tar-like substance. Walter, armed with an artist's brush, had proceeded to paint their naked bodies with oil paints. The connection to Maria was that he had identified one of the two women as Antonina. Her special nose had betrayed her again. The second woman might have been Maria, but as the heads of the women had been shaven at the time and Maria did not bear an easily distinguishable facial feature, the witness was not confident enough to be absolutely certain.

"What exactly is this documentary going to be about," I had asked Ludwik when the hubbub in the small office subsided for a moment.

"It will be about Poggenburg and Maria", he replied and explained that a series of documentaries had been made about the conditions in Poznań in 1939 at the beginning of the war and particularly about the people who had later been imprisoned in Fort VII and Poggenburg. The last programme would be made on Wednesday with my help. It was to be about Maria and her book!!!

The full picture of what was planned came as a mild shock. Since 1995, I had exchanged many letters with dr Wozniak. Each letter had to be translated word for word with the help of a dictionary and as any language translator knows, this method can lead to misunderstandings. Sometimes the result had made no sense and required a certain amount of guesswork to extract the meaning. The end result therefore could not be relied upon for accuracy. Despite these hazards, I had sensed a feeling that as time passed, dr Woźniak had become happier with Maria's manuscript. As each item had been checked, and found to be possible, more credence had been given to those points for which there remained no evidence. But, I still found it hard to believe that he had committed his approval so far as to agree that a whole forty-minute programme should be devoted to her story.

'Go with the flow,' I told myself.

The film producer also called into the office that morning. Forget the Hollywood primo in grey raincoat and sunglasses. This one was female for a start and wore her blond hair in a plait – an unbelievably long plait. Waist length would have been impressive, but this plait reached almost to the back of her knees. Only Rapunzel could have possessed a longer length of hair.

Dorota Latour was in her early thirties. She wore no make-up and peered through small round glasses. She spoke some English, but was wary of practising it beyond that which was absolutely necessary. Her manner was almost brusque and she negotiated with the 'smart gentleman' in an abrupt tone, making short statements and awaiting comment before she uttered the next.

She did not stay long and departed with a cordial handshake and a suggestion that I avoid 'white' in my clothing, as the camera did not like it.

Go with the flow, I reminded myself again. Stay calm and ride the waves of destiny!

The next morning, I enjoyed not having to stir at a godforsaken hour. Monday had been a 6.30am start.

My time was my own and I sauntered out into the square to do some window-shopping and souvenir hunting. I also needed to purchase a new dictionary. The old one was disintegrating.

I called into dr Woźniak's office for a cup of coffee. He was entangled in a plethora of Agnieskas in the Szymanski family, none of whom seemed to share the same birth date from one reference to the next. Agnieska was the name of Maria's mother's younger sister. Locating her in the records was proving a problem.

More practical shopping was next on the agenda concerning the essential matter of food.

Climbing the stairs again to my room, I encountered the young man who had so kindly found me a bed at the Ministry of Culture. He

Dorota Latour

seemed momentarily very surprised to see me again. I thanked him, remarking that the people that I had been meeting in the shops and on the street seemed more relaxed, more spontaneous and less reserved than in 1995. The difference was quite noticeable. He conceded that I might be right, but for him, the main difference between then and now was the huge increase in private cars. It was becoming a problem. The roads were not built for a large volume of traffic and the cobbles were suffering. Also, too many youngsters were out of work and car theft had become an alternative occupation. He concluded smugly, that he avoided both difficulties by clinging to his bicycle.

I spent the evening in front of the TV, grazing on the fodder that I had purchased earlier and exercising my dictionary.

The news on the screen reported that airports in Britain had been affected by IRA bomb scares. Somewhere in East Europe, a terrorist bomb had actually exploded. There had been casualties. The world was still a crazy place, showing the same inhumane tendencies today as the text that I was busy translating.

Wednesday morning found us all assembled in the execution yard of Fort VII. No timetable had been drawn up and Woźniak, Ludwik and I wandered around the bunkers of the Fort, while filming was taking place inside the museum. It seemed that the doctor was not over familiar with the place. I had studied the only diagram available of the construction of the Fort and when I asked him where a certain set of steps had been, he shrugged his shoulders. At the time, we were standing at the top of a short flight of steps that led down into an alcove to an entrance of some sort. The doorway was bricked up with a small barred opening at the top. Inside, the room was intensely dark.

I balanced my camera on the lower edge of the opening and pressed the button. The camera flashed. When developed, the photograph revealed railings emerging from the floor on the back wall, indicating a stairway down into the prison below. This entrance is not shown on contemporary plans of the prison!

Soon, our presence was required in the yard below and I began to follow instructions with the camera whirring.

The initial sequence took place in a narrow passage, which descended beneath the level of the outer yard. It was not open to the public and dr Woźniak became excited at the idea of venturing deep into the bowels of the Fort. He had not known that such tunnels existed.

The sloping passage led to a small vaulted room. The brick arches curved high overhead to a point. At one time it must have formed part of a corridor. Newer brickwork at the far end of the small space suggested a blocked access. An old coffin, of the shape used to bury prisoners, was stored on high shelving. Vertical indentations in the wall of the passage indicated where doorposts had once been, and a deep horizontal groove worn into the brickwork where something broad and solid had repeatedly scraped the wall. It was not difficult to imagine the misery and desolation of those who had been forced to pass this way so many years ago.

"Try not to look at the camera."

I marched down the tunnel several times before Miss Latour was satisfied. For me, the whole scenario was like a film in itself. My involvement was minimal, as I understood so little of the discussion. I had the space to withdraw into my own speculative world and draw my own conclusions.

A group of chattering children entered the yard. A school group was booked to visit the museum. As kids will, they were not paying attention to what was around them as they waited to be ushered into the little museum. Filming stopped and we all waited outside.

When they emerged ten minutes later, their demeanour was almost shocking to see. They were silent, each wrapped in their own world of thought. Had the gallery of photographs of elegantly dressed men and women, some with their children, or the faces of young men in uniform, who could only have been a couple of years older than themselves, or the images of elderly gentlemen caused their faces to become so solemn. Perhaps the sight of the guillotine had shocked them. Possibly it was the line of cement filled holes in the ceiling of the main prison cell that had disturbed them. They marked the place where the rings for the hangman's noose had been, eight of them above a wooden platform in a cell containing one hundred and fifty people. In close proximity to friends and family, the victims died each time the wooden bench collapsed.

The children had been transported back to a terrible period of Polish history, which their grandparents could still remember. Their eyes were glazed, their tongues silent.

All visitors were gone.

The museum was now empty and the camera team was ready to start. I recognised a familiar face that I had not expected to see. Jurek was assisting the sound engineer! Now I knew how the rumour of my arrival in Poland had filtered to the farmhouse in Dzieduszyce.

Dr Woźniak sat at a table beside the programme presenter. He spoke carefully, wary of his new teeth. I had been told that it had only been with great reluctance that he had been persuaded to take part. His mouth was extremely sore and he was not confident that he could speak clearly in front of the camera. His self-doubt was misplaced. He appeared as a very serious, thoughtful person and his teeth did not let him down.

The museum itself had been 'sanitised'. The photographs that had filled the walls were nowhere to be seen so it was not they that had sobered the children. In the main cell, display cases stood in regimented lines. As I wandered among them, the prison mug shots of a teenage boy caught my attention. His chubby face expressed youthful naivety. In the first profile shot, his eyes held a fear mixed with a curious astonishment that had disappeared by the time the camera had recorded its third photograph. My guts heaved. He was so like my own son at home: brash, sometimes stupid, sometimes irritating, but basically harmless. The young Pole died in Fort VII in 1942. How many like him had suffered the same fate?

Dr Woźniak and Ludwik retired to their desks after the filming in Fort VII and I boarded the transit van, adorned with the Telenova logo. I had been abandoned to cope on my own. It felt lonely.

From Fort VII, we headed back into the city centre, stopping for more filming at the church where Maria had been baptised, one of the few in Poznań that had remained open for Catholic worship during the Soviet occupation. The next stop was at the apartment block where she had been born. My task there was to stroll in and out of passages and pose 'in thought'. It did not require too much effort.

Jankowski's house, the agent to whom Maria had delivered a suitcase full of German currency, had been located in a tree-lined avenue overlooking the largest public park in Poznań, a ten-minute walk from the Stary Rynek. 'Solidarnosc' was scrawled on the front wall. It provided another short filler for the documentary as did the interview of a nun as she leafed through an old photograph album that showed schoolgirls on a picnic by the river and several scantily dressed maidens posing on stage.

The last stop before driving out to Zabikowo was the site of the newsagent shop once owned by Maria's grandfather. The frontage was narrow, the shop itself a long broad corridor, situated in a busy thoroughfare. It had recently been refurbished and was still a newsagent.

Zabikowo had also been sanitised since my first visit in 1995. The approach road was no longer pitted with potholes. The entrance had been moved back with new ornate gates leading to a broad gravelled avenue through the centre of the camp. A surfaced car park avoided the necessity to park by the roadside.

Dr Woźniak was again in attendance and the party adjourned to the museum. That too was different. Externally, the dour concrete plaster had been decorated with a modest wall plaque displaying a museum sign. Internally, the place had been spruced up beyond recognition. Instead of the prison identity photographs, family snapshots were displayed on the walls. A model in the centre of the room defined the size and shape of the prison. Another cabinet displayed a canister of Cyclon B. I asked dr Woźniak 'why'. Zabikowo was not a 'death' camp and did not have a gas chamber. It is not even known whether it had a delousing shed. Cyclon B was originally used to kill lice and therefore the canister would have been a legitimate exhibit on those grounds. Did dr Woźniak have any light to shed on the matter? No!

He was more interested in the relief model of the campsite. Tut, tutting, he flapped his arms in despair. He was not happy. The model was misleading. Bits were missing. He explained to me that the map which was generally cited for reference had been drawn by a prisoner who had not had access to the whole camp, nor was he accurate about the function of different huts. Dr Woźniak was frustrated that the museum had not been more careful about presenting inaccurate information to the public. The incident underlined the existence of disinformation in Poland. The Poles themselves had problems getting the facts straight.

In the car park the smartly dressed gentleman from the previous day's conference in the office became impatient to start. He instantly sought the attention of the director, Dorota Latour, talking with such animosity that he barely paused to draw breath.

Miss Latour, bustled about her business, issuing instructions to the camera crew, dogged at every turn by a torrent of words from the excited gentleman. To silence him, she was almost rude. The sequence was supposed to involve me listening to the good fellow's account of his time in the camp. Men and women had normally been segregated, but the sadistic commandant was guilty of causing the 'accidental' death of many of his prisoners and also amused himself by acting out quaint idiosyncrasies at the expense of his charges. In his case, the victims had suffered the indignity for eight days.

The poor man must have been rehearsing his story for weeks. As the camera started to record, he started on his speech and continued relentlessly to the end, despite Miss Latour signalling to the camera to cease filming when her attempts to stop him had failed. A retake resulted in the same monologue repeated to the end. He was asked to pause for breath occasionally and although he seemed to have understood, on the third take, he quite obviously had clearly not understood. He rattled through his lines in the same monotonous tone, with not the slightest hesitation.

This was going to take a while. Once engaged the needle had to keep going to the end of the record.

Miss Latour tried to provide a ploy to distract him. It was my duty to shove a photograph in front of his nose, with the intention of allowing him to recognise Maria's mother.

There were two problems with this idea. In the first place, his recital did not provide the suggestion of a pause for the photo to be introduced. Secondly, when an interruption was achieved, he was unable to continue as he had forgotten the next line!

He became upset with himself and angry that he could not be expected to tell his story without interference from the director. The air filled with recriminatory tones. It was brought to an abrupt conclusion by Miss Latour, who announced that, having seen the playback, there was sufficient material recorded for the session to be concluded. The great orator, marched off, his discontent and irritation apparent in every step.

The episode had taken place in the car park outside the fence of Zabikowo. Since my first visit, the foundations of the prison barracks had been tidied and filled with gravel and a pathway led to a memorial erected in the centre. The drinking water well still had water in it, but the reservoir with its embankments rising eight feet above the rest of the camp did not. Watchtowers at the corners of the fencing were no longer on their original sites and only a single wire fence now surrounded the camp area rather than the double fencing separated by a track wide enough for guards and dogs to patrol.

Today, only half the camp area has been cleared. The kitchen garden where Maria's mother had held sway was now under cultivation by a local farmer, and the furthest part of the camp, some ten feet lower than the main camp, where dangerous political prisoners were held, was still overgrown and impenetrable. Trees had been planted many years ago, that had grown to a majestic forty feet, forming a natural cathedral over the site that had been destroyed by fire and discovered soon after the German retreat.

Footage was taken of the camp and I was required to answer a few questions about the subject of the film and Maria. 'Forget the camera and concentrate on articulating words clearly and slowly,' a simple enough task unless your aunt is called Malaprop!

By this time, I was suffering from caffeine withdrawal symptoms and I pleaded for a break before we continued on to the convent near Otorowa, where Maria had attended boarding school. Miss Latour seemed to survive on air but the all-male camera crew rejoiced that I had dared to suggest that the schedule should be interrupted. On arrival in the village, we found the one and only café, hiding in a scruffy yard that backed on to the main street. The local 'gossip shop' provided a very basic menu. But the soup was hot and the coffee strong. The meal was accompanied by the vociferous opinions of three drunken men, imbibing at the table next to us.

We were not permitted to linger long. Our director was urging us to remember that time was passing and the daylight would soon be gone.

It was my first sight of the convent, but immediately, I could recognise it from Maria's descriptions. The old palace stood on a slight rise in the ground, its facade topped by a series of baroque crown shapes that might appear as turrets to a child. There were the steps at the front of the building down which the Reverend Mother had descended, her habit billowing, and there was the lawn on which Maria had auditioned for her dancing lessons. It had not changed in seventy years. Even the Ursuline nuns were still in charge.

The role of the school had changed. As it had been in the nineteen twenties, it was once again an orphanage. A smiling, cherry-cheeked nun opened the door to us. Behind her, a small boy sat in the middle of the room, studiously assembling a jigsaw puzzle, the pieces scattered around him on the carpet. The nun could not, however, provide answers to our questions. All records had been destroyed.

A young nun showed me an album of photographs taken of the previous pupils as they danced and acted on stage. Their costumes were anything but prim and proper and revealed a remarkable flamboyance that would not have been out of place at the end of the twentieth century.

Standing alone on the lawn in front of the camera, I was quizzed with more questions. Most I could answer without having to pause too long for thought.

Then out of the blue, came the stinger.

"In your opinion, was Maria a heroine or a traitor?"

I did not know. There were still too many voids. Suspicions I had, but a black and white opinion, I did not. I pleaded for a few moments respite to sort out a coherent answer.

If they wanted me to proclaim her a heroine of the Polish nation, I honestly could not do it. Her motivation in the war years had been a theatrical career and it was her determination to seek stardom that had caused her downfall. Drawing from my own acquaintanceship with her, I had become aware of her selfishness. Conversely, within her personal relationships, she was a heroine. She had not betrayed either her mother or Herbert when faced with the brutality of the Gestapo or the awe of the court martial. In her heart she was not a traitor.

In the same instant, I was reminded how much I regretted being unaware of Maria's background while she was still alive. She had numerous eccentric moments, when she had behaved quite unreasonably. She had occasionally told me stories, hinting at a mysterious past, but to my shame, I had not taken them too seriously. I attributed to her a wild imagination and believed that her stories had acquired colourful embellishment. I now realised that she had understated the truth. Surrounded by the comforts of a modern Britain, it was hard to conceive how survival in such circumstances was possible. I recalled Josef Garlinski's mournful expression in 1995, as he explained the lack of interest of the British islander in the fate of Poland.

"Take my advice and forget it," he had said, "The British don't want to know"

Such distractions had to be shoved aside and I had to concentrate hard to give a logical reply to the question. The woman I had known was proud of her nationality and would never have betrayed Poland. Somehow an answer stumbled forth for the benefit of the camera. I opted for the middle road, describing Maria's love of the theatre above all else. She had stars in her eyes. The older woman that I had known was devious and scheming. Her antics made her few friends, but she had a kind heart and she had loved her Poland until the day she died. Her mother Antonina on the other hand, was a strong woman who made most of the decisions for Maria, shielding and protecting her daughter. Perhaps it should be she about whom such a question should be asked.

Heads nodded in approval after I had finished. The only problem was that turning the focus on Antonina was futile. If she had been heavily involved with the Polish resistance, she had been a very successful agent, and had covered her tracks. Apart from her daughter's account, practically no archival evidence remained, if it ever existed in the first place. It was the nature of the 'intelligence' game.

The driver of the van was eager to get back before dark. He was pacing back and forth beside the van, urging us to board without delay. Ten minutes later, the five of us were squashed into the three-seater vehicle with the equipment stashed in the rear. The Telenova logos on the sides of the van had caused the locals to gather and stare in silence. We waved a cheeky goodbye.

It was necessary to cling to the seat and anything that was bolted down in order to survive the G force of speeding around the tight bends of the narrow lanes. When we joined the main road, the drive became even more uncomfortable. The road had only one lane in each direction, with gravel either side of the tarmac. The traffic was heavy, and a continuous line stretched into the distance on both sides of the road.

This did not deter our intrepid driver. For him, the oncoming traffic was no problem when he decided to overtake. With brash confidence, he would swerve out from behind a vehicle and simply put his foot down, regardless of whether there was a sufficient distance left for the oncoming traffic. Unbelievably, without fail, (I live to tell the tale) the approaching vehicle took refuge on the gravel, allowing our driver room to monopolise the wrong side of the road. Most of the journey, as I recollect, was spent on the wrong side of the road. The practice felt suicidal to the passengers. The expression of the oncoming drivers facing imminent doom was not dissimilar to watching a horror movie. The last-minute wrenching of the wheel to avoid a head on collision was repeated time and time again.

Our driver was deaf to reasoning. He had only been married for three days and we could only conclude that he had made a mistake and had developed a death wish to end it all. Miraculously, his desire was not fulfilled and somewhat shaken but still in one piece, we disembarked at the TV station headquarters.

The programme was broadcast a few weeks after I returned to England. The copy that I received was in Polish, a voiceover drowning out whatever I had said. When checked, the translation was reasonably accurate.

Preceding the acknowledgements was an appeal for anyone who had known Maria to come forward. I had not anticipated this bonus and had to patiently await a response for many months.

19

In England, the General Election was taking place. New Labour, led by Tony Blair, was making a strong challenge against the Conservatives. There were fears that the IRA would cause chaos by planting bombs, but in the event, it turned out to be terrorising by threat only.

Far removed from British Politics, I spent the day in Kórnik in the company of dr Woźniak and Ludwik. It was a day of pleasurable interest mixed with reminders of the terror invoked by the Germans when they invaded Poland in September 1939.

On arrival in the small town, our first stop was at the allotment area where four years earlier, dr Woźniak had acquired a small garden. A fellow coffee addict, he immediately disappeared into the small cottage on the site to put on the kettle. Though supplied with water and electricity the interior of the building had only basic furnishings. The sink was a plastic bowl perched on a broken chair; the kitchen occupied the far end of the main room with a large table and an enormous television filling the remainder. On the ground floor there was also a toilet and washroom plus a separate bedroom. A cramped space in the roof provided further sleeping accommodation.

The outside of the hut was freshly plastered with sturdy grids over every window to deter intruders. The bars across the outer door were thick enough to keep the most determined hacksaw at bay. A large veranda looked out over the garden to the fields and a lake beyond, on the other side of which lay Kórnik itself.

The next-door neighbour was in the process of building a two-storey house of brick. Technically it was not permitted to erect 'permanent' structures, but as Ludwik explained, "This is Poland. We are glad that someone has the money to spend on such things." The allotments were each a standard forty square metres and there were 150 of them with gravelled service roads between each row. Parking on the road was not permitted and only access for loading and unloading was allowed.

The garden was neat and tidy with mature fruit trees. Woźniak admitted that it was his wife who was the gardener as his knowledge of such things was very limited. Tulips and primroses were in flower and the apple and cherry trees were covered in blossom. The flora was very similar to an English garden. I spotted a weed and pulled it out of the soil. A fine, grey sand, drifted away from its roots like dust in the wind, reminding me of just how gluey Essex clay was in contrast.

Over coffee there was some discussion about what may happen to Maria's story. Apparently, Dorota Latour had made enquiries about making a full-length film about it. This would require the magnificent sum of 9,000,000 zloty and even with financial assistance from public funds, it was a figure that could not be raised. I began to realise the importance of the heroine/traitor question. If I could give them the answer they wanted, 'a heroine', it would make a positive contribution to finding funds for such a project. It also became apparent to me that I was expected to arouse interest outside of Poland.

I inwardly cringed at the notion. I lacked the confidence and panache to bluff. As yet I still knew too little about the mysteries of Maria's survival, Herbert's role in the German forces and a host of other enigmas that her story presented.

Dorota had also suggested that my own story of how I had explored the background to Maria's story could make an interesting read in itself. It was the first time that such an idea had been suggested. I had written magazine articles before and had invested in a course for creative writing, but the notion of composing an epic of book proportions was a daunting task that I dared not contemplate. I was not organised enough. My life in England was not conducive to sitting alone for hours on end with pen in hand. Each day disappeared with the speed of light, fielding phone calls, running errands, making coffee for those who called in unannounced, besides a large house and garden to tend when there was a slack moment. Me – write a book! Impossible!

But the seed had been sewn. Having unsuccessfully endeavoured to find material that had been published in English, I was aware that I was treading on unexplored territory. The history of Poland during and after WWII had been tragic and the details barely recognised by the West. Gradually, I was beginning to understand some of the reasons for its neglect. Inaccessibility to the facts featured high. Destruction of documents was yet another ingredient. The Poles themselves were only now able to access the truth. Under Soviet occupation, everyone learned to keep what they knew, to themselves. Over fifty years later, their memories were not totally reliable. Sorting out the reality was dr Woźniak's task. Establishing facts for the encyclopaedia that he was collating was driving him to desperation at times. The witnesses that he interviewed rarely gave similar accounts of the same event. The complicated equation of family history, national loyalties and political attitudes distorted the memory. Every family had lost grandparents, fathers, mothers, brothers, sisters, uncles or aunts. Loyalty to the national bond united them. Forty-five years of suppression by the Soviet Union had kept the knowledge concealed.

Ludwik had provided the transport to Kórnik for dr Woźniak still did not possess his own car. Normally, to reach his garden from Poznań was a complex journey involving trains, buses and finally, a taxi. The reason for today's expedition was to attend a meeting of the allotment owners to make plans for new water pipes. Driving around the lake back to the town, Woźniak bemoaned the lack of a telephone link to the gardens, mobile phones being as yet a novelty in Poland.

As we drove down the main street of Kórnik, we passed the gas works. The house beside it was dr Woźniak's birthplace. His father had managed the facility and in 1942 he had died there. As leader of the local AK group, he had opted to leap into a tank of heating oil and drown rather than fall into the hands of the Gestapo who were knocking at his door. If he had been arrested, he knew that he was doomed. The resistance expected him to remain silent for 24 hours under interrogation and torture. Thereafter, a prisoner was not deemed to be a traitor if he yielded, but the longer he held out the better the chance his contacts had of 'disappearing'. As an AK leader, however, Woźniak senior would have known too much. He would have endangered too many of his colleagues and their families. Execution would inevitably have followed had he survived the beatings. He chose to die by his own hand rather than risk betraying his friends.

We visited his grave that afternoon in the tightly packed cemetery where his wife lies beside him. She died in 1976. Neither grave showed signs of age or neglect. Like most others in the cemetery, fresh flowers and removal of weeds indicated that they were still not forgotten.

As we passed the council offices in the centre of the town, Ludwik pointed out the high wall surrounding the yard where his uncle, an official on the town council, had been shot in September 1939. As soon as the Germans arrived at any village or town, large or small, the most influential members of society were arrested. The twenty men that were arrested in Kórnik included his uncle. Less than 24 hours later they were dead, executed for the crime of being a responsible Polish citizen.

Why did the Nuremberg lawyers have difficulty in establishing that war crimes were part of the German agenda from the very start of the war? Surely the fate of men like Ludwik's uncle could not have been overlooked – or could it?

My Polish vocabulary increased by two words on the road back to Poznań. Dr Woźniak had remained in Kórnik. With Ludwik once again behind the wheel, I became the navigator following directions according to the map. Prawo/lewo – right/left. At the junction with the main road, the 'lewo' came too late. Ludwik stamped on the accelerator instead of the brake and we shot across the main road and up the bank on the far side. The 'lewo' was finally achieved on to a farm track on the top of the bank. Driving parallel to the highway, we eventually 'levoed' at the next opportunity back down to the highway again. Fortunately, the traffic was sparse. In the rush hour we would not have escaped unscathed.

New Labour was rumoured to be crowing from the hilltops. They had won the election in Britain but the rejoicing did not feature prominently on Polish TV. The success of Britain in the Eurovision Song Contest was more important for them. Friday had been a quiet day. My head, reeling with the events of the past week, had rebelled with a thumping headache. The eyes of the boy prisoner in Fort VII still haunted me. They begged me for some recognition of his predicament and fate.

Dorota's suggestion that a book was the logical consequence of Maria's story was also causing me some discomfiture. There were still so many loose ends that needed to be tied up, loose ends that were connected to her story but were as yet unexplained. From the mud of ignorance, rose a large bubble. Who was Herbert Kurzke, the German that Maria married in 1941 and what role did he play in the German forces? It had become an obvious priority that his service record had to be somehow traced.

I started to make lists of the questions that needed answers, thinking that where to look for the answers was a mere complication of the research. I deluded myself!

Now that Maria's manuscript had come to be accepted as a reasonably accurate account of her life, a baffling problem reared its head. Why had she not mentioned her connection to the resistance in more detail? Written shortly after the end of the war, had it still been indiscrete to admit involvement in clandestine activities?

Another problem with the manuscript concerned the chronology of events. Maria had implied that she had spent three summers in Poggenburg and that was just not possible. Why had she made the mistake of suggesting that she had been imprisoned in the camp for two and a half years, when in fact she could only have been there for a maximum time of eighteen months? The error was too obvious if she had written the story herself. Had another hand been involved in the writing of her memoire? My head spun.

In the back of my mind lurked a possibility. Was the 'other little project' that Alfred Weideman had referred to in his letter dated 1947, the manuscript? If so, how would I ever find out the truth?

The recent 'near death' experiences on the Polish highway, deterred me from further excursions outside the city. I wandered around the narrow streets close to the Stary Rynek trying to locate places that I had seen two years earlier. I found the council building from whence we had hijacked a car and chauffeur. In my wobbly condition that year, it had seemed that we had walked for miles. In fact, it lay very near to the market square.

Relaxing with a book in my hand on a park bench, I read in the sun and indulged in people-watching; the courting couples, the dog walkers, the grannies exercising the toddlers, the teenage boys feeding the pigeons. It was a seductively normal scene and redressed a balance to the horrors that I had encountered during the past few days.

It quite suddenly turned chilly and as I walked back to base camp, I noticed that instead of the small bars that had occupied the entrance halls two years ago, each door that I passed had now become a minute kiosk or shop selling a variety of travel items; postcards, newspapers or a few sweets and cigarettes. The grocery shops (they were hardly big enough to call stores) were not apparent to the passer-by. Few of them displayed goods in a window and often they were at ankle level, the customer having to descend steps to reach an anonymous entrance to a cellar.

The plasterwork on the buildings appeared cleaner, some window and door frames had been painted. Eight years on, the greyness of communism was gradually being erased.

A delegation from the Woźniak household met me in the lobby in the late afternoon. Dr Woźniak, Małgosia, her little sister Marta and their older brother, the proud owner of a car, carried me away to their home to celebrate their father's name day. Apparently, birthdays are not celebrated in Poland – only the saint's day of one's name.

The meal consumed, a discussion developed around Solidarity and the Free Europe radio station. Dr Woźniak rooted out his video about the revolt in 1956 and the riots in Poznań, remarking that the communists were prone to produce remarkable propaganda films about misconduct in Poland as well as broadcast items of news to illustrate suppressive activities of the USA.

A Pole could not believe anything that he saw on television and the broadcasts made by Free Europe (Wolna Europa) were the only means by which real news could be obtained from the world beyond Soviet influence. Proudly, dr Woźniak produced a small radio that he had built himself. When radios were forbidden, it was the only way that a Pole could maintain a contact with unbiased opinions. The BBC World News was a lifeline for many years and the radio still worked, cheerfully throwing out a modern tune with clarity.

The first major post-war revolt against the Soviet rule took place in Poznań. Children, as young as thirteen years old lost their lives. Every two years or so there would be further demonstrations – with bloody results. The Poles were restless subjects. It was not until 1981, when Lech Wałęsa led the dock strikes in Gdansk and Solidarnosz became the by-word for the struggle for freedom, that the light at the end of the long tunnel began to get brighter.

"In a way," boasted Woźniak, "it could be said that the seed for the failure of communism and Soviet control was sown in this very city." Certainly, since the Gdansk riots in 1981, the movement had snowballed until the Russians sudden withdrawal from East Germany in 1989. Their communist world had imploded and the Berlin wall was torn down. Nations on the Eastern borders of Europe were free at last from communist occupation. The subject matter of the conversation changed.

I asked dr Woźniak his purpose for the TV documentaries.

He told me that five in the series had already been filmed. The one featuring Maria Weychanowa would be the last to be broadcast. Working on his encyclopaedia, he had reached the conclusion that he needed material to fill some of the holes in the incomplete archives. The idea to use television had occurred to him in order to encourage the generation of people who could remember, to come forward. He was presently coping with a bulging mailbag each day.

I watched examples of previous programmes. None of them featured Poggenburg. For the most part, they referred to prisoners that had been executed in Fort VII or the Młynski criminal prison. Woźniak had featured in each documentary; the 'studious historian' looking for the most part like a grumpy owl with his spectacles perched precariously on the end of his nose. In the comfort of his sitting room, he roared with laughter at the sight.

What would the documentary about Maria turn up?

20

Dr Woźniak's eldest son, Małgosia and her eight-year-old nephew collected me the following morning with a car. We were off to explore the lakes north of the city. My head was suffering the effects of the previous evening. It was not surprising. The mixture of homemade wine and vodka had challenged the digestive system.

Woźniak's son (who I was too embarrassed to ask his name for the third time), spoke English reasonably well. He was married to an English teacher after all. He was also another car driver who was new to the joys of owning his own wheels. A bicycle had served him well until six months previously and at times he still drove at the same speed, tending to slow down to change gear and to stall the engine too easily. The ride was, however, less noisy than Ludwik's war with the gearbox and certainly more cautious about defying other road users than the TV van driver.

Northwest of the city, beyond the Hippodrome, we passed a 'camping' site with spacious looking log cabins, previously holiday homes of the pre-1989 political elite. In every way they mimicked the dream house of today, surrounded by trees, secluded and a lake beach nearby. Different was the tall fence securing the boundaries. They underlined the privilege of the communist party member versus the restrictions of the rest of the populace who lived in cramped apartments in the ten-storey blocks in the city.

Sipping coffee, we sat on the patio of a cafeteria overlooking the large lake. The day was dull and a cold wind blew. A group of horse riders ambled by. Macadam covered the paths. The grass was trimmed as for a city park. This was the official tourist park for the citizens of Poznań, neat and tidy, open space, fresh air and places to stroll without getting one's shoes dirty.

A few more kilometres down the road, it was a completely different picture. This lake had proved difficult to access and it was only after taking several wrong turns and ignoring large warning signs, that we eventually arrived at a pebble beach.

Ten years previously, it had been realised that the untreated sewage from the local villages together with the chemicals draining from the fields had killed the equatic life. Stagnant water lay to a depth of fifteen feet below the surface where it was impossible to find a single bubble of oxygen. Three machines with long paddles were in action to activate some life into the lake, stirring the dead water. They seemed to be fighting a lost cause. The only plant life they had generated was a brick coloured scum of algae. It lay inches thick on the bank where it had drifted to the shore. Like oil slicks, islands of the growth could be seen floating on the open water. The smell was not attractive.

Turning south again, we arrived at an artificial lake on the outskirts of the city. Malta, as it was called, was designed for water sports and canoeing and rowing events were regularly held there. 'Freedom Hill' overlooked the complex. Created from the earth removed from the hole dug for the lake, the large man-made hill served in communist times as a ceremonial mound where officials could march importantly up and down for their various celebrations. Today, private enterprise had converted it into a dry ski slope and laughter filled the air.

Driving back through the city, we passed large chalet-style houses.

"It is where the people who cooperated with the communists lived," explained the chauffeur. "Some of them still live there, but they have been without an income since 1989."

The comment opened up a discussion about the transition from the communist regime to a capitalist system.

"Most people welcomed the change and appreciated being able to earn more if they worked harder. For some, those who under the communists received the same income as their neighbour, regardless of how little they did, these people are unhappy. They cannot come to terms with the idea that today, everyone is not on the same level and are extremely jealous of success, however small."

Back at base, I dined on a very large ham salad and coffee for the princely sum of £2 (10zl) in the small restaurant in the basement of the Dom Polonii. Since 1995, the exchange rate had become more generous to the English pound, however, there had been a significant rise in the price of food. Afterwards I climbed the stairs to the second floor where I made myself a cup of coffee before making the final ascent to the third floor to find my bed.

The lights went out! I had woken early in my roost on the third floor and started to read, take notes and think. The TV had kept me company, grumbling to itself unintelligibly, but the flicker of the screen was a source of movement in the stillness of the room. Suddenly, the screen went black and the bedside lamp switched itself off. I waited for the power to return. Nothing happened, so I took my book to the window and continued to read.

Two hours later, the power had still not returned. There were several errands that needed my attention and it became apparent that it would be necessary to descend the stairs to find nourishment. Although outside there was bright daylight, with no windows, the stairwell was in pitch darkness.

Darkness without any reflected light whatsoever is like existing in a black soup. Once I closed the door of my room behind me, I was enveloped in a void. Arms held wide, I found the turning to the top of the stairwell. Clutching the handrail for support, the slow task of descending the stairs commenced. Hit the top of the step with the heel and drop. Ten steps, the landing, turn right and start again. Four flights had been negotiated when thankfully the glow of a torch greeted me on the first floor.

"Are you alright? Take this!" The torch was thrust into my hand.

"We have another in the office." Effusive thanks! With a light source, the last two flights were a doddle. The electric locks on the door were disengaged and useless, but I had escaped.

Returning the torch to the receptionist in the foyer, I walked across the square to dr Woźniak's office, hoping to photocopy some papers. He too had been affected by the power cut. We sat drinking cold coffee and exchanged a few words in Ponglish Deutsch. In desperation, he summoned a very pleasant woman from the main office who translated my message for him. I needed to telephone Berlin to discover whether the archive had unearthed information about Herbert Kurzke. But the telephone line from his office would not connect to phones outside Poland for some reason and we would be obliged to go to the Institute HQ across the square.

It took two calls to the Bundesarchiv to track down the quarry. Yes, he remembered the two English women who had invaded his office, but no, he had not managed to find any trace of Herbert Kurzke. His tone was enthusiastic and he promised to let me know as soon as anything turned up.

The response was disappointing. If Herbert could not be traced by the largest archive in Berlin, where should the next enquiry be directed? I had assumed that he was in the army, the Wehrmacht, but there were several other alternatives including the SS or Sicherheitspolizei that might prove more rewarding.

The electricity supply remained dormant. On returning to Woźniak's office, we found his assistant pouring over pages of corrections for the encyclopaedia. Dr Woźniak fetched the six volumes of *Armia Krajowa w dokumentach 1939–*

1945 that he had generously presented to me, together with a collection of statements and information about the AK. They weighed over three kilos and were written in Polish (of course). Getting them back to England on my flight luggage allowance would be a challenge.

Published by the Polish Underground State study group in London, it was possible that the six books had already been translated into English. That afternoon, I could only make sense out of the letters that had been printed in their original language (i.e. English). Volume V for example started with a letter from Lt. Col. Perkin to General Tabor, informing him that the SOE (Special Overseas Executive) was definitely planning to send a party of three officers and two signals personnel to Poland. Led by Col. Hudson, and including a Pole, Lt. Pospieszalski, the mission intended to contact the AK and investigate the validity of reports that had reached London, indicating that the Soviets were acting improperly towards the Polish resistance army.

My 'holiday' reading was *Fighting Warsaw* by Karbonski. When Ludwik called around midday, we discussed a number of questions arising from the text. He was able to throw light in dark corners.

"Dr Woźniak says that Karbonski is a political animal. What he says may be correct but dr Woźniak is suspicious of the name dropping that he indulges in." We also mulled over the traitor/heroine question. It was bothering me too.

The electricity was reconnected before Ludwik left. The stairwell was no longer a hazard. The repeated treks up and down to greet visitors meant that I was getting fitter by the day.

Waldemar, (Woźniak's son – I had remembered his name at last) phoned up to my room from the foyer late in the evening. He had volunteered to book a seat on the train back to Berlin for me. He had phoned the station but had been told that red tape required his presence in person.

Waldemar, a man in his thirties, who had grown up under the occupation and spoke English, was a prime target for me to interrogate. The result was a comprehensive lecture on the political structure and ethnic content of various regions of Poland; Wielkopolska (West) versus General Government (Central) versus Upper Silesia in the South. I tested my conclusions of how Poland and its wartime treatment fitted into the larger plans of Nazi expansion and sought his opinion of how right or wrong I might be. Perhaps he was being polite, but I do not recall any sense of patronisation on hearing what must have sounded to him a naive summation.

The ticket had to be collected that night for he would be away the next day.

At 10pm, Waldemar hurried to complete his mission, returning an hour later. He had a satisfied grin on his face. The reservation of seats from Poznań was half the price of those booked from the Berlin end! I thanked him for his trouble and offered apologies to his absent wife for keeping him so late.

A second visit to the citadel was on the schedule for my final day in Poznań. The purpose was to visit three exhibitions concerning the AK covering periods before, during and after the war with Ludwik as escort and guide.

The tourist would have by-passed the first exhibition without noticing anything special. Housed in the service passage where, once upon a time, cannons had guarded the long ramp to the top of the outer defences, there was no billboard or even the smallest of notices to direct attention of the casual passer-by to the entrance. It seemed a case of masterful understatement.

"The schools know where to find it," was Ludwik's excuse!

Once inside, the receptionist switched on lights so that we could view the exhibits and we signed the visitor's book.

The walls of the wide corridor were lined with glass-fronted cabinets displaying photographs, artefacts and memorabilia; samples of supplies dropped by the British included small arms; portraits of the five AK leaders of the region who met their deaths in various ways, two of them beheaded by the guillotine in Berlin. The supreme commander of the AK, who was based in Warsaw, only ventured into the Reich Territory of the Wartegau once. He stayed barely two days before retreating back on to his own patch, declaring that there were too many Germans about for effective action to succeed…

Resistance groups started to form as early as October 1939, but the AK was not officially existent until 1943. It ceased to be active after 1945. The organisation was controlled by military officialdom, to which the civilian underground was affiliated at a lower level

In spite of the scepticism of the commanding officer from Warsaw, the AK in the Wartegau was busy with acts of sabotage. Reprisals and arrests had followed. Any 'terrorist' action from the Poles instigated draconian revenge by the Germans.

The crimes could be minor. The first civilian to be executed in Posen, was convicted for carrying a handgun, he did not use it. He was shot on 13th September when technically Poland and Germany were still at war (Poland surrendered on 28th September). Refusing to hand over ones assets also became a criminal offence that automatically warranted the death penalty. Even complaining about confiscation of property resulted in a death sentence. In some cases, 'complaining' was not dependent on words. A defiant expression or a raised eyebrow was sufficient.

Posen itself suffered minimal damage from German bombing in 1939. The Americans inflicted substantially more in 1943 when they bombed the military factories that were scattered throughout the city. The destruction shown in most of the photographs on display occurred in January/February 1945 when the Soviet army attacked the heavily fortified city. The battle lasted over a month. The Russians bombarded the northern side of the city mercilessly. But the Germans retreated into the citadel, where the century old defence system still proved impregnable even for modern weapons. Only when their ammunition supply was depleted, did the Germans surrender.

Among the prisoners taken were AK fighters. Their HQ had been in one of the hundreds of tunnels that lie under the defensive ridge surrounding the fortress. When the siege began, they had been discovered by the Germans and given two options. 'Die now, or help us defend your city and families against the communists.' They dreaded the communists and the lawlessness of the Red Army more than they despised the Germans.

As we emerged from the exhibition, the lights were switched off and the minder followed us out of the door, locking it behind him. Were we the only visitors expected that morning?

It was now midday and the sun was shining down oppressively. We found shadow in the lea of a crumbling ruin at the centre of the 'park' where we found a small coffee bar.

"It is pleasant enough here during the day," remarked Ludwik. "But it is dangerous at night. The place is so vast with too many trees and wild shrubbery and there is no watchman."

It was not the first time that I had encountered the attitude that places that are not 'watched' are unsafe and dangerous. The 'haves' had not so very much, but were the 'have-nots' jealous enough that they would lurk in darkened places in order to ambush the unwary? Or, were the habits of a lifetime under communist rule hard to shake off? The NKVD had vanished, but their shadows still lingered.

We dined at Ludwik's apartment that evening. His vivacious wife, a handsome blonde woman, talked incessantly – but only in Polish. Fortunately, I was beginning to understand snatches. I could discern separate words and could make some sense of conversation as long as it flowed in a single direction. Argument and discussion were still impossible but with Ludwik's assistance, the language barrier was lowering.

The couple had moved from their house to the flat on the tenth floor three years ago. When their son's wife was expecting their third grandchild, it became obvious that their apartment was too miniscule for two adults and three small children. New accommodation was difficult to find and the problem was resolved by swapping with his parents, who had lived at the time in the ground floor of a house with a garden.

Ludwik's wife had prepared a banquet of Polish dishes. She was an excellent cook. We chatted about the visible improvement in the Polish economy. Western goods were available at prices that a Pole could afford and confidence in general had improved. I had noticed that since my first visit, the market stalls in the street were now flush with wares. Shoes, clothes, fresh fruit and vegetables spilled over into the walkways and customers were spoiled for choice. In the nineteen eighties, 'Only bread, no meat and food that had the bland taste of floor boards was available,' Ludwik claimed.

A potted history of Poland was served with dessert. It enlarged upon what dr Woźniak had told me. The resistance against the communists was most active in Poznań. In 1956, the first revolt was quelled by the military. Tanks occupied the city and one hundred people died. Other rebellions followed.

Poznań was the old capital of the Prussian Empire prior to 1918, while the rest of Poland was under Russian control in the east and the Austro-Hungarian Empire in the south. The fight for freedom and self-autonomy started before WWI. Post WWI, the Prussian Empire was gone, the Austro-Hungarian Empire was gone and the Bolsheviks had revolted, establishing communism in Russia.

Poland had risen out of the chaos and the Treaty of Versailles had established her borders. Many Prussian traditions had been inherited by the inhabitants of Wielkopolska. Among them was the divorce law that had ended Antonina's marriage. It was a region rich in both industry and agriculture when most of the world was in recession. A visitor from Sweden in the nineteen twenties was shocked by the luxury compared to Swedish standards of living at the time. The region of Poland that had been under Russian control did not enjoy such wealth, however, and this had led to an internal competition of one-upmanship between the two regions.

Post 1989, a certain amount of envy still existed. The very name 'Wielko' meaning 'Great' was still a source of political sniping.

Invasion by the Germans had deprived Poland of her independence in 1939, and when the Russians took over in 1945, the fight for freedom renewed against another enemy. East Poland merely returned to the control of the previous occupiers and they were more resigned to their destiny. They did not rebel, for them, it was a return to a lifestyle that was already familiar.

The age of invasion in England is way beyond living memory. Its population has not had to suffer change in its way of life by the dictate of an occupation. Traditionally we have forgotten what that could entail. It was as though the Polish nation had been required to change its political colour like a chameleon, the skin colour disguising its true identity and nature. For nearly twenty years between the two Great Wars, the nation had the opportunity to be itself. September 1st, 1939, brought the celebration to an abrupt and tragic end.

The final office conference on the morning of my departure yielded three more gems. To illustrate a topic we had discussed earlier, dr Woźniak produced maps showing the radio network used by the resistance during WWII. They showed clearly how messages had been sent from the General Government, the centre of Poland, and relayed through Sweden, Switzerland and elsewhere to London. He had been right, none of the radio routes emanated from the Wartegau. The AK in Poznań was as cut off from the HQ in Warsaw as it was from the rest of the world.

He also showed me a copy of a statement made by the inspector of camps (Gerhard Wiebek). The statement was typed in German and had been obtained by the Americans after Wiebek was arrested in 1945. It described the conditions in Poggenburg and the murderous nature of the commandant.

A third curious document seemed to be a declaration for the Wehrmacht to support the Polish struggle against undue force! Mystifying! Apparently, all the papers had been sourced in 'secret files' held in German archives.

The photocopier was not functioning, but dr Woźniak promised to forward copies so that I could make a closer inspection at leisure.

We all gathered for a farewell lunch in the restaurant in the centre of the Stary Rynek. The dishes of Polish fare were bland in comparison to the culinary skills of Ludwik's wife. The note at the bottom of the menu caused an eyebrow to twitch. 'Indigestion tablets are available in reception.'

They would not have cured my mental indigestion. I was suffering from information overload and was beginning to look forward to creeping back to the familiar surroundings of home.

21

The reading of popular fiction, whether romantic, thriller or detective novels, became insignificant frivolity against the study of books about Hitler, his henchmen, the Holocaust, the concentration camps and the wartime conditions in Germany itself.

Every two or three weeks, I exchanged letters with dr Woźniak. The possibility that Maria and or her mother, Antonina, were double agents or collaborators, had cropped up before the filming episode, but he had not disclosed the reasons for his suspicions. He was still making enquiries about the 'facts' disclosed in Maria's writings. He had for example, traced the address in Poznań where the two women had gone into hiding after escaping from the Gestapo HQ in January 1945. It had been the home of the sister of Vera Novaczyk's (Maria's maid), but today there was no longer any link to the Novaczyk family.

He had also tried unsuccessfully to find the divorce records for 1924 where conformation of the end of Antonina's marriage might have been found. They no longer existed. The quest to source information about the various aspects relating to Maria was possibly a distraction for him from the arduous task of editing the encyclopaedia.

"Editing the encyclopaedia is burdened with a great number of red herrings," he wrote. "People are used to untruths more than honesty after a lapse of fifty years. Those still living tell splendid legends. It is extraordinarily difficult to find the real truth. The period of the Polish People's Republic made holes in the morals of mankind."

The emotions evoked by trying to remember were also a stumbling block. He had recently met an ex-prisoner of Poggenburg who had mentioned Maria's name. When interviewed, she did not remember Maria at all, but started to relate her own experiences. Suddenly, she changed track, totally avoiding the issue of remembering her torture in the 'House of Jews'. The interview was proving useless and Woźniak had to desist from further probing, hoping that she would be more coherent another day when she had had time to think. He admitted that the hope was fragile. People are afraid of the consequences of unlocking terrible secrets. The terror that they had encased in mental concrete, was safe. Shatter the concrete and the terror escapes, as alive as it had been fifty years previously.

Woźniak's suggestion that Maria and Antonina could possibly have been double agents, had given me a shock. It had been established that they were AK members of the Bloc group in Berlin and that Maria had been in touch with the AK again while working at the munitions factory in Posen. Neither of these contacts had she deemed worthy of a mention in her story, although certain ways that she described events suggested that hidden between the lines, there could have been a concealed story. It was why I had taken the manuscript to Poland in the first place. A double agent or collaborator was not what I had expected to find. It was necessary to discover why dr Woźniak was thinking that way. But without identifying the role of Herbert Kurzke in the German forces, the double agent and collaboration issues were open ended.

That January, a free bonus marched in the back door. A friend, working as a rep for the distribution of animal foods, had met a Mark Marriot on her travels. Maria had called herself Marriot when I first met her in 1975. Mark had lived with her for six years from 1968 until 1974. He knew her well. He had also known both Antonina and Herbert Kurzke. Having already met him once on the horse riding circuit, I was soon making a telephone call to him to renew the acquaintanceship.

From him, I learned about Antonina's death in a dark Oxfordshire lane in 1972. There had been no telephone link direct to her house and she had been forced to go to a neighbour to make a phone call late at night. The neighbour lived on the other side of the unlit lane. While crossing the road, she was knocked down by a car and died from her injuries. A check with the Oxfordshire Police showed that the file regarding the accident no longer existed. Antonina had become a statistic.

Mark had liked Herbert. He felt that he was a man who could be trusted. He was discreet and powerfully self-controlled. "If my life depended on someone, I would have chosen Herbert a long way ahead of Maria," he declared. A failed relationship could be said to have biased his opinion. However, having come to know Maria moderately well during the last ten years of her life, I had learned that discretion and self-control were not obvious characteristics. Her reliability in a threatening situation would have been dubious.

I recalled the occasion in the early eighties when Maria had announced out of the blue, that while she was in prison during the war, she had been condemned to death by the Gestapo.

At the time, I had been a bit nonplussed. Was my friend a little mad? She had a habit of exaggerating things. Was she stating fact, or was her memory playing tricks on her? I had bluffed my way past the moment, retorting that if the Gestapo had sentenced her to death, I must be talking with a ghost. Maria's face had settled into one of her enigmatic smiles.

"You'll see," was all she said and immediately drew my attention to another topic.

This short but poignant conversation had lingered in my subconscious. We met infrequently. Horse matters usually dominated the discussions. Maria was an obsessive horse woman. The animals intruded into every waking moment of her day and the past was rarely permitted time to raise its ugly head.

Only once, when the influence of alcohol had lowered her defences did I meet the ogre that haunted her. I was spending the night at Maria's cottage. She had produced a bottle of whiskey and we had chatted about everything under the sun until the early hours of the morning. Maria was a little drunk and confused when there was a loud crash outside the kitchen door. I heard a cat jumping off the dustbin and dislodging the lid. Maria heard something far more sinister.

She visibly shrank into herself, pleading with me to go and see what had made the noise. She would not accept that it could have been a cat on the prowl and was convinced that the noise had been made by a human and that the intruder had dangerous intentions. Her obvious stress was making me nervous and I too was becoming uncertain of how useful I would be if she were right.

The terror on her face forced me to make a decision. Getting to my feet, I started to raise my voice and make extraneous noises, more to bolster my own courage than to allay Maria's extraordinary fear. If there were an unwelcome stranger in the vicinity, with luck, he would retreat peacefully.

But Maria was only satisfied after I had unbolted the back door and stuck my head into the cold night air to inspect the pathway. When I came back to the lounge, she was pouring herself another tot from the near empty whiskey bottle, her hand shaking uncontrollably. When I enquired what had caused her to react so violently, she almost cried.

"Sometimes", she said, "certain things frighten me." It was a side of Maria's persona that I had not encountered before. Always appearing to be super-confident and self-opinionated, her transformation into a jabbering wreck in just a few seconds had shaken me. Her eyes had searched the room as though looking for a hiding place and I had the impression that if the chimney had been big enough she would have attempted to have concealed herself within it.

Minutes later, her adrenalin ceased flowing, for suddenly she became inordinately exhausted. It was with great difficulty that I managed to half-carry her to her bed where fully clothed, she was overcome by deep sleep.

The explanation for her behaviour remained obscure until the third incident that left an indelible mark. The conversation had meandered towards the war. Maria had probably engineered the direction of the discussion. I was both ignorant and naive and for her, sharing memories with a disinterested foreigner would have been difficult. We had no common language of experience.

I chanced to mention in her presence, the heroic contribution of the British forces during the war. It was a mistake! Maria had rounded on me.

"You English make me sick. You are so self-satisfied with yourselves," she screeched at me. I gaped foolishly at her. What was upsetting her now?

"You have no idea of what it is like, living constantly in fear of betrayal; having to watch every word that you say; suspecting everyone of being a possible enemy," she added. "You smug British have absolutely no idea of what living with war is really like." I could not argue with her.

I had no recollection of the WWII. My knowledge had been influenced by the cinema; inspired by feature films like *The Dam Busters* and *The Great Escape*. I had never even thought to question my parents about the trials and tribulations that they had undergone at the time. Yes, we were smug about our heroes and we were proud of them. Maria's outburst had injected an element of doubt. What had it been like to live in occupied Europe under the Nazi regime? I learned no more.

Maria, as though ashamed of her indiscretion, had clammed up and I was left to wonder.

Mark Marriot had lived with Maria for several years. He reminded me of the assertion that I had heard from Maria's own lips. "Antonina was not her real mother you know. She was adamant that her real surname was von Brockmann," he said. It was yet another aspect of the puzzle that remained unresolved. Was Maria's genetic identity really suspect or was a rift between mother and daughter the cause for her recriminating accusations?

22

JUNE 1997

The documentary about Maria and Zabikowo evoked a good response from viewers. Pelagia Novak, the younger sister of Maria's maid, Vera, had contacted the Institute. She was able to supply a number of addresses and to describe who lived where and when. She had also maintained a contact with her sister and the Weychan family after the war. Her sister, Vera had accompanied Maria and her new British husband, Mark Chevalier, to England at the beginning of 1947 and had lived in Malden, Essex until she died in the early nineties.

The family of her husband (Florek) had been known to Antonina. It had provided the labour on the farm belonging to the Szymanski estate. Old though she was (now 87), she clearly recalled that her sister had worked as a housekeeper for Antonina in the 1920s. She was also able to confirm that Antonina was a wealthy woman, who had owned a chain of shops and had extensive social contacts. She had known Maria's grandfather, who in 1939 ran the small paper shop in Glogowska Street in Poznań that featured in the documentary.

Maria's pre-war life was coming together. The scraps of information coming to light were endorsing the social position that she described in her book.

Her most important contribution to the puzzle directly concerned Maria and Antonina. It was to her home that the two women had fled after escaping from the Gestapo headquarters in January 1945. Maria had been extremely ill. She was emaciated and very frail and for some days, Mrs Novak had feared that death was hovering close by.

The bonus for the archive had been new information that the documentary had elicited about Mosina, the village from which the women with whom Maria had shared a cell in Fort VII had come. Today Mosina has grown into a small town. It lies south of Poznań on the route to Zabikowo. Today, the virus that was used in the experiment in 1942 that killed two Germans and a cow would be called 'a weapon of mass destruction' with a potentially for destroying both man and beast. The Germans understood the threat and acted accordingly. The families of those arrested were now coming forward with their memories of the event.

In August, dr Woźniak sent a letter, giving me further details of what was known about Gerhard Wiebek, the German camp inspector. Wiebek's photograph had been briefly shown to me in 1995. At the time, I had not grasped the significance of the stranger. What dr Woźniak now explained added a glaze of shifting intrigue over the whole puzzle.

In the spring of 1943, Gerhard Wiebek had been appointed to the disciplinary court of the SS Headquarters in Posen, engaged in the task of investigating corruption and abuse within the SS. He had come into conflict with the Gestapo and had made progress only through incidental enquiries made on his own initiative. There are no surviving documents to support this except for the statement that he made himself to the US Army Investigation Officer and CIA agent, Captain Gutmann, delivered at the front near Munich.

Wiebek's principal informant in Poggenburg was Otto Riebe. A lawyer from Berlin, he was accused by the SS of being a member of the AK. Riebe was thought to have had a connection with Siatke A (Group A) of the AK in Posen. Little is known of the group, except that it seemed to consist of folkedeutsch sympathisers and operated from the munitions factory where Maria worked. Towards the end of 1944, Riebe had been arrested and after a spell in Poggenburg, was transferred to Sachsenhausen in Berlin. He was a strong candidate for Maria's 'Herr Blum', the manager of the munitions factory who had given her clothes and food.

Dr Woźniak had also unearthed evidence that Otto Riebe had known Maria personally, referring to her and Antonina as 'two prisoners in Poggenburg who do not feature on the normal transfer lists' – and 'why not?' was the obvious question.

The explanation for their preservation was proving elusive. What was so special about Maria and her mother, Antonina, that they did not suffer the same fate as other prisoners? Was dr Woźniak right? Had they been double agents? Or was there another explanation for their survival?

Wiebek had arrested Hans Walter, the commandant of Poggenburg on October 4th 1944. Three days after the arrest, Walter was found hanging in his cell. Maria had described how she learned of his suicide. The news filtered back into the camp several days after she had been found alive in the pit where corpses were stored before being removed for cremation. I could now pinpoint the day that Walter had punished her by forcing her to keep a dead body company.

According to Maria's account, she was punished for smuggling food and clothes into the camp. It was one of Walters little jokes to torment his prisoners by bizarre methods. When she was pulled out four days later, she had been barely conscious. She had been too ill to attend roll call the following day and according to Maria, "the other prisoners concealed my absence." The day after that "a miracle happened… For the first time since we have been in Poggenburg, there was no roll call." Several days later, rumours of the commandant's suicide circulated in the camp.

With my Sherlock Holmes hat on, I arrived at the conclusion that 'the miracle' was due to the arrest of Walter (and nineteen of the garrison staff) by Wiebek. There would have been insufficient staff left to control the prisoners and count their number. Recalling Woźniak's claim that Walter had been arrested 'for causing the death of a prisoner without the appropriate bit of paper,' I began to consider whether it was Maria that had been the prisoner concerned. The possibility that Wiebek knew that the confirmation of her 'death sentence' had been 'lost' in transit, made Maria the one prisoner in Poggenburg that should not die an 'accidental' death.

Afterwards, Wiebek had interviewed the prisoners and a list of names survives of the prisoners who revealed the sins of the Commandant. 'Maria Weychau', a dancer appears on that list, strangely obvious, for her description fills two lines on the page against all the others that fill just half a line. Why? Was it a subtle means of ensuring that her name would stand out from the rest? In conversations with Wiebek, Maria apparently admitted her connection with the AK. In addition, recorded in the notes of the Polish War Commission in 1945, is the fact that Herbert may have known Wiebek before the war started.

The Americans had not at first believed Wiebek's statement. At a time when German suspects were distorting the truth in order to save their own skins, a horrendous tale about a German camp commandant's wrong-doings was not what they particularly wanted to hear. The horrors of the vast concentration camps smothered all reference to smaller camps such as Poggenburg. In the spring of 1945, Poland was already deep within the Soviet jurisdiction and an investigation into the camp at Posen was beyond their remit. From the American point of view, the Poles and Germans were condemned together, 'forced to drink from the same well'. Dr Woźniak pointed out that the Americans and the Polish War Commission 'did not bathe in the same washtub' when it came to their interests in grasping details. The Americans had been focussed on Jewish persecutions, while the Polish War Commission had concentrated on the persecution of Polish nationals.

23

SEPTEMBER 1997

Some material emerged from the Bundesarchiv in Berlin. It did not make sense, however, and I was unconvinced, that they had found the correct man although several options were offered. Herbert had certainly not spent time in Norway as was suggested. An H. Kurzke had been found on lists referring successful candidates for a driving course at Oranienburg but there was no clue as to his military function. Few of the other items of information compared sensibly with what Maria had suggested. The search for Kurzke in the main archive of Berlin had failed miserably. It was disappointing.

The disappointment did not last for long. Within a week, another small package arrived from Berlin. I had sent another letter of enquiry to the military archive in Freiberg. It had been forwarded to Aachen and thence to Berlin. This time, my enquiry had reached the right target. This time, the details fitted Herbert's profile.

On 8th March 1939, Kurzke had become a member of the Schutzpolizei.

In September 1939, 'he drove a large lorry, transporting prisoners through hostile territory' – for which he was awarded the Iron Cross in 1942.

He served in the 12th Company of the Police Battalion 103.

In 1943, he was promoted to Hauptmann.

In June 1944, he was wounded on the eastern front.

There was no reference to a court martial in December 1943. That he had been court marshalled, had been established from Herbert's own statement to the High Court of Berlin in 1963. Neither was there reference to his presence at the Police School in Oranienburg.

The second item on the list caused food for thought. In the first instance, it confirmed that he was a vehicle driver who was entrusted with special duties. But, who were the prisoners that he had transported and what was the definition of a 'hostile' territory as opposed to a war zone? His deed must have been out of the ordinary. Driving prisoners through a war zone would in itself, not have been sufficient to merit the Iron Cross. Therefore, what was so special about these particular prisoners?

The new information was relayed immediately to dr Woźniak to see what he could make of it. The glee in his reply was vibrant. It was known that a police battalion had been in charge at Główna, the main railway station, during the mass transportation of Polish citizens during 1939/40, but the identity of the battalion had remained elusive. If, as Maria had described, Kurzke had known the staff at the transit camp, it must have been his own Police Battalion. It explained why he had been able to inform Antonina of which districts the SS would raid each night, and also how he knew about the procedure of the form filling required for the movement of a prisoner.

It was a breakthrough. The crust of physical events had been cracked, revealing a magma of intrigue beneath. Kurzke had been playing a double game from the very start. It invited a closer look at the repeated visits that he made to the Szymanski apartment during the October and November of 1939.

He had often been in the company of 'a jolly fellow from the Rhineland', who according to Maria took a shine to Maria's distant relative, Ina. While Kurzke remained in the apartment with Maria, the Rhinelander took Ina out. 'They are having an affair', she was told.

In the back of my mind I was aware of what Maria had told me when she gave me her manuscript, that not everything happened to her and that she had borrowed a little from the experience of other people. The journey that she described of how she had travelled from Lichtmanstadt to Posen in September 1939, had long been suspect. A German general had given her and her mother a lift in his official car!

Several authors had written about Halina Szymanska. She too was given a car lift to Posen by a German. The German had been Admiral Canaris and he had advised her not to go home but to seek alternative accommodation. This she did, finding refuge with 'distant relatives'. Heinz Höhne offers an alternative version of how Halina bumped into the admiral. She had almost been run over by his car in Posen. Maria describes both incidents in detail. Were these 'borrowed' events?

Realising that Kurzke had been involved in antics that were to the advantage of the 'enemy', suspicions were strengthened that he had contacts within the Abwehr, the German intelligence at the head of which, reigned Admiral Wilhelm Canaris.

I was now able to seriously consider Maria's chapter concerning the Szymanski apartment from a different angle. If Ina, the distant relative, was in fact Halina Szymanska; the 'jolly fellow' who often accompanied Kurzke was possibly Pickenbrock (he became Chief of Abwehr I in 1940) and described by Höhne as a 'jolly Rhinelander'. What Maria described as a 'clandestine affair' between the Rhinelander and Ina would have been a cover story for her visits to Canaris. Reinforcing this scenario is the fact that Maria claimed that friends helped Ina to leave the country in November. It is documented that Canaris arranged for Halina to be secretly driven to Berne in Switzerland at that time.

The fairly obvious conclusion to these deductions was that Kurzke was an intelligence agent of the Abwehr and at the same time was attached to the police battalion. Did Maria know? Was this what she had hidden between the lines in the text of her manuscript?

Delving into the world of intelligence was like searching for a mirage. The sands of time had blown away the traces of what little was recorded at the time. The security of the agent was paramount both for British as well as for Reich intelligence staff and the details of their activities were rarely committed to paper. Halina Szymanska was my only definite link into the secrets of the Abwehr and it seemed a worthwhile venture to investigate that line of approach.

The British Records Office in Kew, London holds the records of the SOE (Special Operations Executive). Whether they could reveal any surprises about Kurzke was doubtful, but they might prove profitable with regard to Halina. My country-bumpkin soul would have to reconcile itself to venturing down to the capital to investigate.

24

1998

I received a copy of the documentary in February. A toneless voice-over translated the spoken English into Polish and it was necessary to obtain help from the late Mrs Olszewska at the Polish Underground Trust, to discover the details of the text. I lent her my copy of *Straty i martyrologia Ludwosci Polski w Poznań 1939-1945*, written by her namesake Maria Olszewska and printed in 1991. It was a book that was unknown to her. The Trust was well versed with the conditions and activities of the AK in Central Poland, but hardly acknowledged that the resistance existed in the Wartegau. The information to which she was now being exposed was uncharted waters, and she had been horrified by what she learned.

A composer for Hollywood films visited in March. Jan was in his late thirties and was revelling in the 'American dream'. He wanted to try horse riding and he was invited to mount 'Yogi', a 28 year old veteran who should have been quiet enough. They had walked solemnly around the sand school for a few minutes when Jan decided that he wanted to go a bit faster and he started to flap his legs. Despite his years, Yogi took offence and charged out of the gate, scrabbling to keep his feet when he hit the tarmac road and with Jan miraculously still aboard, disappeared towards the stable yard. Instantly, images of a mutilated musician flashed through my head. But, seconds later, to my relief Jan reappeared, leading the horse by the bridle.

"It is OK," he said. "The horse only went back to his garage."

Jan's family name was Kasczmarek and originally, he came from Mosina.

A fifteen year-old girl, who had been imprisoned in Poggenburg, was one of only two witnesses to have made recorded statements that included a reference to Maria and her mother. Her family name was Kasczmarek and she had lived in Mosina. Coincidence is sometimes shocking.

On the 2nd April a letter arrived from dr Woźniak. He confirmed that

Maria and Antonina had definitely been associated with 'Bloc', the AK cell in Berlin. At last he revealed why the accusation of traitor had arisen. 'Bloc' had been broken up during the summer of 1943. Some members had been arrested. Others had disappeared. Had Antonina or her daughter betrayed them when they had been arrested in March of that year? The shadow of 'traitor' was still cast over of the two Weychan women.

Dr Woźniak once again described the information that he had received about Kurzke as 'truly sensational' and furthermore, he had been able to confirm the connection between Herbert Kurzke and Wiebekk. Their association was established in Berlin before the outbreak of the war. Dr Woźniak did not know that there had been a police training school in Oranienburg. He knew only of the concentration camp at Sachsenhausen, sited north of the suburb. Here Kurzke had been stationed in 1940–42, which meant that he was not involved with the Einsatzgrup, the criminal police that wiped out whole communities of Jews in the East of Poland during 1941–42.

The 'Pill', the girl who had betrayed Maria and her mother to the Gestapo had also received some of his attention. Dr Woźniak had discovered a convent educated woman born in 1925 who was known to have worked with the Germans. Her true identity was unknown, but it was not impossible that the two women were one and the same.

The pebbles of established fact were gradually forming a substantial heap.

Frustratingly, the finer details about Kurzke remained elusive. He was a mirage that dissolved the nearer one approached.

Sources were broadening. There were so many options with regard to cause and effect that it became necessary by deduction, to endeavour to eliminate the impossible. The net was cast wide, the antennae alert to small details that would normally have passed unnoticed. For example, while watching *Schindlers List* on television on 18th October 1997, I had learned that it was Schindler, who had provided the Polish uniforms to the Abwehr for the scenario at Gleiwitz in 1939 that provided the excuse for Germany to attack Poland. While the anxieties of the British were being diplomatically soothed, Hitler had been colluding with the Soviets and preparing for his attack on Poland. The catalyst for the war was carefully planned. German criminals were to be dressed in Polish uniforms and 'killed' while attacking the German radio station at Gleiwitz, close to the southern border The resulting evidence of Polish aggression would provide the excuse to invade Poland. After delays, the 'attack' took place in the early hours of September 1st, 1939.

Admiral Canaris was involved in the plot to the extent that he was asked to obtain the Polish uniforms. According to Höhne, Canaris was unhappy when he discovered the use to which the uniforms had been put. His supposed diarist, Lahousen, recorded that a member of the Abwehr staff had driven the uniforms down to Gleiwitz. Höhne spells the name of the driver 'Kutchke', which is not that too far away from Kurzke especially for a historian who equates Chimanski to Szymanski. I could not help wondering if the doomed prisoners were wearing the uniforms at the time and whether Herbert's Iron Cross for 'transporting prisoners through hostile territory' could be connected to the action. It was a mind-bending thought and my head almost ceased functioning at the idea that I could be dealing with a man who had been so intrinsically involved with the start of WWII.

Ania came into my life that summer. She was visiting friends in Cambridge during her annual holiday in England to brush up her English. A translator by profession, she was aware of how language develops in subtle ways and conscientiously tried to keep abreast of those changes. She lived in Lódz, a city that had featured in Maria's story.

A mutual acquaintance introduced us and a friendship rapidly grew. She showed a great interest in my on-going project, picking up on the claim for compensation that Maria had made against Germany in 1963–4. Her father-in-law was involved in a new movement in Poland to claim for war losses against Germany. It was not meeting with much success as the continuous claims by other powerful ethnic groups had inevitably drained the pot dry.

Łódź became an alternative port of call to Poznań for my next trip to Poland.

25

1998

There had been suggestions about the making of a second documentary. This time it would be filmed in England, with the idea of following Maria's life after the war. I had not taken the proposition too seriously, but had mentioned it to Mark Marriot in case the idea became concrete. He had put me in touch with a woman who had been Maria's landlady in the 60s and Harriet Wye, who had known Maria during the last twelve years of her life, was another person that might agree to be interviewed.

The TV crew arrived at 8 o'clock one Sunday morning in June. I was still in my dressing gown when I stuck a tousled head outside the back door to investigate the cause of the dogs' hysteria. They tumbled out of their van, boldly inscribed with logos for Polish TV, grinning at my expression of surprise and horror.

The journey had started on the Friday with an intention to drive through the night across Europe. They had not anticipated the problems that they would meet at the Polish border and had been refused at three crossing points before they encountered an official who approved the papers for the van and filming equipment and allowed them to pass into Germany.

It had taken them the whole of the previous day to travel across Europe to Calais, snatching only three hours sleep on the ferry. They had been on the road for thirty-six hours.

There were four of them; Przemek the driver and sound technician, Piotr the cameraman (who had also sat behind the wheel to give Przemek a rest), Dorota the director and Yurek, my farmhouse host. They were all very weary and hungry. Breakfast and a shower revived Dorota and Yurek while Przenek and Piotr retired until the afternoon in order to recharge their batteries.

My task for their project had been to contact people in England who had known Maria and persuade them to be interviewed in front of a camera. I had netted the two 'volunteers' suggested by Mark; Harriet Wye who had worked with

Polish television van arrives in Essex

Left to right: Yurek, Przemek, Dorota, author, Harriet, Piotr

Maria for twelve years and Diane Porter-Harris who was one of her landladies. A second landlady declined the ordeal but Mark Marriot, her partner for ten years during the 60s and 70s, was happy to oblige.

I had met Harriet in 1975 when she first worked for Maria. As a teenager, she had been a very introverted and shy young lady, tall, thin and shapeless, a mop of straight blond hair crowning her head. She had rarely spoken. When she did, she emitted only two or three words in a deep husky voice.

Harriet had first met Maria in 1974 and had been employed in the stable yard to groom and work the horses. Maria had taught her the art of dressage on Epona Samson, a horse that despite its reputed parentage had matured into a Percheron in size and weight by the time it was eight years old.

The physique of the horse belied his agility. He obligingly learned to go sideways in shoulder-in and half-pass and had sponges in his feet that allowed him to elevate off the ground as he moved. From a distance he had the proportions of a Welsh Mountain pony until one realised that it was not a child aboard but a fully-grown adult. Sadly, when Harriet could no longer devote sufficient time to ride and train the horse, nobody else could be found to take over the reins. Most ridiculed the idea of sitting astride a 'carthorse' in public.

Eventually, lack of work and overweight had caused laminitis, the pedal bone dropped through the sole of the hoof and the horse had to be destroyed. Maria had been devastated.

Harriet had been involved throughout the tragic scenario. She had provided Maria with help in various projects and supported her through the tragedies. She knew Maria's emotional repertoire possibly as well as anyone.

Mark Marriot had also worked with Maria in the mid 1960s, as a jockey for the Arab horses that she trained for racing. He had met Herbert Kurzke, by then a High Commissioner with the Hamburg police force, and had liked the man with elegant hands. In 1968, Maria had taken three thoroughbred horses to Germany. Mark was to have ridden them on the racetrack, but the rules in Germany prevented him from doing so for six months. The bills for stabling and feed mounted and the project soon ran into financial difficulties. The German bank denied them access to funds, saying that they did not hold cash in the bank. In desperation, Mark had leapt over the counter and flung wide the safe door, revealing heaps of bundled notes.

Such behaviour should surely have caused big trouble, but Herbert was with them. Taking control of the situation, he had talked hard and fast and managed to extract the over enthusiastic Mark without an arrest being made.

The incident seemed powerfully exotic to me; that Maria could excite men to behave in such an extreme fashion. The story revealed a side to her character that I did not recognise.

The third 'volunteer' for the proposed Polish documentary, Diane Porter-Harris, still owned the stable yard in Salcey Forest that Maria had leased in the early 1970s.

Dorota and Yurek spent the morning working out the logistics of how to fit together the three interviews during the two days that they had for filming. In order to meet them all, they would be travelling several hundred miles, as they were scattered around Northamptonshire, Oxfordshire and Norfolk.

My role was to be the presenter, the common denominator that linked the three interviewees on screen.

Piotr reappeared in the afternoon, refreshed and armed with an enormous camera. He loved animals and amused himself filming the dogs, the horses and the carp in the pond, amazed that they were so tame that they swarmed to the bank and permitted a human hand to stroke their backs.

Przemek, the driver, was back on form by breakfast time the next morning. We squeezed into the limited seating of the van and set out for Salcey Forest, which lies to the southeast of Coventry. Sitting in the front of the vehicle, I was armed with the road map and was soon exercising my Polish vocabulary, using the three vital words, lewo (left), presto (straight on) and prawo (right). Przemek proved totally deaf to instructions given in English.

Two hours later, we were bumping down a long drive between cultivated fields to the house of Diane Porter-Harris. Ahead lay an island of mature trees, the remains of an ancient forest. Dead oak trees dotted the landscape, their bleached and stunted branches clawing skyward like petrified ogres pleading with eternity.

Salsey Forest ancient oak tree

Dorota Latour inside an oak tree

Przemek parked the van in the cobbled stable yard. Piotr espied cats and gave chase with his camera, while Dorota studied her surroundings, plotting her tactics. Diane and her husband had seen us arrive from the main house, a fortress of a building with no windows below the first floor level. The whole place had an eerie atmosphere.

We were offered refreshments and were regaled with stories about the forest and its trees. It was said to be haunted. Two figures had been seen by a number of different people. A woman dressed in wispy white, followed by a man in a dark cloak. Their clothing suggested the sixteenth century and they had been seen to disappear behind one particular oak tree that grew by the entrance to the spinney. Intrigued by the tale, Piotr set out with his camera to film the location and was missing for what seemed like hours. Somewhat shamefacedly, he admitted on his return that the trees had taken hold of him. He had found some veritable monsters, totally hollow yet still in leaf, in which four people could stand together. Dorota was not amused.

A stable door was chosen as a suitable spot for my interview with Diane. The camera would catch glimpses of the grand interior of the stable itself with the painted Victorian bars that separated the stalls. Piotr would also be able to capture in the background, a cat or two, the chickens and an elderly goose that ruled the yard, its breastbone sunk so low that it barely cleared the cobbles.

Maria had lived in the flat above the stables during the late sixties and drama had followed her even to this secluded and peaceful corner of England.

Diane recalled the evening when two gentlemen of eastern origin had appeared unannounced on her doorstep. They were looking for Mark Marriot. They were aggressive in their manner and Diane was relieved that Mark was not on the property at the time. It had been clear to her that their attitude was anything but friendly. She had reassured them that their journey had been in vain and sent them on their way.

When she next saw Maria, the full story emerged. Maria had conversed with the visitors and complained to them about Mark's treatment of her. Maria could be passionate and powerful with words and had inspired the two men to seek revenge on her behalf. Diane had been witness to the extent of their ambitions. Maria had been repentant and had made haste to deter the avengers and restore Mark to favour.

The incident brought home to me just how volatile Maria could be in her forties and how charismatic she must have been to the opposite sex. The tale sounded so exotic that it could have originated from the Arabian Nights.

The interview over, we had to pack up and leave quickly, delayed only by Piotr lying on the cobbles, clicking at the goose. It obligingly waddled forward and pecked at the camera lens. Was it suggesting that enough was enough?

By 3.30pm, we had negotiated miles of narrow lanes to reach Brackley. Piotr was getting anxious that he would soon lose the daylight.

Harriet's home was a large rambling farmhouse surrounded by railed paddocks. Among the three horses that she owned was Monger, the last foal that Maria had bred. Now in his late teens, he was elderly and rather stiff but enjoying his retirement. There was something very nostalgic about the horse trotting away into his field against the glorious red and gold of an English autumn sunset. Piotr did not miss the spectacle with his ever-ready camera.

With the evening closing in, Harriet's interview took place in her lounge with the large window as backdrop looking out over the garden. Dorota had scripted the questions. It was my task to develop them according to the answers. When asked whether Maria had ever spoken about her activities during the war, Harriet replied that she claimed to have worked for the resistance as a courier, no more. What that entailed Maria had not revealed. For whom, where or when, she had kept undisclosed.

When Maria's manuscript was first translated, I had sent a copy to Harriet. She had known of its existence but had taken little interest in its content, basically because she could not read German. She had been as disturbed as I had by the story.

The manuscript mentioned only the one occasion on which she had acted in the 'role of a courier'; namely in March 1943, when Maria had smuggled a suitcase full of German currency into Poland on behalf of a resistance group in Berlin. If there were other occasions, Maria had not mentioned them to Harriet.

Before we left, she presented me with three scrapbooks that had belonged to Maria, each brimming with photographs and each relating to a different chapter in Maria's life. They made an invaluable addition to the private archive that was accumulating on the bookshelves at home.

It was another brisk start the following day. Before the weekend, the weather had been grey and miserable. The Polish visitors brought the sun with them and for the second day running, it shone out of a clear blue sky.

The terraced houses lining the streets of Saffron Walden had caught Dorota's eye. She was curious to know how old they were and what materials were used to build them. When told that many of them dated back to the seventeenth century her mouth dropped open. She compared the lathe and plaster construction to adobe huts in Africa.

"It is true to say that houses in England are no better than in Poland, but yours are so pretty," she remarked. "Perhaps it is because they are all painted and have nice curtains at the windows," she added.

I had seen many examples of village houses when touring through the countryside in Poland the previous year. Chunks of plaster were missing from the walls, unpainted wooden window frames were rotting and grey netting was draped carelessly across the windows. Concrete grey, the colour of anonymity, was universal.

Heads turned as we cruised around the town in the Telenova van. Piotr sat in the passenger seat pointing his camera at the sights. Several times, Dorota ordered us all to get out for him to capture a particular scene that she thought may be useful for her documentary. Several times she gave instructions to the wrong person in the wrong language, but it only caused laughter. They were a good team and I could only wonder at their effortless co-ordination, their ability to understand almost immediately what Dorota wanted and how to execute her wishes with minimal discussion.

After lunch, we were on the road again, speeding toward Great Yarmouth to meet Mark Marriot. He had been scheduled to meet us at Salcey Forest, but had cried off at the last minute in deference to his state of health. He suffered shortness of breath leading to asthma attacks when under too much stress.

He seemed bright enough when we invaded his bungalow in the middle of the afternoon and talked excitedly as we sipped the tea served by his wife, Jean. A new environmental situation, another part of England, Dorota immediately assessed the options for the interview. We were very near to the coast and the sea and sands of Great Yarmouth sounded attractive to her. A decision was made and we were on the road eastwards within minutes.

Mark and I strolled up and down the beach as instructed, dodging the wavelets that lapped gently on the sand. We were 'deep in discussion'. The camera was a hundred yards away. The close-ups followed as we scrambled over the dunes, Przemek discreetly following us with the microphone.

The conversation revolved around Maria's love of drama, a factor that influenced her whole approach to life. She had even persuaded Mark to test the boards himself, a fact that had previously eluded me, and that I found quite extraordinary. Somehow, I could not imagine Mark and his rather self-effacing personality, tolerating the spotlight.

An aeroplane flew overhead and Przemek signalled for a pause. It had interfered with the sound recording and we had to start the scene all over again.

With no 'script', this was not so easy. Both Mark and I were momentarily confused as to where to restart and how to draw the conversation in the same direction. I turned, tripped over a tussock of grass and lost my balance. My legs flew skywards as I somersaulted down the sandy slope. As I sorted out my limbs and stood upright, a roar of laughter erupted from the audience. The spill was on record for Piotr's eye was still firmly glued to the camera. 'You've been framed'. Bin there and got an earful of sand if not the T-shirt.

On returning to the bungalow, Jean and her mother provided more tea for the 'presenter', while Mark was filmed reading his poem about the ancient trees of Salcey Forest. The exertion of the afternoon had tired him and the effort of reciting caused repeated coughing bouts. Dorota was in half a mind to call a halt to the filming, Mark's coughing and breathing difficulties were making her anxious that he was causing himself harm. But Mark insisted that they continue, and by introducing long pauses between sentences, he managed to complete his task.

Afterwards, I showed him one of the albums that Harriet had given me the day before. It was a fortuitous move, for Mark was able to identify many of the photographs, could put names to the faces and recall the events when the photographs had been taken. The album also contained a press cutting that related to the time that he had spent in Germany with Maria in 1968. The article reported a doping scandal involving one of the racehorses that Maria had taken with her from England. Mark elaborated.

It was not the only scandal that had afflicted the German racing industry at the time. Races had regularly been 'fixed', either by nobbling the horse with drugs or the jockey with bribes. The racing circle in the north of Germany had been rife with malpractice and any outsider who threatened to upset the system had to be wary. Maria had been too trusting. Her horse started well, then faltered and dropped back to last by the end of the race. A dope test revealed the reason for its poor performance.

He described another incident that had resulted in the death of the animal concerned. A promising young horse had arrived from the south of Germany. During its very first race, it was ridden into the rails alongside the track and broke a leg. Kaput!

Maria escaped comparatively lightly with only a doping problem to concern her.

On the way home, Dorota confided that she had a little surprise for me. The events of the past two days had been full of surprises; one more would be more of the same. Little did I know the significance of this one though and Dorota would not enlighten me further.

"Tomorrow," she said.

The reels of film were apparently incomplete.

"We need to fill the gaps," announced Dorota during breakfast. The whole exercise had been a mystery to me. I still had not determined the point of the film and where it was leading. The 'gaps' were a mercurial aspect that left me in a void of incomprehension.

Anchored to home base for the day, the schedule was constantly interrupted by the telephone and visitors to the farm. "Have you found your Rottweiler?" asked the policeman on the other end of the line. Gismo grinned up at me from the floor of the kitchen.

"I didn't realise we had lost her," I replied. Six months earlier, she had gone walkabout and we had reported her missing. The local police were checking out unresolved cases.

The vet called in to administer an injection to one of the horses. She saw the TV van and was curious.

"Does the local press know?" she asked. "Mmmm – no!" I replied.

"I'm going to tell them," she said and as proof of her word, a photographer appeared during the afternoon and hovered while I was busy 'researching' among my papers.

An old friend and her daughter dropped by unannounced. They had cups of coffee thrust into their hands and were entertained by a video about horses. Someone phoned wanting a dressage judge for the coming Sunday. It was as though the farm was a magnet for diversity. I spent the day fielding the interruptions, and at the same time trying to focus on the needs of the film crew and retain some sense of decorum in front of the camera.

Dorota had more than one surprise up her sleeve. As a result of the documentary made the previous year, Pelagia Novak, who dr Woźniak had mentioned in his letters, was looking forward to meeting me when I next visited Poland. Pelagia, the sister of Maria's maid, Vera, was in her mid-eighties. Piotr busily filmed while I wrote a letter to her, asking whether she could confirm that she visited Maria while she was imprisoned in Poggenburg and whether it was she with whom Maria and Antonina had stayed when they escaped in January1945. Both facts had already been confirmed in an interview with dr Woźniak, but they provided a suitable topic for the letter that was destined to travel to Poland and be used as the basis for another interview with the old lady.

Dorota selected the grandfather clock in the hall for the back-drop of my 'interview'. She was crafty. The first questions that she asked were simple to answer, putting me at my ease. Then, out of the blue, the one that had caused me problems in Zabikowo.

"Was Maria a heroine or a traitor?" she asked in an innocent voice. I still did not know the answer. The question itself gave me a clue as to the purpose of the documentary. They wanted a heroine, someone who could be presented to the Polish nation as a symbol of national honour. Maria, a named member of the Armia Krajowa, a survivor of Poggenburg, who before the war had been a glamorous darling of the Polish stage, was a candidate. Suddenly I realised that what was required, was for me to take the lid off and let the cat out. I could not do it. Maria had been a courageous young woman certainly, but her own story cast too many shadows for me to state categorically that she was a heroine in the epic sense. She had been a creature of destiny, adapting to each situation as it arose. Her motivation was not inspired by a loyalty to her homeland and the resistance but by her devotion to her German husband, Herbert, the man who had rescued her from transportation in 1939. True she hated and distrusted the German regime, but she claimed that it was the memory of her father and grandfather, whom she was told had been executed by the Nazis, that persuaded her to smuggle money into Poland for the resistance. Furthermore, it was her personal ambition to become a film star in the German film, *Die Grosse Freiheit* that had been the reason for her precarious return to Poland in the first place. She had needed to obtain legitimate identity papers before UFA would confirm her contract.

I had learned too much about her to be willing to promote her to 'heroine' status. She had loved her Poland until her death in 1986 and had always wanted to return. During the war, she had done nothing to endanger Poland and there remained a strong possibility that she had played a more significant role in the function of the Polish resistance than she had realised. To be added to the equation was the role played by her mother, for without Antonina constantly by her side, Maria would almost certainly not have survived.

The mystery of their survival still remained a tangle of ifs and buts. Fragments of the conundrum had been unravelled, but there remained many unanswered questions. If Herbert Kurzke, Maria's husband, was an Abwehr agent, how did that relate to 'Nana' and 'Jaga', members of the Polish AK and to what degree was the teenaged Maria aware of the intrigues? Most mystifying of all was that although Maria had written down her story, she had only hinted at her involvement with the resistance.

The film crew were almost done. Przemek retired to bed for a few hours in preparation for the long drive back to Poland. They planned to leave just before midnight in order to catch the first ferry crossing in the morning. Piotr was busy filming the photographs from the scrapbooks when Dorota produced 'her surprise'.

She had checked in the Polish film records and had found a list of all the films that Alfred Weidemann had produced until his retirement in 1979. It was possible that, nearly twenty years later, he was still alive. She was curious. Were Alfred Weidemann (scriptwriter – 1947), Alfred Weidenmann ('Canaris' – 1954) and Alfred Weidenmann (a witness at the High Court in Berlin – 1963) all one and the same man? It might be an obvious conclusion for a fairy tale, but coincidence could surely not be that generous in real life – or could it?

Thirty canisters of film were checked into a wicker basket. Dorota panicked, thinking that she had missed one and they were all carefully removed and replaced while a recount was made.

Przemek was roused from slumber and a full mug of coffee shoved into his hand. Sandwiches were made and they were ready to leave. Yurek had found his English tongue and made a speech of farewell before martialling the crew into the van.

As they drove away down the drive, they left a vacuum behind them. The turmoil of the past few days had gobbled time. Suddenly there was stillness, a peace disturbed only by the sigh of the night breeze as it stirred the leaves of the ash tree above my head.

26

The film crew had departed. The emptiness that remained behind them felt like the end of the final chapter had been reached. I had identified all the individuals that Maria mentioned in her book as she predicted I would. What more was there to discover?

The feeling was misleading. Rather than an ending, it proved to be the beginning of a new chapter and was merely a lull, a pause, an intake of breath, before my experience of Poland, broadened on several planes.

Jurek had proffered an invitation to return to his farm. Dorota had insisted that I visit her when next in Poznań. The cameraman, Piotr, had offered to introduce me to Kraków and Ania, the woman that I had met in Cambridge, was urging me to visit Łódź. In November, Dorota sent me a book on the pre-war cars that had been available in Poland. I had complained to her that it was hard to find photographs of the period that Maria had described in glowing terms. The photographs in the book illustrated well the affluence of the time; gleaming autos, fur coats and jewellery. There were several photographs of Polish entrants to the Monte Carlo Rally as well as famous racing drivers. These were the 'untermensch' that Hitler and the Nazis so despised.

That autumn, my mother made what proved to be a significant addition to the growing library. One morning, she rolled up to the back door in her wheel chair, clutching a book that had been written by our family neighbour when we lived in Bury Green, a hamlet some two miles south of Bishop's Stortford.

"I've never actually read it!" she admitted. "It's not my sort of subject. But it's about Poland and I thought you might find it useful." Having delivered her parcel, she engaged the electric gear and zoomed off. Mum was like that – to the point and no hanging around to pass the time of day.

I remembered Reuben Ainztein quite well and knew that he had written a book. We had moved house in the early 60s and I had not realised that his work had been completed and was published in 1974. Over 900 pages about the fate of the Jewish population of Poland was a tough read.

Now that Kurzke's role in the German forces had been defined, the police battalions came under scrutiny. Until I obtained the book in its translated version, I struggled with 'Ganz Normale Männer' by Chris Brown in its German form.

Brown discussed the various activities of the police battalions and from whence they drew their recruits. Kurzke conformed in the latter case. The German civilian police force was the main source. Kurzke, as had his father before him, served in the Hamburg force before enrolling in a police battalion. Brown also noted that the men from Hamburg were not particularly pro-nazi and that within the Hamburg force, there was an opinion that Hitler was overstepping the rules of ethical behaviour. Kurzke would have fallen in line with that opinion.

He also reported the type of speeches that encouraged the men of Police Battalions 101 and 105, the two battalions of Ordnungs police that slaughtered many thousands of Jews in East Poland during 1941. The haranguing referred to Bolsheviks and communists and not specifically to Jews. It was puzzling. Daniel Jonah Goldhagen in his book *Hitler's Willing Executioners* was critical of the omission. Reuben Ainztein suggested a resolution. A large percentage of the population in eastern Poland was Jewish, refugees from the upheavals in Russia twenty years earlier. They were not speaking German, using either Yiddish or Russian as their everyday language. From the German point of view, they were identified as Russian communists and revolutionaries and not necessarily just Jews. That their victims happened to be Russian Jews as well was circumstantial coincidence.

The promotion of the Holocaust since the 70s, took a different view, whereby only the persecution of the Jewish race featured. The possibility that the Germans might have viewed the Jew as a communist, a Bolshevik or a partisan (a terrorist in today's terminology), was not taken into consideration and chipping through the literature regarding traditionalised concepts in order to reach the beliefs of the protagonists at the time, is complex. Like layers of old paint, each coating had hardened and was resistant to the chisel.

As I was mulling over such thoughts, Clinton was preparing to send US forces into Iraq once again. He was becoming impatient with Saddam Hussein who did not seem to be complying with the weapons inspectors and was not admitting to possessing the weapons that they sought. Perhaps he had none to show. Perhaps Saddam had created a convincing myth only to protect himself from threatening neighbours. If so, he was sitting now between a rock and a hard place. The Americans were suspicious and Saddam could only wait to be attacked at some time in the future. Iraq was complaining that her efforts to co-operate had not resulted in receiving any relief from sanctions and the health of her civilian population was being affected. America did not seem to be listening and remained determined to poke her nose into Iraqi affairs in the name of international security.

On 16th December 1998, the United States of America attacked Iraq.

On 22nd December 1998, a copy of dr Woźniak's encyclopedia arrived; a two and half inch thick volume that listed the members of the Polish AK in the Reich Territories of the Wartegau. Although printed in Polish, it took only seconds to locate the entry for Maria as well as my own name in the index as a contributor. As I turned the pages, I began to realise the immensity of the task that Woźniak had undertaken. That he had taken so much trouble to encourage an ignorant foreigner was humbling. The research, the collation, the checking and rechecking of the material would have been an endless nightmare. And yet, he had found the time to send me so many letters that I had filled a file, two and a half inches thick. It would probably take me as long to translate the completed work as he had taken to assemble it. It was taking forever to transpose the contents of 'Okreg Poznański AK' and that was a mere leaflet in comparison.

'Okreg Poznański AK' was one of the titles that I had been given in 1995. It is easier to translate a text that deals with a sequence of facts than one that contains discussion. Hence, I had delayed tackling the 'Introduction'.

When I did so, over the Christmas period of 1998, I discovered that the little booklet had been the forerunner of the encyclopaedia. The first post-1989 publication by the Zachodni Instytute, initiated an investigation into surviving wartime records that would not be restricted by the political correctness required during the Russian occupation. My continuous nagging of poor dr Woźniak to see the project of the encyclopaedia concluded and in print is perhaps why he had kindly included me in his prologue, where he had entitled me 'dr'.

Had I mysteriously been promoted?

27

FEBRUARY 1999

Ruminating over the traitor/heroine question and consulting Woźniak's encyclopaedia, I began to appreciate that Siatka 'A', the AK group that operated from the munitions factory in Posen, was possibly another contributory factor for the 'traitor' label. The Gestapo had investigated the management at the munitions factory. Their folkedeutch leader had been interned in Poggenburg, sentenced to death and transported for execution. Had Maria said anything when she was 'arrested' in the camp and been found in possession of matches?

A letter from dr Woźniak announced that a 'Mrs S' had contacted him as a consequence of the first documentary in 1997. She claimed to have been at school with Maria near Otorowa. It was an opportunity to clarify many hitherto unknowns about the convent school. 'Mrs S' had excused herself for not responding earlier. She had been away at the time of the broadcast and had heard about the programme on the grapevine. To meet her became the core reason for another visit to Poland.

Ainztein's book came under scrutiny that spring. He quoted a speech that was purportedly given by Himmler on March 15th, 1940. The contents supported something that dr Woźniak told me during the 1995 visit to Poznań.

"If the Germans had won the war, there would have been no Poles left after ten years," he had informed me several times (with Ludwik's help). "In 1938, the Polish population in Posen numbered over 270,000. By 1944 there were no more than 27,000 Poles left in the city." What did he mean? For me, it had been an outrageous statement and I had enquired for more input. My knowledge of such things referred only to the Jews and the Holocaust. The idea that Hitler had intended to stamp out the whole Polish nation seemed incredible.

In Ainztein's book, I found a report of a speech by Himmler to his camp commandants on 15th March 1940. It ran as follows:

"It is essential that all our staff, men and women, should know that our chief and most important aim is to capture all Polish leaders... so as to render them harmless. You gentlemen, being in charge of the camps, know best how to achieve this. All skilled workers of Polish origin will be utilised in our war industries. Then all Poles will disappear from this world. In the course of this responsible work you must root out all Polishness quickly and within planned stages... It is essential the great German people should regard it as its chief task to destroy all Poles."

The Polish nation had clearly been at the top of Himmler's list for total destruction. A.K.M. Poszpieszalski was quoted as the source of the speech. He featured in Woźniak's encyclopedia. A lawyer, in 1943 he had been appointed by the AK to collect evidence of war crimes.

But, where did the Jewish race feature on this list of 'planned stages'?

Enlightenment as to the planned destiny of Jews could be gained from a second clue, a memorandum sent to Hitler by Himmler in May 1940, also quoted by Ainztein:

"We are to the utmost degree interested in making sure that the peoples of the eastern region do not unite but that, on the contrary, they shall as far as possible be broken up into small branches and groups. As regards individual nationalities, we do not intend to help them to consolidate and increase, and even less to foster their material consciousness and national culture. On the contrary, we are interested in breaking them into numerous insignificant groups... I hope that we shall completely destroy the concept of 'Jew', as there exists the likelihood of a mass resettlement of all Jews in Africa or some other colony. A little more time will be needed to ensure the disappearance of such nationalities as the Ukrainians, Lenkis and Gorales from our territory. Everything that has been said about these nationalities applies even more strongly to the Poles." (Source – Prestupleniya nemet-sko-fashistkih okupantov v Belorussi.)

These two extracts contradicted so much that has become lore in the West. An enigma that still remained a mystery was – where did Ainztein find his material?

Reuben Ainztein was a Polish Jew. He was fluent in seven languages; English of course, German, Polish, Russian, Italian and two others that I do not recall. He had worked for Reuters as a translator and in the fifties and sixties when he was busy writing his book, he also launched into acquiring a knowledge of Chinese. We were all in awe of him as kids. His high, broad forehead was a sign of his intellectual powers although his control over his dog would leave us in fits of laughter. 'The Red Indian' we dubbed it, a red setter that behaved like an idiot most of the time, was adorned with a long flowing coat. Deaf to its master's voice, the dog bounded across the fields, ears and tail dancing in the jet stream with Mr Ainztein stumbling in its wake, pleading with the hound to come to heel.

His book was published in 1974. It dealt with the Jews in Poland during the war. The author died a bankrupt in 1979. The book stripped him of everything as the lawsuits piled high with attacks on its content.

Holocaust was not a term that he used. In the fifties perhaps, the word had not gained the momentous connotations that it has today. The contents of his book seem to be well informed; the names of people and partisan groups, the numbers of casualties and explanations of the whys and wherefores of different events were described in detail. Over two inches thick, the book was a conscientious history collated by an intelligent man. Yet it drew the wrath of the Jewish lobby on his head and it destroyed him. Why?

Letters to and from dr Woźniak were still being exchanged several times a month. It was a 'thinking' time for me. My various theories about Ina's identity and Maria's involvement with Walter's arrest by Wiebek were offered to him for scrutiny. He accused me of having a vivid imagination and being too reliant on instinct. He could not, however, deny the facts and it did not need too wayward an imagination to relate the data.

Dorota wrote at the end of February. When she had returned to Pelagia's address, she had found that the woman had died. It was a blow. I had been looking forward to meeting her on my next trip eastwards. She had shuffled off her mortal coil, happy that 'her angel', Maria, had received some recognition and grateful that she had made some contribution in acknowledgement for the food parcels that had been sent from England to Poland during lean years.

Sadly, the grave had swallowed a witness who might have explained many things. The loss was typical of the race against time to salvage memories of the living where documentary evidence had vanished.

I was still studying Ainztein's book. Bursting with facts and figures, I wondered how he had managed to source so much detail about events to which no one else appeared to have access. He had once tried to teach me Russian. The first lesson was the last. Discovering that the alphabet consisted of forty something letters to learn, with 'Ps' becoming 'Ts' or vice versa had proved far too confusing for a thirteen year old. In that respect, the Polish language is far friendlier. Though many words are similar to Russian, the Poles express themselves in print using the same alphabet as Western Europe. Some of the consonant combinations (e.g. przy) are mind boggling, but the phonetics, once analysed, are consistent.

It was March, a depressing month of the year, when the winter always seems endless and the glimmering hope of spring still too far away to be more than a faint glow. The previous month, an 83 year-old Pole had been in court, accused of war crimes committed over half a century ago. Someone had identified him as being present when Jews were slaughtered. His crime is a drop in the ocean. Many of those who murdered Poles have remained unnoticed.

In answer to a letter, Mrs S replied in impeccable English. She confirmed that the convent school near Otorowa had been patronised by international aristocrats and refugees from East Poland and that after WWI it had been an orphanage for such children. It had become a school in the early1930s. She also admitted that she had not known Maria well but would try to help.

As the day for departure to Poland neared, the situation in Bosnia became more dangerous. The Serbians were attempting to expel the Albanians from Kosova. If the USA interfered, the USSR threatened to defend the country and keep the American troops out. The situation in the east of Europe was simmering ominously. Was it a wise move to set off in that direction before the political situation settled?

Two days later, I caught the early bus from the bottom of the farm drive to Victoria Street where I re-embarked on a coach to Poznań. The journey would take another twenty hours and travelling long distance by bus was a novelty. It was not as bad as it sounds. The first break was on the ferry where a good meal was available to prepare for the diet of biscuits and nibbles that would follow.

Coffee was available on the bus itself, served by a steward. We motored across France and Germany without delays, stopping every four hours at a roadside service station for the drivers to swap over and for the passengers to stretch their legs or 'powder their noses'. There was a toilet closet on the bus, but only if one was adept at squeezing into such facilities at sea would it have been a useful amenity.

The plan was to drop most of my luggage in Poznań, before catching a train to Kraków where I would meet an English friend, who had delayed booking her ticket until the last minute, too late to purchase a seat in my coach which was already fully loaded. She had taken a coach direct to Kraków. Reunited, we would indulge in the habit of tourists – sightseeing – something that had not featured before on my agenda.

The journey was delayed by a German customs official at the Polish border. The bus was full. Nevertheless, every single passenger was obliged to disembark and to identify their luggage as it was hauled out of the hold. Every single case and bag had then to be opened for inspection. 'Sir' strolled through the sea of exposed belongings, casually flicking up the edges of clothing with a long black rod. I did not observe him dig deeper or scrutinize hard. The whole exercise seemed to be a kind of power game for him. When he spoke, everyone jumped. There was no real purpose and after half an hour of suspense the episode was concluded with the order to close the bags and to continue on our way.

It is remarkable how efficiently that luggage was re-stowed and how speedily the passengers flowed back onto the bus. There was no pushing, no raised voice. With silent agreement everybody cooperated with each other to escape swiftly before the official changed his mind.

Dorota met the bus and whisked me away to her apartment for a shower and a long chat before I caught the afternoon train to Kraków. She had arranged that Piotr Augustynek, the cameraman, would meet me at the station in Kraków that evening. It felt like a parcel, being posted and delivered safely to its destination. In a country where few spoke English, it was very reassuring that an eye was being kept on my whereabouts. I realised that they had a certain anxiety that I should not stray too far from the supervision of my hosts. I appreciated their concern for the safety of a lone female traveller.

My English friend 'Liza' had already installed herself in the room that had been reserved on the top floor of the University Hostel. She was already in her pyjamas and ready to jump into bed after her twenty-four hour journey from Victoria Station. She had already studied the tourist guide and was bubbling with enthusiasm about visiting the Wawel, the amber market, the salt mine in Wieliczka and perhaps Auschwitz if we had the time.

Breakfast the next morning was served in the basement. The accommodation was not normally available to foreign tourists and we respected the silence in the room, not wishing to become conspicuous. Piotr picked us up in his new car at 9am and soon we were driving south to explore the salt mine. He lived in Wieliczka and en route we stopped to collect his wife, Ania. A dainty woman with dark curly hair, she spoke no English but was fluent in French. Liza was in her element and chatted away with vivacious enthusiasm, while I took a back seat, rummaging around in my school day's memory store for sufficient vocabulary to follow the conversation. In fly on the wall mode, I watched with fascination how two women from different cultures began to use the gestures that accompanied a language that was foreign to them both.

The salt mine was 350 metres deep and lay directly under the oldest part of the village. It has been the raison d'être for the community for hundreds of years.

Mining as an activity had now finished. The deepest levels were flooded and the risk of subsidence had become too great. Salt was still extracted by drying the salt water that was pumped out every day, but the production was much reduced.

The tourist had filled the short fall.

There was a queue for the tickets and a queue to take the ride in the miner's cage down to the 3rd level. There were many visitors and the queue was long.

The salt mines in Siberia are supposed to be the end of the road. Impossibly cold and windswept, I had often wondered how the miners had managed to survive. I was about to discover the answer.

A mining community can actually live underground in the mine itself. Salt is white and easily reflects light, unlike coal. There could be permafrost above but within the mine itself, the temperature remains comfortably above freezing. The air is dust free, dry, and with a clean almost ozone-like taste. Accommodation within a salt mine is supplied by the salt crystal. The centre of each crystal is extracted leaving a two-metre shell that prevents it from collapsing. To comprehend this concept, it is necessary to magnify a grain of salt in a saltcellar many billion times to understand the size of a 'crystal'. There is space enough to build a cathedral in the largest one at Wieliczka. It is magnificent. A wide staircase, complete with balustrade, sweeps down into the huge cave, at the far end of which is an altar, diminished in size by the tall canopy above it. The walls are adorned with detailed carvings of the Stations of the Cross. Every item is carved out of the salt.

The tradition that developed such grandiose works had evolved from folklore. Once a crystal had been mined, it should not be abandoned and left empty. The mining company employed artists for the sole purpose of carving figures from the salt, that could 'inhabit' the subterranean voids and placate any malicious spirits that wandered by. The choice of subject was broad. We found Scandinavian type gnomes, squatting behind their beards, their long, pointed hats trailing to the ground, sculptures of man and horse labouring and life-size figures of saints and religious icons. Some of the oldest carvings dated back several hundred years although age and discolouration by the contamination dragged in by the tourists has almost obliterated the facial features.

Liza and I dawdled after the main group who seemed mesmerised by the expressionless monotone of the guide. Suddenly, we were surrounded by a group of men in overalls. They were in a jovial mood and showed us lumps of salt that were fresh from the cavern wall. One of them spoke a little English and explained that Pope John Paul was soon to visit the mine and someone had realised that a rest room would be required for his Holiness. The gang, busy digging out the required space, had taken time out and encountered us as they made their way to the cafeteria.

"Please take the salt – it will be a special memento." It was special. Where else could one acquire salt from a Pope's toilette facility?

Lunch at the Augustynek family home followed. Ania's cuisine skills reflected her ability with the French language. It was a family gathering, with her eight year-old daughter and two boys in their teens taking turns to serve at the table.

Returning to the centre of Kraków in the afternoon, we headed for Kienierz, the Jewish quarter to the south of the main square. We found and photographed the steps that featured in *Schindler's List* that are a permanent fixture. The other side of the street depicted in the film was artificial. In reality, it is an empty area of weedy grass.

The central square of the wartime ghetto area was surprisingly small. The tiny synagogue and graveyard lay at one end, and a large bookshop for tourists at the other. The area was, for the most part, drab and neglected. In the graveyard, the capped headstones tilted in all directions. The graves themselves were scruffy. As we walked back towards the centre of the city, we noticed a plaque on a high wall. It marked the boundary of the pre-war ghetto, built to keep the natives out.

Before nightfall, we went shopping in the covered amber market. It filled the centre of the main square and permanent kiosks lined the central passage that ran the length of the building. Amber of every shade and size was on offer. Pendants, rings, necklaces, carved figures and animals were in abundance. Fossilised flies and other insects were common. We were spoiled for choice. Too spoiled! After inspecting many different artefacts, Liza settled for a wooden salt scoop!

Painfully blistered feet had become a problem. I had worn the wrong shoes for so much walking. But next day, we were up with the lark and breakfasted by the time that Ania collected us. The Wawel was our destination; the castle home of the Polish monarch until Warsaw became the capital of the country. A confusion of different architectural styles, the Wawel complex is situated on the inside of a bend in the river. It was surrounded on three sides by water.

As we climbed the ramp up to the castle, Ania spotted her uncle. Every day, he spends two hours praying in the royal chapel. The friends and family who did not survive the war still haunt him. He was arrested in 1940 and spent four and a half years in Auschwitz with his brother. In 1945, he had been transported into a camp in Germany from which he had managed to escape. During a river crossing, thirty-three men had leapt from the ferryboat (including the German officer in charge) and had evaded recapture.

Ania posted us into the tour of the main church, a mausoleum full of sarcophagi. Over the centuries, chapels had been added to make additional room for the dead. From the outside, they look like a series of highly ornate carbuncles, all different, each clinging to the side of the church as though feeding from the mother core.

We descended to the crypt down a long straight flight of steps. In the round room at the bottom, the coffins of the nobility were laid out on shelves. Only one shelf remained unfilled, perhaps awaiting the corpse that would decay for two years in a locked rotting room halfway down the staircase. Only when it was odour free, would the remains be moved to the crypt. What a strange species the human race is? While they are alive, the aristocracy and wealthy are often wished elsewhere by the masses. Once dead, are they allowed to rest in peace away from the public eye? Oh no! Put them on display and the same public will pay to wander among their remains.

The sounds in the church were muted. The guides spoke in whispers – as did the spirits. We escaped into the morning sun and washed away the silent echoes with conversation and a coffee. Ania had promised to meet us after 'the tour' but there was no sign of her. She had been going to accompany her elderly uncle home and was probably delayed, so we ventured forth to explore the palace before she returned.

The residency of the monarch of Poland was suitably grand with its high, vaulted, beamed ceilings, decorated walls and a singular sparseness of furniture. The throne, a chair dwarfed by the size of the room, perching timidly on a platform in the centre. One hundred faces, many carved in caricature, glowered down from the ceiling above. If they represented the council available to the king when he needed advice, the king would have had a problem! They were inspiration for a nightmare.

Auschwitz had been eliminated from the agenda. The tour required a one and a half hour bus ride each way and the trip would have taken all day. Liza was booked to bus back to England in two days and she still had some shopping to do before we caught the train to Poznań. The schedule should have been reasonably simple.

The next morning, we walked around the ancient walls of the city, spending time to study a large exhibition of paintings by local artists. Liza was searching in every shop she could find that sold crystal glass and I kept a check on the clock.

We had just enough time to rush around a museum in the home of a Kraków statesman, before collecting our bags, hailing a taxi and catching the train. That was the plan. It did not allow for Liza's bright idea.

"Let's drive to the station in one of those horse-drawn carriages from the square." What a lovely idea it would have been, if she had thought of it an hour earlier.

"It's getting a bit close to the train time to arrange that," I protested. But Liza was undeterred and raced off down the road, heading towards the square. I manoeuvred all the luggage down the stairs, settled the bill, then lugged all the bags to the pavement where I sat and waited… and waited.

A quarter of an hour before the train was due to depart, my dear friend came hurtling down the street from the other direction. Between gasps she explained that the road was closed to vehicles, the carriage would have taken too long to reach us and she had a taxi waiting. While she was talking, she had grabbed her suitcase and I had fallen in behind her as she tottered towards the waiting cab, the doors already wide open.

We threw the bags into the boot and bundled into the back seat. We were now very late and it would be touch and go whether we made the train. There would be another one leaving in eight hours that would arrive in Poznań before dawn next morning – but it was not an attractive option. The taxi driver was on our side. It was a ten-minute drive to the station and we were held up by traffic. Unfazed, our chauffeur made use of the pavements and verges, tooting the horn and waving cheerfully at the raised eyebrows. He was a hero, getting us to the train with just thirty seconds in hand.

Seven hours later, the train pulled into the station at Poznań. The platform was all but empty except for a waif-like figure peering short-sightedly up and down the carriages. The knee length plait meant that it could be only one person.

"Dorota," I squeaked. How can she have known to meet this particular train? I had been told that she was busy editing a film with a deadline looming and I had deliberately not let her know our schedule. The receptionist in the hostel in Kraków had kindly located a room for us for the night and I had intended to contact her on the morrow. But somehow the jungle drums had transmitted the news and here she was.

"My aunt is lending you her apartment for the night," she announced. "You will be comfortable."

"But…" I was lost for words. There was no argument for such generosity.

Aunt Bozena greeted us warmly. She chatted with enthusiasm as she explained the protocol to the temporary residents. It was most important she drummed into us, if we went out... we must shut all the windows.

To this day, I do not know where she spent that night. She had abandoned her small flat to two women from England, neither of whom she had previously met. We were both extremely grateful to her. The three days in Kraków had been exhausting and the train journey, boring. To be able to chill out in a cheerful apartment with food and a shower to hand was an unexpected blessing.

As she wriggled down between the sheets, Liza noticed the saintly pictures and crucifixes that surrounded her bed.

"I've never slept in a holy bed like this before," she remarked reverently. I assured her that the experience would be restful – and it was. With no street noise to disturb the slumber of country bumpkins, we slept soundly until eight the next morning.

We summonsed a taxi. The young driver had not been to Fort VII before and was curious as to why we wanted to go there.

"It is the past," he said. "There are more interesting places in Poznań."

Liza fell uncharacteristically quiet as we entered the museum. As she observed the gas bunker, the prison cell, the entrance to the main communal cell in the yard where prisoners were obliged to crawl on hands and knees as they descended into the bowels of the earth, the steep concrete steps beside the huge metal door into the main prison, she remained silent. She was obviously deeply moved by what she saw and very much relieved when a time shortage brought the inspection to an end.

"I don't think that I would have coped very well with Auschwitz," she admitted as we sped in the taxi towards the citadel. Less claustrophobic, she found the military museums less stressful. The trees were coming into leaf and birds sang. The atmosphere was not sinister. It raised her spirits and she remembered that she still had some more shopping to do before catching her bus back to England.

We walked south from the citadel to the Stary Rynek, found a restaurant for lunch and parted company. Liza was seeking her crystal glass, whilst I got lost in a book and waited for her to return. Again, the wait was prolonged by the inability of my friend to understand the passing of time. Again, there was an undignified scramble to reach the bus station on time. We managed – just. The bus was late. It had not yet arrived from Warsaw and I bade her safe journey before continuing the drive back to the apartment in the taxi. I was unaware that after all the dashing about of the past three days with barely a second wasted, the bus would indeed be four hours late. Liza had ample time to slow down while she took a turn at waiting... and waiting.

Two days later, Dorota and I visited 'Mrs. S'. She lived on the other side of the city and Dorota was unfamiliar with the area. The apartment blocks were only six floors high with plenty of space between them, unlike the crowded district where her family lived.

A spacious foyer soared to skylights in the roof of the block. Opposite the entrance, an open staircase led upwards. We located the apartment of 'Mrs S' on the first floor.

'Mrs S' herself opened the door, her back badly bent, she looked up and greeted us with enthusiasm in her voice – in Polish. Her letter had been written in perfect English, leading me to believe that she was a fluent speaker. It was the first disillusionment. She must have been in her mid-seventies, but her facial make up was so cleverly applied that her skin revealed no signs of any wrinkles, creases or sagging. It was a remarkable face, the complexion and colour, that of a young girl – another illusion?

We were ushered into a cramped sitting room. Cups and a plate of heavily glazed Easter cakes were ready on the table. Having seen her two guests settled in the only two chairs available, 'Mrs S' vanished to find the coffee.

"Did you notice her face?" asked Dorota.

"Yes, it's amazing," I replied.

"It is very difficult to produce that effect with even stage make-up, but it cannot be real – she is too old." Dorota, with her theatre hat on, knew what she was talking about.

'Mrs S' bustled back into the room with a heavy coffee pot. She chattered incessantly but I had to rely on Dorota to both ask questions and log the answers.

Firstly, the function of the convent school was cleared up. 'Mrs S' confirmed that the 120 students had represented different categories of pupils. Eighty of them, the daughters of refugee aristocrats who had fled from East Poland and Russia after WWI, slept in the dormitories at the top of the building. Their parents could afford little. The full fee-paying pupils had superior accommodation on the first floor. The rooms were large enough for five to seven beds and she herself had shared a room with Maria and her friend Tuta.

In her letter, she had claimed that she hardly knew Maria and now I had learned that she slept in the same room for a period of time. Unless the two girls did not get along, the close proximity of the sleeping arrangements would have dictated more than a passing acquaintance. The age difference might have played a part if they were in different class groups. 'Mrs S' admitted that Maria was a year older than herself, but she claimed that she shared a classroom with Maria, a class of just fifteen students, so the lack of knowledge did not evolve for that reason.

Praying that the sticky cake would not remove a filling, I munched and concluded that there had been no friendship whatsoever between 'Mrs S' and Maria and that it was possibly that they had in fact disliked each other.

The school educated the girls to 'O' level matriculation. For 'A' level, they spent two years at the High School in Posen. This was in accordance with Maria's story.

The nuns wore black habits and this highlighted a mistaken assumption that was made in the 1997 documentary. Then, an interview was made with a nun in a grey habit from the convent in ul Niepodleglosci. The Ursuline nuns wearing black habits, taught at the Sacré Coeur in Tasczaka Street which was destroyed in 1945.

Maria had been known at school as Mira, confirming Maria's claim to the nickname. Her friend Tuta had survived the war and her last known address was in Paris, but 'Mrs S' did not know if she was still alive. At this point, she produced two old photographs of a group of schoolgirls, pointing out herself, Maria and Tuta. Immediately, I recognised Tuta. There was a full-length photo of her in school uniform amongst Maria's collection that I had at home. Maria stood in the front row. She appeared of a more stocky build than in other photographs that I had seen of her at a similar age.

Dorota enquired about the dancing lessons at the school.

"The nuns would never have permitted such a thing," replied 'Mrs S'. The answer was unexpected. It was contrary to Maria's account of her initiation into the world of ballet.

"A man would never have been allowed to teach the girls to dance," she continued. The existence of Maria's ballet master was denied – but he had existed. According to dr Woźniak, Szcurek was still teaching in 1949.

More contradictions followed. The French teacher, whose manner of dress and deportment so impressed Maria, was not French but English. The French teacher had been of Polish nationality, although 'Mrs. S' conceded that it was possible that Mademoiselle D'Etienne had taught at the school earlier, before 'Mrs S' first started at the school.

The 'Pill' may have been the nickname for the nun who was in charge of the infirmary. 'Mrs S' adamantly denied that the title was bestowed on any of the pupils.

On the positive side, 'Mrs S' confirmed that Maria had spent much of the holiday breaks at the farm belonging to Tuta's family. In contrast, she had been somewhat surprised that Maria had been described as beautiful. She remembered her as being rather tall and chubby with a face that was not particularly pretty. She recalled that Maria had a crooked nose. The Maria that I had known also had a markedly crooked nose. In the photos of her as a young girl, her nose appeared straight. Her nose may possibly have been modified during the interrogations by the Gestapo in 1943.

By this time, both detective Dorota and I were aware that we were being fed disinformation and prolonging the interview was becoming an embarrassing confrontation. We made a mutual agreement to beat a polite and dignified retreat.

Waiting for a taxi to pick us up, we were both reticent to speak. I tried to summarise my feelings about 'Mrs. S'. I sensed that something was not quite right; that the woman was being evasive and avoiding direct questions. She had dodged the issue of naming other girls who had attended the school and had become restless at the mention of the 'Pill'. A horrid thought started to wriggle into the equation. Was it possible that 'Mrs. S' herself was indeed the 'Pill'; the girl who had betrayed Maria to the Nazis in 1943?

Dorota had spotted the taxi approaching on the other side of the street and was waving her arms in the air to attract its attention.

"Dorota!" I said quietly. "Do you think that we may have just interviewed the Pill?"

"It is going through my mind too," Dorota responded. "I think it is very possible."

A few minutes passed, each mulling over the situation and its implications. We both tried to break the silence at the same moment.

"You first," said Dorota.

"She is old and frail and it was such a long time ago," I said.

"She is and it was. If we are right, she has already suffered for many years," said Dorota. Our thoughts had obviously travelled along the same track.

"We say nothing?" I offered.

"We say nothing," agreed Dorota.

She had made notes of the conversation. It transpired that the woman had hardly noticed the war. Her father's estate had been confiscated, but he had been hired as the estate manager. 'Mrs S' had become friends with the daughters of the new German owner and had admitted that the only time that she had suffered anxiety was when the German family left and the Soviet troops swept by in 1945.

How had she and her family remained untouched at a time when people of her ilk were under severe pressure? Had collaboration provided the umbrella? Dorota was right. If she had collaborated, the post war years must have been filled with fear of discovery. She would have paid for her disloyalty and even now she still had to live with her conscience.

The notion that the sins of the past should be forgotten and forgiven was not peculiar to Dorota. She demonstrated an attitude that I had encountered frequently. The oppression that followed the war, taught the Poles to live and let live. There were too many daily problems to surmount to be distracted by the luxury of witch hunting and revenge. Surviving the Soviet occupation required a talent for keeping one's head well below the parapet and assuming a grey cloak of invisibility to the prying eyes and ears of the NKVD and later, the KGB. The Soviets dealt with the German criminals that they found and harassed prominent members of the AK that they could track down. Polish civilians closed ranks, protecting their own against the vicissitudes imposed by the occupiers of their country.

Dorota recalled her experience of stepping out of line. Then a teenage student, she had distributed an underground newspaper. A friend, that wrote articles for the clandestine press, had been arrested. Nothing had been heard from him for several weeks and his family was anxious about his fate. Dorota had volunteered to go to the police station to make enquiries.

"I never did anything like that again," she said. She had been detained in a cell for forty-eight hours and had not been permitted to contact anyone. She had been terrified. Questions about why she wanted to know about the young man, how well she knew him and who had sent her were repeated again and again. Just when she had resigned herself to staying in custody indefinitely, she was told that she could go home.

"It was like stepping into another world when I walked out of the police station," she said. "In just two days, I had become much older and wiser. I will never forget that feeling of helpless fear," she concluded.

28

A brand new super store had been built on the edge of the estate of apartment blocks where Dorota and her family lived. A ten minute walk from the flat, past two nursery schools where small children played noisily among the trees, the shopper stepped into another world. The goods for sale ranged from cheap jewellery and glassware, through ranges of children's clothing to food of every description. The prices of chocolates and cigarettes were low by British standards, roughly a quarter of that which I would normally expect to pay, but slightly above the norm for the Polish market. Imported plastic toys and electrical goods reflected prices outside Poland. The 'carrots' were already installed. The car on display was the first prize in a lottery.

The trollies passing through the checkouts were piled high with goods. Conspicuous in their uniforms were the security guards. Three of them strolled to and fro with their hands clasped behind their backs, glaring repeatedly at any customer that dared to linger.

Until the weekend, I spent a lot of time on my own. Dorota was busy editing a short film about a Polish artist. Ciurlionis had lived at the beginning of the twentieth century, had suffered from depression and died young. To a degree, he was a surrealist, but his paintings were simple to understand and illustrated a gentle humour.

The Instytut Zachodni had relocated to a modern office in Mostowa Street. Dr Woźniak looked out of place in his new airy office. Gone was the clutter and chaos. The surface of his tidy desktop reflected the sunlight shining through the large window that overlooked green trees and red rooftops. Gone were the grimy windows and the back of the town hall that had been his previous uninspiring view. With the encyclopedia behind him and in print, he was able to be more relaxed. People were still coming forward with memories of the past, but the pressure was off. Even the coffee arrived on a tray carried by a smiling secretary!

There was time to indulge in other pursuits than exploring the past. Knowing that horses featured prominently in my life, Dorota organised outings to horse establishments in the area.

The first outing took us to the riding school of Antoni Chlopowski. By accident of birth, he was a Count, but was not interested in using the title.

His stable contained 150 horses, ranging from Shetlands to Hanoverians. The majority of the animals were ponies, imported from England.

He had lived in Sweden for 25 years occupying himself by driving on the Formula I racing circuit and horses. As soon as it was possible to return to his homeland, he did so, reclaiming his family estate and setting up the riding school.

"The Poles have forgotten their horse knowledge," he said. Horses were kept on state farms during the occupation and the public rarely saw them. It is my theory that they have to learn again from the start, so I cater mainly for the younger generation," he continued.

"But you can see here," he added, waving his arm in the direction of a family group that was wandering around the yard. "The parents are also wanting to ride and even the grandparents are showing interest."

Shoeing was another subject that Chlapowski earnestly promoted. Skilled in the arts of a farrier, he held courses at the riding school for aspiring blacksmiths. "Horses have not been shod properly in this country for over forty years," he complained. "I am trying to help."

The energy of the man was incredible. His family home was too enormous for him to live in by himself and he was converting it into a 20–30 room hotel. Instead, he had opted to live with his Alsatian dog in a labourers' terraced cottage behind the main house where he was quite happy.

Two large, long barns housed the horses. Hay was stored in the loft of one, while in the other, there was sleeping accommodation for visitors. Fully lined with Swedish pine, the rooms were large, bright and welcoming.

He had built a restaurant on the side of one of the barns, where we adjourned for lunch. Sitting at a large table, surrounded by a décor that resembled an American ranch house, Chlapowski regaled us with stories about his dogs, his horses and his hopes. Afterwards we toured his latest project; an international sized show jumping arena. The roof was up and it was possible to envisage the finished building. Above the seating for the audience, a gallery on three sides would accommodate the restaurants and boutiques. Fifty stalls in a lean-to against the building would stable the visiting horses.

It was time for the 'interval training' hour. Nine riders and nine horses of various sizes and breeds were assembled, the smallest – a Shetland pony. 'This is a joke', I thought. Chlapowski, a small man, was mounted on a four year old Welsh pony stallion. The group headed away from the yard towards some jumps at the far side of a grassy plain and we followed on foot. The fitness training began. The horses first walked and then trotted for a predetermined period. I was waiting for the cantering to start, anticipating that the Shetland at least would show signs of reluctance or resistance. How wrong can you be?

Both the Shetland and the young stallion behaved impeccably, cantering for exactly the same amount of time as the larger animals.

Jumping was the last exercise on the agenda and I was convinced that the Shetland would faulter. But no! His attitude to the 80cm obstacles was positive. At no time did he flinch or hesitate. I had never seen a Shetland perform like it before and I had to admit that I was impressed.

In contrast, the five horse riding school on the outskirts of Poznań was a tribute to ingenuity. Jurek Lukomski had rented a small farm. The stables were in a poor state of repair and his fields were unlevel and full of small hillocks. In winter, he erected a marquee in which it was possible to exercise a maximum of three horses at a time. More, and the accumulating condensation caused the tent to sag dangerously.

Lukomski had worked with horses most of his life. He had been a groom on a state farm together with his father. The latter was anxious to restore the 'Polish horse', a breed that had been reduced to just 32 mares. He showed me two of them, grazing in his field. The bright tan coat colouring and dorsal brown line reminded me very much of the Norwegian Fjørd pony. It was not dissimilar in height either except that it was of a lighter build. We discussed his concern about the lack of a national horse organisation that could establish a standard of horse care. Currently, the enthusiasm for restarting the horse culture in Poland was causing the blind to lead the blind with unhappy consequences for the horse. Meetings that his father attended were in progress, but the tradition of the Pole to argue every point was limiting progress. Amidst adieus, I promised to send him some literature about how the British organised their national horse society.

It was a Tuesday when Jurek collected Dorota, her son, Jas and myself and we all drove westwards to the farm near Gorzów. It was dark by the time we arrived, but in the moonlight the gap between the ridge of the roof and the end wall was clearly visible. The two dogs emerged from their shed. Only one barked. The other shook its head violently, rattling the heavy chain attached to its collar. The farm was to be my lodgings for the next week or so. Jurek had been burgled twice in the past six months. When his car was absent, it had been an open invitation to the intruders. The house was isolated and old sheds prevented the passer-by from observing anything unusual. Loose boards over the windows had not deterred the assailants.

I was to be the 'house-keeper' for the next few days while Jurek was away, a sort of unchained Rottweiler patrolling the ramparts. Dorota and Jas returned to Poznań by train the following day and I retrieved Maria's manuscript and my Miss Marple hat from the depths of my suitcase. I was looking forward to the several days of uninterrupted solitude and the opportunity to compare Maria's story with the facts that had accumulated during the past five years.

The insertion of date pegs for the different events in the text was the first project. To the 2nd March 1942 when she signed the contract with UFA, could be added a string of others. She had been arrested in Posen on 28th March 1943 according to Herbert's 1963 statement to the High Court in Berlin and interned in Fort VII where she shared a cell with the women from Mosina (arrested December 1942–January 1943). In the late spring she was transferred from Fort VII to Poggenburg with the last of the women. In December of that year, again according to Kurzke's statement, she was a witness at his court-martial in Königsburg. She was punished by Walter the commandant of Poggenburg at the end of November 1944 for she heard the rumour of his suicide on 7th October a few days after her rescue from the pit where the corpses were temporarily stored. Lastly, Pelagia had confirmed in a recent interview that she had given both Maria and her mother shelter in January 1945 after they had escaped from the Gestapo HQ and before they left Posen for Berlin.

Miss Marple's hat started to vibrate in excitement. I had considered the idea before. Was it possible that Maria's near-death experience at the hands of the commandant was the reason for Wiebek, the inspector of camps to arrest Hans Walter?

According to her account, the day after she was found alive in the pit, Maria had remained concealed in the women's quarters. She was too weak to attend the daily roll call. Had the camp authorities known that she was still alive, they should have come looking for her. It did not seem that they did. It was possible that the prisoners that cleared the pit each week managed to smuggle her body past the guards successfully and her survival kept from them? Perhaps! On the second day of her recovery, the roll call was cancelled. It had never happened before.

What could possibly have caused such a dire disruption in the camp routine for the roll call to be neglected?

Could it be that it was the 4th October, the day that Wiebek had marched into Poggenburg in the early morning and arrested the commandant and nineteen of the garrison? The more I thought about it, the more Miss Marple's hat wriggled. Commandant Walter had hung himself in his cell three days after his arrest. The rumour of his death had reverberated around the camp according to Maria.

Wiebek's accusation against Walter was 'for causing the death of a prisoner without the appropriate piece of paper.' Collaboration between Walter and the Gestapo had always ensured that an appropriate piece of paper had materialised when necessary... until the beginning of October. Who had Walter killed that had allowed Wiebek to take action?

A letter had arrived at the Zachodni from an old woman who had been a prisoner in the camp at the time. She described how Maria's mother, Antonina, the black-eyed dragon from the vegetable patch, had wailed outside the cart shed, screaming out for her daughter. The uproar would not have passed unnoticed and Wiebek would surely have had his own spies among the staff at the camp who would have reported the incident to him.

If Kurzke and Wiebek had known each other before the war as dr Woźniak claimed, it was quite possible that they were in contact with each other during the war. If this was the case, Wiebek may well have been aware that the confirmation of Maria's death sentence had 'got lost in the post' and with this knowledge, he assumed, without the shred of a doubt, that when he received a report of Antonina's behaviour, Walter had committed an unauthorised killing.

The irony of the whole situation was that the 'victim' was not actually dead and it was Walter who died.

Miss Marple's hat stopped wriggling. It was a 'eureka' moment. It was a viable explanation of otherwise bizarre facts and when related together, they fitted snugly. A large chunk of the complicated puzzle was complete. It was time for another cup of coffee to celebrate. The house mouse sitting in the sun on the window sill, carefully cleaning his whiskers, froze then bolted for cover.

29

I found plenty of little jobs to do. The grass area in front of the house contained a variety of neglected cultivated plants that were threatened by vigorously growing weeds. I endeavoured to redress the balance by spending a few hours each day weeding and replanting. When the weather was grey, I attacked the crumbling plaster in the kitchen. Continuous damp was reducing it to a state where a light tap would cause it to crumble and form small heaps of fine sand by the skirting board.

On the third day of solitude, I heard one of the dogs bark a couple of times, then voices outside in the yard. Peeking through the kitchen window, I observed three young men approaching the house. One of them I recognised. He had spent a few hours playing with Jas at the weekend. He would have known that the house should be empty for Jurek's car was missing. Drawing myself up to Jane Brodie height, I swung open the front door and smiled benevolently down at my visitors. The chatter ceased instantaneously and the lads stopped in their tracks.

"Can I help you?" I asked them, knowing that it was unlikely that they had any idea what I was saying. They stared back. I repeated the question.

One of them mumbled something. They turned in unison and retreating speedily across the yard, they vanished behind the barn. The Rottweiler had done her job. Several months later, two lads in the small village were found to be guilty of purloining goods that they did not own.

Jurek did not desert me completely. Possibly fearful of what he might find if he allowed me to too much time to knock his house about. He proposed that we should visit several interesting places in the area, among them the old town of Kostrzyn and the lake where swans came to nest each spring.

On the Saturday, we set off in the car towards the German border. It was some time before I started to recognise the route. It was the one that the bus had driven when I entered Poland. Eventually Yurek stopped and parked on a bare patch of earth. Expecting to see a town of some kind, I was perplexed but not for long. Old Kostrzyn was in total ruin; left as it had been in 1945. The Germans had made a stand in the walled city and after the Russians eventually ousted them, the city had been totally flattened.

The outer walls bore the scars of the battle. Feet thick, they had withstood the shells of modern warfare. But the evidence of the conflict was obvious. The walls, surrounded by a moat full of water were pitted where shells had struck.

The bridge across the moat was in a very poor state. Both sides of the narrow path in the centre of the roadway were covered with loose shingle that sloped away towards the water below. The damaged archway over the entrance tilted at a precarious angle. We proceeded with caution.

What awaited us beyond the gate was another world. As far as the eye could see, tall mature trees and silence. The broad main street stretched into the distance. It was lined by a four-foot high bank of grey stones, undisturbed for fifty five years. As we walked up the main street, it was possible to identify the outline of housing. Between them, the narrow alleys were choked with rubble. Trees and undergrowth had taken root in the ruins, concealing them under a cloth of green life, a natural shroud for those who died long ago and whose remains may still lie beneath them.

The long avenue opened out on to what was once the market square. Here the trees had not grown. The area of around ten acres was totally bare of any intrusive vegetation. Beyond it, the one wall within the whole city that stood more than ten feet tall was the chancery end of the church. Close to it was what was left of the castle. Razed to the ground floor, it was a jumble of stone. The arches that had supported the cellar leaned at crazy angles, reluctant to lose their elegant form. Two and a half metre square patches of bright, modern tiles, with a copper pipe protruding in each suggested that modern toilet facilities had once been installed. The splash of colour amid the greyness of the shattered stone made a poignant comment about the futility of destruction. The once proud city had been reduced to nothing. Only the moat and massive defence wall had survived in any really recognisable form, the rest for the most part, was a sea of crumbling stone.

The Kostrzyn that was rebuilt after the war was over half a mile away. Material was recycled from the old town for the foundations, but otherwise the old site had served no purpose. Jurek spoke of proposals to create a tourist attraction out of the place. Projects to install safety measures, to clear some of the debris and to provide refreshment kiosks were under discussion. I was disappointed. It would destroy the magic, allowing the tinsel trash of modern times to intrude on the peaceful serenity that nature had established over the years.

En route back to the farm, we drove around the edge of a huge bird sanctuary.

"Swans come in the spring to nest when the lake is big," explained Jurek. "The water is dammed to flood the plain for them." Flocks of swans drifted back and forth, gleaming white and surrounded by sequins of light reflected by the rippling water. Jurek attempted to take a short cut. The road disappeared under water and he was obliged to reverse the car. "You can drive this way in the summer," he muttered. "Today it is too deep." We drove along the top of the dyke, stopping at an isolated cottage by the sluice gate. While Jurek exchanged gossip with the gatekeeper, I hunkered down by the lake to watch and listen. A bull frog croaked and within seconds a deafening carcophany erupted from the reeds as his mates joined him in chorus. The din waned, only to swell again a few minutes later. There must have been thousands of them to have created the noise that detracted from the otherwise idyllic serenity of the scene.

Dorota and Jas were back that evening, Dorota clutching two rose bushes for the garden and a spade. Jurek's tools were few in number.

A discussion followed about how best to tame the garden. Jurek had borrowed a saw from a neighbour and the next day Dorota and I were hacking down elder bushes and brambles while Jas and Jurek tended the bonfire. It took them two hours to persuade it to catch fire but once alight, they fed it twig by twig from the enormous heap of branches and foliage that we ladies had accumulated. By evening, not a leaf remained. Meanwhile with the boys busy outside, Dorota and I had retired indoors to knock more plaster off the walls!

We did leave some of the house standing although Jurek was careful not to leave us again on our own! Friends and relatives visited with their small children and we all went for walks deep into the forest, where the moss grew a foot deep. Mushrooms were the quarry although the party usually returned empty handed.

It was a pleasant interlude and a break from the sober study of Polish history. Returning to Poznań the following week, I called into the Instytut Zachodni to see dr Woźniak. I reported on the interview with 'Mrs S'. He was not surprised at the conclusion that Dorota and I had drawn.

He had been trying to discover whether there was any retrievable material in central Poland concerning evidence from the 1939–40 transportees from the Wartegau to the General Gouvernement. He had drawn a complete blank, finding that when the Poles had arrived from the west, the inhabitants in the middle region of Poland had regarded them as displaced Germans and had not made them welcome. How many survived the transports was unknown and by all accounts, nobody on the reception end cared. My next contribution to the discussion was to tell dr Woźniak that Dorota's father and grandmother had arrived in Posen from the Ukraine in 1944. "Impossible!" decreed Woźniak. "People who had been resident in Posen prior to 1939 were allowed to return. People from other regions were not allowed to settle here until 1975." He would investigate.

It was an example of the eternal problem of information from different sources in Poland failing to cross reference satisfactorily. When I mentioned my conclusions about Maria, Walter and Wiebek, the response was a non-commital shrug.

"It is possible," said dr Woźniak. "but... it is too obvious." Trained to seek the obscure, he was not willing to accept a simple solution. He did agree, however, that the scenario was a serious possibility.

Dorota saved one of her little surprises to the very last minute. While waiting for the bus that would whisk me back to England, she casually said, "Did you know that Alfred Weidenmann is still alive and living in Switzerland?"

I did not.

30

SUMMER 1999

So... Alfred Weidenmann, film producer and scriptwriter, was still alive and living in Switzerland. Dorota was keen that I should write to him on the chance that he was the same Weidenmann who had made a statement on Maria's behalf for the Berlin court case in 1963. The fat chance could be a slim possibility. Conceivably, he was the same Alfred Weidemann who had written to Maria in 1947. There was the small matter of the missing 'n' in the surname, but the 1963 Weidenmann precluded that he and the 1947 individual were one and the same. If one did not enquire, there would never be an answer. My cousin, living in Switzerland procured his address and soon a letter of enquiry was on its way. I nervously awaited the reply.

One week passed by; a month, two months. Then one morning when I had almost forgotten the matter, an envelope arrived in the post with a Swiss stamp on it. Eagerly, I tore it open to find that it contained my original letter. The wave of disappointment was half-registering when I noticed some handwriting added to the bottom left-hand corner of the page.

'I am as accused', and signed A. Weidenmann.

Disappointment instantly dissolved into triumph. I had hit the jackpot. The slim chance had transformed into fat reward.

A thousand new questions bounced onto the agenda. How did he come to meet Maria? Did he know that she could possibly have met Canaris and almost certainly Piekenbrock? There was a problem obtaining the answers. Mr Weidenmann was obviously not generous with the written word. I needed to speak to him. Another phone call to my cousin, urging him to search through the Swiss telephone directories, yielded the number that I required.

Weidenmann himself answered the phone and I introduced myself. I so wanted to interview him, but he was reticent. I told him that I had seen his 1954 film on Canaris and he was curious as to how I had obtained access to it. I asked him how close his portrayal of Canaris had been to the original. Viewing the film had been a point in my favour, questioning the authenticity of the main character was a mistake. The voice on the phone hardened. 'It was a true portrayal of the man,' I was told. My request to meet him met the rising wall. It was inconvenient for him. He was to spend Christmas on a cruise and he could not be specific about his timetable. He was still too busy with film projects. I could take a hint. He was unwilling to cooperate.

In the New Year, I tried again. The same voice answered the phone. He was more relaxed this time and I made progress.

He had met Maria through Antonina's advances. Mother and daughter had frequented the American parties that were held every night in Berlin in the wake of peace. It was her mother who had been the lively one and it was she who had suggested that Maria should write her memoirs.

"Didn't you realise that I wrote the book for her?" he said.

I spluttered helplessly. Since the start of the project, I had nursed a suspicion that someone else other than Maria had written her book. I had even considered that it just might have been Weidemann after finding his letter dated 1947. The confirmation that the theory was correct came as a shock, however. Many more questions rose to the surface. It seemed unlikely that I would get to meet Weidenmann in person and it was necessary to glean as much as possible over the phone.

"Do you know how accurate the manuscript might have been?" I enquired.

"I wrote what she told me, adding a few frills to make it more readable, but I did not alter the storyline." I was speaking to a celebrated scriptwriter. It was no wonder that friends who had read the manuscript had suggested that the book would make a good film.

Writing the book had caused Weidenmann to be arrested by the Russians in 1945. He had been busy typing his notes when the door burst open. Into the room marched Russian soldiers. Suspicious of what he was writing and unable to read German, they had carried him away to sit in a cell for a week until the text of the typed pages had been examined. It was as well that Maria had not referred to any clandestine activities. The incident had frightened him badly but it threw some light on the reason for the Soviets arresting Maria.

She had told me a strange story of two men knocking on the door of her room and 'inviting' her to go with them to sign identity papers at the office. It was not an office to which they escorted her, but a Soviet prison cell where she remained for two weeks. When her mother returned to the empty apartment, she realised that her daughter had mysteriously disappeared and she had gone straight to the British authority to raise the alarm. According to Maria, her mother had raised 'merry hell' and eventually the Russians admitted that they had abducted her. Maria was released from custody and the two women were listed as priority evacuees to England. Maria never could explain why the Russians had taken an interest in her but as the source and subject of Weidenmann's writing, she would have aroused their curiosity.

The conversation got into difficulties when I started to quiz him on details in Maria's story. It was written so long ago and he had lost his original copy during frequent house moves. Could I forward a copy to him? I agreed and followed up the telephone call by sending a copy of the manuscript and letters. The months drifted by and there was no response. I rang again but no one picked up the phone.

31

Sarah escorted me on my first visit to the British Records Office in Kew. I was somewhat allergic to London, the throng of people, the lack of oxygen and the sense of claustrophobia, all tended to induce mild panic attacks. Taking pity on me, she had offered a bed for the night and her company on the journey across London to the BRO. I had accepted with gratitude.

When we travelled to Berlin, she forgot an essential item. Then it had been her passport. This time, it was her pass to get into the document room of the archive. Only after we had arrived, did she discover her oversight and while her activities were confined to the reference room, I, with new passes, was able to roam anywhere.

There were two trails that I wanted to follow. The first concerned two women working in the Abwehr HQ who had successfully and anonymously acted as agents for Canaris. They had superseded Halina Szymanska when it came to the supply of military intelligence, when Canaris had found it too dangerous to relay it via Halina. My theory was that, if I could locate the information received from the women and if that the source had abruptly ceased to function in March 1943, it could be argued that Maria and Antonina could possibly have been the women in question. They were in the right place at the right time and Maria was married to a man who had connections into the Abwehr. Furthermore, being mother and daughter, there was very little likelihood that they would intentionally betray one another.

The second quest was much simpler – to find when Maria's passport had been issued in 1947.

First, I had to discover how the archive functioned and in which of the filing categories to look. Using the second line of enquiry to help the learning curve, I found myself leafing through several thick books; the records of British passports issued between 1945–6.

Among Maria's affects that had been sifted in 1985, were several old passports. She had married a Mark Chevalier before she left Berlin and travelled on his passport. After two hours of studying strange names and becoming fascinated by the huge number of passports that had been issued to people from every corner of Europe, my eyes gave up. The exercise though unproductive, had proven worthwhile. I had learned something about the protocol of the BRO and how to find, order and where to study the documents. I would be back.

In the middle of March, the local paper published a short article about a local writer. Jeffery Bines was pictured with his latest book, *Operation Freston*, the story of the last mission sent into Poland by the SOE. A phone call led to a meeting over coffee and he was commissioned to enquire of the only survivor of the Freston Operation, a certain Antoni Pospieszalski whether his older brother was either the Karel Pospieszalski that was quoted by Ainztein or the one included by dr Woźniak in his encyclopaedia. It was a very long shot but coincidences were becoming the norm.

It sounds almost banal to announce that the two men were indeed found to be brothers. Antoni confirmed that his brother Karel had been involved with the AK and though 94 years old was still alive and mentally agile. Where did he live? In Poznań of course! Coincidence could not let me down on such a minor detail.

By this time, I was making regular trips to the BRO. I took advantage of a lift offered by Jeffery who was in the habit of driving his car up to the archive on a Thursday, when the place closed its doors at a later hour and it was possible to avoid the evening rush hour for the return home. He introduced me to some of his colleagues who took an interest in what I was doing. I told them how I was trying to locate the information that Halina Szymanska had relayed to England and to ascertain its content and when it changed from 'immediate' data (in December 1940, she had relayed the news that Germany had taken the decision to attack Russia) to a more general descriptions of Hitler's ideas and notions. It was not so easy a task and I was beginning to think that I was seeking the impossible when one of the small group that gathered for coffee breaks took me to one side.

"I don't think that you are going to find what you are looking for here," he confided. I looked at him aghast. Surely the vast collection of documents housed in the mammoth labyrinth of the British Records Office would yield something that would be helpful.

"You might be interested in this file though," he added and passed me a slip of paper with a reference number written on it.

"What is it?" I asked.

"Get it out and you will see," was his reply and he hurried off before I could quiz him further.

I duly ordered the file at the desk and absconded to the cafeteria until it was retrieved. Two hours later, I collected a slender folder and settled down at one of the reading tables to find out what the documents it contained would reveal.

Initially, I established that they were the reports from an agent. Could this be Halina Szymanski I wondered? Flicking through the papers, I noticed a handwritten note in the margin of a document that related to August 1941. It suggested that attention should be paid to this particular source. Disinformation, half truths and blatant lies had been a part of the 'spying' game at the time, so what had caused someone to earmark this particular agent as legitimate? If the agent was Halina Szymanska, the information that she had given in December 1940 about Germany's intention to invade Russia had, six months later, been proven to be accurate. Though the British on the receiving end had absolutely no idea about her integrity, she had relayed news on a matter that showed that she had a contact very close to the heart of the German hierarchy.

Assuming that this was Halina's file, I turned my attention to the content of her reports. The first one was of substantial length and described Hitler's ambitions with regards Europe. The word 'Federation' leapt out at me. I checked the date on the top of the page, 1941. I was aware of rumours that Germany and France had discussed a European Federation in 1943, but here I was reading a document that stated that it was in Hitler's head in 1941. I turned the page.

The next part of the report made my eyes pop. To make the federation work, a common European currency would be introduced. The third page described how the USA would be isolated from European affairs. I really could not believe what I was reading. In the past twenty-five years Europe had travelled a long way down this road. Rather than guns, financial incentives and security had been the carrot with the Ecu as the currency. Could the day come when Hitler would be regarded as the architect of Europe?

European politics aside, the document demonstrated that by 1941, Halina had already been 'side-lined' with regard to up to the minute information and presumably the task had fallen to the two unidentified women in Berlin.

When I tried to confirm from my helpful colleague whether the agent had indeed been Halina Szymanska, I was met a bland smile. The lists, identifying the real name of agents were mysteriously not available. I was not given a denial.

Plans for another bus trip to Poland started to speed up. I needed to speak to Karel Pospieszalski as soon as possible to confirm whether or not he was the source of Himmler's speech of 15th March, 1940.

Warning bells rang when in mid April, David Irving lost his case in the law courts. It cost him £2,000,000. I had not followed the case but during the television interview afterwards, he was howled down when he claimed that there was far more to the Holocaust than the persecution of the Jews. He also pointed out that an evolution of events had lead to the 'Final Solution' and that it did not suddenly erupt out of the ethos. This suggestion was rapidly glossed over, if not totally ignored.

The trail that I was following had certainly already indicated a deviation from the accepted norm. The ethnic cleansing of the Polish population from Posen (Poznań) in the New Reich Territories had by 1944 reduced their number by 90%. Dispossessed of all but a suitcase of belongings, Polish families were transported out of the region en masse between October 1939 and April 1940. At the same time the prominent citizens, the handicapped, the intellectuals and those who showed any sign of resistance disappeared into Fort VII for execution.

Meanwhile the Jewish population had been segregated and confined to the ghetto on the outskirts of the village of Zabikowo. There they stayed until an unspecified date in 1942. These facts might suggest a slightly different agenda to the one that, since the war ended, has received prime attention.

In the spring of 2000, it was curiosity that dictated the next step. Chance had repeatedly surprised me. With no particular purpose in mind, I had drifted on the tide of fortune; a stone, rolling slow enough to gather moss. Maria's book had been significantly unravelled and, as she had predicted, most of the characters in her story had been given an identity. I had researched the background to the tale and the trail was heading into a fog of enigmas that still required explanation. Dorota had suggested that I write a book about my adventures, but I was not an author, neither did I have sufficient windows of time in the home environment, to generate a book-length script.

Besides, the trail still led onward and I was hooked on the idea of following it to its end. In May, I returned to Poznań.

32

MAY 2000

I caught the commuter bus from my home town in Essex to Victoria bus station. It was an early start, but it was the only way to ensure that I would catch the bus that left London for Poland; a bus that left Victoria Station at around 11 o'clock. I was the only passenger holding a British passport and the only one to be travelling to Poznań. Disappointingly, the route had been altered. Instead of a three hour break, roaming the deck of a cross-channel ferry, the bus piggybacked through the tunnel on a train. It was a boring and claustrophobic experience. Sixteen hours later, I stepped off the bus for the final time at my destination, hailed a taxi and found the apartment of Dorota's mother. I had walked a maximum of 550 yards during the whole journey!

My distraction for the trip had been *Operation Freston*, the book written by my neighbour Jeffrey Bines. It inspired yet another line of enquiry as to what was really going on in Poland with regards the persecution of the AK by the Soviets. The departure of the Freston mission was delayed for over nine months while British bureaucracy procrastinated and it was only permitted to leave England at the end of 1944. Its aim, which was to discover whether there was any truth behind the rumours that had leaked out of Poland, was thwarted by Soviet interference.

The dinner table was full that afternoon. At last I met Aunt Bozena, who had so generously provided Liza and me accommodation in her flat. Tomek and Marek, Dorota's brothers were present and of course her mother. Dorota and Jas joined the throng later. They had just returned from the farm.

The following morning, with Dorota's help, I phoned Professor Karel Pospieszalski. His daughter, Donata, answered the phone, saying that her father was out walking but that he would return my call on his return. It was in fact Donata that phoned back to say that her father had just come out of hospital and as he was recovering from bronchitis, he was too unwell to receive visitors.

When my query about Himmler's speech was relayed to the professor, however, he insisted on speaking directly to me. He would have preferred to have spoken to me in German but struggled manfully in English. At first his voice was weak but it gathered strength as he warmed to his subject.

"You know about the General Plan East?" he asked. I had to admit that I did not. "Ah!" he continued. "You must understand about the General Plan. I have written much about it. Many articles!" he concluded.

"Can you tell me where to find your articles?" I asked.

"Many have been published in books," he replied.

He told me that Himmler's March 14th address had been included in the Nuremberg Trial records. It could be sourced in London at the Imperial War Museum. He also recommended that I access 'Documenta Okupaczone Volume 6' and other papers, some of which were in English. Oh joy! But his illness left him short of breath and the conversation had to be rapidly brought to a close. If I wrote him a letter, listing all my queries, he would be very happy to answer them at length. I thanked him. I knew where I would be heading as soon as I returned home.

The following day, I scoured the second-hand bookshops with Dorota in search of any book that had been written by the professor. We were disappointed. Acquiring a copy of Pospieszalski's published work was not as simple as hoped. Most of the material had been written a long time ago was long out of print and therefore a chance find among second-hand books was the only possibility of acquiring a copy of any of his publications.

During a meeting with dr Woźniak and Ludwik at the Instytut Zachodni, it was confirmed that Karel Pospieszalski's work was indeed out of print. They would try to obtain some of his books for me. Dr Woźniak also promised to find documentary evidence of the Nazi plan to annihilate the Poles over a period of ten years. It was to the General Plan East to which he had referred when he had told me once before 'that if Germany had won the war, there would have been no Poles left after ten years'.

When asked about the Jewish population of Posen and the Wartegau, he became vague. For him, it was more important to emphasise that, of the estimated 6,000,000 Jews that were murdered in Poland, over 50% of them were of Polish nationality. (Ainztein gives a pre-war figure of 3,500,000 Jewish inhabitants in Poland.) The Polish losses in the concentration camps were estimated to have been in excess of 6,000,000, 50% of whom were Jews, but that was only a national disaster and not considered worthy of being credited holocaust status. He was somewhat indignant about the omission.

Ania and her teenage son Piotr had stayed with me in England for a few days the previous summer and they had invited me to look them up in Łódź when I was next in Poland. The day after the meeting at the Zachodni, I boarded a bus for the four and a half hour journey to the city, known during the war as Lichtmanstadt.

33

Ania was also keen to show me the remnants of war in her city.

We had taken the tram into the centre of Łódź to find the Children's Camp or what was left of it. The extremities of the camp were marked by single boulders, the only vestige that remained of the original site. Apartment blocks now occupied most of the area and it is practically impossible to discern the full dimensions of the prison that had been abducted by the HSB for Germanisation and included blonde blue-eyed children, awaiting adoption by German families.

They had ranged in age from two to sixteen years old, the older children taking care of the younger. Some 1,200 juveniles were incarcerated at any one time, with a school and play area that enabled them to lead relatively 'normal' lives. The living conditions in the camp were severe, earning it the title 'Little Auschwitz'. Many did not survive. The trauma of being torn from their families and dumped into a strange environment caused deep psychological problems. Those that showed no signs of developing a more congenial behaviour were transported to the death camps. Many just lost the will to live and succumbed. The records as to who these children were, where they came from or what befell them, have been lost. It is thought that of those who were adopted, many could still be alive. Now in their 60s and 70s, are they aware of their origins?

I recalled noticing a group of very blonde headed youngsters in Kostrzyn when Sarah and I had spent a couple of hours wandering around and passing the time before she caught her train back to Berlin. We had suddenly been surrounded by school children, aged between eight and ten. Every single one of them had white blonde hair and pale blue eyes. It was very odd and I made some remark to that effect to Sarah.

"That's a very racist remark!" she had responded sharply. I was taken aback. What was racist about an observation of fact? Visiting the site of the Children's Camp caused me to wonder. In 1945, just how far did the evacuation transport from the camp get? Had the journey never been completed, halted by the prolonged battles between German and Russian troops along the banks of the river Warte?

It is estimated the 2,250,000 Polish children died in the camps scattered around Poland. A further 250,000 that were blue eyed and blonde, were adopted by German couples. Of these, approximately 100,000 were returned to their homeland after the war.

A large memorial has been erected in the public park close by. A graceful column, split at the base, it soared skyward. Shaped like a falling tear, the structure is simple, yet moving with its symbolism. To the side, a long row of tombstone-like slabs, record the towns from which the children came. Nearly every large urban population was represented, including Posen. It was to this place that the children of the women from Mosina had been transported in 1943. Most of their parents did not survive. Did the children?

After a quick sandwich on a park bench, we walked to the museum in Radagoszcz where 1,476 Polish political prisoners were burned to death during the night of 18/19th January 1945.

The prison had been a factory before the war and was converted into a camp for 'high security prisoners', the pseudonym for members of the Resistance. As in Poggenburg, they were at the mercy of the Gestapo, enduring interrogation before sentencing and transportation.

The Soviet army entered Lichtmanstadt on 17th January and met little resistance. By the 18th, it was said to be in full control of the city centre. It was too late for the Germans to organise an evacuation of the prisoners held in Radagosz and possibly the gunfire of executions would have attracted the attention of the Soviets. Another method had to be employed to destroy the prison and its contents. Gasoline was poured over the 1,500 men and the prison was torched.

The full story as to why the German garrison burned the prisoners alive remains a mystery. The horror of the local people who discovered the heaps of charred bodies next morning and the general chaos of the shifting war situation meant that the question has remained unanswered.

Twenty-four men survived by leaping into the water reservoir at the top of the building. Clinging to the sides of the tank in increasingly hot water, they remained concealed for several hours. Those that opted to leap from the first floor windows in order to escape the flames, were shot in flight by the guards waiting in the yard below.

A small museum commemorated the event, but when we made enquiries, we discovered that most of the facility was currently occupied by an exhibition concerning the Katyn forest massacre.

We joined the school children milling about among the exhibits. A large map on the wall showed the Katyn site and others. Also the prison camps where prisoners had been held before being slaughtered. It was a detailed chart of the entire operation. I was curious knowing that the Russians had admitted culpability in 1990 but totally unaware that other large mass graves had been found. Outside the exhibition at the museum reception desk, I bought a booklet on the subject. The concierge chatted with us and told us if we were prepared to wait, we could meet the archaeologist who had arranged the exhibits. This seemed to be a wonderful opportunity to learn about one event in Poland that had mystified the West for decades.

As we waited, I studied the text of my new purchase and rapidly became engrossed.

The discovery of mass grave in the Katyn forest had been made by a German/Polish investigation in 1943. The grave was opened and the thousands of bodies exhumed. Many were identified, including one Polish General. The International Red Cross filed a report on the findings. Evidence was given that the massacre had taken place in April/May 1940.

The Soviets had vehemently denied responsibility. They accused the Germans of the crime, claiming that the men had been executed after the Wehrmacht had taken control of the area. As I read on, it became clear that the Katyn forest burial site containing nearly 5,000 men, was only the tip of the iceberg. In 1940, approximately 15,000 prisoners, the officers of two Polish armies had been assembled by the Russians some 500km east of Warsaw. In 1940 the Katyn forest was still a part of the Soviet Domaine. If the massacre had occurred that spring only the Soviets could have committed the crime. But the myth that the Germans were to blame remained the accepted international and political version until 1989.

The families of the dead men knew that all communication from their fathers and brothers had ceased in the spring of 1940. The Katyn Family Association was formed and pressure applied to obtain answers. Finally, in 1989, Breznev delivered the prison lists that led to the uncovering of further mass graves in Miednoja and Charków.

In 1993–4, the newly discovered graves had been excavated. They contained the remains of an estimated 25,000 bodies, many more than the number of missing officers. Who else was buried with the army officers? Learning more would have to wait. The pages at the back of the booklet were translated into English, but it was only a short summary compared to the main details written in Polish.

Professor Maria Blomberg had disentangled herself from the party of school children who had been visiting the exhibition. She spoke no English but via Ania's interpretation, confirmed the findings described in the booklet. We had been shown into the lecture hall of the museum and had been joined by the museum curator. Most of the ensuing discussion went over my head as Ania explained what I was doing in Poland.

When Zabikowo was mentioned, the curator showed interest. He had found a film showing the awful results of the fire at Radagoszcz in January 1945, but mixed with it was footage taken of another camp that had been burned to the ground. The film had been rescued from a rubbish bin during a clear out of superfluous artefacts and there was uncertainty as to the identity of the second camp. Perhaps I could help.

Ten minutes later, triumphant, he returned with the film, set up the projector and switched off the lights.

The images of the devastation caused by the fire were sickening. The sight of heaps of bodies, the skulls blackened beyond recognition was horrendous. Suddenly, the scene changed – to Zabikowo, with for me the now familiar row of charred corpses found in one of the barracks and a view across the compound. Without the least hesitation, I was able to confirm the location. There were satisfied smiles and congratulations all round.

Why an Englishwoman should be the one to throw light on the problem, was to me mildly amusing if not bemusing.

That evening, I telephoned Ludwik in Poznań and told him what I had been doing. My enthusiasm shrivelled to embarrassed silence when he calmly informed me "my father died in this prison on 18th January 1945."

The world was too small. Under every stone, a scorpion lay waiting to strike.

My short telephone conversation with Professor Karel Poszpieszalski started another ball rolling. When I returned home, I contacted the Imperial War Museum to enquire about evidence that had emanated from the Poles. Using the speech made by Himmler in March 1940 as a 'marker', I hoped to trace the possible source for the material in Ainztein's book. The speech could not be traced.

I sent the professor a letter asking him how Himmler's speech had been obtained. The content had been contentious like the Wannsee Conference and the meeting must have been held in highly secure circumstances. I also asked him if he could throw any light on why it seemed to have disappeared from the reference annals of the West.

His reply arrived a few weeks later via his brother, Antoni. The speech had been overheard by the German soldier who was guarding the door. He had been horrified by what he heard. It was not unusual for such men to have sympathy for the Poles and he had reported what he had overheard to interested parties. As mentioned before, in 1943, Karel Poszpieszalski was officially appointed to collect evidence of war crimes by the AK. At the end of the war the evidence that he had collected was submitted via the Zachodni Institute to the Nuremberg investigations.

According to Poszpieszalski, it had got no further. The Soviet Commission at Nuremberg dismissed the evidence on the grounds that all information sourced from the Poles was 'unreliable'. Hence none of the material was taken into consideration for the trials. It was in effect 'buried'... unless Reuben Ainztein somehow had managed to get hold of it?

34

Kurzke's strange nightmares and his receiving of the Iron Cross 'for driving prisoners through hostile territory' in September 1939 remained a puzzle for a long time. Only when I discovered that the attack on the Gleiwitz German radio station was just one of three phoney attacks that took place in the early hours of September 1st, 1939, did I discover that the Gleiwitz attack had involved only one corpse, whereas the Customs Post at Hochlunden resulted in four victims that had been kitted out in Polish army uniforms.

Research into Kurzke's nightmares suggested that he witnessed the murder of the four criminal prisoners during the phoney 'attack' on the German customs post at Hochlunden during the early hours of September 1st, 1939. The action was one of three false flag operations that were undertaken by Heydrick and his Sicherheitsdienst (SD) who were commissioned to enact the 'attacks'; the radio station at Gleiwitz and a deserted keepers house being the other two targets. The exercise was devised to demonstrate that Poland had made the initial attack.

If Kurske had delivered the Polish uniforms, he may well have also driven the truck of an unmarked commando that delivered the doomed prisoners into Poland. What followed, the attack on the custom's post, and the murder in cold blood of his passengers in order for the press to take photographs of the corpses for propaganda purposes, would have been a rude introduction to the evils of the Nazi methods for the debonair football player. Nightmares could well have followed.

The above scenario conflicts with chapter 17 of Maria's memoir where Kurzke was supposed to be in Warsaw on the 1st September, 1939. Research reveals that all reservists and medical teams had been called up over a week earlier, and the scene described would have occurred well before the Germans invaded. A curious note is written at the top of the relevant page of the original manuscript that is written in German. It indicates that the page was drafted several times.

Was Maria creating an alibi for the man she adored?

The language barrier had always been a problem and it was not until the author had semi-mastered the art of reading the Polish language, that I seriously consulted the encyclopaedia that had been edited by dr Woźniak. The book concerned the Polish Resistance 1939–45. Listed alphabetically were the names and fate of members of the various underground groups.

Wozniak also described the groups themselves and their function, among them, the identity of the 'friends' that haunted Maria's story!

Many covert factions became active at the very start of the German invasion. The Arme Krajova (AK), the Polish home army directed by the Polish Government in Exile, only began to emerge as an organisation in 1942. Long before, in the new Reich territories of Greater Poland, groups had come together to assist their fellow countrymen. Printing presses hidden in cellars, provided news sheets as radios were forbidden and neither television nor iPhones had been invented. Identity papers and travel passes, etc. were forged and hiding places provided for those being hunted by the SD (Sicherheitsdienst) or Gestapo. Acts of sabotage in the region were few. The Nazi retribution was fatal for too many innocents.

In the General Government, for the first eight months of the war, numerous charities emerged to accommodate the hundreds of thousands of transportees that had been banished from Greater Poland. They needed food and shelter. With winter closing in, homes rapidly filled with two, three and four families. The trains, full of several thousand people continued to arrive each day. Massive overcrowding resulted. Unheated schools and factories became shelter for many, but destitute and desperate, the old and very young began to die.

Tens of thousands fled across the southern borders of Poland, travelling on foot through snow-covered mountains to Rumania and Hungary. With Germany to the west, Russia to the east and East Prussia in the north, it was the only possible escape route.

Understandably, the Poles hated the Germans and their Nazi methods and rallied to help their countrymen. Amid the frenzied chaos, however, an alien resistance group took root that historically has slipped under the radar.

Network 'A' (Siatka 'A') agents were of German origin! The 'folkedeutsch', families of mixed Polish/German extraction, had been horrified by the murder and deportation of their Polish relatives and friends during the first six months of the occupation and were united by a strong bond of anti-Naziism. Though sheltered from persecution, they were obliged to serve the German war effort. They were despised by the ethnic Poles – as traitors. Most men were drafted into the Wehrmacht. But some were posted into very different sections of the German system. An army of filing clerks were required to keep abreast of the mountain of paperwork that was generated by Gestapo arrests. Thus Siatka 'A' infiltrated the Gestapo HQ in Poznań; trojan horses that were able to confuse the records by mislaying files, altering names and planting disinformation.

The network escaped detection by the Gestapo. A few officers were arrested, but under interrogation, none betrayed the existence of the organisation. Surviving details of their activity are fragmented and lack cohesion. The connection to BLOC, a similar multinational anti-Nazi group in Berlin, is tenuous. It is possible that the Abwehr, the German intelligence service headed by Admiral Canaris was using BLOC to disperse financial support to agents. In March 1943, Piekenbrock, chief of the Army Intelligence division (Abwehr 1), was dismissed. He was suspected of having provided funds to a 'Major' who was of interest to the Gestapo. In the same month, Maria carried the suitcase full of deutschmark into Poland. Though supplied by BLOC, who was bankrolling the donations?

It is possible to surmise that Siatka 'A' formed a branch of Canaris's intelligence network. Throughout WWII, the Admiral had discretely combatted Nazi activities and the Folkesdeutch in Poland would have provided an excellent source for reliable agents.

Antonina had signed the Folkeslist. That she had been born and educated in Germany, possibly identified her as being German although both her parents were Polish. She naturally spoke fluent German with a genuine accent. She had already shown her courage and audacity at the very beginning of the war, when, having learned of the streets that would be cleared that night from Kurzke, she hurried out of the apartment to warn Polish friends who lived there.

Kurzke, serving in the police battalion from Hamburg and seconded to the Abwehr as a driver, was Antonina's direct connection with the Abwehr HQ in Berlin. On reaching Berlin, she would have been introduced to BLOC members. Working in a restaurant frequented by the Gestapo, gave her access to casual conversations that yielded sometimes important information.

The Gestapo had arrested, interrogated and executed all BLOC members during the summer of 1943 except for two women, one of whom had been employed in a restaurant!

Maria and Antonina had returned to Posen in March that year, escorted by Kurzke. Canaris agents possibly muddied the waters between the Gestapo HQ in Berlin and that in Posen so no connection was made with regard to the suitcase supplied by BLOC or its courier. Recognised by the Pill, mother and daughter were betrayed to the Gestapo, who arrested them initially for evading transportation in 1939. The suitcase was discovered later, incurring a death sentence for Maria as a 'dangerous political prisoner'.

At about the same time, an edict was issued by Berlin that any prisoner under a sentence of death could not be executed without the confirmation by the Berlin legal authorities. 'Accidental' deaths would no longer be acceptable. Was this an Abwehr ploy to protect their two agents? Was the delay of Kurzke's court marshal another? Losing the court confirmation of Maria's death sentence was certainly achieved with the help of Siatke 'A'. It is they who would have caused the piece of paper to go astray before it reached the commandant of Poggenburg.

It was also possible that the young guard with very shiny boots was a member of the network for, not only had he been sympathetic to Maria on at least two occasions. Immediately after Maria had been thrown into the ice pit for a second time, someone alerted Wiebekk, the camp inspector.

In a statement to the Americans after the war, Wiebek claimed that he was behind the release of twenty political prisoners from the Gestapo HQ in Poznań in January, 1945. At the time, his claim could not be substantiated. Only now is his statement confirmed, for Maria and her mother would have been among those he rescued.

Maria buried the identity of her 'friends' deep inside her memoire. Her occasional reference to them gave an eerie quirkiness to the text. Those references, however, acknowledge and give evidence of the existence of Siatka 'A' and the effectiveness of the network. If they had not existed, Maria would not have survived.

Beneath the glamour and drama of her own life experience lies evidence of a German anti-Nazi conspiracy and exposes methods used by German resistance agents. It is perhaps why she did not publish her memoire in her lifetime – too many of them were still alive – and the hawks were still hunting.

EPILOGUE

Maria, it still remains a mystery why you gave the manuscript of your story to me in 1986. Douglas Sutherland, the historian, spent many weeks in your home. Why did you not give it to him? He knew of its existence for his wife once asked me if I had it in my possession.

How you could foresee that I would one day be able to identify the different characters in your story is also a mystery to me. Did Stepanska teach you to read the cards when you were in Poggenburg? Could you see into the future? With coincidence playing a significant role throughout the investigation into your book, there were many times when predestination seemed to be in control. I do not subscribe to such ideas, but could not help but notice that time and again the project took on a life of its own.

The final answer to the question of whether you were a traitor or heroine is complicated. You collaborated with the Germans, treachery in Polish eyes. The collaboration was, however, with the sector of the German population that opposed the Nazi regime; a sector that schemed against Hitler and endeavoured several times to assassinate him. Does that make you a traitor to Poland? The same circumstances apply to your mother. She, though, was considerably more committed to the anti-Nazi cause and at the same time shielded her precious daughter. Does her courage and daring not earn her a claim to heroism?

Without the help, encouragement and support of many Polish people who warmly welcomed me into their homes, I would not have travelled so far down the road of discovery. Many of them have already joined your side of the divide between life and death. Dr Woźniak, Alfred Weidenmann, Mark Marriot and others are now sadly deceased. They all gave witness before leaving, however, and a thick file of documents concerning your case was lodged in the archives of the Instytut Zachodni by the industrious dr Woźniak.

Maria's Memoir

1

Could life ever have been so full of love and laughter, of innocence and light? It is like a shimmering dream, a delusion, as I recall the heavy wooden doors of the church, flung wide open in a welcoming gesture to the whole world; their solid majesty, a symbol of everything that was permanent and safe. I was just twelve years of age.

The air was crisp and clean on that Sunday morning in the spring of 1934 as the parishioners gathered to celebrate Holy Mass. In front of the church, the villagers crowded around the foot of the broad steps, the embroidery of their costumes mingling in a shifting mosaic of colour.

From the high altar, echoing down the pillared nave, came the faint tinkling sound of hand bells. The weather-beaten faces of the farmers turned towards the inner sanctum, where the priest raised the host aloft with both hands, stretching his arms upwards toward heaven. Heads bowed in united devotion. As the bells sounded again most of the villagers sank to their knees, the women gathering their voluminous white skirts in their arms as they knelt. The men, attired in tight lambskin trousers, merely bowed their heads until their chins rested on their chests.

The absolute silence was disturbed only by the priest's Latin words of prayer, reverberating from the distant altar deep within the church. In the pews and crowding the aisles, the worshippers were on their knees, paying homage at the moment of consecration. Shoulder to shoulder they stooped to venerate the host, their eyes cast down towards the flagstone floor. Had lightning streaked forth from the tabernacle which towered over the altar, it would have passed unnoticed, such was the devotion of the moment when the unleavened bread was turned into the Body of Christ and the wine transformed into His Blood.

The bells sounded for the third time and the kneeling congregation stirred. Mademoiselle Detienne slid onto the seat in front of the church organ and silently started to adjust the various knobs above the keyboard.

She looked up and glanced in the direction of the waiting girls. Catching my eye, she smiled and gave a slight nod of her head. She was ready to play and in the same moment, she had delivered a message of encouragement.

The music started on a low nostalgic note. It swelled in volume, wrapping itself around the marble pillars, the paintings, the golden angels and the statues, resounding down from the gallery to the flower laden altar below, resonating past the tightly packed congregation then drifting through the open doors to the crowd waiting at the foot of the steps.

The teacher looked up from the keyboard once again and her eyes flashed a signal in my direction. It was my cue. I was on my own. Stepping forward from the line of school girls, I stood apart, took a deep breath and started to sing.

"Mary, Queen of the May, we welcome you." The volume of noise softened, to allow my soprano voice to slice through the air, soaring over the ponderous tones of the organ.

As I sang, I was aware of the statue of the Virgin Mary, standing on a plinth beside the altar. It glowed in the light of a hundred candles, a golden crown around the head and surrounded by an abundance of blue, yellow and white flowers. The statue of the Mother of God, "Mary, Queen of May..."

The nuns, teachers and pupils from the boarding school visited the village of Szamotuly every year on the four Sundays in May, to attend Mass in the old church. The girls from the convent provided the choir and would assemble in the gallery, pictures of demure innocence in their neat, dark blue dresses. As I, like the church, bore the same name as the Holy Virgin, it was my lot to stand beside the organ that faced towards the altar at the far end of the nave and sing the hymn of the Mother of God "Mary, Queen of May..."

Tuta, Nina and all my other friends at the school envied me for the privilege of singing the solo. Their envy gave me not the slightest pleasure. To be honest, I was uncomfortable with my name, 'Maria'. I hoped that the beloved Mother of God would forgive me when I, with sincere reverence, would confess to her that after only a few religious lessons with Father Sylvester, I had experienced some disturbing thoughts.

As children will do, I imagined myself to be this saint or that apostle, identifying myself with the heroes of the wise old priest's stories. I felt physical pain when listening to the tale of 'The Sufferings of Saint Sabastian'. When we were taught about Prince Eugene, my imagination took off, riding on horseback against the satanic hordes, flags thundering aloft.

When it came to the Holy Virgin, however, I could not understand why, according to the Holy Book, she stood calmly at the foot of the wooden cross on which her son hung, dying in agony. How could she accept the situation without question? Why did she not scream her horror to the skies or take a sword, like Petrus or the Maid of Orleans and seek her revenge against His murderers. I could not understand her. Her reaction was contrary to every instinct that I owned. Yet I bore her name and the responsibilities that came with it.

The volume of noise from the organ increased, pulling me back to the present. I had been singing the hymn at the same time as my thoughts had been wandering. I felt so resentful about why I should be singing in the first place that I was not paying full attention to what I was doing. I did not care. Singing the solo was not so important to me and within seconds my mind continued on its deviant course.

Somewhere in Poland there had to be a hero or heroine that would fulfil my dreams. I had searched in books and sat expectantly in lessons, waiting for that special person to be discovered. Dear Lord, why did we not have a Joan of Warsaw or Łódź?

Why was Napoleon born in Corsica and not in Poland? Why was I called Maria? Why was I a girl? Female though I was, could I not take a sword and fight against the exploiters and enemies of my fatherland?

Reflected in the benign smile on the face of His servant, Father Sylvester, God always seemed to give his answer.

A bright ray of sunlight fell through the tall, narrow church windows. It slid, like a fine translucent veil, over the Madonna and came to rest on the carved, wooden statue of the holy man, Saint George, lance in hand, clad in shining armour astride his prancing charger, the slain black dragon twisted into a contorted heap beneath its hooves. The light shimmered around them. My thoughts shimmered in unison and I realised that the service was over and together with my class mates, I clambered down the dimly lit spiral staircase into bright sunshine.

"You sang very beautifully, Maria Theresa Weychanowna." Mother Superior said to me as I left the church. She gently laid her hand on my head and softly made the sign of the cross on my forehead with her thumb.

"Thank you, Mother", I responded, bending my knee slightly in a little curtsey as I had been taught. Sister Bonaventura too came over and smiled at me, endorsing the benediction of her superior. Her chubby face swelled into the frame of her white wimple. She had the open, good-natured features of a country woman, her healthy complexion somehow at odds with the severity of the pure white habit of the Ursuline order. She was popular and it was feared that we might lose her as our class Sister after the holidays.

We put on our dark blue straw hats and lined up in pairs, ready for the walk back to school. Tuta waited beside me, who else? Long ago when we first met and at the time unbeknown to each other, we had each sworn mutual, everlasting friendship. She seemed very slim in her school uniform, her narrow face dominated by a pair of large black eyes; eyes that never seemed to rest and were ever wide as though in endless question of everything about her. Those eyes fascinated me. They were like bottomless silent wells. Tuta was so self-controlled and quiet in many ways, a contrast to my impulsive nature. At times, when she lacked enthusiasm for my ideas and failed to respond to my persuasive arguments, she would begin to bore me. At such times, I would attach myself to Shefa, who possessed a somewhat wilder and more adventurous spirit, possibly inherited from her Hungarian mother. Sooner or later, however, I would return to Tuta where friendship meant peace and security.

The blue and white crocodile wound its way down the road. In front of me, walked the 'Lady', so dubbed because she was the daughter of the English Ambassador to Posen. When speaking Polish in class, her accent invariably caused peals of laughter. Far from taking umbrage, she would actually join in the merriment and laugh heartily at her own efforts. She rarely revealed her feelings and in the main lacked any signs of sentimentality, showing a sparkling degree of sober minded realism and maturity for her age. We were all, however, very wary of her critical sense of humour. This she could competently aim at her opponents with devastating effect. Her wit easily rallied laughter on her side, and the poor victim, in this instance, little Helliant, would suffer humiliation in the eyes of the attendant audience.

The 'Lady' had been the first to return to school after the holidays with varnished finger nails.

Mother Superior had been extremely annoyed by this act of defiance which prompted me to suggest to Tuta that we should include the 'Lady' in our League of Friendship. We had just read Caesar's *Bellum Gallicum* and the idea of the three of us forming a 'triumvirate' seemed an appealing possibility. But Tuta had reservations and suggested in reply that we should wait before issuing the invitation. Promising though the candidate seemed to be, she had been at the school for only a short while. Should she not come up to expectations, much unpleasantness could erupt from a broken agreement. After all, Tuta argued, there were plenty of examples in history that lead to war. She had made her point, and I had to agree. A few months were to be allowed to pass in order to assess the 'new one'.

The boarding school was built on a gentle slope, surrounded by park land. It took an hour of walking from Szamotuly before the towers and arched facade of the palace-styled convent came into view, the tall trees which surrounded it, competing with the turrets for the sky.

As soon as we were out of sight of the village, Mother Superior allowed us to break ranks and proceed in small groups of our own choosing. The 'Lady' immediately joined us and, linking arms, we marched abreast.

"She is wearing silk stockings, did you see?" Talking was forbidden whilst in crocodile formation. Tuta's words must have been burning her tongue, for they came, bubbling out of her mouth like water bursting through the wall of a dam.

We had all noticed of course that Mademoiselle Detienne was wearing sheer, silk stockings. Such things could be seen every day in Posen, but we were not used to being exposed to such luxuries in the convent enclaves. Not only were the stockings silk, but her shoes were the ultimate in fashion. Her cotton summer dress had a low neckline, not too low, but by convent standards – daring. Her general appearance was not blatantly ostentatious, and would easily have blended into the street setting of a small town without attracting attention. Here, however, compared to the dull school uniforms and the habits of the nuns and in contrast to the formal high buttoned black dresses of the rest of the staff, our Frenchwoman seemed to us to be like a ballerina in a sea of bad taste. Singled out by the footlights of a thousand envious eyes, she was the centre of our universe. The whole school loved her for her ability to maintain her individuality and flaunt it with the natural confidence of a star. As the theatre goer loves the heroine, so the school loved our French Lady, if only for her courage.

Mademoiselle Detienne was absolutely French, from the topmost hair of her head to the tip of her toe nail; in all her movements; in the charm of her accent and in the unconcerned way with which she continued to dress herself as though she was still teaching at the Seventh Preparatory school in St. Forbourg, near Paris. She was indeed very beautiful.

It was customary for the staff to wear long skirts. Mrs Szulkowa, our maths teacher used every available centimetre to hide her limbs, thus denying our mocking tongues a rare feast of gossip. In contrast, Mademoiselle Detienne did not need to be ashamed of her legs. She could reveal them even to the critical eyes of her students and be confidant that they would meet with approval. The same could be said for her hips, her waist, her bust, her shoulders and her neck, although most of those parts of her anatomy were, needless to say, modestly covered. Her slender hands with their long fingers for me, were her most enviable asset as they stretched over the keys of the organ, held a book or took hold of my own small hand. Everyone loved her, with the deep ardent passion that continues until death, so admirably described in the romantic novels that we read by torchlight under the bedclothes.

'The Lady' would laugh at us. "What is so special about her? She should use less rouge and she would look less like a painted whore." How I hated the English one when she was so destructive and, as now, when she mockingly swayed her hips and warbled "Ooh-la-la".

Mademoiselle Detienne must have heard what was going on, for she hesitated, then stopped and waited for us to draw level with her. She smiled at me.

"You have been known to sing better, my dear," she remarked. She alone had noticed that I had not been paying attention during the solo and was not afraid to criticise. She alone would not pay me any cheap compliments, unlike the Mother Superior. I felt a hot wave of blood rush towards my head, travelling up my neck until it tingled in my hair line. I must have looked pretty helpless and rather crimson. Mademoiselle Detienne laughed at my discomfort.

Oh, what perfect, pearly white teeth she had.

2

Pietro Cardell was a Spaniard. He was very slim and very tall with very shiny, black hair that waved down to his collar.

His arrival at the convent was contrived by Tuta's mother in league with my own. After Mademoiselle, he was the second arrow of inspiration that the twentieth century shot over the high walls into the seclusion of the nunnery.

He arrived at the gates of the Ursuline stronghold one fine spring morning, in a little car that puffed and panted as though suffering an asthmatic attack.

Little did he appreciate the significance that was attached to his advent. It had been anticipated since the previous term, when the rumours had circulated that petitions for ballet tuition to be added to the curriculum, had been successful. Now he was here, the Maitre de Ballet (no less), of the opera house in Posen. The Sister who guarded the gate admitted him without question. She had her instructions and, however much the look of disapproval on her face contrasted with her actions, she obeyed her orders and let the strange guest enter unchallenged. The religious order demanded blind obedience and Sister Monica had no intention of jeopardising the salvation of her soul by showing her true feelings with any obstructive behaviour.

Hence Pietro Cardell proceeded through the grounds, his car staggering along the drive as though it was the last journey that it would ever make. He was greeted by the Mother Superior who descended the front steps with ponderous dignity, her immaculate white habit giving her the air of a rotund ghost. Her manner was reserved and she betrayed no enthusiasm, but like Sister Monica, she appeared uneasy with the intrusion of the male visitor.

It had required a good deal of tactical persuasion, on the part of the mothers of a number of the girls, to influence the Ursulines. The idea of 'dancing' was the first concept that had to be introduced. Selection of a suitable teacher was the second hurdle. For the latter to be male as well, must have caused great consternation and caused considerable anxiety in the inner sanctums of the nuns' community. To point out the necessity of updating educational methods and keeping pace with modern trends would, in itself, have been insufficient argument. Tuta's mother, the Countess of Niemjewska, president of the Polish Women's Organisation, and my own mother who had only the previous year donated new furniture and curtains for all the dormitories, both gave the project their full support. Neither of these two ladies were used to having their wishes denied and thus it was, that Señor Cardell, the well known master of the art, was enlisted to teach their offspring the intricacies of the art of ballet dancing. The 'auditions' took place that same afternoon. We had put our books away a good half hour before the normal time for the conclusion of the day's lessons and assembled on the grass in front of the main building. Everyone was agog with curiosity and all eyes were riveted on the slender Spaniard. Señor Cardell seemed to be oblivious of his importance, nor did he appear to take much notice of the disapproving expressions on the faces of the nuns, which clearly illustrated their scepticism.

First, he stripped off his jacket and threw it, with a certain finesse, onto the grass where it fell into a crumpled heap. The nuns fidgeted a bit at this exhibition of flamboyancy. For a gentleman to take off any of his clothes in the presence of the opposite sex was definitely doubtful behaviour. To do so in front of a gaggle of school girls, was scandalous.

"So ladies!" He clapped his hands and rearranged the rather loud orange handkerchief that he was wearing under his open shirt. "En avantos. Please step forward – one at a time!"

In silence, he observed each girl as she advanced self-consciously from the ranks. His eyes scanned each individual with the sharp precision needed to make a quick assessment and select the most suitable candidates from the large number of applicants assembled. He had us walk on tip toe for as far or as long as we could manage before we lost balance and made us lift our arms above our heads as we turned full circle. In a strong no-nonsense voice, he divided us – "To the right! To the left! Left, left. To the right!"

It soon became obvious that the group being marshalled to right contained the girls that were of interest to him. Tuta and I were elated to find ourselves among them.

The whole exercise lasted barely twenty minutes. The nuns and teachers stood in a group, observing the proceedings, not making any attempt to interfere or object to any of the decisions except Mademoiselle Detienne, who, with a determined expression on her face could not resist intervening on behalf of one of her protégées. Mother Superior too, suddenly jolted out of her statuesque stupor, vigorously nodded in agreement when the French woman said, "With respect Señor, this young lady…"

The unsuspecting Spaniard was at that moment in the process of dismissing the 'Pill' to the left side. The little Wysieczka had earned her nickname on account of her sickly complexion. The general consensus of opinion blamed her lack of colour on her consumption of too many pills. It was a family failing as far as we were concerned. Her mother had the reputation of suffering from ten different complaints each day and subsequently took many different kinds of pills to cure each complaint. The 'Pill' only followed her mother's example! However, the 'Pill's' mother was also the wife of Poland's Deputy Minister of Agriculture and therefore a State-political personage, which made her frail and spindly daughter, a State-political child. Her very presence at the school was a State-advertisement for the convent. So it was unthinkable that she should be allowed to remain among the rejects on the left.

The Spaniard was not in the least bit impressed by the explanations that Mother Superior whispered discretely in his ear. He stepped back and bowed before her with faultless grace, at the same time managing to display a touch of irony. Disregarding her desire for confidentiality, he announced in a firm but melodious voice – "With regret, most gracious lady, the body is a gift from nature and dance is dependent on that gift. The pupils that I have selected on my right, represent a temporary choice only. More than half of them will fail to cope with the training and will join those on the left. Let your girls take part in gymnastics and sports. Everybody can do that and should." He put the tips of the fingers of his left hand to his lips like a connoisseur savouring the thought of a sensational taste. The fingers of the hand sprang wide, "But dancing is something very select and exquisite. Only a very few people are born to dance."

He bowed again as though he was on his opera stage acknowledging the applause then, sweeping up his jacket and casually throwing it over his shoulder, he turned his back on the astonished nun.

As he walked towards us, his charisma immediately had us spellbound. Nothing existed outside that small world.

"Well young ladies, now to work…" The afternoon bell broke the spell.

As I lay in bed that night, my thoughts were in turmoil. There it was again; the excellence; the inspiration; a role model that could provoke and stir one's inner being to burn with passion; an invitation to admire; to emulate and to worship – like Xerxes in *The Tempest*. That extraordinary man stood on the shore of the Hellespont and ordered his soldiers into the water, to whip the sea. The sea had aroused his fury by washing away his bridge of boats in a storm and thus prevented his army from crossing to the other side. He did not think to order the building of sacrificial altars or sinking offerings of gold in the waters to put the Gods into a favourable mood. No, he punished the sea itself, for daring to revolt against him.

Mother Sophia used to teach us ancient history, but seemed to lack any imagination or enthusiasm for the momentous stories in the school syllabus. She had the ability to make the sagas of the Persian king, Herodotus, sound like a biography of the tax department. With her spectacles perched on the end of her nose, her emaciated body bent over the book, the blackboard behind her half obliterated with obscure mathematical calculations, she could transform monumental magnificence into dry dust.

Instead of the classroom, we should have been sitting on a rock beside the sea with the eternal sound of breaking waves in our ears. A young Greek hero should stand before us in his chainmail vest, his arms stretched towards the sky. It would be he who told us of how Xerxes had ordered the execution of Sisamnes, one of the royal judges, because he had passed false sentence for monetary gain. He was to be skinned alive, as punishment. The golden-haired narrator would tell us how the king had ordered that the skin of the dead man be cut into strips and stretched over the judge's chair; and how he then demanded that the successor should sit on the same chair when making judgements. The successor was the son of Sisamnes and he was constantly reminded by the chair on which he sat, about the ethics of making suitable and fair judgement when passing sentence.

However dreary and monotonous the story sounded when crawling out of the mouth of Mother Sophia, to me, every word had colour and I was deeply disturbed by the tale. I began to love with more and more passion anything that was unique and outstanding; everything that reached out for the stars and beyond. My whole body would tremble with excitement when I felt the breath of inspiration upon me.

Was there not something greater than the power that man wielded through steel and cruelty? Was there no way to transcend to the soaring heights without the use of force; a way in which a woman could travel? Had the Spaniard not said only yesterday that dancing was something special, something uniquely wonderful?

The early morning Mass was the only hour of the day that we mentally had to ourselves. In the little chapel, kneeling on the wooden benches, I could forget the world about me. It was good to be alone with my thoughts and dreams. The dim, low-ceilinged room, filled with the subdued rhythms of prayer and the hum of the harmonium, provided a soothing ocean of sound in which to bathe. Even though the close proximity of my school friends caused our arms to physically touch, with my eyes closed, I could drift happily away from them all. No one could talk to me or interrupt my spiritual wanderings during the hour-long service of Holy Mass.

I did not think of myself as being less devout or even a sinner for such self-indulgence. True, Father Sylvester would threaten us repeatedly with a mountainous penance of prayer for such inattention to duty. But, as my thoughts lifted up my heart and my feelings echoed the holiness of the occasion, I was firmly convinced that I was not sinning. My religious fervour was never satisfied by the endless repetitions of traditional prayer. An original word, spoken from the heart, and an independent thought, inspired by the uplifting mood of the moment, should surely bring me closer to my Maker than all the formal incantations of the High Mass.

I considered my opinion was beyond reproach and had Father Sylvester reprimanded me for my attitude, I would have looked at him with astonishment. He would have had to possess psychic powers, however, as he could not have known unless I admitted it to him in the confessional. But as I did not consider that I was committing a sin, I did not need to confess!

As the Sanctus bell sounded through the chapel, I realised with a shock that my feelings towards the French woman had abruptly cooled down. The thought of her no longer caused me to tremble and I did not suffer pangs of jealousy when I saw her giving her attention to other girls. The idea of throwing myself from the highest point of the staircase to the flagstone floor below in order to demonstrate my anguish, seemed now to be a rather quaint, childish idea. Something new had taken over my life completely. It would seem that my loyalties could not be divided. There was no mourning for what had been. Instead, since the appearance of the Spaniard, dancing, with all its intangible vistas, filled every crevice of my mind.

Fifteen girls of all ages had been finally selected from the original group. Tuta, the 'Lady' and myself were among them. Señor Cardell visited the school three times a week, travelling back and forth from Posen in his dilapidated car. He usually found us already warming up in our gym slips, carrying out a number of exercises that had to be practised as often as we could manage during the daily school routine.

The assembly hall, the only large room available, had been fitted with bars along the wall so that we could use them to help maintain balance during these exercises. We determinedly made steady progress.

"Fourth position! Fifth position! Chassé! Plié." Señor Cardell was a merciless task master. It was not difficult to see, on the perplexed face of the Sister in charge of the wash room, how little she understood our enthusiasm for an activity that could transform her sweet, dainty angels into drooping rags, flushed with exertion and drenched in perspiration. Sister Bonaventure alone, instructed to provide the seemly presence of an adult female during the lessons as chaperon and to keep an eye on the Spaniard, only she showed any sign of comprehending the situation. She came to realise what effort was required and to applaud the eagerness with which we tried to do our best. She appreciated, as well as an observer could, the hard work and physical strain involved.

She did not, however, understand what sense or purpose could justify our efforts. She did not appreciate the effect the dancing lessons had on the other items on our time-table. She noticed that we paid less attention to our normal lessons and often fell asleep, especially during the maths period! Slumbering through the evening service in the chapel became a regular mishap. The lively ballet training sessions were detracting from our efficiency in dealing with academic demands and this did not meet with the approval of the sceptics. It did, however, inspire me to even greater application of mind and soul to my dancing, if only to defy them.

Each year, at the end of the summer term, a number of important officials from the school authorities in Posen, would arrive to oversee the complicated exam procedures. There always seemed to be enough of them to field a football team. The convent had a reputation to maintain and the nuns saw to it that we obtained the best marks that we could from these gentlemen. Mother Superior nursed the ambition that we should achieve higher marks than any other school in the country. The summer term that featured Señor Cardell lessons, was not a booming Academic success.

On the morning of the exams, I attended Holy Mass as usual. The harmonium, standing in the sacristy near the altar, began to play the final hymn. Father Sylvester turned from the tabernacle to deliver the blessing and Mother Superior rose to her feet and walked with sober dignity to the altar rail. Every morning, she was the first to receive Holy Communion at the end of the service. The other nuns, the lay teachers and class after class of girls, followed in an orderly file, hands clasped and heads bowed in reverence.

When I felt the cold altar steps beneath my knees, I could see, by squinting sideways, first the shoes and then the hem of the robes of the priest as he approached nearer and nearer. I raised my eyes for a short moment to glance at the gold ornamentation of the door of the tabernacle.

"Oh Lord in heaven, please let me be a great dancer, and, don't let me fail my maths."

The exams over, the distinguished dignitaries from the school examination board departed fully satisfied after a sumptuous farewell dinner.

The little Studienraf (master of secondary education) had left with them. This diminutive figure of a man, with his red face, who looked so clever and superior in his steel rimmed spectacles, had failed to notice that I had recourse to blow my nose rather frequently during the written maths paper. A heavy cold had not been my problem. Gaining access to the hieroglyphics that decorated my handkerchief had.

Afterwards, as we had filed out of the classroom, a hand fell on my shoulder. "Good, keep it up my daughter!"

Why was the little man congratulating me?

3

My one possession, adored above all else, was my pony. I yearned for his company and eagerly looked forward to the beginning of the holidays. At school, I would dream of the excitement and freedom that I enjoyed during our wild gallops.

When the school term was over and we were together at last I could be heard shouting with glee, "Castor, my gallant steed, faster. It's the holidays! Do you know what that means?"

The pony would lay his ears back into his flying mane. The grass reached upwards to his sweating belly. The soil, churned by his galloping feet, was black and heavy.

'Poland is fertile. Poland is a land blessed by God.'

The wind tousled my hair and as we swept past the cornfields that lay on either side of the road, the heavy ears on swaying stalks rose and fell like huge ripples on water; a golden yellow ocean.

We would career up hill and down for some time, my stallion leaping the tracks and pathways. Sparks flew whenever his iron clad hooves struck stone. Trees and bushes streaked past and I felt his mane lash my face whenever I ducked low to avoid overhanging branches.

Castor had been a gift from my father. He had been given to me when he was a tiny, awkward foal and I had watched him grow into a strong, handsome animal. I had always wanted a horse of my very own. Father and Grandfather both rode their own horses as was right and proper for any man. Castor had been my prize for persistence. I had begged long and hard for him.

Mother had been very upset when my dearest wish was fulfilled and had strictly forbidden that I should ever learn to actually ride him. "A girl should do other things," she would declare obstinately. To this end, she arranged for my hair to be permed, put me into organza or silk dresses and dragged me off to tea parties and other suitable female functions. But, she fought a losing battle.

When mother was away on a visit to Uncle Joseph, a Deacon in Witkowo, my father would ask for his horse to be saddled. He would sit me in front of him and take me out to ride until I was able to become one with the movement of the horse at all paces. In time, I was allowed to ride without him behind me. Thus in my mother's absence, I had learned to balance safely on my own without support.

I never learned to ride in a side-saddle, which was the ladylike way of sitting on horse back. My father would insist that to become part of the horse and ride well "One must feel the horse's body between the thighs." Hence he taught me to ride astride, like a boy.

Castor was now fully grown and I could ride where and when I wished, but I remember well one particular day when little did I realise how complicated life would become as a result of innocence. I felt elated. My beautiful steed stretched out his nose as we sped at full gallop towards the Niemrowski's farm, Tuta's country home.

An open carriage, drawn by two chestnut horses and decorated with meadow flowers drove along the rough farm track that ran along the edge of the wood. The surface of the track was so full of pot holes that the little vehicle, with its high spindly wheels, behaved like a ship caught in stormy weather.

"At last! You've got here. We were getting bored waiting for you. Where have you been? Władyhas absolutely no idea how to behave as a bride. He's hopeless!" cried Tuta, standing on the upholstered leather seats and brandishing her white top hat. Her brother, two years her junior, climbed up to join her.

"It's no use," he shouted. "Three people are needed to play weddings and it doesn't work with only two. Where have you been, Maria? You're supposed to be the priest, not a wild brigand!" Włady gesticulated with his arms, indicating his approval of his sister's verdict and giving emphasise his own frustration. He looked not a little comical, standing next to Tuta, clad in my white summer dress. A lace curtain was secured to his head for a veil and in his hand he clutched a bunch of wilting flowers.

I was unable to stop myself giggling as I steadied Castor and adjusted his speed to ride beside the carriage. Frantisek, the groom, turned to look at me from the driving seat, and grinned. The stable lad had been told to accompany us for protection and supervision, but the expression on his face suggested that he was enjoying the fun and would join in the spirit of the game.

"I want my trousers back!" complained Włady. He had realised that, dressed as he was in girl's clothes, he was the source of our amusement and was very near to tears.

I took mercy on him. "Over there, in the stables," I said. "We can't change here, it's too public. We could be seen by just anybody." Władly accepted this, but his face bore evidence of his dissatisfaction with the delay.

Earlier that afternoon when we had been playing in the stables of the farm, I had tricked Władly into swapping his trousers for my dress. "How would you like to be the bride for a change?" I had suggested and he had eventually agreed to my idea. My ulterior motive had been to get my hands on his trousers, as they were far more practical for riding than the frilly summer dress that my mother had chosen for me that morning.

Tuta had not been too pleased at first. Her height demanded that she always played the groom and she therefore felt that should have had some say as to who should play the bride. Hitherto it had naturally enough been my part to play. To expect any finesse from a younger brother in such a role was asking for the impossible. He hardly looked the part. My dress was too big for him and it drooped sadly from his shoulders and the veil did not disguise the fact that he had short hair. Nevertheless, after a lot of argument, I had my way. To compensate, I had promised them an outstandingly moving sermon in my new role as the priest, a feat that would have been beyond Władly's capabilities.

With reluctance, Władly had taken off his knee-length trousers and thrown them over the partition into the next stable where I waited to put them on. It had been a bit of a squeeze, getting into them and the clinging fit would have caused my mother's hair to fall out had she seen me. But I was not worried, only anxious to be ready to escape on my pony... to freedom. My dress, I had carefully passed back to Władly across the feeding trough.

Frantisek had fetched my pony and lifted me into the saddle, I had trembled with excitement. At last, I was sitting astride my little black stallion, dressed as a man should be. Castor was keen to be off and soon, I was singing my heart out to the world as we cantered gaily away from the farm.

"The sermon!" said Tuta. "We haven't done the wedding ceremony yet, and you promised us a good sermon. You went off on your own and left us, so we haven't really started yet!" Tuta did not want to miss out on the grand conclusion of our game. Władly, however, had lost all enthusiasm for such a charade. Tearing the veil from his head, he again demanded in belligerent tones, to have his trousers back. He was eleven years old and well past the age for a boy to be dress up as a girl.

Frantisek suddenly took matters into his hands. He cracked his whip and urged the two carriage horses forward. I closed my legs on Castor and turned him to follow the departing carriage. Within a few strides, all the horses broke into a trot and past the big oak tree, where the field track joined the road, the speed increased to a canter. The barns and cow shed flew past, Castor now competing with the harnessed horses to take the lead. On approaching the office building, we slowed down and proceeded at a steady trot to the stable yard, decorum restored.

Although my father did not approve, I had always enjoyed riding straight into the stable rather than dismount in the yard. Frantisek knew this and after he had unhitched the two chestnuts from the carriage, he opened the double doors leading into the stables so that I could enter the cool gloom beyond.

The big stable block was quite empty. All the other horses were out working in the fields. The sweet smell of hay mingled with leather greeted me and as I rode down the passage between the boxes, Caster's hooves making a hollow ringing sound on the cobbled floor. The noise magnified and echoed until the whole stable seemed to be filled with a battalion of chargers. When I reached his box, I threw the reins up Castor's neck, kicked my feet free of the stirrups and swung my right leg over his back to dismount.

Frantisek appeared from nowhere. He must have abandoned the carriage horses and followed me down the passage. His shirt sleeves were rolled up to his elbows, exposing his deeply tanned arms. They reached up towards me. I started to slide off the saddle but instead of supporting me until my feet touched the ground, he swept me up in his arms. I wanted to shout as he hugged me so tightly to his chest, that I feared I would break, but found that I could not utter a sound. I was so hot and breathless after the ride and so surprised by Frantisek's boldness that I was literally struck dumb.

Unable to call for help, I tried to wriggle free of his grasp, but to no avail. His arms were strong and he – determined. As he buried his face in my hair, the only thing that I could do, was to stretch my head away from him as far as possible.

I suddenly realised that I was not in the least afraid. The initial hot surge of panic cooled abruptly as though I had taken a cold shower. I found myself staring at the stable lad's face. Frantisek had his eyes closed and I was fascinated by the strange contortions that were distorting his features. The more the muscles of his jaw protruded, the more the dark vein on his forehead swelled and the harder he crushed me to him.

He gradually seemed to become aware of my stillness and opened his eyes slowly, uttering a deep sigh. The look in his large black eyes at first seemed vague and dreamy. Only on meeting my questioning gaze did they snap into focus. Immediately, the lad eased his hold and as though I were made of the finest china, he lowered me down carefully to the floor. He tried to smile, but embarrassment turned it into a grimace which seemed to express regret, apology and a plea for secrecy, all mixed up together.

Without a word, I turned and walked away from him, down the passageway towards the yard doors. Tuta was standing in the exit and from the look on her face I knew that she had witnessed the whole episode. She followed me silently into the corner of a stable, where the impatient Wład20 sprawled on the straw, struggling to extricate himself from my dress. I heard the groom moving about with a bucket as he started to water my pony at the other end of the stable block. The straw bales were stacked to the roof and I hid behind them to take off Włady's trousers.

I pulled my dress down over my head and as Tuta helped me by buttoning up the back, she whispered in my ear.

"Do you know that when a man holds a woman really tight to him and has certain thoughts, the woman is going to have a baby?" She was flushed with excitement and her words tumbled in a breathless gabble.

Suddenly my arms and legs felt as heavy as lead. I could still feel Frantisek's powerful embrace and could see his grotesque face, eyes closed, jaw set, blood vessels throbbing, coming closer, closer, ever closer.

Tuta's words had reminded me of the innocent chatter and speculations that thrive amongst school girls. I was still very confused as to how babies appeared in the world. Gossip and rumour were our only teachers on the subject. The cinema camera always remained discretely outside the bedroom door and sex education in a convent school got no further than the Immaculate Conception.

I longed for the 'Lady', with her fund of worldly wisdom. It would have been a relief to talk to her about our new and terrible secret. I recalled a multitude of occasions when our feelings and ideas had been so muddled that we were at our wits end. We only had to present the 'Lady' with our problems and her clear headed thinking would instantly unravel the strands and provide solutions that should have been obvious to us from the start. We often wondered why we had needed to consult the English girl at all, when the answers to this or that question were so simple.

But, we always did refer to her for her opinion because she had the perfect strategy for dealing with any problem. Her intuitive logic pointed us in the right direction so that we could find our own conclusion. It was as though she held the key and when she loaned it to us, we could open the lock ourselves.

Unfortunately for us, the 'Lady' was not available for consultation. She was far away on a luxury cruise liner, floating about somewhere on the Atlantic Ocean. Her parents had decided that she should travel with them to New York during the summer holidays. Only the previous day, a picture postcard with multi-coloured Portuguese stamps had arrived, bearing her signature in an illegible flourish. The 'Lady' and her practical logic were inaccessible.

Tuta was at my side, however, giving me moral support and treating me like a Madonna. My every word was her command. We renewed our bond of friendship behind the wash house door and swore to keep our mutual secret absolutely to ourselves, until the birth of the child made it no longer possible. How long this would be, Tuta vowed to discover. We talked it over and agreed that it would be safer if I did not ask that particular question. If I aroused suspicion, it might lead to the drama of an early confession.

Even so, I could not resist the temptation to discuss the circumstances of my own birth with Vera, our maid. Her mother had worked for my family since time began and Vera herself had grown up within the household. She had cared for me since the day that I was born, always with a special affection and love. I was cautious how I brought the conversation round to the subject matter that dominated my thoughts, for I was unsure of her reaction. I need not have worried. She seemed to feel honoured that I had thought of approaching her about such a topic and answered freely. Such questions as to how I had looked on arrival, what food a tiny baby eats, details about health and sleeping habits and so on, she answered as though they were the simplest and most normal things in the world.

She told me with considerable pride, about her own contribution to my upbringing and at no time did the kindly, genuine soul seem to suspect the true nature of my sudden interest in child development.

4

During this period of my life, my deepest love belonged to my father. I was an only child and he saw in me, the son that he did not have, a young companion and friend and he treated me accordingly. My mother, on the other hand, tried to prepare me for the demands that are expected of a young lady in society.

She would take me with her to her salon to select dresses in keeping with the latest fashion. At the hairdresser, she made sure that I received the same attention as she did herself. My interest in music was encouraged and, of equal importance to her, was the understanding of the subtleties of facial make-up. A dainty white piano, a true work of art, built by a well-known master craftsman in Warsaw, found its way into my room and by the opposite wall stood an equally expensive dressing table with its matching stool. I should have been delighted by the angled reflections that could be seen in its folding mirrors. They invited experiment with different hair styles and cosmetics, but somehow, they did not amuse or attract me as they should.

Father's bicycle, with its tubes, tyres and a dynamo was something else. It was also thrilling to drive his car, sitting in front of him in the driving seat, the steering wheel in my hands. He would work the pedals and change the gears and I would concentrate on keeping the car on the road as we sped faster and faster. Sometimes, he would take me rowing on the lake in his boat and then, I would lay my head on his shoulder as he pulled at the oars, savouring the moments which the two of us spent together. How I enjoyed his company. It meant so much more to me than the feminine temptations offered by my mother.

My father was a tall broad shouldered man. His walk was not light and expressionless like the town dweller who is used to treading on asphalt. In contrast, he walked with a purposeful stride that carried him easily over uneven meadows or along rutted tracks, just as his forbearers. There was always the delicious smell of the forest on his clothes when he returned from shooting or hunting.

He was a descendant of the free Mambry, a mountain people. Members of this clan were easy to recognise for their height which was above average and the proud way that they carried their heads. In evening dress, at dinners and dances they would stand out in a throng, mainly because of their regal bearing. I adored my father and everything about him, not least because he was descended from a brave and famous family. One of his ancestors had once received honours for disposing of a bandit, called 'Capitan'. The rogue was beholden to no law and had been much feared in the region, until one day he met my great-grandfather.

My great-grandfather had been unarmed and therefore had to use his bare hands for the fight, but it had taken him only seconds to catch the villain in a vice-like hold. He gradually forced the head back, until suddenly it was over, 'Capitan's' neck snapped and his nose pointed in the opposite direction. This feat was commemorated by a plaque for all to see in Posen at the Raczinskihaus (town hall) in Wilhelms Square.

My father had inherited those big strong hands and I could understand how helpless his opponent would be, if he ever used them in anger.

My enthusiasm for my father suffered the first heavy blow, when he mentioned during lunch that he had received a visit from a certain Spaniard. Señor Cardell, for it could only have been he who had tried to persuade him that his daughter showed talent and promise and should train to become a ballet dancer. This had not met with my father's approval. As he spoke to us, his voice was peppered with a biting irony. At the time, it had never occurred to him to consult either my mother or myself for our opinion and if he had not been so affronted by the Spaniards impudence, we might not have heard about the interview at all. In his own mind, he had completely dismissed the idea of his daughter taking serious dancing lessons with the intention of making public appearances on the stage in the opera house. The whole idea was unthinkable to him. He had reached for his favourite French wine, making derogatory remarks about crazy ballet masters and laughing at his own wit.

Suddenly, he was a stranger. I did not recognise this arrogant fellow who was so derisive of something that I cherished. From this day forth, my love and affections turned in my mother's direction.

It had been at my request that Señor Cardell had sought my father's blessing on the scheme. He was preparing a ballet with children at the opera house in Posen for the Christmas celebrations and had asked me to commence training in order to dance two of the solo numbers. Naturally, I had wanted to accept the challenge. I had been truly excited by the idea. The Spaniard had first spoken to me one morning at the tram stop. Vera had been with me and we had just climbed down from the tram when Cardell accosted us. He had been in a very cheerful mood and his smile had stretched from ear to ear. His proposals for the children's ballet had just been accepted at the stage meeting and he was positively glowing in his triumph. It was a project for which he had fought long and hard. However, he would depend on my support for the production and implored me not to let him down. I assured him that I would do anything to help, but insisted that he met my father to seek his blessing on the idea.

However, judging by his casual dismissal of the whole idea, it seemed that my involvement to date with dancing had passed unnoticed by my father.

My mother protested on my behalf. She was adamant that my father should not have the last word. After his outburst at the table, she consoled me as best she could. At breakfast the following morning, I was aware that she had continued the battle into the night. The bedroom had become a place of tournament and with lance and shield, she had attacked and parried, fighting for her daughter's ambition, but, as the sun rose on a new day, it was apparent that the opponent was still in the saddle.

My father watched me warily. He did not speak, neither did my mother. He seemed to be trying to picture me on the theatre stage and could not reach a satisfactory conclusion. He had not finished his breakfast, when he suddenly got up from the table, announced in querulous tones that "Surely, we are not a family of circus acrobats" and marched out of the room, slamming the door behind him.

Mother decided that it would be best if I let her deal with my father on her own; that she would make greater inroads into his stubborn attitudes if I were absent for a few days.

"You'd best go and stay with Uncle Joseph for two or three days," she suggested. She detested delay and in a trice, I was popped into a coach and was on my way to Witkowo.

Vera travelled with me, dressed in her Sunday best, an embroidered costume which her mother had worn before her. On her knees, she balanced a large travelling bag that contained my personal necessities for the short visit and a packet of refreshments for the journey.

It was not far from Posen to Witkowo and the horses had covered the distance by early afternoon. Uncle Joseph had visited us only a fortnight earlier and had been very nice to me. He had cordially invited me to spend a few days at the deanery before I returned to school at the end of the holidays.

I had found the somewhat stout but handsome man quite likeable, with his badge of office, a golden cross, hanging from a golden chain, in the centre of his chest. His little eyes would dart mischievously from one person to the next as he chatted about the colourful episodes that he had experienced during his parochial duties. He had proved amusing company.

The dean was not actually a blood relation of mine. I called him 'Uncle' as was customary when addressing close friends of the family. He had been an old school friend of my mother and it was she who had given him financial support during his theological studies. This continued, when he later took up his first appointment in a country parish and he had experienced hard times. It looked at one period of his studies, as though he would forsake his clerical career to find a more comfortable way to make a living. My father too, had helped him when first married to my mother until life gradually improved for their protegé as he received promotion after promotion. Finally, heaven had blessed him with the appointment to the rank of a dean, although in earthly terms, the news arrived in the form of a letter from the bishop.

"Our 3,000 zloty have grown well and pleased the Lord," were my father's words of greeting when Uncle Joseph came to see us soon after his latest elevation to higher office. Father had, I think, been referring to the small fortune that he and mother had contributed over the years.

"Are you hungry, Maria?" The faithful Vera had opened the travel bag. The mention of food was usually guaranteed to arouse my interest, but on this occasion, I was so deep in thought that I failed to even reply to the woman's question. I was dreaming. The events of the last few days had left me thoroughly confused. The future was suddenly so very unpredictable. The disagreement between my parents had shaken me and with the possibility of a baby looming in the distance, my safe little world seemed to be on the verge of disintegration.

I found some comfort in the broad back of the coachman in front of me. He was an elderly man from the neighbourhood, who had been enlisted by mother at short notice and as a matter of urgency. His brown cord jacket was badly torn with a large black patch down the left side. He was obviously poor, but his stolid figure was somehow a reassurance that the world was real and not an intangible nightmare of disappointment.

I did not complain when my mother proposed that I visit Uncle Joseph. When he had shaken hands with me on his departure, I had found his strong, firm grip convinced me that here was a man that I could trust.

We reached the paved road of the outskirts of Witkowo in the early afternoon. At first the houses on the right and left were scattered, but as we progressed, they increased in density until we drove through streets, lined with rows of small dwellings, huddled close together. At last, the coachman reigned the horses to a standstill in front of a two storey building, set back from the rest. The porch was supported by two pillars and the double doors beneath it were each decorated with an imposing cross, carved deep into the wood.

Our arrival had not gone unnoticed. An elderly woman emerged through the doors and came down the steps to meet us. As she paused to tie the strings of her apron, Vera and I climbed down from the carriage and approached the house through the meticulously tidy front garden.

"The reverend is out on business, I'm afraid," she said, then added hurriedly, "...but he is expected back within the hour."

She ushered us into the house and relieved me of my coat and hat, explaining that the dean had mentioned that a young lady might soon be visiting for a few days, but had not been able to tell her exactly when it would be. She assured us that he would be delighted that I had arrived so unexpectedly and that it would be a nice surprise for him on his return. She took the travelling bag from Vera and offered some refreshment.

Having assessed that I was in safe hands, Vera declined her hospitality and requested that she be permitted to return home without delay. The coachman was anxious to cover as much as possible of the return journey before the daylight faded. This made me a little apprehensive. It had never entered my head that my companion would leave me quite so soon and I panicked when she made to leave.

Vera knew me well and recognised the signals. She promptly enquired of the housekeeper if my room was available and escorted me up the stairs to my temporary accommodation. Her air of quiet efficiency restored my confidence and I was able to release her. We parted, Vera promising to return on the following Saturday to collect me. It would only be a short visit of three days. My little room looked out over the front garden. From the narrow window, I waved a tentative farewell to Vera, who waved back from the open carriage as it disappeared down the road.

The bed was high and narrow. It would have been more at home in a country house from whence it had probably originated. I poured water from the china jug into the washbowl and rinsed the dust from my hands and face. Afterwards, I found the study, where I decided to wait for the dean's return.

The housekeeper bustled into the room with a white tablecloth folded over her arm. As she busied herself laying the supper table for two, she asked me all sorts of questions. She was curious to know how my parents had become so well acquainted with the dean and why the friendship was so amicable. She seemed to assume that I would enlighten her without realising that she was trespassing on knowledge that she had no right to know.

Like many adults, she made the mistake of assuming that a child (she obviously regarded me as such) will automatically respond openly. I resented this and my answers contained little useful information. My mood, as a result of recent experience bruising my innocence, did not permit me to trust the older generation as blindly as I had earlier.

At last, she was finished. The cutlery had been moved several times in order to create a delay so that her inquisition could be prolonged. But duties in the kitchen eventually called her away and I was left alone. For the first time I became aware of the room itself. Its dreariness started to drag my spirit lower. The corner in which the writing desk stood was overcrowded with dark green leafy plants. The arm chairs were covered in brown leather and the sofa in which I sat had certainly seen better days. Pictures of the sufferings of Christ adorned the walls.

Suddenly, Uncle Joseph stood in the doorway, laughing merrily, his eyes twinkling and his arms outstretched in greeting. "Look who is here... Maria! Dropping in like a stray leaf, blown by the wind! What a delightful surprise!"

He threw his hat in one direction and his coat in another. The golden cross on his chest glistened as he stepped into the stronger light of the standard lamp behind the sofa. He chatted and joked, sometimes with the housekeeper, sometimes with me. He checked his mail, reading aloud the contents of the letters. He took off his town shoes and found his slippers, rattled the canary's cage by the window and the dark and depressing room was transformed. Suddenly it was brimming with the boisterous cheerfulness of the Dean.

"A bottle to celebrate the evening," he ordered, as though his living room was a restaurant and the housekeeper a waitress.

Soon, we were seated on opposite sides of the little table and the Dean offered me food and wine. His behaviour was that of a host trying to make a good impression and he treated me like a lady. It was not long before the effects of the wine and the novelty of being spoken to as an adult affected my tongue and I too became talkative. The whole situation was a step into the unknown. Never before had I sat at table in a strange house with a lone male, nor was I used to being treated by a respected personage as an intelligent and witty person in my own right. Soon, I felt my cheeks glow. I could not sit still. Like my host, I became animated and bobbed about in my chair in my enthusiasm, never still for a second. When the dean extracted a liqueur from his wall cabinet, however,

I declined. This would have been going too far. At home, I had been given the occasional glass of wine, but never liqueurs or brandy.

"It is not a sin today, little Maria! Absolvo te!" he joked, as he made the sign of the cross on my forehead, "and such a small glass won't do you any harm."

We drank to the health of my parents… and another to my visit… and a third, (at my suggestion) to the health of the Very Reverend. In the interim, the table had been cleared. We rose eventually from the empty table and settled into the comfortable arm chairs. The dean lit a cigar and as he relaxed behind a cloud of smoke, the bubbling fountain of conversation dried up. The rhythmic ticking of the clock seemed to fill the room, having a mesmerising effect on me and my eyelids became heavy.

Uncle Joseph noticed my drowsiness and, lifting me from the armchair, he carried me to the sofa where his soft hands gently removed my shoes. Suddenly a thought raced through my head like a herd of galloping horses. Were these not the hands that had transmitted trust when I shook them? Would they betray the pledge that I had sworn with Tuta? I would never have the courage to talk with my parents about our secret. But Uncle Joseph, surely, to him, I could tell everything. He would understand.

"Uncle Joseph, tell me… I have a…" I tried to make sense, but my words and my brain seemed to pull in different directions. The dean, who had just put my shoes on the floor, rose and looked at me inquiringly. I was in the full light of the lamp and he could not help but notice my flushed face.

"What is worrying my little Maria?" he asked, sitting down beside me and placing both of his hands on my arm.

"It's rather difficult, Uncle Joseph, and I've sworn not to talk about it actually…"

Another thought struck me and I heard my mouth saying, "A priest has to keep a confessional secret, has he not? Does this apply to a dean too?" If this were true, I could be quite open to him about my problem.

Uncle Joseph smiled, but his eyes were not dancing any more. They gazed down at me, the carefree sparkle missing. "Is it so hard? What has my little Maria got to tell me that is so secret?" The dean then leant over me, peering intently at my face, his golden cross dangling close to my lips.

"It's not that I want to confess, I mean, it's… because no one must find out what I am going to tell you, especially my mother or father."

"No one in the world, little Maria!" His voice was soothing, inviting confidence.

"The thing is..." again I faltered. "The thing is, Uncle Joseph, Frantisek, the stable boy at the Nieumrowski farm, he, he... he..." Suddenly my heart stopped. My mouth repeated mechanically "he... he..." again and again.

The man leaning over me, his golden cross touching my lips, had inserted his hand under my skirt and was stroking my thighs. The limb felt heavy against my flesh and cold like a stone.

I leapt to my feet, thrusting the dean aside. He looked surprised and his eyes flickered nervously. Grabbing my shoes, I fled from the room. I yanked open the huge front doors, racing down the steps and through the garden into the street before the Very Reverend had time to recover himself.

Barefoot, I ran headlong down the road and into the night.

5

The wind was cold and lashed my face. The trees seemed to applaud, their great shadows heaving as I raced past them. When I could flee no more, my breath reduced to sobbing gasps, I crumpled into the shelter of a wall. It was some minutes before I could start to think and reducing the cold became my first priority.

I spent the night in a barn on the edge of the village. I had heard that it was warm to sleep in hay.

I was not warm. I shivered until I fell into fitful sleep. When I heard the first horse drawn carts rumble by, I left my hiding place and crept back to the neighbourhood of the vicarage, slipping behind trees or into doorways, whenever I heard approaching footsteps. I found a hiding place in a small stable close to the deanery where I could observe the front door through the feeding rack. Dawn had broken and most of the farm labourers had already left for the fields with their animals. Before long, Uncle Joseph left the house, wearing his hat and coat. He passed so close to me that I could have touched him. But he seemed preoccupied, ignoring totally a woman who greeted him by respectfully bowing her head as she passed.

The next few minutes seemed interminable. I emerged, cautiously watching the road in case Uncle Joseph should unexpectedly return. But, there was no sign of my treacherous uncle and I slid out of the stable, wishing that I could make myself invisible.

As I approached the house, I tried to imagine what the housekeeper would have to say when I asked her for my coat and bag.

Curiously, she said nothing. She neither argued nor demanded an explanation. She even helped me to find transport and promised to give to the dean the letter that I had written in which I excused my sudden departure and assured him, in a gesture of youthful generosity, that I would tell no one of the incident. The unexpected cooperation of the housekeeper seemed oddly well rehearsed.

On the journey back to Posen, I had plenty of time to think about the events of the previous evening. I was very confused. The adventure with the stable lad was inevitably included in the tangle. I found myself remembering a scene in a theatre play, when a sailor had thrown himself over a woman and smothered her with kisses. My impression at the time had been that he was doing his best to suffocate her. I had seen too, lovers in the evening, absorbed in each other. Slowly I was associating all these things together.

Was there something inside us that had a willpower of its own; something that hides within us like a crouching animal waiting to spring? If that were so, if the wearer of a dean's golden cross could not tame the beast, Frantisek's misdeed could almost be excused.

Father Sylvester preached that the God Almighty could see and hear everything. He had also said that the Heavenly Father loves mankind. Then why did he not provide men with the ability to free themselves of this serpent? A twitch of His left hand could have done it! Yet, and my reasoning folded back on itself, maybe, this was the sin of Adam and Eve? God had permitted the animal then, to rear its head. Why should he do otherwise now?

It was only when we arrived home that the problem occurred to me of how I was to explain to my mother the circumstances of my premature return. I had no money and had to ask the coachman to wait while I found Vera, so that she should reimburse him with the necessary fare for bringing me home. Hurtling in through the front door, I almost collided with an unfamiliar young man who was on his way out.

There was a dark blue car parked in the drive. The boot was open and the young man in brown uniform was engaged in transporting pieces of luggage into the house. It looked very much as though my grandfather had returned from Yugoslavia and I assumed that possibly the young man was his personal valet. The uniform that he wore was that of 'Sokol', a youth organisation which had recently been formed by my grandfather.

The driver of the car was indeed my grandfather. His unexpected appearance had turned the household upside down and as a result I was spared the necessity of explaining the reasons for my unscheduled return. Grandfather had already asked after me and expressed his disappointment when he learned that I was away from home. Thus, when I suddenly appeared in their midst, no one thought to ask where I had been or how I had managed to materialise from wherever it was. Such queries were quite irrelevant compared to the excitement of a family reunion.

The old gentleman wore a grey travelling suit. He lifted me up and whirled me about the room, laughing merrily as he did so, before setting me down by the sideboard. On the top of the sideboard lay a traditional Serbian national costume, made of white silk and covered with beautiful hand embroidery... and to my delight, I realised that it was for me!

Without delay, I had to try it on. Vera helped me, but even she did not question me as to why I had not stayed with Uncle Joseph until the Saturday, occupied as she was with the arrangement of the dress to perfection. Minutes later, I was the central attraction, parading up and down before an admiring audience in my new finery.

Eventually, Grandfather sat me on his knee and I became aware of the four elderly gentlemen, sitting at the table with my parents. Two of them wore the uniforms of Polish officers. Tobacco smoke filled the room and a lively discussion, which undoubtedly I had interrupted, was resumed.

"They are more alert down there. The Serbian nationalists have already joined up with the Croats and Czechs. Every fish wife in Zagreb knows what we should do in a crisis."

"If Gdansk is only an excuse, don't imagine they are building planes and tanks like mad, just to drink duty free Gdansk Goldwater yet again."

My Grandfather vigorously stubbed out his cigar in the ash tray, causing me to slip from his knee as he abruptly rose to his feet and called loudly to the young man who I had seen unloading the luggage.

"Come here, Janek, here to the window." He sat down again and the boy stood to attention in front of him.

"It is up to you youngsters, Mirka," (his pet name for me), "to strike a spark and wake up our sleeping society. Look at his uniform, Mirka, already more than 300,000 young people wear it – from Sarajewo to the Alpine mountains and throughout Czechoslovakia. There are as yet only a few hundred in Poland, but I shall not rest until every boy and girl of your age knows what the options are, so that they can decide whether or not to defend their fatherland. As sure as I'm your grandfather, I shall see that they are forewarned. You shall shout 'here' and stand up to be counted, not hide in mouse holes like your parents – Jeszcze Polska nie zginela! (Poland is not yet lost!)"

He invited the young man to the table, poured out two glasses and proposed a toast.

"To the future!" he boomed.

Everyone rose to their feet, raised their glasses and drank.

6

The holidays neared their conclusion and I was looking forward to returning to boarding school with mixed feelings. On the plus side, I wanted to hear about the adventures that my school friends had experienced during the summer vacation. I was anxious to find out which nuns and new teachers would be taking the lessons during the forthcoming school year. Most important, I was impatient to show off the various presents that I had received from my parents and relatives. I would not be the only one flaunting my possessions and admiring envy was the reward awaiting the owner of the best.

On the negative side, I feared going to chapel for the first Mass of the term. At home, it had been possible to deceive my parents when they had taken me to church for Communion on Sundays. On one occasion, I had 'absentmindedly' eaten cake beforehand, which automatically excused me from receiving the sacrament.

On other occasions, I had mysteriously become separated from my mother at the altar rail, losing myself in the crowd and returning to my seat in another queue. There I would kneel with hands clasped in devotion as though I had just received the host. In the school chapel, however, where the pupils came forward pew by pew and row after orderly row, I would not be able to escape.

Tuta, the only one who knew my secret and understood my predicament, knelt beside me. Her glance expressed immense compassion and mutual sympathy. It also signalled her uneasy fear. I had few options. I could stay behind in the pew, but by refusing to receive the host, I would immediately become the centre of attention and all eyes would be upon me. Everyone would be trying to guess the nature of the sin that prevented me from going to the altar. I did not feel brave enough to play the part of Magdalene so obviously.

Neither did I have enough courage to go to confession. I would not have known where to start or what to say to the priest, hiding behind the wooden grill.

I was not quite sure exactly how to define my sin; there was no prayer that I knew that included it. Yet, I felt very deeply the burden and blemish of having sinned and was totally helpless at finding a solution. Perhaps this was the meaning of the deadly sin – there was no way back, no means of resolving it.

God is wise and surely loves mankind. He, who sees everything from his throne above the clouds, He knows that I have not broken any commandments. He knows that there is no need for confession. He could see into my heart better than any priest. I had learned from Father Sylvester that the greatest sin one could commit was to approach, unclean, the altar to receive the sacred host. No sin is more profound; no punishment more horrific… than eternal damnation.

"Dear God in Heaven, you know my 'secret'. Here on earth, it is only Tuta who knows about it. You also know of the wild, uncontrollable beast that you have created within us. Tuta has yet to encounter that beast and does not know of its power."

I knelt at the steps of the altar. Father Sylvester was approaching with the chalice. I felt that if I had been transparent, like a wine glass, Mother Superior, Sister Bonaventure, the French woman, my mother, the 'Lady', all the other girls in the chapel, indeed all the Christians in the world could have seen through me and condemned me for receiving Holy Communion. Or, they would fear for me, as Tuta did.

"I put myself completely into your hands, Dear God. You are the Truth and the Light. Father Sylvester is standing before me and I am looking up at him to receive You from his hand, against the will of everyone who believes in You and Your prayers. Heavenly Father, should You reject me, I expect to be struck by lightning hurled from Your avenging hand; for the walls of the chapel to crumble." I closed my eyes, terrified that my end was nigh. The altar steps seemed to disappear from beneath my knees. The space around me became empty and infinite. Existence should disintegrate; an almighty thunderbolt would announce God's displeasure.

Nothing happened. When I opened my eyes, returning from another world, the priest stood before me with the communion cup in his hand; his old, wrinkled face, surrounded by a halo of silvery white hair, smiling down at me with infinite kindness.

7

Four years later, the girls from the lower classes streamed through the big portals of the Sacré Coeur and scattered into the Marczinkowska. They were chattering happily, their lessons over for the day. Small groups of mothers and nannies had collected by the railings in front of the impressive building, waiting for their charges to appear. A number of girls travelled every day from their parental estates outside the town and their cars and carriages were parked on the opposite side of the road. Some of the younger children, who lived close enough to walk home, gathered at the toy shop, or bought ice creams and turkish delight in the nearby Badsergasse. They would gaze in awe, tongues licking busily, at the senior students as we descended the school steps with the dignity befitting our superior status. We, the members of the highest and final year, acknowledged their deference by blatantly ignoring them.

The approaching finals meant hard work, glory and freedom, in that order. The juniors still had a long way to go. They would have to tolerate the burden of lessons, homework and restrictions for some years to come before they too would graduate to the fourth door from the staircase, on the fourth floor of the Sacré Coeur; the classroom where the final exams took place.

Tuta and I wore light coloured summer dresses now, instead of the dark blue uniforms that we had been obliged to wear to the Ursuline convent. We were both very aware that it was not only the eyes of the girls that followed us. There were a good number of male students about at that time of the day. They all managed to find a reason to be in the vicinity of the Sacré Coeur when the girls were released at the end of the day. It was therefore essential to be seen looking one's best.

Our respective parents had transferred us to Posen for our final year of study. It was a traditional thing to do and the last year spent in a public school seemed a good and gentle transition from the seclusion of the boarding school to the great school of life. Tuta went home by carriage. It was usually waiting for us by the Café Arkadis. I rode my bike, although my parents did not altogether appreciate my insistence that I should cycle to and from school each day. My independent attitude was contrary to the conventional idea that a sixteen-year-old daughter should be escorted everywhere. Every day, after lessons, the old school caretaker, Woźniak, brought my bicycle downstairs on his shoulders. 'Unia', the name of my bike, was my beloved 'locomotion machine', its silver frame, the envy of many. I used to give names to all my belongings. My comb was called 'Pinntek'; the white summer dress with its pleated skirt was 'Bzelutha'; the fountain pen with which I wrote letters and used for school was called 'Piotr'. My faithful Vera was familiar with the names and when I asked her to get 'Helioszek' out for me, she would put my waterproof on the hall stand.

As we crossed the Gdanska, I noticed a slim young officer, waiting by Tuta's coach. My friend blushed slightly when I grinned at her. "This is he? The one you've told me about?"

The lad had seen us and came to greet Tuta. In the middle of the road, between the tram tracks, I was introduced to Kasimir Rybarski. His healthy, boyish face was dominated by his eyes, alert and sparkling. He wore the uniform of a lieutenant, his peaked cap tilted over his left ear at a rakish angle. It was obvious that, like most young men, Kasimir Rybarski loved life and pretty girls – especially the latter.

Tuta and I had remained very close friends. She had confided in me every detail of her acquaintance with Kasimir, and she had shared with me all his glowing and lyrical love letters. He had a lively way of expressing himself on paper which did not prepare me for the rather cool and casual reception that I received when I first met him in the flesh. His behaviour was very reserved. It contradicted the sentiments that he expressed with his pen. But in conversation with young ladies, the young man seemed to take refuge in irony for fear of revealing any emotion.

The lieutenant kindly offered to fetch my bike and as soon as his back was turned, I took both of Tuta's hands in mine and whispered my approval. Tuta beamed with delight.

"You must definitely allow me to get to know you better," said Tuta's gallant, as he wheeled the bike around the back of the carriage. "I want to get to know about everyone and everything that Tuta loves," he added, as he handed me my bike and touched his cap politely.

"Would you and Tuta like to visit me on Sunday?" I asked, offering the young officer my hand. The encounter had made me late and I needed to delay my departure no longer. He took a card from his breast pocket and handed it to me. He saluted, lifting a fist with two fingers extended to his cap and clicking his spurs together. In his best officers' mess voice, he solemnly replied, "I am pleased and honoured to have made your acquaintance and gladly accept your invitation." Having dispensed with convention, he relaxed and added with a grin, "It would be nice if we could be on our own."

"You'll have to put up with mother's presence," I responded, for I could foresee that my maternal parent would have been shocked at such a suggestion. I nodded my farewell to Tuta and, as I moved off down the road on my bike, I called over my shoulder, "Until Sunday! Around four then!" Tuta waved and her admirer saluted yet again. He seemed to like saluting! I concentrated on the traffic ahead which was always busy at that hour.

It took only five minutes to cycle from the Sacré Coeur to the opera house. My teacher would be waiting for me in the vast, empty hall of the ballet school. Today, I was very late.

Ivan Szczurek was a Russian from St. Petersburg. He had replaced Señor Cardell who the previous year had been called back to Barcelona. The change of tutor had altered my attitudes and radically affected my approach to dancing. The Spaniard had aimed at a completely relaxed style. His own movements had been full of southern charm and graceful gallantry and he had taught his pupils accordingly. The Russian, however, demanded pedantic discipline and tense control. He held himself very straight and upright and walked with short, energetic steps. His everyday posture was the personification of his teaching methods.

The soloists at the ballet had openly revolted against the Russian during the first weeks of the Szczurek epoch. There had been many heated arguments in the practise hall. The manager had almost been driven to despair. He had campaigned hard to acquire the services of the famous Russian dancer, but was beginning to doubt the wisdom of his choice.

Using the few dancers who had decided to follow his interpretations, Szczurek had choreographed a routine for a matinee production. Within a short week of tough and unrelenting rehearsal, he had achieved the impossible. His nerves had been at breaking point and his temper shortened during those long hours of practise, but the dancers benefited far beyond their expectations. It was indeed a privilege to study under his critical eye during that frantic week; to be awakened to and infected by the fanaticism of a great artiste.

The performance that resulted was a resounding success for the Russian. The audience seemed to be electrified. A spark, set off by the unforgettable 'Czambaione', ignited both the stalls and the circle. The house burned with feverish enthusiasm. The severe style of classical dancing was new to the Posen stage. The applause it evoked seemed endless. The press reviews that followed reflected similar excitement and praise.

The Russian was immediately established as the indisputable ruler of the ballet hall. Those who had rebelled now submitted to his leadership with unwavering conviction. No one dared to challenge his merciless demands.

Szczurek was intolerant of argument or resistance. He seemed to follow a straight and narrow path, from which he could not stray; a path, invisible to others. Both chorus and soloists feared his scathing criticism which even encroached on the personal life styles of some of the dancers. Others he gave to understand that they were as yet far from perfect in their dance technique and that they certainly had not earned the right to put on the airs of a prima Donna.

He always appeared for rehearsals wearing a black silk blouse, buttoned to a Cossack styled collar. His lean narrow face with its high forehead resembled that of a formidable repentance preacher. It was not difficult to imagine him in the role, swinging a whip in holy rage and demanding absolute obedience to the Commandments of the church.

The only outward acknowledgement that I had been among his small band of dancers at the matinee was that he shook hands with me every time we met. He would normally be more reticent when meeting people, face to face. His hand shake was a coded 'you belong to the faithful' signal. It was administered to very few. The other honour that he bestowed on me was that he continued with my private lessons. Unlike his predecessor, Szczurek refused to undertake any commitments outside the official ballet rehearsals. The extra income did not interest him as it had done Señor Cardell. Pupils that found themselves suddenly deprived of a teacher were transferred to the care of the soloists, who well appreciated the extra money. Szczurek was dedicated to his 'mission' and had no time for pursuits that fragmented his energies. I was the only exception.

Three times a week, immediately after school, I cycled to the opera house, usually meeting the theatre dancers on their way out after a hard morning's training. Today, Tuta's lieutenant had made me ten minutes late. The Russian would have had to wait for me.

When I entered the hall, he was sitting at the piano playing the theme music for his current production, the march from the end of Mozart's Scherzo. He leapt to his feet as soon as he heard me and started towards me. I had feared some reproach and before his tongue could hurt, I started to apologise. He seemed not to hear my excuses and behaved as though I was perfectly on time. He inspected my costume, that I had put on somewhat carelessly in my haste and then scrutinised the fit of my shoes, an important item that was checked before each lesson. Satisfied, he clapped his hands as though to shut out everything unimportant and gave the signal to start.

"First position! Second position! Third position!"

He never failed to start with the five basic principles of classical dance. It was as though Señor Cardell had never existed and that I had not already been practising these same positions for four years. The Russian stood five paces away, motionless, his arms folded and his legs apart. He observed every twitch of every muscle. The hollow echo of his commands sounded harsh in the empty hall. "Forth position! Fifth position! And again first position! Second position!" he drilled me relentlessly.

From the other world, the sound of the occasional car horn or the rattle of a tram drifted through the high narrow windows; a faint reminder that a normal world existed beyond the walls of my chosen prison.

8

The former carefree relationship with my father had never been re-established after the evening when he had finally given permission for me to study dancing seriously. The resistance that he had made many years before to Señor Cardell's scheme, was as nothing to his obvious displeasure at the thought of me taking up dancing as a career. For a long time he had stubbornly refused even to discuss the matter and had finally given in for reasons that were connected more with his new personal responsibilities, rather than family considerations. In 1938, in league with my grandfather, he became involved with politics. The scraps of conversation that I overheard, led me to believe that he was neglecting his business obligations as a consequence.

His political work was mainly concerned with the Polish emigrants who had left the country after World War I. Unemployment in Poland had been so high at that time, that large numbers of people had crossed the border with Germany and had settled there, spreading as far as Westphalia. My father and grandfather felt that another war was on the horizon and that it was important, therefore, to gather these emigrants and form a Polish Nationalist organisation with the aim of weakening Germany's strength from within Germany itself. They did not doubt that Germany would become Poland's enemy. Indeed, one would have had to have been deaf not to be aware of the main topic of conversation. Everywhere, in cafés, in the tram and openly in the streets, people were gossiping and exchanging opinion about only one matter – the deteriorating relationships with Germany.

The conflict of our interests may have motivated my father to change his mind about my ambitions to become a dancer. He was, at the time convinced that war with Germany was inevitable. The thought that his wife and daughter chose to deny the fact and remain as ignorant as Pilsudski's government in recognising the approaching danger, was to him more painful than anything else. He was not prepared to fight indefinitely over such trivia as the career ambitions of his daughter. There were other things of far greater importance and urgency to occupy his mind.

Only on one occasion did the old affection become apparent between us. I still can feel an empty void in my stomach as I remember how my father embraced me in his strong arms when he received the news that my school, the Sacré Coeur, would become the headquarters of the L.O.P.P. The organisation had amalgamated with the movement that my grandfather had started over half a decade earlier. Its main aim was to make youngsters more aware of contemporary politics and to give them pre-military training. The instructions given for National Defence, went under the guise of 'air raid drill'. The government of Poland, already strongly influenced by Germany, did nothing to prepare for an attack from the West and it had been necessary to camouflage under an official banner any preparations made by more enlightened activists.

My father had been pleased by my choice of the Sacré Coeur for my final year at school, but now, for the last time, he questioned my decision to become a dancer. Under the current circumstances, he sincerely thought that it was impractical.

"At the moment, Poland needs young boys and girls like you, to think of nothing else than the protection of their country. We can all think about our personal ambitions when it is all over, Maria. If we survive and are together again afterwards, then, you can dance to your heart's content and I shall give you every support that you need. But now is not the time. It is not right to be thinking of theatre and entertainment. Can you not taste the sticky poison of war on your tongue, even as you breathe the air?"

His plea was passionate, but he could not persuade me to take him seriously.

"You are seeing ghosts, Papa," I replied. "You have been talking of war for such a long time, that you cannot see clearly any more. Marshal Pilsudski was in Berlin only yesterday, and his visit was welcomed with loyalty and friendship. You have been forecasting war for years. It looks as though things are quite peaceful at the moment so how many more years must we go on listening to your omens. I cannot wait. A dancer needs to start as young as possible. Every day that I lose, is lost forever. I cannot regain it."

The pressure on my arms relaxed. He released me from his grasp. When I looked up into his face, the expression in his eyes said everything. The light was extinguished by his bitter disappointment. His own daughter had failed to understand the magnitude of the impending catastrophe. Instantly, I regretted what I had just said. I would have given anything to undo what I had done to him.

Had he answered my rebuff and asked me just once more to change my mind, I would readily have capitulated and sacrificed my dancing. But, he remained silent; stunned. What had I done? I wanted to throw my arms about him to beg his forgiveness, but he had already turned away. The moment had passed. It was a tiny fraction of two lives, but the consequences of those few seconds echoed long into the future.

It was getting dark. In silence he crossed the room and switched on the light. As he opened the door, not sparing me a glance, he said in a monotone, "I have given your mother the money for Salon Mlynekk. You can go tonight if you wish..."

My mother had ordered my first evening gown from Mlynekk's. It was ready. We could collect it. Why did I feel so miserable? How did I know that something intangible had irretrievably shattered, leaving me drifting helplessly away from the one person that I admired and loved above all others. I think for the first time in my life I experienced the pain of betrayal; the guilt and the shame. In those few seconds I understood that I had a responsibility towards others and not to myself alone. For the first time in my life that I could remember, I wanted and needed to cry.

9

Lieutenant Kasimir Rybarski's wish to spend Sunday afternoon alone in the company of two young ladies was thwarted. He arrived with Tuta punctually at four o'clock, presented my mother with a bouquet of flowers and produced a box of chocolates for Vera.

The coffee table was laid in a small side room, adjacent to the drawing room and the home of the piano and gramophone. My mother remained with us and it may have been her presence that was the cause of the rather stiff and formal behaviour of the young officer. Once again he showed his impeccable manners to make polite conversation. It was not until I remarked that he would never retrieve the cost of the flowers and chocolates if he paid so little attention to the coffee and cakes, that the tension was broken. Kasimir changed into the natural, easy going person that he truly was and we all had a good laugh. From then on, the chatter was light hearted and full of fun, just as if we had all known each other for a long time.

Eventually, my mother was called away to deal with household matters and we were able to play the gramophone. Tuta and I took it in turns to dance with the gallant young officer and did not wait for each record to end before we swapped places. Poor Kasimir was quite breathless after ten minutes.

Our amusement, however, was short lived. Kasimir had just poured out three glasses of iced lemonade and we girls were sprawled on the sofa, feigning lady-like exhaustion, when we heard footsteps and voices in the drawing room. Almost immediately the intervening doors flew open and in marched my grandfather.

"There you are," he boomed at us. "I've found them. They're hiding in here!" he added, bellowing over his shoulder to the figure standing behind him.

"I'm sorry that your tête a tête has been interrupted, but I have a few guests with me and I must introduce you to them, Mirka."

Kasimir, recovered from his surprise at the initial intrusion and jumped to his feet, coming to full attention.

"Sir! Lieutenant Rybarski, 5th Cavalry, 2nd Company."

Three elderly officers materialised next to Grandfather, one of whom announcing his elevated rank by his uniform, that of a general no less. This was probably a bit more than the new recruit, Lieutenant Rybarski of the 5th Cavalry Regiment had bargained for It must have been a very strange experience for him, verging on embarrassing, to be addressed on equal terms by a general.

We were obliged to join grandfather and his guests in the drawing room. Kasimir's discomfort was increased when the amiable general cordially enquired about his fiancé, Tuta, and invited him to be seated beside him on the sofa.

The conversation soon turned to the topical themes of Gdansk, Pomerania, the border question and the prospect of war in general. The atmosphere in the room became heavy with tobacco smoke; the glass tumblers were repeatedly replenished with brandy. Tuta passed an occasional glance in my direction, rolling her eyes in the direction of the music room, where the table had yet to be cleared and the little feast still awaited our attention. Her meaning was not difficult to understand. Kasimir tried hard to follow the discussion, paying special attention to anything that the general said. However, even he, though he was doing his best to appear interested, now and then caught my eye. The message written clearly on his face was not very flattering to Grandfather and the guests!

To make the hopeless situation even worse, it started to rain heavily. The storm which had been brewing most of the afternoon, announced its impatience with a prolonged rumble and rain started to beat against the windows. This only seemed to encourage the ferocity of the debate among the elders. They were after all, in the comfort of a warm and dry drawing room and lively discussion was a welcome alternative to braving the elements outside. On the other hand, neither could we fugitives escape to the great outdoors. Nature had connived to spoil our afternoon with a thunderstorm.

As the three of us wallowed in our individual frustrations, Vera slipped quietly into the room and signalled that she needed to talk to me. With relief I excused myself and, approaching her, listened attentively to her whispered message. Apparently, there was a young lady in the hall who wished to see me.

The girl who waited by the front door was soaked to the skin. Her dark hair stuck in thin strands to her face and huge, dark patches of dampness spread over the shoulders of her blue coat. She had come from the opera house for I immediately recognised her as a member of the ballet chorus. I invited her to stay a while to refresh herself and dry off a little, but she assured me that she must return immediately, as she had to be on stage again for the third act. She had been free during the second and for that reason, the ballet master had asked her to deliver an urgent message to Miss Weychanowna. The letter that she handed to me was rather wet, "Please excuse the envelope... but I must return with a reply!"

Inside the soggy envelope bearing Ivan Szczurek's name and address, was a card. On the back of it, written in a slanting disjointed hand, were the words, "After performance. Stage door! Message from Warsaw!" Nothing else! The brief note sounded more like an order than an invitation.

"Tell Mr. Szczurek, I shall be there. And thank you for coming in this awful weather." I had been so intrigued by the nature of the demand that I had not given a moments thought to how I would be able to comply with the request. My answer was spontaneous. I knew only that I must be there, however inconvenient.

I returned to the drawing room and sat down in my armchair again. In the corner facing me stood a tall clock which I studied carefully, calculating that I should have to leave in exactly half an hour. It did not occur to me that there might be valid reasons for not keeping the appointment; that the venture was somewhat harebrained for an unchaperoned young lady. I absent mindedly tore the envelope and card into smaller and smaller pieces as I considered the possible reasons for the summons.

Warsaw? A message from Warsaw? Had the Russian already received a reply from his friend, a theatrical agent, in answer to his enquiry concerning my performing there? It was surely impossible. Too soon! Only three days had passed since we had discussed my final school exams and future career. Earlier that summer, I had surprised the Russian by expressing a wish to become a modern dance soloist. I was determined to appear in variety shows and revues and I had asked him to develop my lessons steadily in that direction.

Initially Szczurek had taken offence. He confessed that he had been convinced that I would join the ballet company connected with the Opera House in Posen. Our discussion had become so heated that the doorman had looked in to see what was amiss. A Russian arm had gesticulated wildly in his direction and sent him packing.

For the first time, we had parted that evening without saying goodbye.

At my next lesson, two days later, I was surprised by the Russian's equanimity. He began the lesson in the normal routine, his voice issuing instructions exactly the same as it always did. I had dreaded our next encounter, but was relieved to find that our disagreement had not caused any significant change to his professional attitude. After half an hour of vigorous training, he abruptly asked me if I still insisted on following the course that I had described at our last meeting. When I assured him that nothing on earth could persuade me otherwise, he immediately started to teach me the rudiments of modern steps without further comment.

He offered an explanation when the lesson was concluded. "The one thing that I appreciate in anyone, is a strong will. If you had changed your mind, you would have lost my support forever," he said, and he offered me his hand. He even attempted a little smile, a novelty that I had not witnessed before. "However, I would advise you not to stay in Posen," he had added. "The variety clubs here are just music boxes. You must go to Warsaw, where the stages are bigger and better. A good friend of mine is an agent there and I shall write to him immediately on your behalf." At this point, we had parted. No further arrangements had been discussed.

A reply only three days later was surely impossible.

Yet Szczurek's message could only refer to his agent friend, I could think of no other alternative. Had he refused? Or was my dream coming true?

The conversation around me in the drawing room became more animated. The general, in a great state of excitement, started to sketch geographical maps, illustrating military lines, borders and defence posts on a sheet of paper. When his diagram was finished, he added arrows which crossed the lines here and there. The officers crowded around him and grandfather got to his feet to gain a clear view over the general's shoulder. It seemed an auspicious moment to leave the room. I signalled to Tuta that I wanted to say something to her and she followed me into the hall. Hurriedly I explained the situation. She was not altogether happy that I might soon be departing for Warsaw, but realising how important the meeting might be for me, she promised to make excuses for my absence should it be noticed.

The rain was still falling, although it had now reduced to a steady drizzle. I found Ivan Szczurek waiting patiently at the stage door. As soon as he saw me, he hurried towards me.

"Maria. You've come! I have news from Warsaw." No other explanation. No apology for calling me out without warning on a very wet Sunday evening. It would not have occurred to him that such things would be necessary; all other considerations being non-existent, where work was concerned. He seemed oblivious to the rain as he crooked his arm around mine and swept me off down the empty street.

"I need to move when I talk. Hate standing still," he said abruptly, as he tripped along with short springy steps by my side.

"Have you ever heard of the Café Club?" he asked. "No, I have never been to Warsaw..." I replied.

"You have never been to Warsaw?" he echoed, incredulity reverberating in every syllable. "Well, well! The Café Club on the Nowy Swiat at the Jerusalemski, you must have heard of it? It has the best variety show in Warsaw."

The knot of excitement in my stomach tightened. I felt myself grow physically taller despite the inclement weather. My head was beginning to spin, as I imagined all the opportunities that were rising on the horizon.

"Has your friend got me a booking?" My heart seemed to be climbing into my throat, the suspense was beginning to hurt.

"Yes, he has phoned and he is willing to accept you." Szczurek replied. Everything started to fade into the distance. I could still hear him, chattering on at my side, but he sounded as though he was at the other end of a long tunnel. "Yes, he trusts my judgement. Of course! Now... you'll take your final exams in approximately a month. Three numbers will be required for the Café Club. Let's see. It'll take two months to arrange everything and after that...allowing for Christmas... you should be ready. On this schedule, I have accepted an engagement for January."

He had been talking as though to himself. But his last statement jolted me back to reality. I was stunned. The deal was sealed. It did not seem to have entered his head, that perhaps he might have consulted me before accepting of the offer. It would seem that as he knew what I wanted (and for him, Warsaw would provide the best) it was unthinkable that I would have any other obligations that could obstruct his plans. The offer had been made and, in his view, it was obvious that no time should be wasted before accepting. No discussion was needed. He did not even seem to expect my heartfelt thanks. "I think we'll use a tango and a rumba and..."

"...and a national folk dance," I squeaked, at last finding the use of my tongue again. He squeezed my arm in agreement and as if to say 'that could be something special'.

"Yes, what a good idea... a Polish folk dance with special choreography," he added, nodding his head in approval.

Suddenly, the Russian stopped in his tracks and swung round to face me. He stood so close that the drops of water dripping off his hat, splashed on to my nose and down the front of my coat.

"We must celebrate, Weychanowna! Today is the start of all your tomorrows. A new life! We shall have to frame it like a picture to hang on the wall, so that you will always be able to remember and admire it."

Without another word, he led me through the gate of a bedraggled looking house. Slightly bemused, I began to realise that our aimless stroll had a destination. I was unfamiliar with the area and had paid little attention to the route we had taken and had absolutely no idea where we were.

The narrow entrance passage, adorned with beer posters, led to a cheap restaurant that reeked of Schnapps and the stale odours of cooking. The low ceilinged bar room was empty and it was some time before a portly landlady shuffled over to our table. It was apparent that she had been working in the kitchen, potato peelings stuck to her apron and she clutched a small pointed knife.

Szczurek seemed familiar with the old woman. He referred to her as 'Mammuschka' and stroked her arm affectionately. "We would like to celebrate a special occasion," he said. "Please light the lamp and bring us the best your house can offer. The Dear Father in Heaven will reward you when you meet him up there... one day!"

"If your promises were anything to go by, Ivan, I should not be frightened of dying," the woman retorted. "You call on the Lord often enough when you want something from me, my boy." Ivan assumed a suitably penitent expression. "Don't look at me like that, my lad, I'll make your borsatz for you, don't fret." They spoke in Russian, but I could understand the language sufficiently well to follow their banter.

The landlady lit the old fashioned gas lamp that hung above the table then switched off the single electric bulb that was the only other source of light. The corners of the room were plunged into deep shadow.

"How I love the pale flame and hate the harshness of electricity," Ivan remarked, watching the flickering light settle into a steady glow. "If you fetch a bottle of wine for us now, Mammuschka, it'll save your legs an extra trip." he said, addressing the broad backside of the old woman as she retreated to her kitchen.

Under the influence of the gas lamp, sitting at a round wooden table in a scruffy pub, Ivan Szczurek appeared to mellow. The slim-built ballet master, with his high, intelligent forehead, lost all his usual reserve. His movements were no longer brittle and constrained. His speech sounded neither shrill nor abrupt. His whole body; his entire being seemed to relax and evolve into an agreeable human; a transformation that I would have thought impossible.

"To Warsaw, Maria Weychanowna!" He passed me my glass and raised his own. We toasted. He then took my hand in his and gazing into my eyes, he gave me a serious lecture.

"We shall have to work hard, work very hard. Nothing is free. Indeed, there is no such thing as a free gift. It may look free, but I've found that I always have to pay for it in the end. Nothing falls into your lap. Every success is the result of dedicated hard work. You cannot take short cuts, especially when you are on the threshold of your career."

He poured more wine and stared into the depths of the dark red liquid.

"I can see the tango already. We shall use the music of the 'Nocturno'. As though hearing the tune, his fingers started to rhythmically tap the table. "But you must not dance the same way as thousands have danced it before and thousands will dance it in the future. I hate averages. I hate mass production." His hand closed into a fist and he began to lightly beat the table, causing the glasses to wobble. "Pioneers do not only fight on the battle ground. Courage is needed to climb out of the mainstream and venture into unknown territory. We must be the pioneers of dancing. If you had been born with stiff legs, you could be destined to sell matches on a street corner. But you were born with legs that can dance, so you shall dance... and dance... and dance!"

Outside, the rain was falling heavily again. The sound of running water became louder as it drained off the roof in increasing volume. It reminded me that the same storm was drumming against the windows of the drawing room at home. Somehow, it no longer seemed important that my absence may have been noticed, I was too spellbound by the man who sat opposite me in the flickering gaslight. The news that I had been accepted in Warsaw had triggered a feeling of blissful happiness and I was both bewildered and fascinated by his sudden change of character.

I ate little of what the landlady called 'her best', but the Russian had a very healthy appetite. He greedily gulped down the food and emptied his glass, time and time again.

A cab driver was the only other guest at the inn. He had come in some time after us, giving warning of his imminent arrival by stamping his feet outside the door. On entering, he took off his cap and knocked it on the back of a chair to dislodge the water. His sodden cape, he flung casually onto a seat. Like the Russian, he too seemed to be a regular customer. He walked round the serving counter and straight into the kitchen. Soon, he re-emerged, carrying his food and drink, opting for a table in the gloom by the door. As soon as he was seated, he attacked the steaming mound, shovelling the mess into his face as though it was the first that he had tasted in a week. He paid not the slightest attention to us.

The Russian had put our dirty plates and cutlery on an empty chair. For a long time, he just sat in silence. Now that he had finished his meal, he was relaxed and peaceful. He carefully refilled my glass and raised his, looking deep into my eyes. His gaze lacked focus. His thoughts seemed to be elsewhere – far away – possibly already twisting through the intricate movements of my new dance programme. I was foolish. Misled by my dreams, I misread his intentions.

As he replaced his glass on the table, he appeared to return to the reality of the present. I had felt as though he had looked straight through me, piercing the inner crevices of my mind. Thankfully his eyelids closed for a moment, then opened again to stare at my hands that were coiled around the stem of my glass.

"You will not be able to shut me out of your life, Maria Weychanowna." He delicately caressed the back of my hand and I felt his fingers gently push between mine until our hands were firmly locked. Suddenly they seemed to have a life of their own. That which could not be said with words, was transmitting itself through the sense of touch, the throb, the demanding ache.

"It is wonderful to stand at a turning point in life, especially when danger is involved," he murmured.

"One day you may curse me or even hate me, but you will never forget me."

He looked deep into my eyes. The fat landlady, drifting through the periphery of my awareness, placed a key on the table, scooped up the dirty dishes and vanished back into the kitchen as discretely as she had come.

I could no longer bear his gaze. My eyelids drooped in submission and we rose from the table. As though hypnotised, I followed him to climb the narrow stairs at the back of the room. The old woman saw us leave and climbed the stairs behind us, carrying a bowl of water and a towel. The Russian opened one of the small doors on the tiny landing at the top of the stairs and stood back to let me pass. The room I entered was narrow. With a low ceiling, it was little bigger than a cupboard. Only the white bed linen was visible. The old woman came in behind us.

"The storm is right above us," she said, excusing herself of the need to switch on the electric light. She spoke, barely above a whisper and I sensed that whatever lay ahead had to be carried out in silence and secrecy, like a crime.

She placed the bowl of water on the dim shape of the chest of drawers and shuffled from the room immediately, closing the door softly behind her. Before her footsteps had died away, the Russian stepped close to me and took me in his arms. I felt his kisses on my face and neck. Lightening flashed outside, and the room was momentarily bathed in brilliance. In that split second, I saw his piercing eyes looking down at me. Darkness followed, the pitch black aftermath of a blinding flash. Our lips met. I clung to the body that was pressing so eagerly against mine.

We did not hear the footsteps on the stairs. A knock at the door interrupted our passionate embrace. The Russian gently let me go and stepped outside the bedroom. The conversation that ensued on the other side of the door was not difficult to hear through the thin planks. The landlady, for it was she, wanted payment before she retired as Szczurek would probably get up before her. The Russian murmured something in reply that I did not catch and the woman added, with irritation in her voice, that she was not prepared to wait for her money for over a month as last time – she had the gas and electricity bills to pay, not to mention the rent.

The thought had occurred to me down stairs, when the key had appeared unrequested on the table, that a mutual understanding existed between landlady and customer; that I was possibly not the first. Now, it was evident that I was indeed not the only one that Ivan Szczurek had led up the narrow staircase to this little room on the first floor of the inn; that the bed must already have...

There was a 'last time' or had it been 'one of the last times' when he had left the room in a hurry and failed to pay the landlady the few zloty that she charged him for his clandestine trysts on her premises.

The Russian was still tucking away his purse as he came back into the room. The electric light was on and I stood in front of the mirror, tidying my hair. The brightness of the naked bulb had revealed the shabbiness of the extremely drab little room and it had brought me to my senses as effectively as a cold shower. When we embraced again, and I admit that I did let it happen, I felt nothing. I could not return his passion. The fire had died.

He stepped back, holding me at arms length and looked at me in surprise. I was not yet seventeen and not bold enough to remonstrate with him about his duplicity. I found it difficult not to hurt him, if I told him the truth. How could I do that, held as I was in the gaze of eyes that had filled with child-like sadness.

Mustering every scrap of dignity and fragile self-esteem that I had left, I took his hands and lifted them to my lips.

"You will take me home now, Ivan Szczurek, because I want to remember you with love, not hatred."

A steamy scene could have been anticipated at this point, but, I remember Ivan Szczurek with love.

He was an honourable man!

10

The 3rd January 1939, was a bitterly cold day. The snow had been falling continuously for a week. Tracks and lanes in the countryside were impassable and the drifts were often over a metre deep. Our arrival in Warsaw on the train was delayed by five hours in order to thaw out frozen points on the track, frequent stops had been necessary during the journey.

Vera had accompanied me on the train and when we arrived in Warsaw we enlisted the help of a porter to carry the luggage. We could not see the other side of the Jerusalemski Road as we left the station for the snow still fell, thick and blinding. Cars were travelling very slowly and warned of their approach by muffled but frequent hooting. It was impossible to see further than two or three metres. Passing pedestrians appeared from nowhere and like ghosts disappeared as mysteriously into the wall of whiteness. The weather conditions being as they were, it took some time to find a taxi. Eventually we attracted the attention of a mobile snow drift and thankfully climbed inside.

It was my first visit to Warsaw and, excitedly, I asked the driver of take us past the Nevsky Cathedral with its five golden cupolas. To me it was the symbol of Warsaw. There had been innumerable pictures of the church in my school books and a large illustration had hung above the classroom door at the Sacré Coeur. For me, Warsaw was not Warsaw without the cathedral and I felt that I could not be sure that I had come to the right city unless I had made sure that the cathedral was in place.

"There it is!" said the driver, stopping the cab. He turned in his seat to wipe the condensation from the window with his shaggy fur glove. Of course the falling snow prevented us from seeing anything. I could only discern some stone steps rising from the pavement and a glimpse of massive wooden doors beyond. The street was narrow, but the snow fell heavily and we could only take his word that we were staring in the right direction. When I persisted and asked him for more details about the five gold-plated orbs, he assured me that they were all still there; that he had seen them only a fortnight ago when he drove a party of tourists past the building.

"They looked very handsome with the sun shining on them," he said, "but the weather today is not suitable for sightseeing." His irony was lost on me. He shrugged his shoulders in what I took to be an apologetic manner, as though for some reason he was responsible for the snowstorm, then engaged the gears and proceeded at walking speed towards the Nowy Swiat.

The Nowy Swiat was part of the Krakan district in the centre of the city. It was here that my mother had rented a three-roomed apartment at No. 55 for the duration of my contract at the Café Club.

During the long train journey and the slow drive from the station, I had looked forward to seeing my new home, anticipating a warm, welcoming room to be awaiting our arrival. When the caretaker unlocked the door, however, my dreams were shattered. I gaped in horror at the scene which met my eyes. Furniture and boxes were haphazardly strewn all around the room. Too late, I recalled that my mother had managed to find the apartment only just before her return to Posen. Everything that she had ordered to furnish the place had been delivered after her departure.

To add to our misery, the temperature in the room was sub zero. The snow on our clothes and luggage gave not the slightest indication that it would melt and the stove was covered in a mantle of dust. The caretaker was grumpy and unhelpful, anxious to get back to his own warm lair.

For several moments I marched around the room, disappointment destroying my ability to think. I talked aloud to myself, trying to sort out a logical and satisfactory conclusion. I had imagined that it would all have been so different and I felt sick with frustration. How could we possibly create order out of the chaos that surrounded us. I hurt my toe kicking one of the boxes and suddenly it was obvious to me what we should do. We should find a hotel for the night and in the morning, after a good night's rest, we would tackle the problem.

Vera was used to my tantrums. While I had been occupied venting my anger on the innocent boxes, she had started to fill the stove with wood and by the time I had reached my grand decision, the first flames had started to flicker and dance over the sawdust. Within minutes, warmth began to radiate into the chill air. We were still clad for the blizzard outside, but as the snow that we had brought in with us disappeared, my determination to seek shelter in a hotel also faded. Vera sensed this and suggested that before I made a final decision, I should take a look at the other rooms and perhaps investigate the contents of the boxes. Curiosity, she knew was an overpowering failing of mine.

Soon I had forgotten my anger and frustration. My excitement increased with each box and I realised that I was getting hot in my heavy fur coat. The stove had rapidly heated the room to a comfortable temperature and I decided that perhaps we could make one room habitable for the moment and deal with the rest in the morning.

We were busy trying to manoeuvre a chest of drawers across the room when, just one hour after our arrival, an imperious rap on the door announced our first visitor.

Vera opened the door to find an impressive looking gentleman armed, with a huge basket of flowers. She stood back to allow him to enter. Our surprise visitor swept past her, a slim, dark haired boy following in his wake.

"Welcome to Warsaw, Maria Weychanowna." The sound of his voice resonated into every corner of the room as he strode majestically towards me, flourishing his ebony walking stick. I gaped at him in disbelief, confused and embarrassed. I was in no fit state to receive guests, least of all one with such regal bearing. His elegant cloak, spotless gloves and flamboyant cravat must have made a ridiculous contrast with my crumpled and disordered appearance. The room was still in turmoil. The heat from the stove had eventually caused us to shed our outer clothes and these had been thrown over chairs to dry. Boxes and their contents were strewn about in haphazard disarray.

Our visitor seemed to notice nothing out of the ordinary. He executed a formal bow, as correct and polite as his apparel was extravagant. "Permit me to introduce myself, dear lady. Count Cszapski! At your service!"

Of course, my agent, the friend of Ivan Szczurek! He took my hand and lifted it solemnly to his lips. I remember how his beard tickled the back of my hand. The basket of flowers was presented with a flourish and I endeavoured to receive them with as much grace as the occasion required. I did not anticipate that the bouquet would be so heavy and nearly dropped it as the count passed it to me. My ears were filled with a cascade of effusive explanations as to how he had waited at the station for the train; missed me in the snow storm and after a protracted search, found his way to my apartment.

It was to this man that I owed my thanks for arranging my debut on the Warsaw stage. His bearing was distinctly military, betrayed by his posture and the neatly trimmed beard. What had made him leave the army to open a theatre in Warsaw, I was to learn later, but for the present, he talked as though he was addressing a large audience, gesticulating emphatically to stress a point and hardly pausing for breath. His companion had discreetly perched himself on the armchair just inside the door. He hardly stirred during the count's grand oration and his face remained unmoved. He seemed extremely bored with the entire proceedings as though the count's repeated apologies had all been heard a thousand times before. I did not appreciate then how he had been the determining factor in the count's sudden change of profession.

"It would have been so fitting, to welcome our new star of the stage amidst heavenly confetti. What a picture it would have made to see your radiant young face, savouring the scents of the bouquet, framed in a pillow of drifting crystals. You do not realise how impatiently Warsaw has been waiting to welcome you." I accepted his flattery with mixed feelings. His sentiments were full of romantic nonsense. My nose had been so cold, whilst seeking the services of a taxi, that it was extremely doubtful that I would have appreciated the delicate perfumes of his frozen flowers. The idea of a backdrop of snowflakes appealed to my romantic instincts, however, and I found myself warming to his enthusiasm.

For nearly ten minutes, the count beat his chest in abject apology for the misdemeanour of having missed me at the station. Finally, as if to offer compensation for his lack of efficiency, he drew from his pocket a handful of newspaper cuttings and spread them across the table.

"To show you how much Warsaw is anticipating your appearance, dear lady." He pointed with some emphasis at his treasures. " See here, you have a busy agent, namely myself. I have informed the press of your pending arrival and these are the articles that they have produced to date," he continued.

This announcement caught me by surprise. I was speechless for I had not given a moments thought to the publicity that might be necessary for a public debut. Seeing the disconcerted look on my face, the count added, "Oh, you will find out soon enough, how important it is for an artiste to receive press attention. This is only the prelude, nothing more. The heavy guns are to come and I shall see to it that they fire volley after volley."

He carefully folded his white leather gloves and stowed them in the pocket of his fur coat.

"We have no time to waste. The first night is in fourteen days. The stage will be free for your rehearsals for one hour every day, starting this coming Saturday. The entire orchestra will be available to you on three afternoons each week." Like a military commander issuing orders, he rattled out his plan of campaign. "We shall need portrait photographs and others of you in dancing poses for the programme, posters and the newspapers. Further, I have promised the gentlemen of the press an article on your life hitherto. You know – some love, a little sentimentality – weak lemonade and inflated passion. I've a chap on hand who will contact you about that. He knows what he is doing and is capable of devising fascinating stories. Isn't that so Mario? Ostrowski, you know him!"

The count hesitated, suddenly aware that he had forgotten to introduce his companion. With all the excitement, he had ignored the young man entirely. In dismay, he leapt up from his chair and immediately launched into another confusing battery of apologies.

"Whatever must you think of Warsaw manners. Don't deny it! You must encounter better behaviour in the provinces than you have seen so far here in the capital. I shall be avoided by everyone from Posen for such gross negligence. Mario, you should have given me a nudge to remind me!"

He grasped the young man by the elbow, raised him to his feet and propelled him across the room towards me.

"This is Mario!" declared the count. "His surname is much too long and complicated for us Poles to pronounce, so he is just 'Mario' to everyone. He comes from Palermo in Italy, so he's a long way from home."

"Do forgive me. I'm really not at my best when the weather is like this." Italian he may have been, but his knowledge of the Polish language was fluent. He smiled, revealing a row of perfect white teeth in a mouth belonging to an unbelievably beautiful face. His hair was deep black, as were his eyes. His lashes were extraordinarily long; his complexion like that of a girl… he blushed as he bowed.

The count interrupted the stillness that had settled momentarily on the room.

"May I have the pleasure of your company to dinner?" he asked, retrieving his hat and walking stick from the sofa where he had thrown them during his energetic tirade.

I accepted with relief. The apartment was still in a mess and the inadequate stocks in the larder would have provided only a meagre snack.

"Excellent! We shall have ample opportunity to discuss your contract and we must also talk about your costumes and the stage settings."

11

Two weeks later I was gloating over the printed programme for the evening performance. It lay amidst the jars of make-up cream, brushes and combs on the table in my dressing room. Featured on its pages were details about the orchestra, the compère, the magician, the performing dog, the ballet and the many other international acts which a large variety show could include.

Above my door, the number '7' flickered in a small glass case, indicating that the 'Five Marinellis' were currently on stage. They were a family of Brazilian jugglers which had arrived in Warsaw the previous evening and had run through their 'orienting rehearsal' during the quiet hours of the night. Only three days previously, they had performed on the stage of the Wintergarten in Berlin. They were experienced and true professionals, used to the conditions imposed on a performer. Here I sat, an uninitiated novice, examining the programme with naive curiosity.

After the Marinellis, in the eighth slot, came the Hungarian Musical Clown. He in turn was followed by the four young men from Switzerland, plucking their guitars and singing Hawaiian songs. Their act was tuneful to the ear and colourful to watch. And then... at number 10... came 'Nana Sullivan'.

My father had made one last request before I left home. He had agreed to his daughter dancing in public with one proviso, that I should be known by another name. The Weychan family should not be embarrassed by finding their name on a theatre programme.

A Warsaw advertising agency, with an office by the river Weichsel in the Bednarska, had been commissioned, on the count's advice, to select a suitable stage pseudonym. They had a reputation for dreaming up names for shoe polish and new brands of chocolate, so thinking up an alias for an unknown dancer was well within their capabilities. The gentlemen from the agency had come up with five suggestions within three days each one carried the smug assurance that it was a guarantee for a comet-like career, even if the dancer in question had a wooden leg.

The count had chosen the fourth suggestion on the list. Being totally ignorant of such matters, I could only concur. Now I studied a photograph of myself entitled 'Nana Sullivan' and my cognitive senses took a slight jolt. The face looked like me, yet somehow, it was not me. It was 'Nana'. The name was also the familiar name for my mother, used by members of her family and close friends, and it would take some time to become used to theatre acquaintances addressing me as 'Nana' – or more frequently 'Miss Sullivan'. When anyone spoke directly at me, addressing me by my new name, my immediate reaction was to assume that they were talking to someone behind me. At first, I had actually turned to look for her. Even when I had learned to control that instinctive reaction, it took much longer to mentally respond naturally as though 'Nana' was my real name.

The loud marching music that I could hear through the partition walling, announced the exit of the musical clown. The applause echoed the rhythmical beat and faded quickly as the music finished. A mild panic crept into my brain, but I refused to acknowledge it. Somewhere out there in the stalls of the large auditorium, sat my mother and my friend Tuta. Yesterday, they had arrived from Posen in order to give their support for my first performance. I had begged them not to come to see me in the dressing room beforehand. I felt that I needed to be on my own, not fussed by well wishers, so that I could talk to my reflection in the mirror and tell it firmly that I was calm and was not suffering in the least from nerves.

Milouka did not count. She was adding the finishing touches to my hair and checking my make-up. To me she was more part of the theatre trappings than a person in her own right. She was so delightfully silent; one of the best make-up and wardrobe mistresses that one could wish for; a shadow that was never in the way, but always there when needed.

Count Cszapski had insisted that he should replace the stage manager to call me when the time came. Immaculately dressed in a tail coat, he noiselessly slipped into my dressing room and pointed to the illuminated number '9' that was now displayed in the glass case above the door.

Mario appeared behind him like a shadow. His sallow face, highlighted by his white shirt front, seemed more expressionless than usual. He seemed often to exist in an isolated, secretive world of his own.

I rose from my stool and Milouka instantly attended to the fall of the folds in my full skirt. The count took my hand, ushered me through the door and led me down the narrow passage to a spiral staircase. The mixture of stale air and greasepaint affected my stomach and I became aware of a desperate urge to escape the restrictions of the corridor. I suddenly found that all I really wanted were the wide open spaces of home.

I swallowed hard and told myself to be strong. The count must have sensed my tension, for he turned at the foot of the staircase, smiled and gave my hand an encouraging squeeze.

As if in a dream, I climbed the iron stairway emerging at the top to the view of the stage itself lying below us in a brightly lit square. Hawaiian melodies wafted up to us through the web of chains and ropes that are all part of the backstage machinery. There is nothing glamorous about the paraphernalia that create the illusions for the audience, but for the moment, I did not see them. My attention was focused on the lighted stage.

We descended into the wings, where the girls from the ballet stood waiting in small groups, shivering. In the depths of winter the whole theatre was heated, but cold draughts could not be completely excluded. Suddenly, I too found myself shivering, but not from the chill air. Excitement and apprehension fought their battle and I started to shake uncontrollably.

The stage manager nodded and smiled in our direction. It was an acknowledgment that we were in good time. He was a professional and assumed that all artistes knew their job as thoroughly.

His attitude was a tonic and gave me strength. Every new number demanded changes and rearrangements in the complicated routine of backstage management. A first night performance was as much a trial for him as it was for the artistes. My punctuality was professional and the stage manager had noticed it. I stopped shaking.

Applause sounded from the auditorium. As the curtains closed, shutting out the spotlights, the stage area behind them dimmed. The four Swiss singers stood ready to take a second curtain call, but the clapping ebbed and died into the hum and clatter of many people shifting in their seats. The four boys dropped their poses and with their guitars dangling sadly from their shoulders, they sauntered off the stage.

The orchestra started to play again. A tingling sensation ran through my whole body as I realised that it was the introduction to my dance, the 'Tango Nocturno'.

Stage hands erupted from the wings and with lightning speed, the props were winched up, the chains softly jingling. They were replaced by the gigantic pieces of scenery which had been designed for my act. The setting for a Spanish wine cellar rapidly took shape; a stylized backdrop of an inn, showing a few wooden tables with empty glasses lying on them and some upturned chairs. It was fascinating. The count tried to shake my hand but was interrupted by the manager, who whisked me away to my starting position in the middle of the scenery.

It was an old superstition of the house that a man's shiny leather shoe brought good luck. I could see that the count had removed his left shoe and stood in the wings on one stockinged foot, waving his good luck symbol and smiling.

All activity suddenly ceased and a hush fell backstage. In front of me were the dark red velvet curtains, their plainness exuding a sense of security and comfort. I closed my eyes and made a supreme effort to wipe out the memory of all the distractions about me and concentrate on the steps of the dance. Once I had started, the rest would hopefully follow automatically.

My mind filled instead with a host of possible disasters that might befall me in the next few minutes; my memory would go blank and I would forget the dance routine; a nail would rise out of the floor and trip me; the stalls and circle were filled with ogres that would laugh and ridicule my efforts, slapping their fleshy thighs as they pointed and jeered. Ominous horror scenarios whirled before my eyes. Those pointing hands came closer and closer, reaching towards me. They grew in size and started to fly around me, their grabbing, mocking hands moving faster and faster, ever faster.

I felt as though I was being suffocated. The fitted bodice of my dress seemed to squeeze my body until I had difficulty breathing. I began to tremble and more than ever, I wanted to flee – to escape and hide in some private corner.

The curtain drew back and the brilliant spotlights shone down on me. My eyes were still tightly closed, but the dazzling light pierced my lids. Although I had withdrawn into panic, I gradually realised that the real world was still functioning.

There I stood in my starting pose, quite unable to move; my eyes clamped shut. It took concentrated willpower to force those eyes open. On seeing the familiar faces of the orchestra, lit by the glow of the lights on their music stands, my confidence slowly returned. I took a deep breath and prayed that my stage fright had not been noticed. With blissful relief, I understood that I could see only blurred silhouettes beyond the orchestra pit, not distinct faces. The audience that I had feared so much was sitting in the dark. The paralysis evaporated and I regained my ability to move.

By this time, however, I must confess, I had missed my cue. The kind and considerate conductor, his face framed by silver hair, like a grizzly cherub, smiled reassuringly at me. It was not the first time that a fresh artiste had been reluctant to take her initial steps on his stage. He discretely took the orchestra back to the beginning of the music and on reaching my cue again, gave me the pre-arranged signal to begin the dance.

The tension within me now inspired me to dance with an extravagance that was unrehearsed. The music and steps were those of a modern tango, but my mentor, Ivan Szczurek, my inspiration and master, had added his own style, both strict and disciplined, to the choreography. He could not, however, have anticipated the energy with which I attacked his programme.

As I began to dance, I could visualise the Russian in front of me, dramatically swinging from one position to the next. Now the emotion of the slow deliberate steps pulsed through my veins; every fibre in my body was embroiled with the movement and rhythm of the music. As the tempo increased, my fear of the pirouettes on the twelfth beat vanished. I was free; I was all powerful; I could do anything.

The spotlight followed my every move. The circle of light became my own world. Back and forth I tangoed, the full skirt of my long, black silk dress, a red lightning stripe flashing through its folds, swished emphatically as I pirouetted, posed and spun. I no longer had any inhibitions. I did not care. I was on air, dancing with the mood of the music, unconscious of technique or anything else.

When the applause came thundering across the forestage, I was not immediately relieved or even glad that it was all over. It seemed at the time that the curtain closed unnecessarily quickly, leaving me feeling surprised and somewhat disconcerted at the abrupt conclusion of my 'number'.

My spirits soured as the applause continued. It had not died and there were shouts from the audience for a curtain call. The count appeared, unbidden at my side, his shoe still in his hand. He congratulated me in his usual pompous manner and with a further flood of words, begged me not to take the curtain call. He became adamant. At a first performance, it could spoil one's luck. It would seem that he was totally addicted and influenced by every shade of superstition.

He had his way. I could only laugh at the earnestness with which he made his plea. But I demurred to his request and followed him off the stage while the applause continued on the other side of the curtain.

In the wings, we met Mario. He kissed my hand with grace and permitted himself a shy smile. He had not had the time to retie the laces of his left shoe, I noticed, but something told me that I should tactfully ignore the fact.

The orchestra struck up again as I returned to my dressing room. From the platform at the top of the stairs, we watched the curtain rise for the ballet. The troupe involved some eighty dancers. I had only a little over five minutes to change for my national dance number. Leaving my well-wishers, I hurried down the steps to find Milouka, who was waiting in my room with the fresh costume.

I returned to the stage, not a second too soon. This time, however, the ice had been broken and the wheel was spinning. Nothing could stand in the way of my confidence and joy. If the spectators up there in the circle and below in the stalls had any heart, they would surely feel the great happiness that I felt radiating from my soul.

And they did. The typist, the tax collector, the civil servant, the commercial traveller, the shop assistant and the army officer, the chocolate manufacturer and the stockbroker peering down from their spacious boxes, all applauded generously as the curtain fell. I took curtain call after curtain call until the drums announced the next item on the programme.

A group of Chinese girls fluttered nimbly on to the stage as I left. Item number 11 of the theatre programme was about to start. The show continued.

12

The 'Oasis' night club was decorated like a Moroccan caravan tent. Handsome hand-woven tapestries covered the white washed walls and the low brass tables were etched with eastern designs and patterns. Customers, lounging beside them on large, plush cushions made of maroon coloured leather, sipped wine and filled the air with the murmur of conversation and the smell of cigarette smoke.

Mother and Tuta had gone home to prepare a small festivity to celebrate the triumph of the evening. On the insistence of Count Cszapski, I had been persuaded to accompany him to the 'Oasis' for a more public acknowledgement of the evenings success, but only on the understanding that I was expected back at my apartment and could stay for only a short while. The count fully sympathised with my Mother's wish to congratulate her daughter at a private gathering, but felt that his contribution to the debut merited at least an hour of my company to mark the occasion. His ebullient insistence had eventually argued my mother into acquiescence and with the assurance that I would not be too long, she had left me in the charge of the count. He had certainly taken a very active part in ensuring the maximum chance of a successful premiere. From his point of view, it had been a gamble. He had taken on the responsibility of promoting an unknown dancer, with only the recommendations of his Russian friend in Posen to guide him. As the agent, he needed the confirmation of public opinion to prove that he had been correct to take that chance.

The evening had endorsed his hard work and now he was happily content to continue as my agent. The response from the auditorium promised a bright future – for both of us.

"The evening cannot be concluded with a plain 'good night' as though we had bumped into each other in the foyer of the theatre. I need to go home tonight with the satisfaction of having toasted our mutual success – a bond for the future!"

Mario had not stopped grinning all evening. He too seemed to be relieved that it had all gone so well. The three of us linked arms in jubilant mood and we strolled arm in arm, towards the night club, looking to all the world like a happy family.

The club was a popular haunt of theatre goers. Most of the guests wore long dresses or dark suits. All the theatres closed at a similar hour each evening and the 'Oasis' was convenient for refreshments and socialising before returning home. Count Cszapski and Mario were apparently regular customers. Both were warmly greeted by staff and guests alike, with the exception of an elderly couple at the bar, who made a point of deliberately turning their backs as we approached. I thought this somewhat rude, but assumed then, that they did not know the count well, an example of my naivety. In fact, I later found. they knew the count all too well.

One man in particular did not seem to fit into the general scene. His shocking choice of wardrobe demanded that he should be noticed. A loud check jacket screamed discordantly at his coarse green pullover. His features were sharp, his piercing eyes flashing from beneath abnormally thick, bushy eyebrows.

Stanislaus Sobieski was engaged in a rather heated argument with two other men. Oblivious of their surroundings, they leant over the table until their heads nearly touched. In turn the heads twitched and jerked as the owner emphasised his point, his eyes rolling, aware that he had the full attention of his adversary. Ignoring the intensity of the conversation, the count addressed the wearer of the conspicuous jacket. The man looked up irritably, the flicker of antagonism still in his eyes. On recognising the count, however, like a chameleon, his expression changed to amiable courtesy.

He scrambled to his feet and gave me a short quick bow when he was introduced, a lock of his black hair straying forward over to his forehead. Impatiently, he swept it back into place. In turn, he introduced me to his two companions who, judging by their names, were both of Russian origin. They too were not attired for a visit to the theatre. They were, however, more conservatively dressed than Sobieski.

Stanislaus Sobieski himself, as it turned out, had known the count since their days in the army together. Both had served together as cadets and later in the cavalry. Both progressed at the same time to the rank of lieutenant.

"He shed his uniform earlier than I did," said the count in jovial mood, putting his arm around the shoulders of his friend. "He went to Spain. He had learnt to shoot, liked playing soldiers and wanted to put his skills to practical use.

Poland remained boringly quiet, but Spain smelled of gun powder and war. So he went off to join their war."

"War!" Sobieski spat the word out. With a dismissive sweep of his arm, he freed himself from the count's grasp and preached directly at me, spitting out his words. "In Spain, two different worlds of politics collided with each other. Victory or defeat, everyone's future, yours included, depended on the outcome. I don't expect you to understand or even be the slightest bit interested in my ideals." Without waiting to see if I had an opinion, he raved on. Those sitting near us had stopped eating and had turned their heads to stare at Sobieski as his voice swelled with emotion. "You would never comprehend how a man could imagine that his contribution to such a conflict could influence it in any way: that by leaving his own country, family, home and livelihood in order to fight, gun in hand might help a new world to be created. Spain is not the only place where I've fought for a new ideology. I have ridden with the Red Brigade... and I would do it again tomorrow."

His outburst was now being addressed to other customers around the table, resentfully, as though he knew from the start that his words would be falling on deaf ears. Like me, the rest of his audience gaped at him in astonishment. He could not help but have noticed that even in our taste for clothes, we were worlds apart.

The count showed signs of discomfort at the turn that the conversation had taken. He had anticipated that our time together would be spent in more festive mood, especially tonight. He made a vain attempt to sidetrack matters away from the ominous subject of war by diverting my attention to the reason for our visit to the Club.

"Maria my dear, a theatre in Gdinga has been in touch with me already. They have expressed an interest in your act. What do you think?" I mumbled a reply. I did not comprehend the full impact of what he was suggesting. My attention was focused elsewhere. Sobieski's words echoed in my ears, I had not heard such challenging ideas before. What did he mean when he claimed that I could not understand? Why did he seem to think that we were so different? He was right, I was confused, I did not understand.

The man fascinated me and foolishly, my desire to satisfy my innocent curiosity provoked him further.

"And this new... this other world, which is better than the present one, shall it be created by bombs, assassinations and war?" I asked.

"Does that shock you?" Sobieski turned round abruptly and gave me a hostile glare. "Can a wolf or tiger be trained to abandon the hunt, when it chases and kills its prey before tearing it apart? You are so young and innocent that you cannot know how a bomb in the right place at the right time can bring justice closer to mankind. Just as long as there is someone around who has the courage to throw the bomb in the first place."

And once again I found myself in the midst of men whose topic of fervent discussion was war and its various aspects. Their enthusiasm was infectious and could not fail to affect me. Here was a man possessed. Perhaps he could succeed in such a murderous conflict. However, it seemed to me also that they were afraid of it. Talking relieved their fear and distanced the event itself.

My face must have reflected my doubts. "You must not be frightened. Fear is the greatest enemy. Fear prevents us again and again from tackling rogue laws and legislation," the deep voice spoke close to my ear now. "Mankind is not bad! We believe that man is basically good. It is only the methods of man, media propaganda that is bad. Radios and the press conspire. The human race has to be set free!"

Mario had been listening to the speaker with intense concentration. The Italian was staring in reverent admiration at Stanislaus Sobieski, his hands pressed so hard on his forehead that red marks appeared on his skin. Once more the count tried to give the conversation a new direction. He hailed a waiter and when the champagne that he had ordered arrived, he poured it out solemnly, taking elaborate care.

Raising his glass, he announced, "I propose a toast, to your future, your happiness and your success, Nana Sullivan." At last he had succeeded in steering the attention of the audience to more peaceful matters.

Everyone raised their glasses crying in unison, "Nana Sullivan" and I flushed with pride.

13

The hours in the day seemed endless. I rehearsed every morning for two tedious hours. Until the performance in the evening, I was free for the rest of the day to use the time as I wished. There were of course the visits to the hairdresser and massage parlour and fittings for new dresses at the salon, but these were intermittent appointments that took up too little of the vacuum.

At first, I tried to study; to gain a practical knowledge of German and French, continuing with the languages that were taught at the Sacré Coeur. I bought pencils and paper and attempted to sketch the urban world about me. When I became dissatisfied with my efforts, I redeployed the pencils and paper and tried to write short stories.

It became more and more tiresome to drag myself to the desk or the drawing board. My heart was not committed and I found that my concentration lasted for shorter and shorter periods. In the end, any extended project was out of the question. I could not even start a good book, knowing that I would never finish it as this would require prolonged sessions of sitting still.

Three days were fruitfully occupied. In the suburb of Praga were several furniture manufacturers. Their workshops lay in the Peterburska behind the Alexander Park area. There, one could acquire customer designed furniture. For three days, I was busy planning and designing cupboards, tables and chests which would be suitable for my apartment. Once the project was finished, however, I rapidly lost interest. The hours and days again became empty and aimless and I was aware of a certain restlessness of mind and body that I did not understand. It was more than a desire to absorb the novelty of my new surroundings. Aged just seventeen, the 'monster' inside me was beginning to stir. I began to notice things that previously had little importance for me and gradually, I also realised that my attitudes to the people around me were changing.

My public appearances at the variety theatre and the count's publicity campaign with photographs and press releases, inevitably attracted the attention of male visitors. Every night fifty white roses were sent to my dressing room, but the donor remained anonymous. Letters and visiting cards arrived every day in flattering abundance. I replied to none.

Some of these epistles and notes aroused my curiosity. A distinctive style of writing or an unusual use of a word would cause me to close my eyes and try to imagine the writer; his face; his physique, his dress or the way he spoke.

I was beginning to notice the male sex. It sometimes came as a mild surprise just how much more interest I found myself taking in the men that were introduced to me or in those I observed in the cafés or restaurants. My experience to date, had been of how men reacted towards me, resulting in various evasive actions on my part. I had not 'felt' anything within myself, rather that life was a series of experiments, each to be manipulated as the occasion permitted and twisting them to my own best advantage. Now, I found myself seeking out the handsome face, the well-shaped hands or the eyes that exposed a meaningful soul. I found them attractive. In the theatre, standing on the platform that overlooked the stage, I noticed that one of the rehearsing tightrope walkers had broad straight shoulders; that every muscle was visible through the tight body stockings of the acrobats. In the company of the count and Mario, I fell to wondering why men smelt so very different from women. In the tram, when a soldier pressed close against me in the crowd, the indescribable feeling that was aroused within me, took my breath away.

As much as I tried to ignore these, for me, strange events, my thoughts circled round to the same thing again and again. In spite of myself, my new hobby became ever more fascinating. I became ever more involved with trying to decipher the hidden meanings that lay behind the formal behaviour of the gentlemen who tried to impress me with their gleaming white shirt fronts.

The programme at the Café Club changed in mid-February. I locked my apartment in the Nowy Swiat and moved to Gdinga in the north of Poland. With the move, I hoped that new work and fresh surroundings would occupy my mind and my former peace with the world would return.

The director of the 'Mascotte' had seen my performance in Warsaw and had planned a special coverage in his printed programme. He had chosen to keep the 'Tango Nocturna' but elected to replace the folk dance with my third option, the 'Rumba'. Other modifications were made so that on the Gdinga stage, I would perform together with other artistes on the stage with me.

Vera, my resourceful Vera, once again managed to conjure up an atmosphere of home for us in the hotel rooms to which we were allocated. The town, like Warsaw was covered in a thick layer of snow, but the sun shone more often and for a while, the faithful Vera and I used the free time to explore our new surroundings by horse drawn sled. Before climbing aboard, we would bury ourselves in furs for the cold was penetrating if one had to sit still for any length of time. The horse would set off at a sprightly trot, bells jingling. The frosty air, the views of the town bedecked in its winter finery and shimmering brightly in the afternoon sun, successfully distracted me for a while.

After only two weeks, however, the town had lost its fascination for me and the desires and feelings that I hoped had been left behind in Warsaw returned more intensely than ever. They had been merely sleeping.

Here too, a number of men, both young and old, started to follow me about. They would sometimes get as far as the hotel lobby, intent on seeking to attract my attention and eager to pay their respects. I was not the only one to be so pestered. A Hungarian singer who was on stage with me, was subject to similar treatment. She stayed in the same hotel and we had ample opportunity to discuss the various antics of our admirers.

For me, the situation was becoming intolerable. I needed to escape from my own sensual desires and from the demands of others. The answer, I decided, was physical exercise. Instead of sleeping late as I had done in the past, Vera was commissioned to wake me early. I signed on with the local Master of Ballet for two sessions a day; an hour in the morning and an hour in the afternoon. I started to take riding lessons at the riding academy, where the indoor schooling area was a little old fashioned, but nevertheless spacious. My instructor was a retired cavalry officer who showed little mercy. The third venture involved the local swimming bath, which I visited several times a week, achieving distances that I had never attempted before. I committed myself to all this activity with the firm intention of bringing my body under control once more, providing little time for my mind to speculate.

It was not that easy at first. The temptation to stay in bed was great. During the initial week, I tried to skip the riding or swimming. 'Just this time', I would tell myself. Vera would wake me and I would seriously consider the 'pros' and 'cons' of making the effort to get out of my warm bed. This would only be a delaying factor, however, for the 'pros' invariably won the argument and before the 'cons' could get in another word, I would get up, pack my swimsuit and pull on my breeches.

Once this was done, pride and self-satisfaction would take over and I attacked my self-imposed marathon with enthusiasm. The day arrived when I could sit on the horse in trot without either stirrups or reins. Eventually, I managed to swim twenty lengths of the pool and add a few more for fun. When I had started, the twenty lengths had taken an interminable time and I had climbed, utterly exhausted out of the water.

Within two weeks of the start of the sports project, my body became noticeably fitter and more supple. As I progressed, so I became more ambitious, pushing myself to become more competent every day. The satisfaction of overcoming physical weakness, fed on itself and in turn became even more rewarding.

There were some drawbacks. The producer and my colleagues at the theatre interpreted my rare attendance at their nightly gatherings to mean other things. I was prone to tiredness during the first couple of weeks in hard training and to them, the indications led them to other conclusions. I took no notice of their insinuations and as a result, they regarded me as haughty and arrogant. As the weeks passed, I became more and more isolated from them. Even the generous floral tributes and letters that had been delivered in abundance when I first arrived at the Mascotte, eventually disappeared. The fans, disappointed at my lack of response, no longer wasted their money on flowers and cards for a performer that was rapidly acquiring an unpopular reputation.

The only exception was a basket of fifty white roses. It continued to arrive regularly at Gdinga as it had in Warsaw and every evening it stood on my dressing table, waiting to greet me when I returned from the stage. There was never a note to indicate from whence the bouquet had come and how this determined admirer managed to obtain roses in the depths of winter, remained his secret.

14

I used to thoroughly enjoy my riding lessons. Castor had taught me to ride so that whatever happened, I instinctively remained safely in the saddle. Now, I was introduced to the techniques of classical riding with its reliance on the self-discipline and balance of the rider to achieve results. It was in many ways similar to the discipline required of a dancer and I found it intriguing to discover how to control a horse with minimum effort and at the same time produce maximum effect.

One morning, as I cantered across the hall of the riding school at the end of the lesson, I noticed Mario standing by the door. Vera must have told him where to find me. I nodded to him acknowledging his presence, before I circled the horse to a halt, dismounted and handed the reins to the waiting groom. I spent a few minutes in discussion with my instructor about the technical aspects of the lesson before the next horse and rider entered the riding hall whereupon, I thanked my instructor and collected my coat. Throwing it casually over my shoulders, I joined Mario by the door.

His face coloured as he tried to explain the reason for his unexpected arrival in Gdinga. He was supposedly conveying an urgent message from the count about future business contracts. Instinctively, I sensed that his visit had some other motive. Not wishing to hurt his feelings, I listened attentively, pretending a sincerity of interest that disguised my curiosity. I was protective towards him as if he was my small brother, although in reality he was probably my senior and I felt a need to shield him from embarrassment like a sympathetic sister. Having no brother, however, I could only guess at the identity of my attitude and feelings.

My mother had been too busy to come to visit me in Gdinga, trusting that Vera would cope with any crisis. It was therefore a welcome surprise to see a familiar and friendly face. Although we had not known each other for long,

Mario was a messenger who brought news and greetings from 'home'. Warsaw had become for me, my second home.

That evening, I accepted an invitation from one of my colleagues to join the festivities after the show. With Mario as company, there was no danger of becoming bored by the proceedings. To my cost, I had too often found these gatherings wearisome. I did not enjoy drinking and flirting into the early hours of the morning. It left me incapable of fulfilling my schedule for the following day.

The restaurant where the artistes gathered for drinks and a late meal was not far from the Mascotte. Most performers met there regularly after the show, whether they were singers, dancers, jugglers or acrobats. The walls were covered with photographs of the clientele, autographed and with messages of good will to the restaurant owner scrawled across them. The room itself had the atmosphere of intimacy and leant itself to a feeling of family friendliness, albeit that the members of the family were extremely colourful and varied in character.

The director of the 'Mascotte' was a Jew. He was the only person that knew about my tough training programme. Since I first arrived at the club, he had been kind to me and I had nick-named him 'Tatek' (Daddy) because of his benevolence towards me. This, he had taken to heart and had tried to fulfil the responsibilities that went with the title.

As soon as Mario and I walked into the room, Tatek invited us to sit at his table. Immediately, he found common ground with my companion. Rome had been his home for many years, where he had worked in variety theatres and to put his guest at ease, he took the opportunity to air his rusty Italian. It was not many minutes before he was twittering away in a totally incomprehensible language.

A director is always a very popular fellow towards the end of the month. Payments are soon due and some artistes think that their employer can be wooed better over a glass of wine than in a sombre office when it concerns an advance in salary. It was not long before Tatek was called away from the table by the two 'Orana' Jugglers. They were very clever at manipulating their gold coloured batons on stage but were unable to handle their money with the same skill.

Mario, who had been quieter and more reserved than usual, seemed to welcome the fact that we were now alone. He thoughtfully refilled the glasses with the speciality of the house, a deep red wine, before lighting one of his sweet smelling Greek cigarettes. His movements were so deliberated and careful that it was fairly obvious to me that his thoughts were elsewhere and he was trying to come to a decision.

The tip of his cigarette glowed as he pulled the smoke into his lungs. Slowly, he exhaled and said, "What I said this morning... about contracts and business matters. It was irrelevant... but I think you know that." He took a sip from his glass. "I had to find an excuse to see you. I couldn't really turn up and simply say 'Hi, it's me', or 'Mama mia! Ecosi difficile adire!'"

My instincts had been right. The messages from the count were a subterfuge. The good Cszapski could not take a single step without the young Italian by his side, so Mario had been obliged to invent a convincing story in order to get away for a few days in order to meet me.

I smiled and gave him to understand that I did not have any idea what he was talking about if he insisted on speaking Italian. He looked at me in silence, taking the occasional pull at his cigarette. I studied his face through the haze of smoke as it drifted upward from his lips. He moved his chair fractionally closer to mine and in a confidential voice, said, "Nana, you are the only person I can talk to." I sat very still. He was about to reveal the true motive for his visit and I did not want to distract him. "We have not known each other for very long and I suspect that you, a woman, will not understand what I am about to tell you. From the first moment that I met you, you remember, when the count and I came to see you in your cold chaotic apartment, ever since then, I have felt that it would be nice if you could have been my sister. While the count was occupied with his silly speeches, I had time to study you closely. I liked what I saw and identified with you."

My mind was doing somersaults. What was Mario trying to tell me? Surely, it was not of an attraction to me. I had seen with my own eyes, in which directions his affections lay and that did not include people like myself. To disguise any tell tale expression on my face, I suddenly developed a fascination for the way the lights of the restaurant filtered through the wine in my glass. Mario's voice continued.

"I don't have any brothers or sisters and don't really know what family life is about. My father is dead... and my mother? I have no idea whatsoever where she is... whether she is even alive. She ran off a long time ago. You seemed that evening to be the sister that I've... that I've always wanted and never ..."

The noisy distribution of meals at the tables in the middle of the room, momentarily interrupted his explanations and he swivelled his head to see what the commotion was all about. When he continued, there was a pleading tone in his voice, rather like that of a small boy asking forgiveness.

"You must not feel sorry for me, that is not why I am telling you all this." He became more assertive. "Pity makes us dishonest and distorts our true feelings." He stubbed his cigarette out on the ash tray, pounding it vigorously until it disintegrated. He was perhaps at last getting to the point. I dared not avert my eyes from the wine glass to look at him.

"Count Cszapski met me three years ago in Milano. At the time, I was trying my luck as a singer in a wine bar. Where I come from, in Sicily, the songs are among the most beautiful in Italia. Cszapski was a captain in a Polish delegation that had taken part in a riding competition in Roma. They were on their way back to Warsaw, when they stopped in Milano and visited the wine bar. He asked me to sing at his table and…" He paused, staring into the distance. The knuckles of his hand lying on the table whitened as he clenched his fist. Seconds passed. He was mentally in Milan and seemed to have forgotten what he was doing.

"…it was possible to clear any obstacles during his short stay and I was able to leave with him." I was watching him now out of the corner of my eye. Mario's face had lost its colour. He spoke in a monotone, his mouth opening and closing like a ventriloquist's dummy. What was he trying to tell me? It was causing him a great deal of distress and he had so far only succeeded in confusing me. I burned with curiosity and hardly dared to breathe for fear of causing him to stop talking.

"When we arrived in Warsaw, the count learned of his transfer to Torun. This was a disaster. He left no stone unturned to cancel his commission. He knew the small garrison at Torun and it was impossible for him to take me there. The regiment insisted on his immediate departure, however, so Cszapski handed in his resignation. He then behaved in such a way as to enforce a dishonourable discharge from the army, staining his reputation for ever."

Something started to make sense. It explained why the count was rudely snubbed in the clubs of Warsaw by people whom he obviously knew and who equally obviously knew him.

"What Cszapski did for me cannot be described in words. He deliberately abandoned his career and his honour as a soldier. As the son of an army family, that was the equivalent of losing life itself. He made other sacrifices, both material and idealistic, in the course of caring for me. I could never give an account of everything that he has given me during our friendship, my clothes, my studies, the apartment that he bought for me."

Again he paused and lit another cigarette. His eyes seemed to have sunk into his head, large shadows engulfed them. He stared down at his cigarette, his shoulders hunched in desperation. His voice was barely audible now. "Why am

I telling you all this? Don't be cross with me, Nana! As I said before, you are the only person that I feel that I can talk to... and I must talk to someone. You see the terrible thing is that... I cannot live any longer with the count." He raised his eyes to meet mine, an expression of childlike helplessness on his face begging for my understanding and sympathy. His huge dark eyes glistened as the tears welled.

"I thought that no other person but he would ever enter my life. I have never desired the love of a girl or a woman. He was everything to me. My entire being belonged to him. It never occurred to me that it could or would change. But now..." he reached for my hand "...my feelings have grown cold; empty like an upturned glass. I suppose I could bear this, Nana, but that is not all. The glass has been refilled. The feelings have been rekindled to their original fire but... they belong to another!"

I could find nothing to say. I had heard of the attractions that some men had for one another and was not unaware of the gossip about the relationship between Mario and the count. To hear about it first hand, though, was disturbing. However much my instincts objected to such forms of love, I had to try and understand that some men, like the young Italian, were given to it by nature. Yet in the same breathe, he was making the revelation that his affair with Cszapski was at an end and there was another who had already taken his place. Why had he come all this way... to tell me? I had an ominous foreboding that, somehow, I had become the new focus of his attention.

"Can you recall the night at the 'Casa', Nana? You remember the evening of your premiere... the man in the check jacket at our table?" I felt my whole body relax. "It was with him, as it was with the count, three years ago."

I felt like leaping up from my chair and dancing with relief. So, Sobieski was the one. It did not matter to me who it was, as long as I had not become entangled in his misdirected passions. It was as he said, only a brotherly need to confide in someone whom he trusted that had brought him all the way from Warsaw.

Disguising my jubilation, I spoke in as calm a voice as I could manage.

"Feelings can sometimes deceive you, Mario. It happens that we have to change them sooner or later... Are you quite sure that Stanislaus Sobieski returns your affection?"

"He has been to see me twice at Rozbraticka." Mario replied.

While I had been so absorbed by Mario's confessions, the rest of the tables in the restaurant had been pushed together for everyone to sit around in one huge party. Only our table remained on its own, still separated from the rest by a metre as wide as the river Warta. I had been aware of the hostility that was generating behind my back, but had not dared to interrupt Mario. He had a troubled soul and need to rid himself of guilt. It would have been unforgivable of me to stop him. I could sense that the deep despair of his conflict was breaking his heart. Holding both my hands, as though touch would comfort and strengthen him, he continued in a low voice.

"I cannot go back to Warsaw; not back to Cszapski. I cannot bear to deceive him any longer. I cannot look him in the eye and pretend to have an affection for him which I simply do not have. With the exception of the clothes on my back, I've left everything that he has ever given me in my apartment…"

After a pause, he continued, "I know most of the things I had from him are intangible, but I can't keep up the charade any longer." I felt the pressure of his hold on my hands increase. "I am going to meet Stanislaus in Łódź, Nana. Apart from myself, you are the only person close to the count…"

My face may have been under control, but he must have felt the slight tremor in my fingers, for he hesitated and looked deep into my eyes before continuing.

"…well, not as close as I have been, I admit. He didn't want anyone else but me. But you must explain to him and help him. I know it will be hard for him … very hard." At last, he released his tight grip on my hands, reached into the pocket of his suit and pulled out an object that glinted in the lamp light. "This medallion belonged to my father. It is the only thing that I possess, to treasure his memory by. I loved him dearly. Please give it to the count." He thrust a small medal into my hand. "I cannot send it to him with a letter. Written words are so hard without feeling!" The noise made by the party behind me had grown increasingly louder. Shouts and laughter had almost prevented me from hearing Mario at times. Now, I realised that we were the cause of the din. Our apparent refusal to join them had made us the focus for their jeering.

Tatek appeared at my side and asked us, impatiently, to join the others. Mario, concerned with his personal problems, did not immediately understand the urgent necessity to be sociable. He gaped at Tatek and his hesitation was interpreted as a refusal even as we moved the table to join the others. Some earthy and provoking remarks were slung our way. Mario was still too wrapped in his own thoughts to take much notice. Innocently and possibly to acknowledge the safe delivery of his mission to me, he raised his glass towards me.

This caused more resentment. It seemed to our mocking audience that Mario was deliberately ignoring them. One thing led rapidly to another and suddenly someone shouted the word 'fascist'.

Italy was of course the land of Mussolini. The dictator from the Palazzo

Venezia was renowned for converting even cats and dogs into fascists. The accusations started to rain thick and fast. "Obviously HE was one of them." "What was HE doing here?" "Why was HE allowed to leave the country?" "Did Mussolini fancy Poland?" The train of thought was ugly and their intoxicated brains were working overtime.

The stocky 'pillar man' from the Four Rondellos (the acrobats), more inebriated than the rest and puffed up like an Atlas, muscles bulging, was being particularly offensive. His filthy jokes soon included me.

Gdinga in February 1939 was suffering a bad attack of war fever. I had been called 'Szwab' before, a nickname normally applied to the Germans. My hair was very fair and I sometimes wore it in plaits around my head. It was not to be taken seriously, rather a jest, a light-hearted ridicule of the German threat.

In the present company, however, the word 'Szwab' suddenly became an accusation. I was no longer just 'Szwab', I was a spy for the 'Dwjka'. The acrobat expanded his theories far wider than his chest and added to the suspicions of my colleagues. The fact that I was rarely seen outside performances became evidence for my new crime. I must be an informer, reporting on the theatre activities. And of course, my companion, the hapless Mario – a fascist no less, proved the point conclusively.

The drunken acrobat, revelling in his oratory powers, finally screamed at me.

"Are you a spy for the 'dwjka'? Go on deny it!"

I was so disgusted with his behaviour and so angered by his impudence that I answered defiantly.

"If I were, what would it matter?" Oh the naivety of youth, when it thinks it can defy a river in full flood. As soon as my brain caught up with my mouth, I realised how very stupid it had been to lose my temper. A stunned silence followed. Then, pandemonium broke loose. My arrogant reply caused outrage. As one, the protagonists were on their feet, brawling with each other and shouting threatening insults at me.

Someone retained enough sanity to call the police.

Looking back on that frightening night, I confess, my remark was not only stupid, it was thoughtless and downright foolhardy under the circumstances. I was aware of the tensions that saturated the town at the time and I should not have thrown down the challenge. But the acrobat had irritated me immensely with his ignorant suppositions and I could not help myself. Unwittingly, I had provided the spark that detonated an explosion.

Mario had calmly watched the whole episode as though it was a scene on the cinema screen, detached as he was from the world about him. He seemed totally oblivious of the peril that now threatened us.

We were rescued by Tatek. He strode masterfully between us and our accusers and quickly pushed the pair us into a small side room. He was their respected employer and thankfully, no one tried to stop him.

As he closed the door, however, it was only too clear that he was seriously concerned for our safety. Beads of sweat glistened on his forehead. He knew the police were on their way and explained as rapidly as he could that a legal investigation would mean a long period of detention and berated me for my thoughtless remark. It would be very difficult to convince the police of my innocence after such an incautious outburst. Flight was our only option. With an impatient wave of his hand, he dismissed our objections that he might get into trouble if we should conveniently disappear and purposefully opened a second door, stuck his head through the gap and scanned the corridor to ensure it was clear.

Mario and I followed him down the long passage, through the kitchens and scullery and out of the house. Here the Jew abandoned us, our panting breath forming little clouds in the cold night air. He paused only to shake hands and wish us 'God speed', not waiting to hear the words of gratitude that were on the tip of my tongue. In an instant, he was gone, leaving us standing forlornly at the back gate of the restaurant.

An hour later, I was on my way back to Warsaw. With Vera's help, I had hastily packed some belongings and Mario had managed to hire a car for the journey. Vera herself stayed behind to complete the packing and arrange for the rest of the luggage to follow. Mario was to leave for Łódź. He walked beside the car as it moved slowly away, gesturing and signalling at me through the window. Finally, he pressed his fingers to his lips and blew a kiss. As the car swept me away, his forlorn figure faded into the night.

15

Herbert was a tall broad shouldered man, just like my father.

Since my return to Warsaw in March, I had danced at the 'Adria' and it was in my dressing room, that I saw him for the first time. It was the 17th March, the anniversary of his wife's death.

That evening, the white roses which had followed me to Gdinga and that were always there to greet me when I returned from the stage, were missing. On the little table where the roses normally stood, lay the linen mat, but no basket and no bouquet. I remember how the surprise at not finding the flowers where I expected, caused me to stop in mid-stride, as though I had lost something and could not quite recall where I had left it.

Instead of the flowers there lay a single white card. On the card, the name 'Dr Herbert Kurzke' was inscribed. A movement in the mirror made me look up and... there he was... watching me.

I had become so used to seeing the roses, they had become like dear friends to me. Thus, the man reflected in my mirror, holding a bunch of white roses in his hands, somehow did not seem to be a stranger. At last, he had come. At last he had revealed his name.

Shivers of excitement ran down my back. For so long, I had wondered about the source of so much dogged persistence. The roses had never included a card to placate my curiosity, but, it would have been very strange if, even for one day they had failed to arrive. I turned to greet him.

A handsome man stood before me. He was tall with fair hair that was thinning a little on the crown of his head. He stood proud and straight and bowed with grace and dignity as he presented his flowers to me. My first impression aged him thirty plus for he already had lines etched on his face. His hands, one of the criteria by which I would judge a man on my first encounter, were well cared for and slender. His eyes were a deep blue colour, not cold, but suggesting a friendly, warm humour.

Seated on the small sofa, he offered an explanation for the roses. He told me that his wife had also been a dancer. He produced some photographs and I gazed at them in amazement. Her likeness to me was uncanny. They could have been taken of myself and I could only speculate on how disturbing it must have been for him to find the pictures of me in the papers and then to see me in the flesh on the stage.

"It was as though Katrina herself had been reincarnated," he said. "I had found her again. She died…" He hesitated, took a deep breath, then continued… "She died in an air crash. Her body was never identified." He fell silent for a few moments. He must have loved his Katrina very much. He was still obviously upset by the thought of her horrifying death.

"Then I saw your picture. I had bought the paper as usual and opened it to scan the news as I walked home, when I saw what looked to me like a picture of Katrina. It was crazy, but I immediately bought all the papers that the newsboy carried. I needed to possess everything that was connected with that picture and I suppose, in my shocked state, I was trying to stop anyone having the chance to even see it. It was madness, but I felt that only I had the right to look at her." I listened to him, aware that I was again providing a sympathetic ear to a man with a troubled soul. This man was a stranger, however. His advantage was the bunch of roses and his indisputable good looks. I found him extremely attractive.

My resemblance to his Katrina may well have brought me to his attention in the first place, but I felt no resentment. I felt totally at ease in his company, as though I had known him for a long time.

"Because Katrina had no proper grave that I could visit and leave flowers to remember her by, I sent the flowers to you, her living image. Please forgive me, it was presumptuous of me… but it helped me to recover from her loss."

Fate had deprived him of his wife and her gravestone. Katrina's white roses had found refuge in my dressing room, like homeless wanderers. Herbert's love for his wife had been his reason for sending the flowers in the first place and they had come to mean peace and security to me. That security now transferred to the man himself. I had dreamed for so long about the possible characteristics of the romantic that could so constantly track my theatre career. The reasons for his actions were not quite what I had expected, but far from feeling insulted that I was a substitute for the one he had loved, I felt honoured to have received the attention of such an honest and faithful gentleman. The faith that I had in the flowers made me believe also in the man. To be adored with such unchanging loyalty, after death, reflected back on the source of that love. The man must possess an eternal depth of heart and who was I to deny him. At the age of seventeen, it seemed that fate could not bestow a greater blessing on me.

When spring banished the winter chill, we met, night after night during the clear starry evenings. After the show, he would be waiting for me in my dressing room and gradually I learned his full story.

He told me that he was a surgeon. After the tragedy of Katrina's death he became the victim of a nervous break down and for weeks he had wanted neither to see anyone nor to talk to anyone. He lost his appetite and fell ill.

Friends helped him back to normality and he eventually returned to work, itself a great healer. He loved his work, and apart from his practise, he soon became head of a clinic. Day and night, he had worked on the wards and in the operating theatre to avoid thinking of his own immense pain. Since he had found me, the pain had lessened. At first he could only send the flowers but as the numbness of grief faded and a belief that the morrow was a treasure that could be anticipated with hope, he had decided to declare himself.

Usually we walked along the Zaknoczymska to Glacis, where we could see the view over the citadel and the silver ribbon of the Weichsel. Sometimes, we walked across the Sachsisher Platz to the cathedral, where the five golden cupolas watched over the sleeping town, glowing brightly, when the moon was full. Herbert had the height and strength of a sturdy tree that I could depend upon for support.

And how his patients adored him! With such calm confidence, he told me how he helped them to recover; how he was much respected and was called upon to lecture at the university, despite his twenty-eight years which was half the age of most of the speakers at that venerated institution. His shirts and ties were always selected with careful heed to their suitability for the occasion. His eyes were always kind and understanding. I felt so safe when he closed his hands around mine. I felt so secure in his arms.

We became engaged, three months to the day that Herbert first came to my dressing room.

My mother was delighted. She had been acquainted with Herbert's mother when she lived in Germany as a girl for they had attended the same school. Frau Kurzke was a few years her senior, but the two women had exchanged amicable letters of congratulation, concerning the romance that had blossomed between their children and honoured us by travelling all the way from Hamburg to be with us for the occasion of the engagement. That evening, Herbert did not attend his clinic and I was excused from the theatre. Instead we spent the time quietly celebrating with the family and a few friends.

Our engagement did not mean that I had to give up my stage career. Herbert was happy that I should retain a full freedom to be independent. The relationship was unrestricted by petty rules and our love for each other was not forced into a rigid pattern.

On my abrupt return to Warsaw, I had danced at the 'Adria' for a month. Cszapski then arranged for me to perform in the cabaret at the 'Zuwazck'. He was frequently unavailable during the early months of that summer and in his absence, I attended to the final details and signed the contract myself.

As spring developed into summer, the count became a changed man. The realisation that Mario had left him had a severe effect on him. He took the young man's disappearance exceedingly hard and the depression that followed destroyed his naturally optimistic character. He neglected his work and became careless in his appearance. He would not shave for days. His shirts were crumpled and his trousers unpressed, his shoes dirty and worn. For those who had known him when he was always immaculately dressed in the latest fashion, the decline was painfully obvious. In addition, he showed signs of addiction to cocaine. His eyes acquired a telling yellow tinge.

I had not had the courage to present him with Mario's medallion and message. Since saying 'Goodbye' to the Italian, I had carried his memento on my necklace for safe keeping. On reflection, I had thought it kinder to leave the count under the impression that something serious may have happened to the young man which prevented him from returning or communicating. Although it might cause the count anxiety at first, it meant that at least his memories of Mario would not be clouded by disappointment His frequent absences, however, caused me to wonder whether he was still trying to trace his lover, although he never confided in me. But then... why should he? He was not aware that I had knowledge or that I had innocently become concerned with his amorous attachments.

Although I could not bring myself to do all that Mario had asked me to do, I did try to look after the count. He was frequently invited to dinner for he seemed otherwise to pay irregular attention to his meals. I also helped him with his business affairs as far as I was able. But in the three months since Mario had left him, he had aged considerably and seemed unable to find any motivation or direction.

The time and opportunity to tell him of Mario's disaffection did not happen.

I fully intended that one day, I would talk to him, but the day never arrived. I could only watch his steady down-hill slide, helplessly witnessing him submerge into a morass of despair.

16

Warsaw, in the late summer days of 1939, seemed unchanged. The city, at the time, was supposedly the centre of international concern. Politicians were haggling over the fate of Polish territory and mediators negotiated for partners. For the citizen of Warsaw, life was the same today as it was yesterday and of course, as it would be tomorrow, no different from any of the inhabitants of a national capital in Europe. Taxis and trams drove down the streets. Beneath parasols, the customers sat outside the cafés, sipping coffee, nibbling cakes and enjoying the company of their friends. Children licked ice creams and accompanied their elders in and out of the shops. The threatening clouds of war were of no concern to them. Far more important to me, was trying to decide whether to buy the blue gaberdine outfit from 'Janowski' or the suit in the more expensive woollen material from 'Mirewiez'. Autumn was approaching, so the woollen cloth would probably be more useful in winter!

My mother was a frequent visitor to Warsaw on various missions concerned with charitable organisations. During one of these trips, she announced that she wished to come with me to visit the count. She too had become worried about his physical and moral decline and felt that perhaps she could contribute some positive suggestions. Her experience of such things was far greater than mine.

We left the flat in high optimism that we would somehow help the count, but as we were about to cross the street at Marszalskowa, we were distracted by the excited shouts of the newspaper boys.

"Hitler has declared war on us!" "Hitler has declared war on us!" "Hitler has declared war on us!"

The print was still wet and the boys could not distribute the papers fast enough, let alone return the change if required. They pocketed many an extra zloty that night, simply because nobody wanted to wait. All that mattered was to obtain a newspaper – and quickly.

The headline stood out in bold capitals at the top of the page. With difficulty, I tried to comprehend the small print beneath it. What did it mean? "Hitler has declared war on us!" The impact of the words did not seem to relate to the mellow autumn afternoon. I had not lived long enough to have experienced the upheavals that had bedevilled the history of my fatherland. Grandfather had talked about future trouble for as long as I could remember, but I had no notion of what it all meant.

Would it be, as the history books described, that guns and tanks would guard the border? Could it be that somewhere in the cornfields and forests, hundreds, perhaps thousands of human beings would have to fight and die? It was so unreal; somehow impossible to comprehend.

The sun shone from a calm, undisturbed sky. No shot had been fired and no grenade had exploded within my hearing. It was the age of radio communications and air travel, I reasoned. What could not be sorted out by one means would surely be sorted out by the diplomats who travelled in the planes. They could be seen on the weekly newsreels at the cinemas, flying back and forth, in their black suits, their briefcases tucked under their arms in business-like fashion. It was up to them to lose a few nights' sleep in order to draw up a treaty or agreement to avoid such nonsense as the newspapers declared. Surely these clever brains would succeed.

The headline news made no sense. In a forlorn attempt to deny the possible truth of the announcement, I crumpled the paper and threw it away. My mother linked arms with me and as we walked on, she remarked that perhaps it would be for the best if we returned to Posen the following day.

How naive and arrogant I was. It did not occur to me that aeroplanes could also carry bombs and soldiers, for that would have been a totally unreasonable and unsociable thing to do. It never crossed my mind, that Grandfather might have been right all those years, sensing the import of Hitler's devilish intrigues and predicting the inevitable.

On that unforgettable day, the 1st September 1939, Warsaw was enjoying a peaceful, autumnal day. 'Hitler has declared war on us' seemed a meaningless threat, which did not really involve us at all. Mother and I had slept late that morning. We were totally unaware of the initial air attacks on the military bases near Warsaw. We had not heard the planes that had flown around in the early morning skies. It was as though the newspapers were reporting about another world, another existence, of which we were not a part.

17

But, the war did not stop at the borders. The gentlemen with their diplomatic know-how and bulging briefcases proved helpless to prevent it. It was too late for gentle persuasion. Overnight, the balloon of peace in Warsaw burst.

The following morning, the newspapers reported the first Polish casualties; of villages set alight and burned to the ground; of the dead lying among the cornflowers and fronds of fern, riddled with bullets, torn to pieces by grenades or mown down by armoured tanks. News reached us that a whole regiment had been destroyed; a regiment of human beings, young and old, who only a few weeks earlier had worked in a factory, studied in a lecture hall or nurtured ambitions of moving to a little white house at the edge of the forest to spend the rest of their days in peace and quiet.

There were reports of masses of Germans attacking and masses of Poles counter attacking. Gossip inflated the numbers to thousands and I realised with horror that only the lives of the victims mattered in war. Just as an engine needs fuel, so war needed human beings. Young, old, handsome or ugly, anyone living was the fuel on which it feasted with insatiable appetite.

And Herbert?

As soon as war had been declared, he received orders to report to a military hospital behind the front line. He did not leave until the following day by which time a fuller understanding of the meaning of war was beginning to impress itself upon me. Had he left on the first day that war was announced, I do not think I would have been that worried about him. War to me still seemed something of a great adventure and it was one's honourable duty to join the battle in the tradition of flying the flag, hero worship, Napoleon and the Maid of Orleans... The notion that something could happen to Herbert in this vision of mine, had not occurred to me until the morning when I saw the first wounded soldiers being transported into Warsaw. There was a shortage of vehicles and the men were carried across the Novy Swiat on stretchers, in an endless procession.

Herbert was kitted out in full uniform when he came to say goodbye, later the same morning. I was terrified, angry, frustrated and burning with hatred for the war that was taking him away from me.

When he had gone, unable to think straight, all I could do was to stare at the door which he had closed behind him and at the latch which had been the last thing that he had touched.

It had all happened so horribly fast. Life had been normal two days ago. Only yesterday, I had danced at the theatre as usual and Herbert had collected me from the dressing room, as he did every day. This morning I had seen the first planes over the city, climbing high above the clouds, then diving low, almost touching the spire of the cathedral. The first convoys of battered, mud covered vehicles had driven down the Jerusalemski. The wounded followed. They were distributed into hastily organised, temporary hospitals. The first survivors of war had marched along the Novy Swiat, unshaven, with blood soaked bandages and torn uniforms. Those who stepped aside to make way for them saw the horror in their eyes.

The mountain had collapsed. The thunderstorm hit us without mercy. Warsaw was helpless, its inhabitants unprepared, many like myself having deluded themselves into assuming that it could not happen. The city was in a state of shock.

At the last minute, air raid shelters were being dug and frantic attempts made to reinforce cellars. Police raced through the streets in cars and on motorbikes. The panic buying of food had started.

Crowds fought over non-perishable goods and gas masks in the shops. The latest front line news could be heard from every window as the newsboys relayed information at the top of their voices. Everywhere, huge wall posters called on male citizens to take up arms.

I did not register the warning scream of the sirens. Slumped in the chair where Herbert had left me, I was still staring at the door, hardly aware of whether it was night or day, when my mother and Vera came rushing into the room to drag me down to the safety of the cellar. Mother had been unable to return to Posen, for the very simple reason that the army had commandeered all the trains. All telephone and telegraphic communication had broken down and we had no idea how father and the rest of the family were faring. It was a consoling comfort that she was still with me and I was not alone.

Warsaw had no anti-aircraft guns, no search lights. The city lay unprotected and vulnerable, like a puppy on its back. When the first bombers arrived, the hapless inhabitants of the city could only switch off all the lights in the house and seek shelter in the cellars, hiding themselves as deep as possible underground. Beyond that, the only thing to do was to pray to God and beg him to direct the containers of explosive to other quarters of the town, as far as possible from one's own street.

The city may have possessed no defences, but the Germans were not without organised assistance. As soon as the first squadron reached Warsaw airspace, lamps and spotlights, concealed in the town centre and all other sensitive areas, sprang to life and indicated targets.

The porter of our block of apartments was over sixty. He had been a soldier during the Great War and was a passionate patriot. Alert to the possibility of treachery, he crept outside to investigate what was going on, together with a police officer and a civilian. They observed a light shining from the roof of a building across the street. In the loft, they discovered a complete searchlight installation, the beam pointing towards heaven; a signpost of welcome for the approaching aircraft. The rooms had been disguised as a photographer's studio and had appeared deserted. A thorough search, however, had revealed a woman, concealed within the upholstery of the sofa.

Following that initial air attack on the city itself, aimed mainly at the railway stations and other prime targets in the suburbs, the fear of spies became a general disease. Neighbour became suspicious of neighbour as it was realised that the city had been thoroughly infiltrated by alien sympathisers. Even reliable 'names' were accused and individuals with good Polish credentials were among those arrested. Women were caught with messages secreted into the high heel of their shoe. Men in uniform tried to smuggle information about troop movements under false bandages and splints. One young man was apprehended in the middle of Vjadowski Avenue, carrying a transmitter in a flower pot.

We slept very little that night. After the planes had gone, the suddenness of the attack and the grim novelty of the situation in which we found ourselves, left us all in a state of shock. The women and children remained in the cellar, but Vera and I found mattresses and got as much sleep as we could in the corridor on the ground floor. If the bombing had started again, we would have been down in the cellar in seconds. My mother had been installed on a sofa which we managed to fit into the boiler room. The area down there was dark and without electricity to provide light, so all the candles in the building, new or half burned were collected and mother was given charge of them. She became known as the Candle Queen of the boiler room.

At 4am the next morning, mother woke me. Tuta was with her looking tired, dirty and dishevelled. Tuta! My dearest friend! All seemed quiet for the moment, so we climbed the stairs to my flat on the second floor, where Vera made us some coffee.

With dismay, we listened to Tuta's story. She had travelled through the night in an open truck of an army train. Kasimir, her fiancé, had been wounded near Kutno. He had managed to get a message to her via the guardsman at the station in Posen, telling her that he was being transported to a military hospital in Warsaw. Without stopping to pack anything, she had run to the station and fought for her passage to follow him.

Exhausted, her coat dirty and torn, her hair hanging in limp, bedraggled curls, but fired by singular determination, Tuta had come to find her lieutenant. The gentle, sensitive Tuta that I had known at the Ursuline boarding school had vanished. Instead a tigress, bent on protecting her loved one had been revealed.

The day remained quiet with no signs of further air attacks, so I fetched my coat and left immediately with my friend. The sky still glowed over the old town where fires raged uncontrollably.

There was no one on the street, but at the corner of Jerusalemski, we found a bar that was still open. Bright light streamed through the windows and projected shiny squares onto the pavement outside. It was hard to believe that it was not peace time... for we could hear music too.

I entered the bar in the hope of finding someone that I knew or better still an officer who would give me information about the wounded. Tuta waited for me in the hall. She felt that she looked too dishevelled to be seen in a public place and preferred to stay out of sight.

Every chair was occupied. Some couples were dancing to a silly jazzy record, others sat on the high bar stools, embracing each other. The tables were loaded with bottles and glasses as though the landlord wished to turn his stock into cash before a bomb destroyed his business. There were a number of 'ladies of the night' with their escorts. There were exotic looking characters who were quite openly bartering with narcotics. There were young men who were evading the military uniform and there were the racketeers, the parasites of war... and their business was thriving. The storm that hit us it seemed, had not churned just the surface. It had also stirred up the mud.

It was obvious that I could not expect to find any assistance amongst the clientele of this particular café and I turned to leave. As if from nowhere, Count Cszapski suddenly materialised at my side. I had failed to notice him amidst a group of younger men. His step was unsteady. He wore a tailcoat, but the lapels were stained. His shirt and tie looked as though they had been worn for days. He looked sick, his face sunken and hollow, a colourless grey, the growth of stubble on his chin indicating that he had not used a razor for some time. The man I saw before me, was not Count Cszapski. It was a shell, a caricature, a distortion, vile and decaying. It said; "I have the uncommon honour of welcoming you here. You weren't by any chance looking for me? You can see that I am very busy." He waved his empty glass in the direction of the table where his young companions were sitting, then, his arm dropped like lead to his side, as though the exercise had required too much effort. Only days before, my mother and I had been on our way to help him. We had not found him and the war had interrupted any further search. Now I took him by both arms and eased him to one side of the entrance.

"Come with us Count Cszapski. You can stay with us. You must forget all this. We can find a way…"

His tired eyes held me for a moment in a vacant stare. He seemed to be giving some consideration to what I had said. In answer, he slowly pushed up the sleeve of his jacket, revealing the skin of his forearm. It was sore with needle marks.

"Cocaine! I cannot live without it. My life will be over soon my little angel. Should you hear one day that I have 'shuffled off this mortal coil', possibly from the dustman who has carried off my corpse like he would the carcass of a mangy dog, do let them read a Mass for me in the cathedral. You can deduct the cost from my salary."

He smiled a tired smile, swung his arm dramatically across his waist and bowed his head slightly before turning his back on us and rejoining his friends.

18

For several days, Tuta and I anxiously tried to find her wounded lieutenant. There was a lull in the air raids although on the ground there was the chaos of panic. Information gleaned from medical officers and the Red Cross was frustratingly misleading. They too were totally disorganised and unprepared. We walked from one hospital or emergency depot to the next in our desperate search. Everywhere, we found injured men lying on makeshift beds. There was a shortage of nurses, of bandages, of bed linen and the doctors worked around the clock.

We found him eventually, sandwiched between comrades in the chemistry laboratory of a girl's school. His stretcher lay under a blackboard still adorned with the formula and calculations of the last lesson.

In order to get a better view of the lines of patients, Tuta had perched herself on one of the metal trolleys which were used to transport the stretcher cases. When she recognised Kasimir, she burst into tears and rushed to his side. The stress of the last few days was just all too much for her. Kasimir's face lit up, radiant with happiness on seeing his beloved Tuta. His left arm was heavily bandaged and the proximity of his neighbours meant that they could only hold hands and whisper their joy at seeing each other again.

I learned that the young lieutenant and his cavalry unit had engaged the enemy in one of those futile attacks on horseback against armoured tanks. It could only be called a romantic gesture of patriotism. A volley of machine gun bullets had smashed his arm and killed his horse. He must have been in a great deal of pain which he disguised manfully. As the two of them cooed lovingly to each other, one would think that he had only stubbed his big toe. He was in very good spirits and the doctor assured me that he would be able to save the arm.

If only Herbert were here, I knew he would help. I had not had the time to think about him too much lately. The tensions of false hope and disappointment while looking for Kasimir and the total disruption of life as we had known it, had forced all thoughts of him into the background. Now, as I waited for Tuta, surrounded by wounded men, I missed him deeply. These men needed his healing hands, his calm competence. Suddenly, I found myself worrying and fretting about him, imagining a thousand horrible scenarios that could threaten his safety.

At midday, the planes returned. In the distance, we could hear the rattle of machine gun fire. Precisely, to the minute, at twelve noon, the German hunters appeared and half an hour later the bombers would follow.

Kasimir ordered Tuta to leave immediately. We had barely thirty minutes to reach the shelter of our cellar. The school was no place to be caught in a raid. It was full to bursting with wounded men, the classrooms and the corridors on all floors were lined with stretchers. There were no bunkers and the cellar space was already allocated to the medical staff. The building was undefended and because of its size, it offered an easy target. My mother awaited us in the cellar in Nowy Swiat and would be frantically worried if we failed to seek safety there.

Tuta, however, was reluctant to leave. She got to her feet, promising to fulfil a last minute request from Kasimir to bring some washing items. "I'll bring them this evening," she said. "They can't hang around for ever. It'll be safe then." A few more precious minutes were wasted in another flood of kisses and tears. Finally she managed to drag herself away, but the delay had put us in peril. More hunters than usual were chasing over the roof tops and we kept close to the walls as we hurried along the empty streets. The sound of aeroplane engines rose and fell in the distance, when a new siren-like whine became audible. The stukkas had arrived and the noise of the first explosion confirmed our fears. Identifying the particular noise of the bombers had been a short, unforgettable lesson. In the few days that the uninvited visitors had terrorised us with their bombs and scarred our beautiful city, we had become experts.

We had to climb over mounds of rubble and were sometimes obliged to move into the middle of the street when we encountered a whole row of collapsed apartments. Hence, when the first pack of enemy aircraft suddenly swept down out of low cloud cover, we were caught in the open. We did not hear their rhythmical throbbing in time to conceal ourselves. They flew very low, their bodywork glinting in the sun. We raced down the road as fast as we could, trying to reach the shelter of the nearest undamaged building, hoping that it might give us some protection from the worst of the flying debris and shell fragments. Soldiers were posted in the park at Napolona Square where anti-aircraft guns had been positioned in the corners. The guns were spitting out shells in an endless stream. Above the din, someone shouted "Get down." We obeyed instantly, throwing ourselves to the ground on top of rubble in the lea of a precariously tottering structure. The remainder of the ruin towered ominously above us.

A horse-drawn taxi cab moved along the opposite side of the square. The coachman managed to stop his horses and leapt down to run for cover. Alas, too late! The first bomb blasted the outer corner of the square clean away. Stones and debris from the house flew as far as our hiding place near the arched doorway of the ruin and the pressure of the blast picked Tuta up and threw her on top of me. In the same instant, I saw the coach and the horses and the coachman lift slowly off the ground, as though the tarmac had become a powerful spring board. It seemed to take several seconds to happen, I remember the scene in so much detail. They folded, twisted, then smashed down again on to the road.

Pandemonium broke loose around us. The ground shook. The air throbbed. The pressure waves from explosions caused a deafness through which I became aware of my own heartbeat, thumping violently inside my skull. Buildings crashed to the ground, groaning and screaming like century old trees yielding to the saw.

I found myself clinging to Tuta, eyes screwed tight, trying to shut out the disaster happening around me. The thud and crash that accompanied the arrival of each bomb challenged my entire existence and with each impact, I clung ever tighter to Tuta. She lay in my arms and at first I thought that she was being very relaxed about the whole thing, before I realised that she was unconscious. Now what? The remains of the house above us could collapse at any time. I rolled her to one side and scrambled to my feet, desperately trying to think how I would be able to move her and where to go next, when yet another series of four or five explosions rocked the street. I almost fell and was blinded and choked by the dust storm that followed.

Suddenly all was quiet; no aircraft noise; no more explosions; only the occasional hollow rustle as a lose brick shifted. The silence was eerie. My terror had been so great that I was finding it difficult to breathe. I could feel blood pounding through every limb and a violent throbbing in my head made me feel nauseous. As the dust settled, I tried to pick out familiar landmarks.

There were none, only smoking, jagged fingers, rearing like so many spectres out of the mountains of rubble. Narrowing my eyes, I searched for the tall red-bricked building that we had left only fifteen minutes before. It was not there. The temporary hospital that had housed Tuta's lieutenant and many, many others like him had been reduced to a heap of bricks, wreathed in a cloud of smoke.

It was not shock that had caused Tuta to slide into oblivion, but a heavy blow to her head. Her hair was matted with blood and dust and I found a deep cut above her ear.

It was unthinkable that I should leave her to find help. Where would I find help anyway? No one was in sight and survivors were probably in the same impossible predicament as we were. With great difficulty, I set about carrying her as best I could. I could manage only a few metres at a time and frequently had to stop to gather strength for the next few steps. I had covered a distance of some two hundred metres, when Tuta began to regain consciousness. She touched the side of her head and flinched, but was too dazed to ask questions about what had happened. Thankful that she could use her own legs once more, I slowly led her onwards, careful that she did not get the opportunity to look back towards where the school had stood.

The raid had blasted the heart out of the city. We passed countless shattered and burning buildings. The fur shop 'Apfelbaum' in the Marszalkowska was torn apart, ripped open like an envelope and spilling its contents into the street. Persian lamb and arctic fox lay scattered all over the pavement and already survivors, emerging from the safety of their cellars, were helping themselves to the flotsam of war. A jewellers shop had collapsed. Silver goblets and gold trays lay squashed and bent amongst the rubble. Here too the scavengers were already at work.

Tuta did not seem to know where she was or why, allowing herself to be gently steered through the chaos. At last we reached the Novy Swiat, where our apartment block had escaped undamaged.

Mother rushed out to meet us. She had been keeping watch since the planes had gone, praying that we would come back unhurt. She immediately took charge of Tuta, and set about dressing the wound. Once she had cleaned away the blood and tied the hair back, she revealed a large ugly gash, exposing bone. At once, I was ordered out again to find a doctor.

The clinic where Herbert had worked, had like so many others, been requisitioned by the army. Undeterred by the sceptical looks that came my way, I demanded to see someone who could make decisions, explaining that my friend was in dire need of medical help. I hurriedly gave a description of Tuta's injury and for good measure mentioned that my fiancé had been a prominent surgeon at the clinic until the army had posted him off into the blue. I do not know to this day if my wild boast had any influence on the course of events, but, they agreed to admit Tuta. I even managed to arrange for a car to fetch her to the clinic. The roads in the area had been damaged but were fortunately still passable with a motor vehicle.

I ran home with the good news and within half an hour the car arrived and Tuta, still in a state of shock and suffering from severe concussion was whisked off to the clinic. She could not remember anything; not even that Poland was at war or that we had been searching for Kasimir for the past week. She did not seem to be too sure that she knew who Kasimir was! Poor Tuta, how very confused she must have been. She must have thought that she was living through some terrible nightmare.

Once again I made the journey to the clinic on foot. The car was permitted to carry patients only. Examination of the cut above Tuta's ear, suggested that indeed the skull was fractured and a small operation would be necessary to remove a blood clot. I therefore had to abandon Tuta at the clinic, hopeful that, here in the suburbs she should be safe, as the Germans seemed to be concentrating their attacks on the more prestigious centre of the city.

By the time I returned home, it was late in the evening. The drone of distant planes could be heard once more and everyone was hurrying to the cellar. For several days, the bombing routine had become a predictable pattern; a raid in the morning, followed by another in the evening.

My mother had been worried about me for the second time that day and was much relieved to see me safely back. Just to be together again somehow seemed to lock all the ghastly events of the last twenty four hours into another time dimension. Vera retrieved the last piece of bread from its hiding place and we shared the last two tins of sardines between us. Mother produced a bottle of wine that she had brought down from my apartment and, sitting on her sofa next to the boiler, we celebrated that we were still alive.

That night, the area around the Nowy Swiat was hit for the first time. The thick walls of the cellar absorbed both the noise and the impact of the explosions. The bombs seemed muffled and distant, whispering voices like the sound of a flowing river. We did not feel the fearful shudder of impact and convinced ourselves that they were only dropping incendiary devices. Thus we spent the time during that raid in a world of delusion.

The raids became longer and started earlier. Food was in very short supply, necessitating hurried excursions in the early morning. Our street remained undamaged until the third evening after Tuta had been injured. When the planes had left, those that went out to investigate the possible damage, returned with horror-stricken faces. The entire row of buildings on the other side of the street, right up to the junction with Jerusalemski, was engulfed in flames.

There was no fire brigade. There was no water.

All we could do was to help the victims to rescue as many of their possessions as possible and offer them shelter. The cellar at No.55 was already overcrowded. With the extra influx, it became choked. There was hardly room to move. People were squeezed together on benches, chairs or cushions on the floor. The only ventilation came from the doorway, which during raids had to be closed. The air beneath the house became stifling and I spent most of my time in the corridor of the ground floor. To stay more than fifteen minutes in the cellar made me feel faint and nauseous.

The lack of electricity and water had become an unpleasant inconvenience. Bread had become scarce and most families were too frightened to go upstairs to even collect food from their kitchens. The gas supply too had been cut off. Modern houses were fitted with central heating, but had no coal fires or alternative cooking facilities. Without electricity or gas we had no means of even boiling potatoes. The air was heavy with the stench from broken sewers.

Early the next morning, Vera set off with two buckets to fetch water from the river Weichsel and I ventured forth to find some bread in the suburb of Praga. The city centre was in chaos. Shops had been looted and stripped of their wares and the likelihood of fresh supplies was practically impossible in such confusion. I hoped the suburbs would be less affected.

I had, however, to traverse a corner of one of the most devastated areas. Tram cables were swinging too and fro, severed and useless. Corpses still lay where they had dropped, two or three days previously. Horses, their bloated bellies slashed open and their legs sticking up in the air like wooden bedposts, were still fully harnessed to their shattered carts.

I tried desperately to think of something else; to escape the scene of carnage by taking refuge in memories of the carefree days at the Sacré Coeur. But Kasimir was there too. The blond and smiling young Lieutenant Rybarski greeted me with one of his salutes. He had been so fond of saluting. The war had demanded more of him than just a mutilated arm. And Tuta... and Herbert!

They were all part of that fortunate dream and now were all part of this horror. Where was Herbert? What could have happened in Posen? Were my father and grandfather still safe? Were they wounded? Were they even alive? In all the turmoil of the last few days, I had barely spared them a thought.

Remembering to think about the possible fate of people who were dear to me had succeeded in distracting me. My brain was whirring away on another dimension, but reality still had some shocks in store. Two metres in front of me lay a child, face down in a puddle of water, just as if someone had thrown him down like a discarded doll. The scenes of those streets could not be ignored and I shall remember them for as long as I live. They crushed heart and soul; in a panic-stricken silent scream.

At the bakery, I joined a long queue, receiving a loaf after half an hour's wait, for the princely sum of thirty zloty, ten times the normal price. The baker was a fat, dirty looking fellow who served behind the counter, naked to the waist. His customers protested volubly at his high prices, to which he replied in an angry voice,

"I'm the only baker that's got the guts to work. The rest of 'em 'ave crawled underground like toads. Yer not payin' for the flour. Yer gettin' me blood for yer money. Take it or leave it. If yer want bread, pay up. The next man in line'll 'ave it if you don't wannit. Hurry up or the Gerries'll be back before you've made yer mind up."

I was home again by seven o'clock in good time before the expected morning attack. As I entered the apartment, I noticed that we had visitors. Two greatcoats hung in the hall. My heart missed a beat. Could Herbert have returned while I was away? I rushed expectantly into the sitting room.

There, I found my mother in the company of two total strangers. She introduced them to me with some reserve, the older man, a colonel and the other, a captain.

In my absence, mother had taken the opportunity to visit Tuta. Had I known beforehand, I would have tried to stop her from exposing herself to danger. She had found the patient recovering from the emergency operation on her head. The doctors were pleased with her progress. As soon as she had woken from the anaesthetic, she had asked after her loved ones. The blow had, however, caused some amnesia. She could not remember that several days had gone by since she had been injured, nor could she remember leaving Kasimir, otherwise, she was fully aware of what was currently going on around her. Poor Tuta, she would cry her heart out when she learned the truth about her darling lieutenant.

The two officers had been kind enough to bring mother home in their car. I was suspicious as to what was their ulterior motive for such a display of gallantry. There had to be a reason for their presence in my parlour. The captain elected to explain, the awful implications of what he said stirring more dread with every sentence that he uttered.

"We fight on horseback against tanks. Wherever the Germans position a division, we put in a regiment. One Polish aircraft is matched by a hundred German planes. The troops are short of rations, supplies have failed. There is no doctor available when a bullet stops in your belly. The first aid units have run out of bandages. We are finished. In a couple of days, the Germans will march up the Nowy Swiat."

My mother groaned and sank on to a chair. I rushed to her side to comfort her, but it was she that put her arms around me and I sensed her strength in the safety of her embrace. The captain added, "How can we be expected to risk our necks at the eleventh hour, when all is lost?" Mother slowly shook her head in sympathy. "Perhaps I would think differently if I were a professional soldier," he pleaded. "It would be my job to serve until the end in war. As it is, I have worn this uniform barely three weeks. I am an artist, a painter. It is important to me that my hands survive this war, uninjured."

Mother may have understood his reasoning, but I felt angry. "And the others," I snapped, "the hundreds of others who have not got the option to simply quit?" Indignation boiled within me as I thought of Kasimir, Herbert, father and...

"Is that a reason to risk losing an eye or a limb, just because others can't stop? Your mother has told us that your fiancé is at the front line, but you should not let that cloud your judgement."

The arrogance of the man! How could he dismiss my fiancé so casually as unfortunate war fodder. I stood gaping at him, lost for words, indignant that the man should dare to give voice to such outrageous opinions. But his words made some sense. What right did I have to criticise? I did not have to risk my life in a hopeless cause. Maybe, he was right? Who could judge what was fair or what was unfair in the present chaos? What was right about the idea of heroism in the name of the Fatherland and what was wrong? Where did honour end and dishonour begin? The two men were not the only ones to have thrown down their guns in the face of insurmountable odds when resistance seemed senseless and futile.

They could not all be like Stanislaus Sobieski. News had reached us that he had formed a division from stragglers in the area of Kowno, which was already occupied by the Germans. Apparently, he had found Mario, for the two of them were reported to be together, fighting their own version of the French Revolution; the leader, with flag held high, climbing the barricades, at his side, a boy, beating a drum in wild excitement. Apparently, not everyone was prepared to lose his life for an ideal and those who were not able to prove themselves, should not stand in judgement.

Mother agreed that the two men could remain in the apartment. Even during raids, they showed no inclination to leave, perhaps preferring to risk dying in civilised comfort than to face the criticisms that they would meet in the crowded cellar. They stayed concealed in the flat for just one day and one night.

Meanwhile Warsaw was burning.

That evening the Germans came yet again. The air was alive with the thunderous noise of machines flying in to break the resistance of the capital, once and for all. There was no need for spotlights to guide them. The glow from the dying city must have been visible for hundreds of miles. Wave after wave of bombers passed overhead, releasing their missiles of destruction. At 11pm, the town centre, the Nowy Swiat included, came under heavy bombardment. The whole house shook repeatedly. With each impact dust puffed from the support beams in the cellar. The children woke up and cried. The tension and the lack of air in the confined space could have been cut with a knife.

The heavy door was suddenly flung open. In the gloom, we could just make out the figures of the two men who had been occupying my apartment.

"The whole of Nowy Swiat is burning. The front of the apartment has been torn away!" The captain had his leg in a make shift splint, tied together with a strip of my sitting room curtains. He had obviously been hurt when the wall crumbled.

The danger of the house catching fire was imminent and when that happened, we should have to leave the relative safety of the cellar. The possibility that this could become unavoidable rapidly spread panic among the anxious occupants of our underground shelter. The colonel took charge. He persuaded everyone to keep calm and hold on to reason. At regular intervals, he ventured out with the house porter to check the building, reporting back that for the present, our block of apartments was still safe.

Near the door, two women knelt in prayer, their muttering adding to the morbid depression that fell on the room. An old man staggered to his feet and climbed over the people packed around him to find the water pipe. The increased tension had succeeded in driving him to distraction. Again and again, he put his ear to the offending pipe to listen for the sound of running water, mumbling and wailing in turn that he was afraid that a bomb would hit the mains and he would drown.

"I nearly drowned like this before. Listen! It's coming!" His agitation was extraordinary. There had been no water in the pipe for over a week.

Shortly before midnight, an ear-splitting roar came from the direction of the cellar steps as though huge load of scrap iron had been dropped from a great height. The floor shook and cracked. Everyone was tossed about and fell on top of one another. I flung my arms out towards mother and grabbed her dress, before we were both thrown violently against the boiler. Dust filled the cellar, billowing from the cracks around the door.

An eerie silence followed. Not even the children made a sound. It was as though everyone was holding their breath in unison, trying not to think the unthinkable, not daring to contemplate the calamity that had just occurred. The cruel reality slowly dawned. We were cut off from the outside world. The building had collapsed on top of us.

We were trapped.

Amazingly, there were no hysterics, no screaming or lamenting. A strange peace settled on that isolated capsule, a communal understanding of a shared disaster.

The colonel and the porter tried unsuccessfully to shift the heavy metal door. It was a gesture appreciated by everybody, but we knew that they were wasting their energy. The fallen masonry on the other side of the door frustrated their efforts and after some minutes, they gave up, defeat and disappointment plainly written on their faces. No one stirred. Even the children were still.

The past few weeks had taught us that our destiny was in the hands of others. The value of life had become trivial and unimportant. We were tiny expendable particles in the cosmos; insignificant specks. What did it matter if we all suffocated together in a gloomy hole. Life had become a hell that no longer held powerful attraction.

Slowly, almost imperceptibly at first, individuals showed signs that they had not given up hope completely. The oil lamp that someone had fixed to the ceiling flickered as gradually the human carpet roused itself, realising that life still continued and that perhaps fate did not intend yet, to initiate the eternal journey.

The door had proved impossible to move, perhaps the boarded windows would offer an escape route, but behind these too, we found a wall of rubble. At least we could try to dig our way out as we could reach the rubble through the narrow opening, but the task seemed formidable.

Progress could be measured in centimetres. Many of the bricks were firmly wedged and only one man at a time could work in the restricted space. We had no tools, nothing which could be used as a lever. Each large piece of masonry had to be painstakingly loosened by scraping around it with bare hands. It was tiring, dirty work and after many hours, there was barely a sack full of debris on the floor to show for the bleeding fingers. Slowly, very slowly, the heap on the floor grew bigger.

Periodically, the work ceased and everyone was asked to be still. We strained our ears, listening for the sound of aircraft, gunfire, explosions or optimistically, for the sound of spades and shovels.

Nothing! Absolute silence! We had no idea at all what was going on outside our subterranean prison. Soon we had lost all sense of time and knew not whether it was night or day.

To begin with, we did have some food. Those sheltering in the cellar had taken refuge with whatever food that they had been able to find and a certain amount of water. After a time, however, both the food and water disappeared and the tunnel did not seem to be getting any longer. After nearly two days of digging, the depth of the hole grew little over a metre. But time stood still. Without day and night, it was difficult to estimate its passing. The stale air became intolerable. A little two year old girl became lethargic, her breathing, very shallow and her pulse rate dropped. Gradually she weakened until she eventually breathed no longer. Her distressed mother tried to revive her, trying to force air into her daughter's lungs by closing her mouth over that of the child and blowing her own air down the girl's throat. She continued long after the child was dead.

Soon after, the tunnel started to grow at a faster rate. In the next few hours, the narrow passageway had grown long enough for the boots of the man working on the digging face, to edge out of sight.

Suddenly, he was through. A minuscule ray of light slipped past him as he kicked a stone back into the space behind him. A cool draught of fresh air confirmed that it would not be long before we would be out. More bricks and stones were rapidly passed down through the hole and soon the colonel, for it was he that had been working at the end of the tunnel, called back that he could see out into the street; that all was quiet and that the sun was in the west.

The dead child was the first to be tenderly passed up the tunnel. With patience, we each awaited our turn to wriggle to freedom. Now that escape was possible, it was as though no one was particularly eager to venture into the shambolic world above. Emerging from the prison that had so nearly become a tomb, the sight of devastation that greeted us was horrendous. Only two buildings remained intact at the Pierackiego. Plastered to the wall of one of them a red poster, the slogan written in both German and Polish, demanded the surrender of Warsaw. The paste sticking it to the wall was still wet.

A group of German soldiers came into view, climbing over the mountains of rubble with their guns slung over their shoulders. They ignored us, moving on to their destination without any sign of precaution as if they had nothing to fear.

Their boots were white with dust and they wore the steel helmet, so familiar to us from the cartoonist caricatures of the 'Bosch'.

The two suitcases that we had taken with us down to the cellar were all we had left. My apartment was a layer in the enormous heap of rubble that now covered the site. There was nothing to keep us here. We all faced an uncertain and precarious future and each one had to do what he felt to be right in the circumstances. Mother and I embraced each of our recent neighbours, wishing them well and we shook hands with the two officers and thanked them for their hard labour. It must have been an odd sight to the casual observer, had there been one, a group of tattered beings, formally bidding each other farewell in a sea of ruin. It was strange, that even in such a dire situation, etiquette and politeness somehow mattered.

Vera picked up the two suitcases and we started to walk in the direction of the railway station. We hardly expected to find a train service of any kind, but it seemed as good a place as any to discover a route to Posen.

The Jerusalemski was full of German soldiers and tanks. A bit further on, we reached the area around the Café Club and decided to make enquiries. The theatre was gone, but a few of the employees had gathered in the burnt-out remains as though seeking comfort from their previous place of work. Their homes were destroyed and they needed to retrieve any threads of their daily routine that remained.

Most of them recognised me from my days in the theatre in January. We learned that the Germans had moved into Warsaw the day before. There had been little resistance towards the end. The horrific bombing that had flattened the apartment had been the worst and the last raid.

They listened in stony silence to our story of the buried cellar, offering no sympathy. Each one had gone through a similar experience and our tale had been told already, many times before. The ability to feel any emotion was numbed by the excesses of the recent horror.

The will to help, however, was still alive. The kitchen of the Café Club had been in the cellar and an angel, disguised as the cook, invited us to taste some hot soup. Heaven still existed! I had forgotten how delicious steaming potato soup could be. The aroma alone began to lift my spirits. Perhaps there was a future after all? It certainly seemed possible with the soup safely stowed in my stomach and the worst of the grime wiped away with a damp cloth. That cook could have been an emissary from heaven. His soup surely had the miraculous effect of not only giving the body life but of also reviving hope in the soul.

19

I had to keep pinching myself to prove to myself that I was awake and not experiencing some nightmare of a dream.

Here I was, sitting in the comfortable leather seat of a German limousine. Beside me sat a German general, in full military uniform. He had tucked a travelling rug about my legs and tried to hold a polite conversation with me. My mother followed with Vera in a second car some thirty metres behind.

The entire escapade could be blamed on my mother. I would never have had the audacity to attempt such a plan. But my mother, able to speak German without a tell-tale accent had dared to approach a German soldier and had managed to arrange a lift to Posen by car! The fact that it was a staff car belonging to a general had not deterred her.

We had tried to find a way of travelling home without success. The railway was out of action and would be so for the foreseeable future and we were obliged to set out on our journey towards Posen on foot. We had not walked many kilometres when my Mother, my dear resourceful Mother, simply spoke to a group of soldiers who seemed to be chauffeurs for the fleet of cars parked in front of a large building which had escaped damage. Apparently a gathering of German officers was in progress. Two guards were posted by the entrance with poles by their side bearing banners displaying the Nazi insignia.

Fluent in the language, she claimed that she was a German national visiting Warsaw with her daughter and maid when the war had suddenly broken out. She was half crazy with worry about her family and home in Posen, but was stranded. The question of proof of identification did arise, but she gave them to understand that all our papers and personal possessions had been lost in the bombing. Her fluent German was our passport.

A very tall, blond soldier had been willing to help. He said that he was about to drive General Ludendorf to Posen and if the general approved, perhaps we would be allowed to accompany him.

"The general is in a meeting at the moment," he said, nodding in the direction of the door where the two guards stood stiffly to attention.

My mother blithely continued to pour syrup onto the spoon and asked in the course of the ensuing conversation whether the general was related to the well known commander in the Great War.

The tall officer replied rather stiffly, "Regrettably madam, I am unfamiliar with the general's personal circumstances. However, I would be delighted to know more about the personal circumstances of your daughter." I froze in panic. As with the Russian language, I had a working knowledge of German, but failed miserably to emulate the standard set by my mother. She came to my rescue, explaining as convincingly as she could that she had been obliged to send me to a Polish boarding school and therefore I could not manage German conversation.

We were interrupted by the general himself. As he emerged from the building, the guards lowered their guns with a clatter and raised their right arms in the Nazi salute. Our soldier moved forward to open the car door, and with the skill of a ventriloquist, managed to announce "The General" through motionless lips.

The immaculate apparel of the general was a total contrast to our dusty, dishevelled appearance. Slim and erect, the fringe of his red and gold epaulettes dancing on his shoulders and the peeked cap framing his face, his plain features looked almost handsome. The side seams of his breeches were extravagantly curved and, except around his ankle where the fine leather wrinkled, his gleaming boots hugged tightly to his legs He was so pristine and elegant. Compared to the disorder and chaos around us, he looked as though he had just stepped out of his dressing room.

The driver, true to his word, spoke to him about our predicament. The general did not reject his suggestions outright and directed some questions at my mother. My comprehension of spoken German was not as dismal as my ability to converse and I understood with relief, that he was more interested in the last days of the fighting in Warsaw than in who we were. He also tried to question me, but again mother was quick to explain why I did not speak German. Satisfied with the answers that he received, he cordially agreed that we could ride with him to Posen. His decision that I should ride with him in the leading car while mother and Vera were travelled in a second vehicle caused me to pale. This had not been part of the plan, but to protest at this stage would have risked discovery. My knowledge of German would have become suspect. Why should we conceal the fact that I was familiar with the language? And if this was the only way that we would reach Posen, then I had to be as audacious as my mother and show no sign of anxiety in my behaviour.

The convoy set off without further delay, two motor cycles leading the way. Thus, in an impressive cavalcade, we left our shattered Warsaw. During the journey, the general again tried to talk to me, but I found it very difficult to understand his heavy accent and our conversation soon abandoned the use of sentences. Compared to the Polish generals that Grandfather had introduced to me, this one was definitely underage. They had been in their fifties or sixties, this one had the healthy, pliant skin and shining eyes of a much younger man.

His eyes sparkled mischievously as he tried to mime a word or translate with sign language. There was a ring on his finger and I assumed that he was married. It was common knowledge in Poland that Germans were encouraged to produce a large number of offspring and he possibly played charades with his own children. He proved very adept at it. I wondered whether he would have looked so kindly on me had he realised that I was Polish, not German. I amused myself, imagining the look on his face had I confessed my true identity. He seemed to enjoy the smug satisfaction that goes with a confidence in the conviction that one's judgement is correct. He revelled in his righteousness and I had little doubt that he would not have been forgiving if he discovered the deception. His vanity too would have received a blow, for vain he must have been, with his hair parted in a dead straight line and the immaculate condition of his uniform.

"Je parle un tout peu française!" Anxious to keep him in a good mood, I subjected him to my best school French. I did not want to irritate him with my ignorance of German for too long and cause him to become suspicious in his frustration.

His French proved to be fluent, far superior to my hesitant attempts to form recognisable words in the language. We could, however, at last understand each other although I gave faltering answers to his questions.

We met long convoys of motorised artillery including a whole tank regiment as we travelled westward. We passed heavy guns, positioned in the fields at crossroads and other strategic points. Their size was awesome. The deserting Polish officers had been right. The enemy possessed powerful weapons and plenty of them. It was getting dark by the time we reached Lichtmanstadt.

The motorcycles stopped in front of a large hotel. The soldiers had halted and dismounted their bikes as though they had arrived at a predetermined destination. It looked as though a break in our journey was scheduled.

Once again, fear of the uncertain made me almost drop my guard. I glanced through the window and saw the other car with mother and Vera aboard, was parking alongside. Mother smiled at me. She had every confidence in me and I could not disappoint her so, when the driver opened the door, I climbed out and accepted the invitation to enter the hotel, careful to disguise my instinctive reluctance. We found the hotel lounge full of German uniforms. Soldiers manned the hotel switch board and served the refreshments. It was very obvious who was in control.

It took a little time, even for a general, to explain away his travelling companions. The adjutant appeared to be remarkably slow at grasping the situation, but we were eventually allocated a double room with an extra sofa. It was with sinking hearts that I realised that the delay was to include an overnight stay.

The three of us were ascending the stairs, when the general called me back. He glared at the soldier at the reception desk as if daring him to understand a word at his peril, before addressing me in French.

"Voulez-vous... m'accompaniez à table mademoiselle?" he asked, smiling encouragingly. It seemed that he would be dining with the other officers and I understood that he expected me to escort him. He excused the fact that he could not invite my mother or Vera, but promised that dinner would be sent to them in their room. He expected me to be ready in an hour. It was an order, not an invitation and I did not dare to protest. I nodded my head and raced up the stairs to join mother and Vera who were waiting for me on the landing.

This new development caused my mother some uneasiness. She pretended to me that she was glad that she had not been included in the invitation, as she was wearing her only dress. This vain acceptance of the general's decision did not deceive me. She was beginning to regret that she had ever arranged the lift, daring that it was. So much was depending on her daughter's ability to act a part.

I gave her a reassuring hug and told her that I could take care of myself. After all, was I not the clever daughter of a very clever mother? I do not think she was convinced by my rash reasoning. She took a deep breath, looked long and hard into my eyes then patted my arm gently to reassure me of her trust. She spent the next hour applying all her skill to the task of grooming her daughter in readiness for her tryst at the dinner table.

The dining room had been recently decorated; the walls showed signs of new paint and the chandelier was clean and sparkling. The tables were set as though a banquet was expected, reminding me of happier times. What a strange contrast to the airless cellar where we had remained trapped for several days and the shambles that we had left behind in Warsaw. The hotel was an oasis of normality surrounded by the destructive sands of war.

Twenty five officers rose to their feet as we entered the room. The general escorted me to the top table and politely, pulled out a chair for me to be seated. Public appearances on the stage had not prepared me for this. A sea of shaven faces gazed curiously at me. They were not veiled in darkness and hidden as in the theatre, but clearly visible and so close that I could see every pimple and blemish. I felt sick.

While I was trying to regain my self-confidence, the general was addressing his officers in his heavy dialect. I was far too confused to attempt to follow what he was saying but several times he turned in my direction and I was aware that all eyes were upon me as he spoke. I tried to smile as agreeably as I could, but suspected that I succeeded in producing a fixed grin which would convince no one. With a solemn bow to me, he concluded his little speech. My ears were burning with embarrassment.

In French, he explained to me the content of his brief oration; that I was one of thousands of German nationals who had been freed from the arbitrary dictatorship of the Poles by the intervention of the German invasion. The smile was still stuck on my face. The idea was nauseous. What a fantastic liberation it was that had sacrificed so many Polish people, separating their souls from their bodies! He raised his glass of wine and proposed a toast. "To you, young lady! Your new freedom and all Germans that you represent!" The smile must have looked permanent, my jaw ached, but how I hated the man dressed now in long trousers and a white collar that was just visible under the detestable jacket of his uniform.

The food was delicious! After a period of near starvation, it was heaven sent. There were soups, pastries, salads, various roast fowl and other meats to choose from. I shall never forget the taste of the roast pork, tender as butter and with crackling that was perfection itself. I had to make a strong effort to control my manners, lest I appeared too greedy. My nerves and revulsion of the company did not affect the appetite of a hungry teenager.

Yet suddenly, and it came as a surprise, I was unable to eat another morsel. When the meal started, I had felt that I could eat many plates full of food with no problem, so desperate was my desire to fill my stomach. My hunger, however, was easily satisfied and I could eat no more even before the first plate was clean. The general noticed my abrupt loss of appetite and advised me that after my very recent incarceration in the cellar, I should start eating gradually, a little and often.

"I shall see that food is packed for the rest of the journey tomorrow. You need to eat a little every hour or so."

My stomach full, I began to appreciate another side of my benefactor. He had shown himself to be considerate for my welfare after all. If I had been German, no doubt I would have considered him to be very kind and thoughtful. Being a Pole, however, I had feared him and was suspicious of his motives. Yet he had done nothing to cause me to fear him, only worn his uniform. I watched him as he continued with his meal, fastidiously cutting away any pieces of fat from the meat. Like many vain men, he seemed careful to preserve his waistline. He was human.

My attention drifted to the other diners. I sat there observing all those heads, bowed over their plates shovelling food into their mouths and a wave of disgust swept over me. They had taken our country like robbers and were sitting at a table which did not belong to them. They guzzled at the trough with arrogant self-confidence while thousands of Poles were condemned to eat little or nothing at all. There was the obese one at the far end of the table who was enjoying his roast pork so much that the fat dribbled from his mouth. He closely resembled a salivating dog. Opposite him sat a Luftwaffer officer with freckles on his forehead, pouring butter over his potatoes as if it were custard on pudding. And Poland starved!

The general daintily picked up his bread, using only the tips of his fingers, fingers which a few days earlier had signed the orders for the destruction of my home. Hands littered the table, hands that had so recently carried machine guns, loaded field guns, manned tanks or crewed planes with the object of killing as many people as possible in the shortest possible time. Now that their owners had finished their bloody business, they had simply washed those hands and extracted a clean suit from a suitcase. Their brains must have been first cousins to taxi metres to be able to turn them on and off to order, without any sense of guilt.

I could not bear to stay in the room any longer. My feelings of revulsion were getting difficult to keep under control. The temptation to fling something, anything at those smug, self-satisfied faces was becoming a fiendish urge and I felt a passionate desire to leap onto the table and sing the Polish national anthem at the top of my voice. Suddenly the full portent of the words dawned on me.

"Gasses Polka me zginela."

I had clenched my hands so tightly that my nails were embedded into the palms of my hand. I had to get out before I did something rash and spent the next few minutes plotting a means by which I could escape from the room as discretely as possible.

First I needed to think of a reason to excuse myself without arousing suspicion. My stomach reminded me that I had possibly eaten too much than was good for me and I suggested to the general that perhaps the food was a little rich for me after days of abstinence and requested his permission to leave the table. His show piece was indisposed. His eyes hardened for a moment.

Was it concern, disappointment or frustration that his show piece was indisposed? Either way, he rose from his seat and insisted on escorting me to my room.

I got up from my chair, stuck the smile back on my face and made my escape, the general in hot pursuit. Reaching the door of the bedroom, I felt safe and turned to offer him cordial thanks. For all that the man was a member of the army that was invading my country, he had behaved with impeccable manners and kindness towards me and I felt that I should express my gratitude. But, I did not get the chance, for he suddenly grabbed me in his arms and pressed his face into my bosom, covering my breast with kisses. I desperately sought something to steady myself and my hand found the cold metal of the door handle.

The metallic rattle of the handle seemed to bring him to his senses. Voices could be heard on the other side of the door calling my name. It would have been most undignified for him to be discovered, taking advantage of a daughter of the Reich in a hotel corridor and he released me, straightened up and pushed his hair back from his face. He then took my hand and kissed it in more decorous style, lingering overlong with his lips on the back of my hand. His gesture was wasted. The door did not open for his gallant performance to be witnessed. At last, he released my hand, muttered a few words in German so softly that I could barely hear them then, with slow measured step, he walked away down the passage. I did not understand nor shall I ever forget the expression in his eyes.

20

Posen too had been overwhelmed by the insatiable war, but the damage was patchy and in no way as devastating as that which we had left behind in Warsaw. Fortune, however, had delivered a missile of destruction on the block of apartments where my mother had been living.

As we turned the corner into the street, the realisation that she had lost everything was immediately evident. The house with its little shop on the ground floor was crushed and ravaged by fire.

The general's car stopped by the burnt out shell that had been my home before I left for Warsaw. The area was deserted; there was no one in sight to ask about what had happened to our neighbours. Our benefactor was visibly moved by our second misfortune and showed his concern by offering to find us accommodation. Here in Posen, however, the family was too well known to continue deceiving him for long as regards our real identity. It was essential that he lose contact with us as soon as possible. Mother assured him that we would find refuge with one of our many relatives and thanked him for his help without which we would still be stranded in Warsaw. The general presented me with his card, adding in French "In case you should come to Berlin", climbed into his limousine and the procession of vehicles vanished down the road.

The three of us were left standing on the corner of what used to be a street of large, well maintained houses. All that remained of the buildings around us were the blackened facades. Where the windows had been, were vacant holes, like the empty eye sockets of a row of skulls. I delicately dropped the general's card into the gutter, mimicking his fastidious manner of handling his bread, then picked up one of the two suitcases and started walking.

Grandmother's house, on the outskirts of the town, was undamaged. There we lodged for some two or three weeks. After the trauma and stress of the first weeks of war, her roof was a peaceful haven, where we immersed ourselves in a daily routine that brought some sanity back into our lives. Time was not important and one day was very much like the next.

There was no news of Father, Grandfather or Herbert. There were no newspapers or local radio and rumour was the only means by which information could be relayed. Gossip is unreliable and invariably distorts the facts, but it was by this means that we learned that all captured officers had been put into prison camps. We could only hope that our loved ones were among them. Imagining them behind a barbed wire fence was better than picturing their bodies, lying lifeless on the ground.

Mother and I were in our own self-imposed confinement within the walls of Grandmother's house. It was not wise for us to be seen on the street. Too many people in Posen were aware of the family involvement with the national resistance movement. German sympathisers were many and all sorts of seemingly innocuous characters roamed the streets, only too eager to inform on their own kind in exchange for a meagre handful of zloty.

Vera, my stalwart nanny who had now become my constant companion, did dare to venture out to renew contacts with our friends and, of course, to find food. Since the occupation, the food situation had become the most serious problem that the Polish national had to contend with. Only those who were successful in befriending a German soldier were usually better off. Everything was in short supply and prices soared to astronomic heights. Relatively speaking, we fared better than the poorer Pole as my family was wealthier than most. But you could not buy what was not available.

Ina, my cousin, was also living with Grandmother at the time. She was older than me by over two years and previously I had barely known her as we had attended different schools. We had occasionally met at the Sacré Coeur where she had sometimes assisted the teachers during my final year, but of course this made her very much my senior. Thrown together by chance, we became good friends and when we watched mother and grandmother dividing the meagre rations that Vera brought home, we started to discuss schemes that would improve the lot of the older women. With youth on our side, we could not stand by and do nothing.

The word filtered through that the town was resuming some sort of normality again and we determined to take a look for ourselves. My Mother did not think that this was advisable, but came to realise that she could not cage two eager fledglings indefinitely and so one morning, Ina and I set forth to make our own assessment of the situation in the town.

What we found did not seem as black as we had imagined. Even fewer areas in the town had been damaged by bombing than we had initially thought. Mother had just been very unlucky to have owned an apartment in the wrong place. Admittedly, the army of occupation and German nationals, resident in Poland, were the most prominent and entertainment in the cafés and theatres was presented in the German tongue. On the other hand, we did not find a uniform at every street corner as we had anticipated nor did we get the feeling that spying eyes in civilian clothes were watching our every move.

The excursion was repeated. Each time, mother and grandmother waited at home, anxious for our safe return. They became more confident in our expeditions when we returned with treasures; a 1/4 kilo of butter or a loaf of bread. In the end, my mother deemed it safe enough for her too to put on her hat and coat and venture out to visit her friends.

Over a period of time, we found out in more detail what the Germans had in mind. Initially, they concentrated on tracking down Polish officers of high rank, at the same time removing the first Jewish families at the dead of night. The top priority in our discrete enquiries concerned the extent to which they were interested in the families of Polish citizens who had been politically active against the threat from our 'neighbours'. We became aware that remaining in isolation and ignorance was unwise. Discovering whether relatives and friends were in danger of arrest became our goal and we were prepared to take any measures necessary to obtain that information.

On 13th October, Ina and I once again walked into the town, intent on finding an officer whom we could engage in conversation and hopefully glean some facts. Meeting the general had encouraged me to reach this decision. Apart from his aberration in the corridor, his behaviour had been civilised to a fault. If I had been able to deceive him during the dinner charade, it should not be too difficult to make similar use of one of the hundreds of young men in uniform that roamed the streets of Posen. Thoroughly bored with the lack of war activity, we persuaded ourselves that they should be easy to amuse and distract. We were not, however, equipped to land such fish. The business of how to cast the line with love-sick glances and silk covered thighs had its own set of rules which had to be learnt as in any other trade. We did not know the rules of the game.

By the evening, we had become rather despondent. We had trawled the streets all afternoon in vain. Our net was empty. The hunt had been possibly hindered by the specific qualities of our quarry. Getting acquainted with the rank and file soldier or any of the supplies officers, we considered, was wasted effort, for they would know nothing about the security plans. We had to find someone who was actively employed in the town headquarters. Someone who knew what was going on.

Before making our way back home, we decided to go to the Café Arcadia and order lemonade. We were tired and the soles of my feet hurt. As we perched on the stools at the bar, each sipping through a straw from the one glass, we discussed our lack of progress. Buried in our frustrations, we both failed to notice the two German officers that entered the Café and took the table behind us. Ina spotted them first. She nudged me, lifted her eyebrows and rolled her eyes. I glanced over my shoulder. There was no need for words. Mutual agreement flashed as our eyes met. This was it! These two were the prey we had been looking for. Fortune had played right into our hands, but of course now that the opportunity had arrived, gift wrapped, neither of us knew how to make the next move.

We finished the lemonade and I began to sense Ina's increased excitement. What next? To break the tension, I called the waiter over and asked for the bill. Ina in the meantime had turned her back on the bar and taken a good look at them.

"Not bad," she said. "Take a look for yourself." The bill paid, I carefully looked in the same direction, but deliberately stared past them as though someone else had caught my attention. On the periphery of my vision, I could see the two men, both of similar build. The one with his back to me had blond hair and something about that head seemed vaguely familiar, although at the time, I could not think why. The one facing me had dark hair, an honest, handsome face and a mischievous twinkle in his eye. Ina was right, they made an interesting pair. The owner of the twinkling eyes had been aware that he and his companion were under scrutiny and grabbing the wine list, he started to write busily on the back of it. When he had finished, he cheerfully called the waiter and handed him the note, nodding his head in our direction.

The waiter obligingly delivered the message to us, but we found it was written in German. Although my mother had given us a crash course in the language neither of us could make head nor tail of what was written on the card. The waiter, an elderly bi-lingual citizen of Posen, offered assistance. He translated as he read, "We would like to make your acquaintance. Where and when will you permit us to see you?"

It seemed we had hooked our fish with very little effort. It had been so easy and one might have thought that we would have been jubilant at our success. On the contrary, my instinctive reaction was to feel affronted! It seemed to me, that German men were as conceited as Polish and that a woman was asked by neither species for her opinion. It was his right to take a fancy, her duty to follow. For the privilege of selection, she must show gratitude. I was irritable after a long day on my feet and was probably unreasonable, but I felt resentful, irrespective that the message had been polite in tone and echoed an old fashioned chivalry.

Ina on the other hand, suddenly became very distressed. She was no longer interested in our scheme. While our ideas had been theoretical, she had been eager to support them. Now that we were faced with a real situation, she could not cope. To her, the words were threatening. The enemy had addressed her personally and a finger had pointed her out. She was no longer one of the invisible masses. She had been noticed.

Without another look at the two lieutenants, she slipped from her stool and almost ran out of the Café. I followed close on her heels.

In a fearful temper with herself, she pushed her way through the crowd outside, paying no attention at all to me, struggling in her wake. She walked so fast, that I had a hard task to catch up with her.

"Ina, do be reasonable..." I pleaded with her flapping coat tails, but she was not listening. A crowd, leaving the cinema, enveloped her and for a moment, I feared I would lose her.

"Ina, don't run away!" Still she ignored me. Eventually we left the crowds behind us and I was able to trot alongside her.

"Ina, if you would only think..."

"There are situations when one doesn't waste time, thinking; when one's reactions are instinctive," she snapped.

"You said yesterday, that there are situations when instinct and emotions have to be silenced." I pointed out. I was indignant that she had taken flight at the first challenge to her philosophy and did not feel inclined to let her reformulate her ideals so easily. Sensing my hostility, she dashed off again, running another hundred metres or so before slowing down. The sudden exertion must have chased away her frustrations, for by the time that I had caught up with her again, she was grinning. She slowed to a halt and leaned against a lamp post. She held her hands out towards me and gasped, "I'm sorry, Maria. Please forgive me..." She squeezed my hand. "... but...it all seems so absolutely senseless... The two lieutenants in the café... or that young soldier over there, not much older than we are... why do they not have to fear that their loved ones may be taken away in the night? We love Poland. They love their Germany. Our men folk fought for our country, they for theirs. Now that they happen to have become the victors, they treat the losers like criminals. And God lets them get on with it. We have prayed for victory and so have they over there, on the other side of the border. Why did God listen to them and not to us? Is heaven dispensing its blessings according to national boundaries? Had we lived two hundred kilometres further west, we, you and I, would not have to put up with the arrogant patronisation of our masters."

Ina's outburst set me thinking. I felt that she was only partially right. The coin had two sides and there were so many different aspects of both sides that needed to be taken into consideration. I pulled Ina towards me and embraced her tightly then we resumed our journey homewards, arm in arm.

While trying to conjure up a formula for my own opinion, I was not paying much attention to what I was doing. We were about to step out into the middle of the road when strong arms grabbed us from behind and pulled us roughly back onto the pavement. An army vehicle came racing past, very fast and close enough to whip my hair across my face in the draught.

"Always look first to the left and then to the right when crossing the road," a voice said in my ear – in German. I guessed at the full meaning, but understood 'left', 'right' and 'road'.

"Polka?" came the next query. The answer to this one had been discussed and rehearsed many times.

"No, German nationality, but Polish school!"

Ina echoed my reply. "German nationality... Polish school."

"Kurt Kattge from Berlin."

We were still facing the road. The vehicle that had so nearly mown us down was not yet out of sight. The dust disturbed by its passing still hovered above the cobbles. Ina and I swung round in unison to meet the laughing eyes of the dark-haired lieutenant from the café.

"Herbert Kurzke." His friend stepped from behind him. The world suddenly receded, whirling in a crazy fashion. The sky swung to my feet and the walls above me shifted and swayed crazily. Everything turned into tumbling, swirling chaos. I recovered my senses to find myself in a crumpled heap on the pavement. Arms enfolded me and a voice whispered softly in my ear.

"Maria, Maria... wake up my darling. Maria..."

I opened my eyes and gazed into the face of my Herbert. I shut them again. This could not be right. I must be dreaming. How could Herbert be an officer in German uniform? He was saving Polish lives, he could not be here.

"Maria, it's alright, it's me Herbert," the voice insisted. It certainly sounded like Herbert's voice, but dear God... he cannot be one of them. Can he?

"Maria, open your eyes. It really is me. I'm sorry that we had to meet again like this. Maria, I didn't mean to give you such a shock... But it is a long and complicated story..."

I opened one eye and squinted at him, then flung both arms around him and hugged him so tight that he must have had a stiff neck for days. I had found my Herbert. He was safe and well. My heart was exploding with joy. The man I loved was here, warm and alive. I felt an overpowering sense of relief and security, wrapped in his arms. Dear God, thank you. Perhaps there was some sanity in life after all.

Herbert Kurzke

"Come on, Maria, we've got to get home." Ina's voice pierced my euphoria like a falling icicle. I looked up to see her peering down at me, a quizzical expression on her face.

"Ina, permit me to introduce you to Herbert, my fiancé." I said solemnly.

Now it was Ina's turn to suffer a severe shock to her nervous system. She did not faint, but her face drained of colour and her mouth fell open. Her eyes flashed a message of confused indignation.

"Maria... I had no idea," she managed to gasp before she dried up completely, her lips forming soundless words.

Herbert helped me to my feet. Ina was right, we had to get back before it became too dark. Kurt Kattge had retreated to the back of the pavement and was observing us from a distance. The expression on his face was now serious. He obviously had reservations about the scene that he had just witnessed and Herbert had noticed. Calmly and without drama, he took his friend to one side. The explanation seemed to reassure Kurt for when they returned, the cloud had cleared from his face and the twinkle was back in his eye.

Ina remained aloof, suspicion radiating from every pore. Only minutes before, she had been trying to indoctrinate me with her theories. Now, faced with a complex reality, she retreated into her shell and dared anyone to trespass. Herbert, however dared. After Kurt, he turned his attention to her, using the charm and sympathy that used to put so many of his patients at ease. By the time we reached home, we were a happy, carefree group. At the front door, we said 'Goodbye'. Herbert and his friend had to report back to their headquarters and meeting my mother would have to wait until the morrow. Herbert kissed me, promising that he would be back the following afternoon and then he would explain the full story behind his present circumstances.

21

The Treaty of Versaille at the end of the Great War had created the independent state of Poland. Germany was deprived of most of Prussia in order to make this possible, leaving an area on the Baltic coast, east of Gdansk, under German control. Access from Germany to East Prussia was either by sea or across Polish territory. Arguments about Germany's rights to reach East Prussia by crossing the 'Polish corridor' was Hitler's excuse to make war.

The borders of Prussia lay to the east of Posen until 1919, but after the Treaty of Versailles, the new Polish border lay some 200 kilometres to the west. The people that lived in the area lying east of Frankfurt found themselves to be living in Polish territory. Many families had been there for centuries and until 1919, were part of the Prussian nation. Suddenly they were Poles. It is impossible to change what has already happened. You can change your friends, but never your forefathers. Hence, many of the families living in the region had relatives and friends on both sides of the redefined border and for the twenty years before the outbreak of the second war, we lived in harmony.

We had not moved. We were not new settlers forcing others to leave against their will. We were living in the same place, but we were no longer called Prussians. The borders had moved around us and we had become Polish. The war that started in 1939 put many people into an impossible situation. Their home was in Poland, yet many had close relatives over the border in Germany as well as in their own country.

I had been born in Poland and my parents had whole heartedly committed themselves to bringing up their daughter as a Polish citizen. When Poland gained her freedom, both my father and grandfather had become deeply involved in developing an identity for the Polish nation. They were both very Polish in mind and spirit. Grandfather belonged to the generation that had fought hard in the Great War to create the possibility of an independent Poland.

The memory of Herbert's first visit to Grandmother's house, even now fills me with a glow of nostalgia. I can still see him, sitting beside his friend on the plush cushions of the plum-red sofa. My Herbert! After all the traumas of the previous two months, here he was, real, tangible, no longer a wraith of my imagination. I was bursting with pride and happiness. His uniform had changed, but there would surely be a logical explanation for that. I was just overjoyed that he was once again in the midst of my family, whole in body and mind. Everything else was an irrelevance.

That afternoon, he did not give the full explanation as he had promised. Perhaps the presence of Kurt prevented him from being too explicit and during that first visit, Kurt dogged his every step. He was possibly concerned that the finer points of his adventures should not reach the ears of the German hierarchy. We were given only a sketchy outline of events since we had last seen him. During the days that followed, the rest of the pieces of the jigsaw were added.

When Herbert had left Warsaw, he had misled me about his plans. In the first instance, he had not wanted us know in case we inadvertently leaked information and therefore could be accused of cooperating with his scheme. His mother had sent an urgent message at the end of August, pleading with him to come home to Hamburg. She had been anxious about the ominous conclusions that she had drawn from the rumours that she had heard and wanted her son and his fiancé to leave the Polish capital as soon as possible.

Not wishing to alarm me, Herbert had postponed the journey. The apparent calm in Warsaw had inclined him to think that his mother was becoming a little eccentric in her old age and that she was exaggerating the danger. He was wrong. The war had begun with him on the wrong side of the starting gate. He had been misled by the same belief that it would never happen and that had deceived the rest of Poland.

His plan had been too perilous to include me. He left Warsaw with the intention of slipping through the lines of two armies and making his way to Hamburg. The company of a woman would have jeopardised the likelihood of success, hence he had considered that it was preferable that I remained in complete ignorance. It certainly saved him a lot of argument! Once in Germany, he had planned to negotiate for the safety of myself and my mother, but the devastating bombardment of Warsaw had meant that he had been unable to trace us. We had vanished and he could only assume the worst and that we had become victims of the onslaught.

His call up-papers were awaiting him when he arrived home, ordering him to report for military duties. Because he could speak fluent Polish, he was immediately sent back to Poland, this time to Posen.

I could not believe that fortune had decided to smile on us at last. For days I would wander about, pinching myself to make sure that I was truly awake; that it was not all a fantasy evolving out of frustrated hope or that it was not a fiendish temptation to make me believe that happiness was still possible when in reality it was dead.

My mother had been somewhat displeased that we had not invited Herbert and his friend into the house on the evening of our chance reunion. She needed to see him with her own eyes to be sure that I had not become a little deranged. Ina was my witness, however, and we could not both have taken leave of our senses at the same instant. The following day Mother and Vera worked in the kitchen all morning, baking with what little flour we had in preparation for Herbert's expected visit. Standards of hospitality should not in her opinion be affected by small difficulties caused by scarcity.

Herbert and Kurt arrived punctually as promised. Instead of flowers, they brought bread, butter and smoked sausage. They both refused to taste the cakes that Mother and Vera had baked. Herbert so that we would not be deprived of what little we had; Kurt possibly was following orders that such food was forbidden, subsequent to a number of officers dying a few days earlier from poisoning at the hand of their Polish host.

My afternoon drifted by on a cloud of bliss; a paradise of security in the belief that from now on everything was going to get better. When our visitors got up to leave, I fell with a bump from my cloud of self-delusion. Suddenly the air was cold and hostile again, the centre of my universe was empty.

My mother was fully aware of my misery and chattered ceaselessly once Herbert was gone. She forced me to eat her cakes and we feasted on the smoked sausage, savouring every mouthful. Never had smoked sausage tasted so delicious.

Herbert returned every day, sometimes with Kurt, but more and more frequently alone. Ina left Posen at the end of the month. A message from friends had arrived to say that it was safe to travel and she was glad to have the opportunity to escape the restrictive life in Posen and seek refuge in another land. Kurt had rarely been seen since. He had not wasted time in finding amusement elsewhere as soon as Ina was no longer available. Herbert told me that he had rented a room at the hotel 'Trokadero' where he satisfied his lusts and where the bed did not stay empty for long.

For me it was totally different. Herbert disapproved of his friends randy habits, besides which he was nurturing a relationship that would be life long, not one that would cease when convenient. He was anxious to rebuild the trust and confidence that we had shared in Warsaw. The circumstances in which we had now found each other were so totally different from the backdrop of the theatre. We needed time to rediscover one another. Hence he arrived every afternoon, bearing gifts for the kitchen and keeping us informed of the German strategies regarding the control of the residents of Posen.

We had heard no news of Father and Grandfather. I often wondered what they would have made of the situation. Polish to the core, they would have found it hard to reconcile the opposing facts. My grandmother stayed out of sight when Herbert was around. She could not bring herself to accept a German officer in her house and avoided meeting him in order to reduce her heartache.

Mother's loyalties were shredded in all directions. By birth she belonged to a rich, well known family from Posen, yet had lived in Germany for most of her life. Many of her friends were now supposedly her 'enemies', yet she could not accept that they had changed in their hearts just because Herr Hitler had intervened.

I was as confused. I had been born in Poland and was proud of Polish nationality... but I had fallen in love with a man who belonged to the nation that was now the aggressive enemy of my homeland. The whole thing was a crazy conundrum of mixed loyalties, which in peace time were unimportant. Now we were all caught in a merciless war that required us to look with enmity at each other as though it were possible for limbs belonging to the same body to attack and destroy each other.

A curfew had been imposed as soon as the German troops arrived in the city. People began to disappear. In October the Germans started to systematically clear certain areas of the city of Polish residents. The abductions were given the innocent sounding title 'evacuation', but rumour suggested that a more ominous fate awaited them.

Herbert often called twice a day now to let us know which streets and houses featured on the list for checking in the evening. If he received last minute information, he would send his driver with a note. Kurtchen, with his sun-tanned face, was a rascal from the Rhine valley. He would laugh at my broken German and tease me in his Cologne dialect which seemed to me to be another language altogether.

Thanks to the information provided by Herbert, we were able to warn and save many friends. A timely word was usually sufficient to ensure that they were staying at another address on the night in question. The Germans tended not to search in the same place a second time. But as Christmas approached, the 'evacuation' of Polish families reached its climax. In broad daylight, a whole street could be cordoned off by soldiers armed with submachine guns. SS commandos then searched through the buildings, evicting all the hapless occupants.

Christmas that year was not a time of celebration with family and friends. On the 30th December, Herbert came to visit. He was sporting a star on his epaulette and brought a bottle of cognac to celebrate his promotion to first lieutenant. Mother was persuaded to bring out some of her Christmas biscuits and we sat in comfort around the stove, the crackling of the firewood providing music for our cosy little world.

The intimate conversation was interrupted by a succession of loud thumps on the main door at the front of the house. The noise made a booming echo in the entrance hall.

"Someone's forgotten their key and doesn't like waiting outside in the cold." My mother remarked. It was the responsibility of the tenant on the ground floor to open the door if such were the case. Grandmother's apartment was on the first floor.

The knocking became louder and more persistent. A tingle of premonition ran down my spine. Then I was afraid. Such a continuous pounding on the door could mean only one thing. The visitors were unfriendly.

Heavy boots climbed the stairs and shouts in German could be heard. A series of heavy blows on the door of the apartment itself followed and the doorbell rang out, filling the room with its demanding rattle.

Mother and I stood motionless, staring in horror at each other. I was paralysed. I tried to move but my feet seemed to be nailed to the floor. I looked at Herbert. He, sitting bolt upright in the armchair, had grown pale. The din had become thunderous. It sounded as though they were trying to smash down the door.

With hesitant steps, mother approached the door and unbolted it.

Six tall individuals in the SS uniform that we had come to fear so much, marched into the room. Their rifles were spiked with bayonets, melting snow dripped off their steel helmets. The sight of Herbert stopped them in their tracks. The stocks of their rifles thudded on the floor as they stood to attention and 'heiled' Hitler.

Their leader, wearing a fur jacket and carrying a pistol, recognised Herbert. They shook hands and addressed each other with 'du'. An awful suspicion began to raise its ugly head, but I resisted it and squashed it out of mind before it grew too big. No... it could not be!

"Szymanski – You?" barked the leader, pointing at my mother. She shook her head and explained that the old lady had already retired for the night. It was of course my grandmother's married name.

"So! Who are you? Your papers!" My mother sent me a pleading glance and I fetched our identity cards from the cupboard where they were kept. Herbert conversed in a low voice with the leader of the SS party. The latter had taken a list of names from the leather case strapped to his belt. He took the papers that I offered him and compared them to his list, using the barrel of his gun to run down the columns of names. Suddenly the pistol stopped – and he grinned sardonically at my mother.

"Władysław Weychan! Your husband? Your father? Eh!" The barrel of the gun levelled first at my mother, then at me.

How could we deny it? He held the papers in his hand that clearly stated the fact. Question followed question like an avalanche, committing us ever deeper into guilt and doom. It seemed that both my father and grandfather were on the wanted list as Polish patriots. My grandmother, who they had dragged out of bed, was the wife of a confirmed war criminal and she was registered at this address. They had been looking for my mother and me too, but finding that both the apartment in Warsaw and our home in Posen had been destroyed, they had assumed that we had both perished in one or other place.

Without looking at us, Herbert requested that he might be allowed to look at our papers and the warrant. The SS leader meanwhile strutted around in his fur jacket, boasting loudly about the fat fish that he had caught in his net tonight. Without a word, Herbert gave him back the papers, shook hands and left, ignoring me completely. The cold serpent of suspicion reared its head again and this time, it remained.

We were alone with the SS men and as soon as they heard the front door close, they started a systematic search of the apartment. They opened cupboards and pulled out drawers, helping themselves to whatever took their fancy. The bully in the fur jacket stripped us of our jewellery and emptied our purses of any money.

Not content with that, they removed any clothes or household ornaments that they felt were of value and packed them into our suitcases. We anticipated that soon we would be invited to accompany our visitors and grandmother had found her fur coat to cover her night clothes. They tore that off her back and instead she was thrown a thin summer coat which was amongst the heap of clothing in the middle of the floor. My mother and I had to remove the special dresses that we had worn for the evening's celebration and retrieve clothes from the same pile.

When they had satisfied themselves that there was nothing further worth taking, they herded us down the stairs and into the street, where we were obliged to climb into the back of a lorry and join others who had already been arrested. My poor grandmother found this feat a great trial. She was too frail to lever herself up unassisted and she had to be hauled up by the arms in a very undignified manner. The two guards by the truck watched impassively. A few minutes later, the lorry jolted forward, stopping after a few meters to pick up two more hapless victims.

It was pitch dark and snowing hard. With eyes screwed up against the wind, we could barely see each other and had no idea of the direction in which the lorry was heading.

We crouched, huddled together in the open truck. It was bitterly cold and I found myself shivering from head to toe. I had swapped coats with grandmother, for my winter coat was much warmer than the thin garment they had permitted her to take. The falling snow matted our hair and stung our faces. Oh Herbert! Was the serpent right? Could you have anything to do with our present misfortune?

It was impossible to tell how long we rode in the back of that open truck, exposed to the fury of the weather. I now know that it must have been close on two hours. At the time, it seemed like an eternity.

"Glowna."

An old man had whispered the name as we climbed down from the lorry. He had recognised the wooden barracks, surrounded by double barbed wire fencing.

Glowna meant deportation. The place was infamous in Posen. It was the place of no return, where 'evacuees' vanished for ever.

We were propelled into one of the wooded barracks, which was already crowded. Some two hundred people, mostly women and children and elderly couples, sat in groups on a layer of straw that covered the ground. There was little room to spare for lying down.

There was no heating of any kind and our clothes were sodden. The occupants of the hut shifted closer together to make a space for us to sit. Grandmother was particularly stressed by the situation. The journey in such rough conditions had taken its toll on her strength. By rubbing her frozen limbs to encourage circulation, we earned her a little warmth as reward.

No sooner were we settled as comfortably as possible in that arid desert of comfort, than we heard our names being called out. Stiff and cold, we stirred ourselves once again to be informed that we must go to the office building for admission particulars.

There, in the low, smok filled room, unmelted snow flakes still clinging to his great coat and cap, stood Herbert. The serpent of doubt inside me staggered as the flame of hope leapt to life at the sight of him. Once again, he ignored us, but I sensed that his behaviour was part of the drama and that it would be unwise to give any sign of recognition. I was aware that for some indefinable reason, no one must know of our close relationship.

He was here, that was the most important thing. He could have only just arrived and already he had arranged for us to be summonsed. He had come to fetch us! It was obvious! I thought that there could be no other explanation and my hopes rose.

Our names were checked and entered in the ledger on the desk. Herbert neither spoke nor interfered and the flame of hope started to die. All I could see was his back as he inspected a file that he had taken from the cupboard and when a guard entered and announced with the Nazi salute that the first lieutenant's car was ready, he promptly walked out of the office with not so much as a glance in our direction. I felt myself tumble deeper and deeper into the chasm of despair.

I cannot remember how I managed to return to our patch of straw in the hut. I heard my mother's voice as she took my arm. I felt her breath in my ear, but did not comprehend a word that she was saying.

Without doubt, Herbert was known to the officialdom of the camp. He had never mentioned that he had anything to do with Glowna. What else had he conveniently forgotten to tell us? How stupid we had been to trust a German. My fiancé he may have been, but he had produced so many little surprises during the past few weeks, that I was becoming extremely sceptical about his priorities. After all, I knew so little about him. His romantic charm had swept me off my feet and I had not bothered to delve too deeply into his past. Now, I was paying for the oversight. The German was our enemy and would remain so. Even when they deluded us into thinking that they were friendly, they could suddenly remove their amiable mask and show their hatred towards us. Herbert had perhaps shown some sentiment by refusing to actually look at us in our moment of condemnation. Perhaps he was embarrassed by our misfortune. I grasped at any straw that might excuse his cold, indifferent behaviour. The serpent, however, reminded me that as a child, many a butcher cannot tolerate the sight of blood.

Was Herbert any different? In a short while, would he too learn to stare stonily at his victims.

The nine huts of the camp at Glowna were not adequate to shelter all the people that were dragged thither. Daily, more arrived. After a few days it became totally impossible to lie down to sleep. We could only sit, huddled together, sharing the warmth of our bodies for there was no other protection against the bitter cold. The shifting of the tired, uncomfortable mass of humanity was constant. When anyone wanted to go to the toilet or fetch water, they had to climb over and around the tangle of closely packed bodies. There was always someone on the move, trying to make their way back and forth to the only door in the room. The large number of children added to the misery. At midday a ladle of gruel was handed out to each person together with a slice of bread. There were no other meals and it was no wonder the children cried from hunger or whimpered ceaselessly from boredom. Some of them had been there for a week and more.

Every day when the lorry returned with more prisoners, my mother would search the newcomers for familiar faces. The sound of tyres and the noise of brakes screeching outside the hut would cause her to stare fixedly at the door. To date, she had only found the wife of a Polish officer who had lived in our street in Posen. Her two small boys were with her.

Grandmother grew steadily weaker. Her chest hurt and she had great difficulty getting to her feet. If she was forced to stay in such conditions for much longer, her prospects did not look promising. She was remarkably philosophical about her predicament, however, and remained cheerful, despite her discomfort and failing health.

On the fifth day after our arrival, a guard appeared in the doorway and called out two names, those of my mother and myself. He told us to bring our belongings We had none, so we were ready immediately. As we had no idea why we had been called or where we were going and expected that we would soon be back, we did not exchange more than a '...goodbye, see you soon...' with grandmother. She had smiled, patted the back of my hand and wished me 'Courage!'

The guard did not lead us to the office as we had expected, but straight to the gate, where a car was waiting. It was dark and I could not see the face of the driver, not that it mattered for I assumed that we were being taken elsewhere for more questioning. The driver looked up and I recognised Herbert's orderly. The expression on the face of the normally cheerful Rhinelander was serious. He did not utter a word, indicating with his eyes only, that we should get into the car.

The camp gates opened and a few seconds later, we drove through. Kurchen kept his sombre pose until the camp was far behind us, then he reverted into the jolly fellow that he naturally was.

As the car sped over the snow covered road, he greeted us warmly and passed back some parcels of food. We had been rescued! Herbert, my guardian angel, please forgive me for having doubted you. The sight and smell of the fresh biscuits and sausage, however, caused hunger to take flight. The scent of freedom, so many hopes, so many disappointments, sheer exhaustion, meant that we could not eat anything. Words cannot fully describe the mixture of emotions that stirred in the shadows of the back seat of that car.

We stopped in one of the wealthier districts of Posen. The houses had been requisitioned by the German army during the first few days of the occupation and Herbert had been allocated a small family house, where he lodged with his orderly. The Rhinelander's duties seemed to include the housework. He had set the table and prepared rooms for us before he set out to fetch us from Glowna. It was with some pride and a cheeky grin that he showed us to our rooms where we found ample evidence of his efficiency.

Herbert had thought of everything. There were fresh clothes laid out ready for us to change into and on the bedside tables, we found chocolates and cigarettes.

The full significance of what had happened to us sunk in as I sipped coffee in the warm comfort of the parlour. Our pleasure at the unexpected release from the hut at Glowna was overshadowed by the knowledge that grandmother was still there, cold sick and now, alone. Could fortune not have included her in his pity?

Mother was very tired and excused herself around midnight. For my part, I wanted to wait up for Herbert to return. The obliging Kurtchen provided me with another pot of coffee, before he also retired to his bed. Curled up beside the glowing stove, warm, fed, clean and comfortable, a cigarette in my hand and steaming coffee on the table, I tried to convince myself that the past five days had been a horrible nightmare. But I found myself trembling, unable to put the cigarette to my lips. In spite of the warmth around me, the cold hand of terror would not go away.

It must have been very late when Herbert finally came in. The coffee and my determination to greet him had failed to keep me alert and I had fallen asleep. The sound of the front door closing disturbed me and I heard him quickly bound up the stairs. Suddenly, there he was, the cap in his hand still glistening with snow.

He gazed intently at me and I rolled off the sofa. He took a deep breath, then let out a long sigh as though shedding a tremendous weight from his mind. In three strides, he was across the room to sweep me up into his arms. It was not the fierce embrace of passion, but gentle and enveloping; a union of souls. The face on my cheek was still chill from the winter's night and soon I felt his lips on my neck, his voice whispering my name.

"Maria, Maria, Maria...!"

22

All the cards now lay in full view on the table. No more secrets.

Herbert had discovered that my father had been detained for leading a group of partisans, who had continued to fight after Poland's surrender. Also that Grandfather had been known for his patriotism before the war started because of his involvement in forming the Polish youth movement which encouraged nationalism; that he had been particularly active against the Germans and that he had organised resistance groups until the moment of his arrest. As a result, all members of the family bearing Grandfather's surname were under orders for arrest. For this reason, it had been impossible to free my grandmother.

The situation had looked a little more promising for my mother and for me. They had not been able to trace us, so we had been registered as 'on the run'. Our arrest had been accidental and had happened only because we were in grandmother's apartment when the SS had come to collect her. Herbert had not been aware of their intentions that night and would have warned us, rather than be discovered relaxing with a cup of coffee in his hand. It would have been useless to argue with the arresting squad as he might well have had to accompany us in the lorry, so he had bluffed his way out of the situation and set about discovering how to achieve our release. He had managed to acquire papers that would order us to be transported to a 'remand prison'. By filling in the forms himself, he had arranged that only one of the three copies that secured their release was actually completed. The two other forms, one that should have gone to the remand prison and the other to the records office at headquarters, had conveniently and mysteriously vanished. He personally had presented the sole copy in existence to the camp commandant at Glowna and, using his own car for the transport, it had not been necessary to involve outsiders. If there had been three of us including grandmother, suspicions might have been aroused as to why a car was designated and not the normal truck. The only danger was to Herbert himself if the release forms were ever checked thoroughly at the central office.

This had all been possible because he worked at the local headquarters and information about 'displacement activities' was at his disposal. He had been aware of the necessary forms and routines used by the German security and had misused them in our interest.

Since we had met again in the streets of Posen, I had been presented with a totally different Herbert to the one that I had known in Warsaw. It was with difficulty that I tried to assimilate the two. Under the uniform, the same heart throbbed and his soul was still mine and he would use every means available to him to protect me. However, the demands of his new role in life were so alien to me, that I could not understand how he could willingly be part of the invasive German war machine.

He, for his part, had discovered that I was not a dancer on the stage that could replace his dead wife, but the progeny of a family that his war machine was bent on destroying.

We may have learned a lot about each other in the past few days, but an answer to the riddle was still elusive. While he was inextricably involved with the hated German headquarters, its evil hawk-eye terrorising the town, I was a fugitive, sought by the same detestable organisation. He had obviously not declared his association with me to his superiors as, rather than protect me, it would have jeopardised his own freedom. Having achieved our release from Glowna, we were now totally dependent on him. Should events turn against him, we would both be lost, for the fate of both my mother and myself had become dependent on his. We could not leave the house or show our faces at the window.

All the houses in the area were occupied by German officers and soldiers. The danger was very real and very great for Herbert. No one must suspect that there were two women in his house.

The other danger lay in a messenger calling or a chance visit by an off duty comrade. Suspicion would be aroused if he left them on the door step. The sooner that we moved to alternative accommodation, the better it would be for all of us.

Herbert found an empty three roomed flat in the suburbs and rented it in his name. This was not an uncommon thing for our unwanted visitors to do, in order to provide themselves with convenient love nests. He arranged for a few things to be requisitioned from grandmother's apartment to furnish the rooms as comfortably as possible and we left his house under the cover of darkness. He could have acquired belongings from any of the apartments that the Germans had seized, but as he was in a position to control the selection, that is what he did so that we might feel more at home with familiar objects around us.

When we arrived at our destination, who opened the door to welcome us, but Vera. The ability of the man to think of everything was immeasurable. Dear, faithful, dependable Vera, he had somehow managed to track her down after our arrest and installed her with the furnishings. And there were yet more surprises! He handed new and perfect identity papers in which I was described as a German national. My polish maiden name of Weychanowna had been shortened to Weychans so that I need not fear any controls. No longer would my 'name' appear on any of the wanted lists.

Even so, he advised that it would be unwise to venture beyond the outer door. Too many people could still recognise me and among them were those that reported back to the Germans. Mother also was too well known in Posen and if we acted without discretion, it was not only our own safety that we endangered, but also that of Herbert. He had risked so much already in order to help us and we agreed readily to his restrictions.

Towards the end of January, however, he received orders for a transfer. His section was to be withdrawn to Hamburg. The withdrawal of the German fighting units from Poland had begun. Hamburg suggested a solution. Herbert's mother still lived there and what could be simpler than that we should seek refuge in her home. Mother could renew an old friendship and she would come to know more about her future daughter-in-law.

Since leaving Glowna, Herbert had found various official reasons why he should visit the camp. He had been able to report on Grandmother and supply her with food and warmer clothing. With the news that he was due to leave, he made the trip yet again, but this time, he returned with his parcels. Sick and old, grandmother had been removed soon after his first visit, her destination unknown. In spite of an intense barrage of questions, Herbert denied all knowledge of her fate. Maybe, he was trying to protect me from the heartache of a bitter truth. Mother and I could only pray for her.

On the same day, 24th January, I received further disturbing news. Herbert returned in the evening to give me his mother's address and told me that he was to leave Poland with the troops on the very next day. The war was moving on! What further trails of misery did the German war machine intend to leave? As a cog in the machine, however, Herbert was obliged to comply. This I could understand, but I could not sympathise.

Later that same evening when Vera returned to the flat after visiting some of her relatives, I had another joyous surprise. Who followed Vera in through the door, but Tuta. It was wonderful to see my old friend again, but was saddened by the story that she had to tell.

"They looked after me so well at the clinic," she said. "But when I was well enough to leave, I could find no trace of my parents. Hoping that they had come home to Posen, I made my way here. It took some time, as I walked most of the way and took shelter where I could. But like yours, my home here has been destroyed and there is still no news of my parents. I tried to find you, but had no luck. Then I remembered the close ties that you have with your maid. I found her family and have been staying with them. When Vera came today, she insisted that I come back with her. I hope you don't mind!"

"Mind? Oh Tuta! It's wonderful to see you." We hugged each other and cried, finding the bitter memories of the recent months very depressing. In silence, we looked at each other, studying the scars etched by distress then embraced again and allowed the tears to flow.

Tuta now knew of her fiancé's death. She was still not fully recovered from her head injury and suffered fits of vagueness and loss of memory. How she had managed to get from Warsaw to Posen without help was a mystery... or a miracle.

23

'Bob' first spoke to me, as I was trying to buy a ticket for Hamburg at the railway station. The man in the ticket office had just explained to me that I needed official confirmation of the urgency of my proposed journey. New regulations had just been introduced that a journey had to be 'war-essential'. Vera was beside me, holding the suitcases. I had decided to follow Herbert and risk travelling all the way to Hamburg on my own. Mother had come to the conclusion that she should stay in the flat. There had been no news of whereabouts of either Father or Grandfather and she still hoped that she would hear news of what might have happened to her mother. If she moved to Hamburg, she would remain in ignorance. However, it seemed impractical for the two of us to stay in Posen hiding in the flat and she had encouraged me to leave.

As I put my money back into my purse, the expression on my face must have reflected my disappointment. The German officer standing behind me in the queue took pity on me and asked politely whether he could not be of some assistance.

He wore the SS insignia on his collar and the swastika and eagle on his sleeve. Although I had become used to seeing Herbert in uniform, I still could not help recoiling whenever I met them. I gasped!

A devil inside me urged me to take the risk. "If this is the only way, I dare you to take it," it urged. "Go on, you can trick him into getting what you want." I had to get to Hamburg by whatever means! The little devil was right, I could get what I wanted if I used my head. Without further hesitation, I told him a sad story; that I was a poor orphan of German descent; that my father had been killed in action and that my only relatives lived in Berlin. I just had to go and stay with them, or my life would not be worth living any more – all told in a quaint, pigeon German.

My performance must have been convincing. Bob decided to take me under his patronage and he lived up to his name. Whoever had dubbed him thus, must have known that he could handle anything, quickly and efficiently.

"To Berlin you said? – A bagatelle!" He would see to it! What was this? Certificate of war essentiality? What nonsense! What do they mean by war? Or essential? The war was over! He informed me, by the by, that I had just become his prisoner and he was taking me to Breslau for trial proceedings. He had papers of authorization of course.

The little man in the ticket office visibly shrank behind his desk and speedily produced the required tickets without setting eyes on the papers of authorization. I noted that 'Bob' was not a member of the Gestapo for nothing. If it suited him to use his power, then he had no qualms about doing so and this it seemed included giving assistance to damsels in distress. He was quite prepared to use the system for his own convenience and escorting a prisoner single handed was quite within his jurisdiction.

I became a little nervous and regretted having listened to the little devil, but it was far too late to backtrack now. While 'Bob' hailed a porter to carry my luggage, I said goodbye to Vera. Her firm embrace gave me courage.

A crowd of people were assembled at the barrier, waiting to be allowed through the gate to board the train. Anticipating the scrum that would follow with everyone fighting for seats, 'Bob' went straight to the station master's office, showed his identity card and flashed his swastika. The result of the interview was that we were escorted to the train by the station master himself, nervously flapping his red cap to clear the way. There was no doubt at all. 'Bob' was a smart boy. The railway official did give me some odd looks, as though I were a calf with five legs, but I did not mind. He did not know about my devil.

The control checks on the train were made after we had been travelling for about an hour. Bob explained that I was a Polish prisoner, due for a hearing at the Breslau courts. The luggage, he claimed as his own. They took a look at his papers, saluted, smiled – and were gone.

We arrived in Breslau at midnight and Bob took me to the Hotel Monopol, where he was greeted as though he might have been a regular guest. True to character, he took the bull by the horns, boasting, "I can fix anything, however complicated." He had been ready to give instant help to me and now he was just as direct in claiming his reward. Without a moment of hesitation, he entered me in the hotel register as his wife and booked a double room. He did it with the same confident grin as the one he had used when the control officials had left the compartment on the train. Everything was going smoothly and according to plan, or so he thought. He had not taken my devil into consideration.

At first, he had shown some reluctance to the plan I proposed. I suggested to him that we should go to a night club to celebrate my safe arrival in Germany, the great fatherland. Using all the beguiling charm that I had, I pleaded and cajoled. Finally, he was persuaded.

My broken German provided most of the merriment. I made Bob laugh and as the hours ticked by, I kept him laughing – and drinking – a lot. We went from one bar to the next until the devil succeeded. Bob, who could fix anything, had gone to sleep on a bar stool and crumpled on to the floor, oblivious of everything that was going on around him. I returned to the hotel alone.

I asked the taxi driver to wait and raced into the reception hall. The night porter looked a little astonished when I asked him to fetch my as yet unopened suitcases, but obligingly produced paper and pencil for me to write a hasty note to Bob. My written German was even more ridiculous than my spoken version of the language, but, tried my best to indicate my meaning. I wrote that I hoped that he would not be too disappointed when he returned to the hotel to find that I had already left and that I hoped too that the hangover hurt! Finally, when the porter appeared with my bags, I asked him to send a telegram to Herbert to tell him that I was in Germany. I begged the man not to mention this to my 'husband' and crossed his palm with a healthy tip. He gave me an understanding smile as he pocketed the money and I hoped that I could depend on him. Bob could still catch up with me if my luck did not hold.

The early train to Berlin was late. It should have left Breslau shortly after 5am and a crowd of passengers waited on the platform for an hour or more. Dragging my suitcases which seemed to get heavier by the minute, I weaved my way into the depths of the gathered throng and prayed that Bob was still slumbering. Perching on the heap of my possessions, I then concentrated on sending telepathic messages to the engine driver and the German railway system to make haste and get the train into the station quickly... very quickly... instantly would be even better. When at last the train did arrive, I snatched up my luggage, now miraculously as light as a feather and climbed aboard while the carriage was still moving.

I had to wait another three hours in Berlin for the connection to Hamburg and I used the time to go to the hairdresser. In Fredrickstrasse, a street close to the station, my hair changed from light blonde to auburn. It altered my appearance dramatically and I was secretly very satisfied with the result. The hairdresser twittered about, making a great fuss about having to destroy the 'ideal' natural colour with dye and was further upset when I failed to give his efforts any more than a cursory glance afterwards. I paid him and left. It would now be very difficult to trace me. I would leave Berlin looking quite different from the woman that arrived.

It was late in the afternoon by the time I reached Hamburg. I had to ask directions even to locate the exit from the huge station. Finding my way to the address that Herbert had given me seemed suddenly to be a monumental problem. An elderly gentleman was buying an evening newspaper by the door. His expression looked amiable, and I decided to approach him for advice. Fortunately, he was only too happy to assist and explained to me, pronouncing his words slowly and clearly, that Hamburg 33 indicated the suburb of Hamburg-Burbeck which could be reached on the underground train. A taxi stopped nearby and he immediately stuck his head in the open window and talked to the driver at a speed that I could not understand. When he withdrew his head, he smiled, opened the door, put my cases aboard and invited me to step inside telling me as he did so, that the cab would take me to my destination at Alderstrasse 22. I smiled my gratitude, wondering why it was necessary to go to war, if all Germans were as considerate as this old man.

The delights of Hamburg passed me by unnoticed. Its buildings, shops, bridges and its people seemed much the same as Warsaw. I was relieved to have my goal in sight and so anxious about what I would find at the end of the trail, that I barely looked out of the window. When I did so, I remember only a kaleidoscope of images. Time dragged by very slowly. The hour's drive seemed like a week and I began to suspect that we were going in circles to increase the fare. Eventually we stopped in front of a detached house, surrounded by a large garden. A small spinney grew to one side and a man was mending the wooden lattice work of the fence that ran along the front of the property. I climbed out of the cab and paid the driver with some of the Deutschmarks that Herbert had given me before he left Posen.

Herbert's mother opened the door in response to my nervous prod of the bell button. I was hoping that the telegram which I had sent her had arrived and that she would be expecting me, but her face showed no trace of recognition. I had forgotten my hair. "I'm... I'm Maria Weychanowna." I hiccupped. Immediately, her face broke into a welcoming smile.

"Maria, my dear! Come in!" She pushed the door wide open and took one of my cases. I had been expecting a welcoming embrace from my prospective mother-in-law and sensed some reserve in her manner. However, as she chatted, I realised that she had not expected me and my altered appearance confused her. She would have been prepared to greet a blonde. To find a dark haired stranger on her doorstep must have been a disturbing surprise for her. On the table in the hall lay the unopened telegram. I had addressed it to Herbert. It confirmed that she had indeed not received any warning and she truly had not recognised the waif on her doorstep.

Herbert was expected home later in the evening and his mother suggested that we meet him at the station. The initial reserve had developed into a mutual trust as we became better acquainted. We strolled arm in arm through the drizzling rain. I had answered her enquiries about my mother and passed on greetings from her. We were a generation apart in age, but she made me feel so at home that soon I found myself talking with her as though she was a older sister.

Frau Kurzke would have been in her fifties. Her age was irrelevant, for she seemed a kind, loving, unselfish person who is always good company, whether they are sixteen or sixty. She loved her son deeply and seemed happy to include in her affections the girl that her son had chosen. She was so like my own mother in so many ways, it was amazing. She was also the first German woman that I had met. To discover that mothers in different countries were the same in their attitudes and feelings was a happy relief. It was a proof that there was no fundamental difference between mothers, wherever they came from. The good mothers in the world are alike and share a common bond. Frau Kurzke was a good mother and it strengthened my faith in her son, however many cards he still might keep hidden.

We were sheltering under a tree, watching the exit from the underground, when Herbert emerged. I recognised him at once by the way he walked, although he wore civilian clothes and a dark hat that cast a deep shadow over his face.

He had almost passed us, when his mother called his name. He turned his head and looked straight at me. The street was dimly lit and for a second he hesitated then, with a loud whoop, he threw his arms around me in a fierce bear hug, lifted me off my feet and swung me in a circle before setting me down again. It was the most spontaneous greeting that Herbert had ever given me. He said little, however. Instead, he linked arms with the two women in his life and marched us back to No. 22, Alderstrasse.

He did not say very much during supper either. He asked after my mother, the last few days that I had spent in Posen and how I had managed to get to Hamburg. Only later when his mother retired did he confess that he had been extremely worried about me, but the fog of anxiety was lifting. I was safe and well and the sun was beginning to shine.

He commented on my change of hair colour and on my dress which was the same one that I had been wearing on the evening that we had found each other again on the streets of Posen. It had been among the garments that the SS had left behind in Grandmother's apartment. Without his uniform, Herbert was again the same man that I had known in Warsaw, his slender hands those of the caring surgeon.

"Always look at the hands first," had been one of my grandfather's sayings. "Many a handsome face became damned by a pair of brutal hands." I believed him.

Herbert's hands emerged from slender wrists, his fingernails clean and shaped like almonds. They were almost too delicate to belong to a man; more the hands of an artist than a soldier. The contradiction possibly held the key to his nature and to our relationship. Softly and with infinite reverence, I lifted those hands to my lips.

24

The language, the road signs and place names, the advertisements and the newspapers, the trams which were taller than the ones in Posen and the many unfamiliar flags waved by children, marching in orderly ranks, singing military songs – the impact of these, was Germany.

The man travelling to work on the suburban railway, complaining that his young son had ruined yet another pair of boots or perhaps looking forward to taking his wife or girlfriend to the Reeperbahn on Sunday – he was the German.

Both had two faces.

The other face of Germany had destroyed my home, arrested and imprisoned my family, dispossessed men, women and children and condemned them to an uncertain future. They had destroyed cities, killing the inhabitants indiscriminately with their bombs and they had become inebriated on their blood.

The other face of the German had trespassed over the border, terrorised with rifles and starvation, murdered and looted. They came from towns like Hamburg. They were the sons and husbands of the people around me. They had been put into uniforms, provided with weapons and become part of the war machine. But the hearts beating inside them – surely, they had not changed. Surely underneath, they had not changed.

My grandfather had drummed into me that the Germans were the enemy of Poland, for as long as I could remember. I had since learned, however, that it was unfair to condemn a nation as a whole; to dismiss them as one would a faulty vacuum cleaner or radio set. A nation was made up of individual people. Herbert, his mother, my new friend Herr Kraus, they were all sincere and immensely human – one could not find better.

Maybe it was the uniform that should be blamed for covering up all individualism and dragging everyone into a common porridge. Wearing the uniform meant that you were drugged by persistent propaganda; protection of the common mass took priority and orders were executed without question. It meant that ordinary people were conditioned to become enemies.

Logically therefore, one should not hate the human being but hate the uniform and the devils that designed them.

If only someone in a position of power had rationalised along these lines, the war with all its horrors would never have happened. I was convinced by my own logic, naive that it was and failing to appreciate that such an all powerful and benevolent person did not exist in this world – though many have aspired and have in their turn become the devils.

At that time, when Herbert had to leave me on my own so often, I would have given anything to be a child again. I longed to be able to sit on my father's lap, lay my head on his shoulder and ask him about all the things that I did not understand; for him to solve all my puzzling problems with his clear methodical mind and wrap his arms around me; to hear his deep voice, saying, "Yes child, this is how...!"

But my father was far away and only my prayers could reach him.

The move into our own apartment stopped me from brooding. Herbert rented a small flat in Deseniss Strasse. I was now a registered German national with residence permit and ration cards to prove it. The sight of all those official papers with all their official stamps spread out over the kitchen table, filled me at last with a tremendous feeling of safety.

On the door of my flat, at the town registry office and in all my papers, I was called Frau Weychan. I avoided developing friendships with the other tenants in the building. My German still needed attention and all my free time was taken up by my efforts to improve my command of the language. I was still very aware that my accent aroused curiosity and I did not wish to get involved in a long explanation of lies with the people that lived around me. It would have been too easy to confuse myself!

The Kraus family lived on the same floor. They were the only exception to my self-imposed rule of solitude. They owned the clock shop downstairs and I frequently visited old Herr Kraus in his workshop. The rhythmical ticking of the time pieces gave an assurance that there was a future.

Herr Kraus would work at his bench, his bushy eyebrows at odd angles from the effort of holding the magnifier in his right eye. In his youth, he had worked in a Swiss factory that manufactured clocks and watches and had set up his business in Hamburg a few years previously, hoping to provide for a comfortable retirement for himself and his wife. The war had cast a shadow on his project for his partner, his only son, had been drafted into the navy. This caused Herr Kraus constant anxiety and he sorely missed the company of his business partner.

One afternoon, while he was telling me stories about his family, the porter's wife came in to tell me that an elderly woman was asking for me. I was mystified. Herbert's mother could not be described as elderly, yet she was the only person that knew where to find me. In seconds, my confidence vanished. Immediately, I was filled with dread, fearing that I had been discovered and that all my proofs of identity were worthless.

The 'elderly person' had followed her into the room. It was my mother. She looked twenty years older than when I had seen her last, her face was haggard and grey. She wore neither hat nor coat and there was no sign of any luggage. I rushed towards her and threw my arms around her. "Mother!"

Gone was the composed expression that I knew so well. Gone was the strong, decisive personality which I knew so well. In its stead were the features of an exhausted and disillusioned woman. Broken and weary she may have been, but she was my mother and we were together again. Now it was my turn to provide a haven for her.

"Let's find somewhere private," she muttered in my ear. "I need to sit down."

I thanked the porter's wife and supported my mother as she climbed the stairs. Once in the small apartment, she sank gratefully onto the sofa.

"Maria, you can't imagine how wonderful it is to find you safe and well. Since you left Posen, things have become impossible." I sat down beside her and laid my hand over hers as they lay clasped in her lap, the knuckles white with tension.

"Is there any news of Father?" I asked.

"Nothing!" Her hand grasped mine and closed tightly in a desperate squeeze. "Nothing...!"

I prepared some coffee. Slowly, she told her story.

Leaving Poland had become more difficult. Even Germans needed permission to travel. To circumvent this problem, mother had joined a group of German labourers who were being sent to Blumental. Her natural leadership had been recognised and she soon became supervisor of the girls travelling in three carriages, making arrangements for their provisions and equipment. When the train reached German soil she had taken advantage of the night darkness and during one of the innumerable occasions when the train slowed, she had jumped off. She had to leave everything behind even her hat and coat. Never short of initiative, she had made her way to Hamburg and telephoned Inger, Herbert's mother. Thus she arrived, tired, dirty and dishevelled, but alive and unharmed.

Inger was delighted to see her old friend and was even more pleased than Herbert that Mother had successfully escaped from Poland.

Herbert immediately procured a full set of German papers for her. She no longer needed to worry about the absence of identity documents which had been a seemingly insurmountable hurdle that had dogged her to date. She could now start a new life. Her ability to speak the language fluently was once again of enormous help. It meant that there was nothing to prevent her from looking for a suitable occupation. The few pieces of jewellery that we had managed to keep would not finance us for long and we had to think of the future.

Within the week, my mother had recovered from her hazardous journey. She regained her equanimity and composure and every day became more active. During the last couple of years, while Father's time had been taken up with political developments, mother had taken care of things at the factory, including the wholesale side of the business. Her experience now proved very useful. She was offered the post of manageress at the Patzenhofer restaurant in Stephen's Square. The owner had been called up and his wife had no experience about financial matters. Mother's arrival on the scene proved opportune.

It was a novel position for her. She had to get used to being an employee rather than employer, having to report for work at regular hours. The memories of our carefree life in Posen kept flooding back, however, intruding when they were least expected. Recalling the hut at Glowna and poor grandmother reminded us constantly that fate had provided us with the chance of a new start and it was up to us to make the best of our good fortune.

25

Every letter from Vera was a cry for help. Her stress leapt out from every line. Her last note told us that she had tried unsuccessfully to follow us and that she felt that she could not carry on alone. The threat that she was contemplating putting an end to it all was implicit in the short message and I became alarmed that she would do something silly. I decided that immediate action had to be taken.

Mother was at work when the postman delivered the letter at 9am Herbert was also away on one of his frequent trips to Berlin, where it was impossible to reach him. With no restraining advice available, I decided to go back to Posen to fetch Vera. It was an impetuous and foolhardy venture, but I was still of an age when caution tends to take second place. Vera was in trouble and needed help.

There was a fast train to Berlin at 11am and I could be over the border by the evening. I wrote a note to mother to give myself an alibi. I told her that I had gone to Berlin to see Herbert and that I would be back the day after tomorrow. Vera's letter, I tucked into my handbag, so that mother would not find it and put two and two together.

The journey to Berlin was uneventful. It was at the border that I had to fear the control checks, for I had neither a permit to leave the country nor even permission to travel.

The train stopped for several hours in open country outside Frankfurt. It was only the engine giving trouble, but the delay set my nerves on edge. The five soldiers in my compartment tried to make friends. They talked of their recent leave and gave me chocolates and apples. They wanted to know whether the Poles wore furs all the year round, in summer as well as in winter and whether Warsaw was a more splendid city than Berlin. They belonged to a unit, based in southern Germany and this relief mission was their first time abroad. They were eager to learn about conditions in Poland and had no idea what was in store for them. We chatted and eventually I told them of my predicament. I invented a story about the sudden death of my mother in Posen and that there had been no time to apply for the necessary permit and travel documents as I would have missed the funeral by the time they were issued. Now, I was completely at the mercy of the police patrols.

The young men offered their condolences and after some discussion, concluded that it would not be a good idea to meet the police check head on. One could never be sure how sympathetic the officer on duty would be! It was getting dark by the time the train moved off and they immediately helped me to climb into the overhead luggage rack. They covered me with their kit bags and other gear until they were satisfied that I was totally concealed. The boy who had been keeping watch in the corridor was called back into the compartment and voices assured me that everything was under control; that I had nothing to fear.

The passport control boarded the train at the Neubenschen border crossing point and I was given a whispered commentary on what was happening.

Red Cross nurses came with huge pots of coffee. Mail trolleys passed the window and…

"There are the border police. No fear little lady. They are coming! Lie absolutely still now!"

I heard the door slide open and a voice ask for papers. The soldiers showed their transport and identity cards, chatting and laughing with the officials.

"How's the food in Poland? Any cigarettes? What are the girls like?"

"You'll soon find out," was the terse reply. Then the door slammed shut.

One of the boys made a loud and triumphant noise that could politely be described as reassembling the flourish of a brass trumpet. The danger was past. For safety reasons, I remained in my hiding place until the train was well into Poland, then the kit bags and paraphernalia were removed and I was helped down to the floor again.

Vera stared at me as if I was an apparition from another world. She had peered round the half open door in answer to my knock, then vanished, leaving me standing in the hall. Maybe my dyed hair confused her? I pushed the door open for myself and entered, gave her a big hug and asked her whether my telegram had arrived. She was still behaving like a mute and without a word, produced a piece of paper from her pocket. The contents would not have made any sense to her, but I hoped they would help us on our return journey.

The telegram, which I had sent from Berlin, said that my mother had been seriously injured in a bomb attack on Hamburg. Not many bombs had actually hit the port at the time, but the suggestion might prove to be a powerful enough lever to get the necessary permits.

Luck was on my side. The telegram did prove to be a good enough reason for all my travelling papers to be issued by the following midday. Vera had no documents of any kind, but I was now familiar with the routines of the railway system and confidently plotted accordingly.

The temptation to visit friends while I had the chance was great, but I stayed in the apartment, wary enough to show some self preservation. Vera cancelled the tenancy, explaining that the occupier had been permanently transferred to Berlin and she sold the furniture to the neighbours for a small sum of money. While all this was settled, I kept well out of sight.

That evening a taxi took us to the station. I told Vera to wear no hat and to wear her house slippers. She stood next to me at the barrier with one of the suitcases, while the ticket inspector accompanied by a policeman, looked at my authorization to travel. My papers were in order and I was free to pass, but Vera had no right to come with me to the platform. I pleaded that she was my aunt, who wanted to see me off and that I would have difficulty handling both cases on my own. Vera was dressed as though she had just popped over the road to see her niece safely aboard the train and that she had no intention of travelling anywhere. They let us both through, threatening us with arrest if she did not return.

We mingled with crowd on the platform and Vera helped me to load the cases through the window into the train, behaving perfectly normally for the benefit of an observer. Then she slipped discreetly onto the train and, once in the compartment, she quickly changed her coat and put on a hat and walking shoes, stuffing her old clothes back into the suitcase. As soon as she had completed her transformation, she wandered off to await departure in the corridor of another carriage. My heart thumped to near bursting point in those few minutes. In every policeman that walked past the window, I imagined a hunter.

Only when the train chugged out of the station did I start to breathe more easily. The next hurdle looming, was the border control. The trick of hiding on the luggage rack could not be repeated. The compartment was occupied by all sorts of people and we could not expect that they would cooperate by piling up their belongings as the young soldiers had done. Instead, I sent Vera to the dining car and told her to say that she had left her papers with me in the compartment. As to her ticket – I had, of course, bought two, one of which was not clipped. I corrected this little detail with the help of a hair pin.

The border control official came to me as expected and asked for Vera's permits. I acted as though I was very surprised at his question and told him that I had just taken her papers to her in the dining car. In the end I managed to confuse him so much, that we got away with our little scheme.

We arrived in Berlin early in the morning and reached Hamburg by late afternoon. Mother came home unexpectedly early and found us at the supper table, pretending that it was the most ordinary of evenings and behaving as though Vera had just dropped in for a casual visit. She was of course delighted to see Vera, but was horrified and angered at the danger that I had been in and the risks that I had taken. As far as I was concerned, the adventure had been a success – and that was all there was to it.

We had been lucky. Fate had chosen to smile on us that day and to add a final touch, the doorbell rang three times... and... Herbert walked in.

When mother and Vera had gone to bed, I suggested to Herbert that we went out for a walk. Admitting a satisfaction to having me alone for a change, we sallied forth into the clear, warm, spring evening. It was late. The streets were empty and few windows still showed light. We walked close together, his arm around my shoulders.

How long we strolled like this, is unimportant. We floated silently on a soft cloud of romance. Suddenly, we became aware that we had reached the town centre. We were surrounded by a vibrant night life; brightly lit restaurants; coloured advertisements; revving cars; people; voices and music. After a moment's hesitation, we smiled in unspoken agreement and mingled with a crowd of merry makers.

We were drinking a second glass of wine, when the lights dimmed and the orchestra started to play the 'Tango Nocturno' – my Tango Nocturno. With eyes closed, I listened to the melody and drifted away on a wave of joy and pain. I do not now recall much of the dancer or the stage set as my yearning thoughts drifted back to the previous summer.

When the orchestra continued with a piece of Csarda's music, I became angry with frustration. What might have been if the circumstances had been different? Cardell! Szczurek! Warsaw! Gdinga! The memories exploded in my head. Would I ever be able to dance again – on a stage just like this one?

Herbert must have read my thoughts.

"We must wait, Maria. You will have to be patient...!"

There was some comfort in his words. Things were looking up. Vera was with us again. We had our own home. Were not the days of fear and persecution behind us? And surely this terrible war would end some day? I would not have to hide for ever? Herbert had talked of war with France and maybe Russia! This had to be nonsense! The numbersof dead and wounded during those September days in Poland must have been known in the higher echelons of power. Surely, they would see sense. No one wanted this war. Listening to people on the street, it was clear that they all wanted the return of their sons and brothers alive and well. The will of the people could not simply be ignored and crushed as the ripe cornfields of Poland had been crushed by tanks.

Common sense, dear God in Heaven! Common sense must prevail – and I can again dance one day. Dance, please God! – I must dance!

We left the cabaret and Herbert once again put his arm around my shoulders. I took his hand and squeezed it, believing that everything would come right in the end. I imagined myself to be walking down the Nowy Swiat towards the corner of Jerusalem- ski and I consoled myself with the thought that I was still only eighteen, still young for one starting out on a stage career.

I halted abruptly and swung round in front of Herbert. The streetlight shone directly into his face. How clear were his eyes... and to think that I had doubted the loyalty of those eyes in the depressing hole of Glowna.

How narrow was his mouth and how blond the hair lying on his forehead. I pushed my fingers through his forelock and thought, 'There is much to beg you, for forgiveness Herbert. There is much you don't know and you never will know. But you shall know my love, every day, every hour...'

26

The Germans were a correct people in all things. The incorruptibility of German officialdom was well known.

But, there are always exceptions to the rule. The exception I found was called Dr Berner and the price was 1,000 marks. From him, I obtained a certificate which stated that I was suffering from a heart and lung disorder. By producing this bit of paper, I managed to avoid the women's work force, something that all German girls were otherwise compelled to do. I was advised to take up some other, more suitable employment. As more and more men were being called up to join the war machine, women were required to fill their places in the civilian ranks. My mother found me a job as a shorthand typist. She had business connections with a Mr Frank, a friendly, white-haired gentleman, who was the joint owner of a spirit and liqueur distillery. He sat behind his desk, puffing at his cigar and smiling with amusement when I told him that I could neither type nor write shorthand and that regretfully, my knowledge of the German language was still a little defective. To counter this handicap, I explained that I would not require payment, but would like to learn – and in return for all this I would need employment papers.

Herr Frank's distillery produced mainly sweet liqueurs, but this had not made him less vulnerable to the charms of a precocious young woman. I received my employment cards and he vouched for my occupation at his firm. Officialdom would have preferred to have seen me behind a punch machine. A second request to report to the munitions factory arrived just after I had started to 'work' for Mr Frank, but I had to decline, with regret of course, as I was already in full time employment.

Kind Mr Frank was not too particular about my working hours. I could come and go as I pleased and enjoyed the privilege of ten litres of liqueur per day at wholesale prices.

"Since you are not in receipt of a wage – and have to live…" the old gentleman would say with a smile, pulling at the cigar that was a permanent part of his aura.

Ten bottles of liqueur had great exchange value. One could get butter, fish, bread, milk and dancing lessons with such wealth. At a time when there was a scarcity of everything, a litre of strong alcohol would purchase much more than its equivalent in money. I used to go to a small gymnasium every afternoon. Wolfgang Lubitsch originated from Vienna where he had been a Master of Ballet at the state opera. Two bottles of liqueur was the fee for a two hour session and to begin with, we repeated all the basic steps. Once again, the daily routine of the lesson always started with...

"First position!" "Second position..."

The summer of 1940 was over and winter was upon us. Mother and I led the life of a German family, worried about obtaining sufficient food and living in fear of air raids. The hope that the war would come to an end soon, was ever present.

But 1941 passed and still the war continued. Vera occasionally received news from her sister who had remained at home in Posen. It was not good, only confirming the rumours that thrived among Polish refugees in Berlin.

Posen was gradually being stripped of its Polish citizens. The initial arrests and transportations had continued until the spring of 1940 and at the same time, many of the prominent citizens had just disappeared without trace; the lawyers, the professors, the teachers, the councillors and other people of importance. Then a reign of oppression and terror began, whereby no one could trust his neighbour. Many were arrested for merely thinking aloud in protest at the behaviour of the new masters. Such people were either executed forthwith or transported to one of the big labour camps that had been established in Poland. Few who were arrested were ever seen again on the streets of Posen. Those who were released, could not be trusted.

It had become obligatory to speak German in all schools and public places. The theatre was no exception and only German films were on show in the cinemas. Even the Polish names of the streets had been removed. It was as though the Germans were trying to erase everything Polish, denying that Poland had ever existed.

Many people, like my mother, Vera and myself had managed to flee. Those of our friends who had failed to do so had, one by one, been arrested and disappeared.

Under Herbert's protection, mother, Vera and I lived in the relative safety of Germany and adapted to the German way of life. My only diversion was my afternoon sessions under the tuition of Herr Lubitsch. He inspired me to make every effort to reach perfection. The development of a dancer is, as with so many other things, an endless progression. One works towards a horizon, only to find on nearing it that a more distant vista comes into view – and beyond that another. I realised that the road was long, needing stamina and determination. With little else to distract me, I studied hard and the months slid by.

Yet still the war continued.

Herbert was transferred to Berlin in January, 1942. We only saw him occasionally at weekends. By this time the motor of our daily life was ticking over on a regular beat, but the war could not leave us alone.

New regulations in Hamburg required a recheck of all passports and identity cards that had been issued since the outbreak of war. The shortage of living accommodation had necessitated the new edicts as a large number of homes had been destroyed as a result of the severe English air raids. The authorities were trying to ease the situation by sending the most recently arrived residents to other parts of the country in order that the citizens of Hamburg could occupy those buildings that remained sound. At the time, it was a policy peculiar to Hamburg.

Mother and I were duly summonsed to bring the relevant documents to the appropriate office. No immediate fault was found, but as we had lived in Posen, we were asked to obtain further confirmation from the Polish authorities.

To gain time on the one hand and to prevent further investigation on the other, we hired a solicitor. Dr Koch promised to keep an eye on further developments and keep us informed. He came highly recommended and had access to all the departments in question. We did not give him the full details of our problem, although he seemed to guess their nature and we felt confident that we could rely on his sympathy for we knew from underground information that he was already hiding a Jewish solicitor in his home.

Mother concluded that our only option was to leave Hamburg under our own volition in the hope that we would avoid the glare of official inspection.

While she was preparing to leave her job and Vera packed as much as possible, I went to see Herbert in Berlin.

I found him at his garrison at Oranienburg. He had been promoted to captain and been seconded for special duties. His aptitude for languages had been noted and he was undergoing specialised training in preparation for service in the former German colonies, which by all account, were next on Herr Hitler's agenda.

Herbert agreed that it might be for the best if we left Hamburg and suggested Berlin, naturally, as our new base. He volunteered to find accommodation for us.

But, when he started to investigate the possibilities, he realised that living space in Berlin was at a premium for the same reasons that it was in Hamburg and, as an unmarried officer, he was not entitled to an apartment. Hence, it was the housing authorities that decided our wedding date. To obtain a licence, however, I needed a number of certificates which I did not possess. In 1939, the Folkeslist had been introduced whereby all German nationals in Poland had been registered by a 'district family office' in Posen and it was to them that I was obliged to apply. With luck, they might help. Records were often incomplete or inaccurate since the war started and I hoped this might camouflage the fact that they would not find me in their records. I wrote to them and asked politely for the necessary documentation.

To my surprise, the answer came back within a couple of days. The office had been recently reorganised and a certain enthusiasm for efficiency could be detected.

'Dear Fraulein,

Concerning your request, the required papers can, unfortunately, not be traced. Many records have been destroyed during the recent disturbances, but we are anxious to replace missing documentation. As soon as your application has been verified, we will communicate with you further.'

I really could not have expected more, but the reply from Posen helped to gain a little time. Herbert, meanwhile, had successfully convinced the civilian authorities of his imminent departure to the front line and we were granted an emergency marriage licence.

Mother and Vera joined us in our new home in eastern Berlin. Herbert's name was on the doorbell and I became known as Maria Kurzke on all my documents. My hair was now dyed the deepest blue-black and I had started down a new road that was leading further and further away from the more obvious path on which the authorities might still be searching for me. The intervening trails had become ever more confused and blurred.

27

The war had developed into an epidemic. France, Jugoslavia, Rumania, Bulgaria, Greece, Africa, Russia, Finland, all became infected.

Soon after its birth, war had shown its true face in Warsaw. War could not restrain itself. It murdered and destroyed everything in its path.

And still it wanted more.

Everyone hoped and prayed that it would soon stop, but the manufacture of weapons continued with increasing earnestness. Ever more sons and husbands were sent to the front lines to be devoured by the ravenous monster. War!

Herbert was constantly on the move, be it by car, by train or by plane. I knew nothing of what he was doing. I never asked him. I could only wait for his return, take him into my arms and be grateful that the 'beast' had not taken him nor any part of him. Wounded soldiers, maimed by the loss of an arm or both legs, became a common sight in the streets. Evidence of the madness was everywhere.

Herbert was suddenly promoted to Hauptman. His uniform was decorated with medals and ribbons, but they only inflicted pain on me.

They were in the habit of rewarding the victims before they were thrown into the jaws of the war machine.

He had lost his carefree cheerfulness – not that he was afraid of danger. He was a soldier through and through and ready to die for his country if necessary. As much as he loved life, he was, like a true aristocrat, brought up in the strict tradition of honour. The final crown of honour was, in his opinion, to fall in the front line. Death was nothing to be feared; it meant fulfilment.

His visible unrest and silent preoccupation had quite another cause. He had been in Poland, the Balkan countries, France and Russia. He had met a great many people and seen a great many things. What he saw was in total contrast to his ideals and beliefs. He kept quiet about his doubts. But at times, when his heart and mind were overburdened, he would talk in his sleep – in short, incoherent, unconnected sentences... Poland, displaced persons, bombardments, Father, Grandfather, Mother and me were all on his mind.

He was in a camp of Russian prisoners... he muttered about Jewish ghettos... mixed with this dream, was a general and party leader. He would ramble on about a conversation with an arms manufacturer... of hunted people... of meeting captured English sailors. And there was a little village in France which had been set alight... a circle of fire... and all the inhabitants lying on the ground... felled by machine gun bullets...

...and there was HE, more magnificent than Napoleon, Frederick the Great and Wellington all rolled into one. HE, the one in whom Herbert had believed, from the days of his youth when he had marched, sung and worshipped the flag; the one that God had bestowed upon this nation, in the same way that God had given a Jew to another nation; a man who declared himself a Saviour. He had believed in HIM as sincerely as a good heart could. But the belief was weakening; the undivided devotion, becoming divided. Thoughts – critical, severe thoughts demanded proof. What his eyes had witnessed needed justification, reason and sense.

How I loved this grim man, who was fighting his own convictions. I loved him as much as I had the gentle surgeon that had touched his patients with the healing hands of an angel.

An end to the war did not seem predictable for the foreseeable future. With this in mind, we made our home in Berlin on a permanent basis. Mother found herself another restaurant which she managed on a part-ownership agreement. She had become an expert, thanks to her job in Hamburg. Vera remained with us, as she had done in Hamburg, without being registered.

I was asked, once again, to take up employment. As the papers from my previous employers stated that I was a short-hand typist, I was directed to start work at the offices of the electricity board. Here my luck held, for my job was to translate Polish correspondence. As I had done when working for the kind Mr Frank, I worked only in the mornings. The afternoons were free for training. I was determined to keep fit. I was determined that when the opportunity arose, I would return to the stage. I began to feel confident enough to think that it was possible. The end of the war seemed far away and my passionate desire to dance on the stage again, could not be persuaded to wait.

In addition to my dancing sessions, I began to take private drama lessons, not so much to perform as an actress, more to compliment my dancing ability by adding a certain impact and expression. I hoped too that my German would improve with an injection of study in pronunciation and diction.

One evening, on my way to see Herbert in Oranienburg, where he often stayed between missions, the train stopped at Fronau. A middle-aged man got into the carriage and sat down facing me. He wore a brown camel coat and suede shoes that I remember clearly for their remarkably thick soles. As the train drew out of the station, I began to squirm internally, aware of the intense manner in which he was staring at me. I became embarrassed and the horrible thought that he could be a Gestapo agent began to nag. I avoided his gaze and looked out of the window to watch the landscape flying past. At the next stop, I decided that I would change carriages, but as I stood by the door, waiting for the train to halt at the station, he spoke to me.

"Dr Lorenz! Permit me to introduce myself."

He produced his card from a coat pocket and with relief, I realised that he was a film producer at the UFA studios.

"Please, excuse my intrusion," he said politely. "I was intrigued by your face. I need someone with your Slavonic features to take one of the leading roles in the film that I am making at the moment." He smiled and offered me a cigarette. I sat down again.

"Would you like to visit me at Babelsberg and talk it over? Take a screen test? If nothing comes of it, at least you will be able to see around the studio. We are filming *Grosse Freiheit* at present. You will see Hans Albers, Luders, Fraulein Hildebrand, and Herr Sohnker in action. Perhaps you would be interested?"

Interested! I was dumbfounded.

Bubbling with excitement, I burst in on Herbert. Words tumbled out incomprehensibly in my eagerness to convince him that my chance encounter was a heaven sent opportunity.

He did not share my enthusiasm.

He patiently pointed out to me that the danger of becoming known to too many people and that the risk of recognition was very great. He begged me to seriously consider the possible consequences of accepting a film part. It would make me visible to too many people and we still had to be careful.

He was persuaded, however, by my excitement about the offer and finally agreed to let the gentleman from UFA have the last word.

The gentleman from UFA said 'Yes'.

I had reported to the tall brick-built block near the main entrance to the studios. From there, I was escorted to the 'Nachwuchsabteilung' (Young Talent Section) where I again met Dr Lorenz, who was accompanied by three men who he introduced as two executive producers and a director.

The armchairs in which we sat in for the discussion, were comfortable and formed a friendly semi circle, but the way that they fired question after question at me was more like a police interrogation. The pressure eased when they heard that I was not a complete novice. The stout, elderly gentleman with grey rimmed glasses, the director of the new production, was especially pleased to hear that I had already danced on the public stage and that I was presently attending drama lessons. At the end of the interview, I was invited to return the following day.

Punctual to the minute and brimming with anticipation, I appeared next day. I was taken immediately to a studio dressing room. A make-up artist coloured my face to give me a dark complexion and pinned back my hair. The first test shots were taken. Under dazzling lights and following directions from the gentleman in the grey rimmed spectacles, I turned my head to right and left and looked straight into the camera.

My hair was restyled again and again. More and more shots were taken, most of them in close-up. Sometimes I was asked to reveal my shoulders. The minister of propaganda had given permission for the proposed film and it was well known that the 'minister', Dr Goebbels, was not of a prudish disposition.

The following day, they took still-photographs and filmed two takes with sound. The short text was in broken German and the role was that of a Russian girl. The text had been given to me the previous evening and I had little trouble with the foreign accent. That came only too naturally – much to my frustration.

By the time we left the studio for a quick drink before going home, it was dark. We gathered in a section of the barrack-like canteen that was used for production meetings. It was separated from the main room by thin partition walls and to reach it, we threaded a path through the colourful groups of extras who were engaging in lively discussion.

A large picture of the 'Patron of the German Film Industry', in a broad gold frame, hung on one wall and tinted caricatures of the world of film, decorated the others.

Here I learned that my screen test had caused a minor sensation.

"We do not wish to give you any false hope, but as far as we are concerned, we are more than satisfied with the result. If the minister also approves – and we can see no reason for him not to do so – we shall notify you early next week." Dr Lorenz, standing behind the director, looked extremely pleased with the outcome.

Dr Gobbels himself viewed the screen test on the Saturday at Castle

Schwanenwerder. The director had been specifically invited in order to show the clips of film. The decision was made immediately.

"No objection! Use the young lady!"

On the Monday, I was summonsed to sign the contract. I put my signature on that impressive piece of paper, headed with the UFA trade mark, at 4.00pm, on 2nd March 1942.

Some hours and days live in your memory until the day you die. That time and date are indelibly stamped in mine. It was the confirmation to the start of a whole new vista of possibilities that I had not previously contemplated.

They recommended a particular drama school and I was advised to attend until the shooting of the film began in the summer.

Summer was three months away.

I enrolled at the drama school and looked forward to starting a new career. Destiny, however, had other ideas. The letter from the 'district family office' in Posen which had satisfied the marriage registrar was insufficient for UFA.

It requires no more than a fine detail to change the direction of fate.

28

Repeatedly, my mother and I had been reminded by the police authorities to prove our German nationality by handing in our original identification papers. It had become a nationwide requirement in Germany. UFA now added a new urgency to acquiring fully authenticated passports.

All we possessed were the documents which Herbert had provided for us in Hamburg and these were incomplete. I still had my false certificate from Posen, but Mother had lost all her accreditations from Poland, false or otherwise, when she jumped from the train. The new German administration in Poland was the only recognised authority that could issue valid identification cards for us.

The summer of 1942 was spent in a flurry of preparations. My lack of a complete set of documents became a problem for until they could be presented for inspection, UFA was not going to include me in their 1943 Nachwuchsschauspielerin. We had heard nothing since the letter in answer to the application that I had made to obtain a marriage licence. I hoped that the authorities in Posen had drawn a blank through lack of evidence, but were delaying the conclusion of their investigations indefinitely. If I was to make progress with my career, I would have to force a decision and risk returning to Posen.

Mother could not be dissuaded from accompanying me and Herbert would not let us travel on our own. He requested leave of absence and applied for all the travel permits.

Two days before we were due to leave for Poland, a young girl accosted me in the street. I was on my way to drama class and had just stepped off the No.77 tram in order to catch an underground train from the Zoo station. She addressed me in fluent Polish. I was shocked. How did she know? I hesitated.

The girl was plainly dressed and would have been invisible in a crowd. Her pasty, unhealthy looking face, partly hidden by a mop of untidy dark hair, was also plain, except for the two very large black eyes that defiantly held my gaze. Against my better judgement, I drew back from the curb at the edge of the road. The eyes followed me, challenging me to do otherwise.

"You are expected, Maria Weychanowna – Grischna is waiting for you!" The voice was flat and expressionless much like that of a child reciting its homework. The use of my Polish name was enough to paralyse my whole being. I was unable to answer. The girl turned towards the entrance of the underground and mesmerised, I found myself following.

She already had two tickets and therefore must have assumed that I would cooperate. She walked straight through the barrier and onto the platform, never looking back to check whether I was still behind her. She boarded the first train that stopped. I slipped into the carriage behind her, wondering why it was that I had abandoned my lesson for this madness. The girl had known my name and nationality. I needed to know how and more importantly why.

The thoughts that screamed through my head as I stood beside her on the train are hard to describe. I racked my brain to find some connection with her from the past – trying to place her face. How would she have otherwise recognised me and used my Polish name? Who was this Grischna?

I concluded that my mother was possibly the source that could provide the answers. She had kept in touch with other Poles hiding in Berlin and had been involved with a welfare fund which had started to help those less fortunate than ourselves. Many were unable to find work because they were unregistered and others were obliged to remain in hiding because they had escaped from hard labour camps and were on the wanted lists.

She had contributed to these funds and must have made some contacts with the Polish underground in the process, although for Herbert's sake, she had never involved me in these activities. The only solution that I could think of, however, was that perhaps an acquaintance in one of these circles had passed on my name and description. For these reasons, I did not for a moment consider that the girl might be leading me into a trap.

She got off the train when it reached Alexanderplatz, walked briskly through the ticket hall and climbed the stairs. I had trouble keeping track of her as she hurried along the street and across the square, dodging around pedestrians. She slowed down only when she turned into a series of narrow alleyways. She seemed to be less anxious here and, almost casually, she slipped into one of the many coachmen's pubs to be found in the east end of Berlin. The door was at ground level and we descended a few steps to reach the taproom in the cellar of the building. The interior was grimy and drab, the faded wallpaper peeling off the damp walls. A shaggy dog leapt to its feet and howled, otherwise the place seemed deserted.

The girl spoke to me again. She instructed me to wait at the table near the bar while she told 'them' that I was here and abruptly disappeared behind the threadbare curtains that hung limply across the doorway leading to the back room.

I felt extremely nervous, wondering what sort of mischief my impetuous 'devil' had got me into this time. Alone in that depressing room with only a mangy dog for company, I felt that I was under observation; that the cracks and chinks in the walls possessed eyes.

"Come with me please!" The girl had silently reappeared, holding the curtain back with the crook of her elbow as she stood waiting in the doorway, We entered a narrow passage, climbed some worn steps to the first floor, swept down another narrow corridor and then through what looked like a bedroom of a cheap boarding house. After passing two more doors, we climbed out of a window to a ladder, on which we descended the outside of the building to a small backyard.

The area was approximately three metres square and surrounded on all sides by external walls. The sky formed a square of dark blue, high above us. From here, we followed the main drainage pipes into a cellar vault which was stacked to the ceiling with sacks of flour. I assumed it could possibly have been the back of a bakery store room.

A young man in his late twenties sat in the corner behind a long wooden table. He was dressed in the uniform of a bus conductor employed by the Berlin Transport Company. His collar was open and his cap lay on the table. As soon as he saw us, he got up and leant forward to greet me, offering his hand. His manner and accent indicated that he was an educated man. I remember his face clearly for it was very masculine, hard and with high cheek bones. A deep red scar ran diagonally across his temple and the upper part of his ear was missing.

"Please, don't think me impolite by not introducing myself with my full name. Even my close friends know me only as Grischna. Permit me therefore to be the same to you." Offering me a dilapidated chair, he sat down again. The table was covered with files and papers written in foreign languages and as I sat waiting, I noticed the three other men in the room. They sat with their backs to us in the semi darkness and gave the impression that they were absorbed in something else other than our conversation. Now and then, one of them turned his head which made me think that their apparent disinterest was a pretence.

"You intend to travel to Posen the day after tomorrow?" The fact that he knew of my second secret, irritated me. He owed me some explanation. I opened my mouth to protest, but before I could utter a word, he continued,

"You travel with authenticated papers and in the company of your husband, therefore in absolute safety. After some consideration, we have decided to give you material to take for us to Posen." Something in the way I reacted to this news alerted him to my amazement and rising anger. How dare this fellow drag me here and give me orders as to what I might do for him! I could feel my face burning with indignation.

"Forgive me! I see Nitschka has not told you! I did not realise..." So, Nitschka was her name! I opened my mouth to tell him what I thought of his ideas, but he cut in first.

"You are at the headquarters of a Polish resistance group. This room is the nerve centre of our activities. All our members are Poles, forced by circumstances to live and work in Germany. There are more groups like us, gnawing away at the insides of the system. Our aim is resistance – resistance in any form, at every opportunity. We don't know one another. Each group works independently, but we know that we are not on our own."

He got up and paced back and forth behind the table, his hands thrust deep into his pockets.

"Naturally, we are interested in every compatriot. Every Pole in Germany must have his mission. No one should think only of himself and his own safety. Neither can we manage without the support of our women." He stopped pacing, turned to face me and stared down at me for a long time. My indignation shrivelled.

"You are young, Maria Weychanowna – young and beautiful. I understand! You love life and you would prefer that the relatively peaceful cocoon that you have made for yourself remained undisturbed. You women are less complicated and more practical than we men. You remain closer to nature with your wishes and feelings. You are less likely to be side-tracked by intrigue. You live by instinct..." He stopped in mid-sentence, as though his wandering thoughts had caused him to say too much.

Abruptly, he sat down again and took a fat, sealed envelope from the desk. My eyes followed his every move, my mind absorbing every word.

"Normally, we do not try to endanger our women. I know your mother does for us as much as she can and usually we would ask the men to take on personal assignments, but, there are occasions, when we have to involve women. Such an occasion has now arisen and you, Maria Weychanowna, are the woman!"

Without looking at me or waiting for an answer, he continued: "This letter must get to our agent in Posen as quickly as possible. The letters we have sent him by post have failed to reach him. We must stay in contact with Posen or we are all at risk.

"Your going there seems to be the best opportunity we have available to find out what is going on. All you have to do is deliver this letter and a small suitcase." My mouth dropped open to protest. "Don't worry, it doesn't contain a time bomb. Have a look for yourself." Grischna put a little pigskin bag on the table. He opened it and revealed the contents. It was filled to the brim with deutschmark.

"We cannot finance a large campaign, but a small contribution helps," he added. The three men in the background were all now facing me, watchfully noting my response.

It was beginning to dawn on me just how dangerous the little scheme was that he was tossing in my direction. Was it not enough to live in constant danger of being discovered on one's own account without taking on the responsibilities of the safety of others? What had I to do with these secret groups, their agents or the whole resistance? I had nothing in common with them, except the country of my birth. They could fight for themselves. What right did they have to invade my privacy and steal my secrets like robbers and thieves?

Again, my thoughts must have been written on my face, because Grischna leant towards me and said: "Your father was Władysław Weychan – your grandfather, Jan Szymanski! Is that not so?"

He took a sheet of paper from a file.

"We had no intention of telling you this, except as a last resort, but… Your father, your grandfather, your grandmother, your mother's sister and her children have all been murdered in a camp near Sachsenhausen, Maria Weychanowna!"

The world about me seemed to stand still as the meaning of his terrible words sank into my petrified brain.

Even Grandmother! Even dear, gentle Grandmother! She was the last one of them that I had seen, huddled in the cold barrack of Glowna, wrapped in my coat and sitting on a thin mat of dirty straw. My initial thoughts were only of her. I could still visualise the snow, glistening in her white hair as she had stood in the open truck. Grandmother!

In the distance, I saw two figures, moving slowly towards me – Grandfather! My father!

"You'll be taking the evening train the day after tomorrow?" Grischna's voice also sounded distant. I heard another noise, becoming aware of rhythmical sounds of a passing underground train.

"Yes, the evening 8.18 from Schlesischer Station." I replied automatically and without thinking,

"The day after tomorrow, at 3pm, someone will bring the case and the letter to your apartment. The envelope is addressed to our man in Posen. You will go and see him. He is above suspicion and is actually employed by the Germans."

It was not until Nitschka had escorted me back to Alexandre Square, that I regained most of my senses. The shock of the news about Grandfather, Father, Grandmother, my aunt and cousins had stunned me. The majority of my family were gone. They did not exist in this life any longer. I found it hard to come to terms with the meaning of their deaths. It was like a void. What had been, was no longer. I could not understand their non-existence. For their sakes, I must do what had to be done.

In the train on my way home, I considered how best to carry out my mission without endangering Mother and myself and most important of all, the only remaining man in my life, Herbert.

29

At 3.00pm precisely, the doorbell rang. I did not go myself, for it was Vera's job to answer the door and it could have been regarded as odd or suspicious, if I had been observed doing so. I had worked out every detail of my mission, for that is how I had come to regard it – a special mission – that I was honour bound to undertake on behalf of my country and in revenge for fate of my close family.

When Vera announced that a young girl wished to see me, I duly remarked for her benefit that it might be a girl from the drama school.

The dark-haired Nitschka was waiting for me in the hall. She barely said 'Hello' and hurriedly handed me the little pigskin case and the letter which she took out of her handbag. I thanked her politely, not quite certain that she needed thanking and rather at a loss for anything else to say under the circumstances. Nitschka, for her part, wished me an uneventful trip, abruptly turned her back on me and let herself out.

I told my mother that a friend had asked me to take the case to her parents in Posen and that I could not very well have refused my help. She seemed satisfied with the explanation. Herbert would think that the little suitcase belonged to the few personal pieces of luggage which are necessary for the female making a short visit abroad. We were hopeful of clearing everything in a single day, but the unforeseen could delay us longer.

Although I knew that no fault could be found with our papers this time and that we were travelling in the company of a Hauptmann in full uniform, I was still very nervous of the border controls. Would they insist on checking all of our luggage? Spot checks were not unheard of and a good 'catch' was sometimes made this way.

Herbert tried hard to amuse me by making light-hearted conversation, but I found it difficult to concentrate on what he was saying and preferred to sit quietly in my corner by the window. My handbag, which contained the letter, seemed to burn in my lap.

The two border control officers who came into the compartment, clicked their heels together in salute on recognising Herbert's rank. As to our papers, they barely glanced at them. They could have been blank bits of paper for all the attention that was paid to them. The two men thanked us before they had even seen our permits and saluted again with a smile suggesting embarrassment, implying that duty alone made it necessary to disturb us. We had safely crossed the frontier into Poland.

Herbert had sent a telegram ahead and the night porter at the hotel was waiting up for us. It had been over three years since I had slept in a bed in my home town. But it hardly felt like home. I had recognised few familiar buildings through the taxi window. Names on the hoardings over the shops had changed and everywhere the German uniform was conspicuous.

To avoid unnecessary risk, Herbert aided by the authority of his uniform, suggested that he try to get our passports himself. With luck, we should not be required to put in a personal appearance. It would be too easy to fall into the hands of an over zealous official in a place that was full of opportunists. He would come and fetch us only if there was absolutely no other alternative.

He set off full of optimism and Mother and I had to content ourselves with what we could see of the town from the hotel window. It was a lovely spring day. The sky shimmered blue above the roof tops and the few clouds resembled fluffy puffs of cotton wool. The town itself bore few obvious scars of the invasion in 1939 and the streets had long since been cleared of rubble. Spring was in the air and I remember how the trees were just coming into bright green leaf.

Herbert returned in the afternoon, very satisfied that he had been successful. He had acquired the necessary papers from four different offices and our passports had already been issued. We would, however, have to sign them in the presence of an official. This was usually done in the registry office, but he had managed to persuade one of the civil servants to bring the passports to the hotel for signing. The Hauptman had suggested that financially it would be well worth his while, aware that the man would be working after office hours.

He was in excellent spirits and of course Mother and I were also exceedingly relieved and happy. It was victory at last and we celebrated with coffee and liqueur.

The gentleman from the passport office was not expected until around 9.00pm and Herbert asked to be excused for an hour or two that he might visit some of his former colleagues and old friends.

The time to carry out my secret mission had come. We were alone and dusk was falling on the town. I could deceive my mother no longer and was obliged to take her into my confidence. Now that the danger of the border controls was behind me, the delivery of the suitcase and letter could be achieved by simply taking a walk in the twilight.

I related to her in detail the whole episode of my encounter with Grischna, omitting only the news of father's death and the fate of the other members of the family.

"We must go this minute," was all she said when I had finished and immediately got to her feet to fetch her coat and hat. It was obvious that she had no intention of letting me take the package on my own and that she had decided to accompany me.

The Marzinkowska was in the old town, well away from the city centre. It was tempting to take the long route around by the Adelbert Church and across the Wilhelm Square, to take one more look at the Sacré Coeur, towering above its broad stone steps. It would have been the same route that I used to take with my school bag. But the thought of Herbert made us take the short route. We justified our expedition as a duty to our country. We had no right to jeopardise his position for a mere fancy.

We were about to cross the Pomorska, when a young woman suddenly stepped into our path. She wore glasses and was very elegantly dressed. I could not place her and Mother made no sign of recognition either. Yet the woman acted surprised and expressed her most sincere pleasure in meeting us. As she took my hand and spoke, the scales fell from my eyes.

'Pill!' I was delighted and embraced her. We had been in the same class together at school for years. She had worn spectacles then, but her former sickly complexion now had a healthy glow. The carefully applied make-up could possibly have helped. She had lost her shyness, laughed, shook hands with Mother and asked us to visit her. It was Mother who spoke and thanking her, accepted the invitation for the following afternoon.

I did not contradict her although I knew full well that we were to leave Posen on the night train.

We said 'Goodbye', telling each other again, what a lovely surprise it was to meet like this and how there were many old memories that we would refresh tomorrow. We parted and as though worked by the same set of puppet strings, turned around at the same moment to laugh and wave.

When I quizzed Mother as to why she had prevaricated about meeting the 'Pill' again, she remarked; "It's best if we avoid contact with friends, even good friends. You can't trust anyone these days. Times have changed and so have people."

Franck Jankowski's address was written on the envelope. The weather-beaten plate over his shop proclaimed him to be a shoemaker and indeed, when he opened the door, he wore the green leather apron which confirmed his trade. His manner, however, was cautious and he behaved as though he was very surprised to see us.

His workshop was filled with brand-new army boots. As if on parade, they were arranged in pairs on all the available shelf space. Grischna had warned me that he was employed by the Germans.

Franck Jankowski would have been in his early forties. He was tall, with very broad shoulders. Once back in his workshop, he visibly relaxed and lost his nervous manner. He shook hands with us in welcome and invited us to sit down. With one of the sharp knives which he used for cutting through leather, he quickly slit open the letter that I had given him. As he read it, he glanced now and then at the pigskin case on the floor beside him. Before long, his eyes lit up and a gleeful expression spread over his face. It seemed that he had received good news.

"This is more than we dared to hope for," he said as he folded the letter. "The Germans will get to hear from us now!" His tone of voice was sincere and passionate.

"Should we take back a reply?" I asked. He laughed.

"You have done quite enough for us already, young lady." He picked up the case and opened it. "Yes... quite enough! One of my couriers is going to Berlin next weekend and he can take any messages. I would not be able to get things organised until tomorrow anyway." With a last look at the contents of the case, he snapped the lid shut.

"Ladies, you had best be on your way. It would not be right for you to be on the street after dark. Thank you both most sincerely for your trouble." We wished him well with his schemes and took his advice.

We returned to the hotel well before Herbert and decided to keep quiet about our little outing. When he did come back, he was full of news. Even if we had wanted to, we could not have got a word in edgewise. He was his old bubbly self again, full of high spirits and I realised just how heavily the whole business about our passports and identity papers had weighed on his mind during the past few weeks.

The telephone rang and the hotel porter announced that there were two gentlemen waiting downstairs who wished to speak with us.

"Two? What do you know!" Herbert laughed. "Please, send them up. They are expected." He put the receiver down, clapped his hands then taking me in his arms, whirled me about the room in a wild polka.

"The passports, my gracious lady! And the head of department has come along with his clerk and brought them in person."

The two gentlemen, who had requested to see us, were not the officials with our passports. I remember to this day, the horrible premonition I had, when the knock on the door came – my back grew stiff with fear.

The two men who entered our hotel room were from the Secret State Police. One wore civilian clothes, the other, the black SS uniform.

I lost composure completely and started to tremble uncontrollably. My reaction would surely have been noticed had Herbert not fortunately captured their immediate attention. It gave me time to reach an armchair.

He had put on the jacket of his uniform, but was still in a light hearted mood and did not seem to attach too much significance to our unexpected visitors, possibly assuming that they had something to do with the hotel security and nothing more.

The man in uniform saluted, as he should on meeting a Hauptman. His companion also stood to attention. Suspecting nothing, Herbert walked towards them and asked authoritatively, in the way a general would address a lance corporal;

"Can I help you, gentlemen?"

"Our apologies, Herr Kurzke, but we have orders to check the passports of the two ladies."

Herbert's attitude changed instantly. His voice sounded several degrees sharper as he asked "A direct order? Concerning my wife and her mother?"

"I'm sorry, sir, but those were the orders," responded the SS uniform.

The civilian put his hand mechanically into his pocket and drew out his identity card. He offered it to Herbert.

"If you please!" he said.

Herbert stepped aside. I could see that he was having difficulty keeping his temper under control. Mother and I showed our travel permits and our Hamburg papers indicating German nationality.

"Weychans! Is that your real name?" The civilian, glancing up, looked directly at my Mother.

Herbert interrupted, claiming that we were under his personal protection. The official, however, insisted on repeating his question. He then turned on me and in the same aggressive tone, expressed his doubt as to whether my name was genuine.

Herbert intervened again and angrily made it clear that he refused to tolerate such insults, whereupon the official retorted that he would have to make other arrangements and they would exclude the Hauptman from further interviews. He seemed to enjoy the word 'arrangement', for it flowed like oil from his lips. "I'm arresting the two ladies and require them to accompany me immediately," he concluded and his smug smile sent icicles of foreboding through my heart. Herbert protested volubly, but it was of little use. We 'ladies' were helpless. The doubts that the civilian expressed about the authenticity of our papers, were so terrifyingly justified.

"We shall arrange the whole thing quite inconspicuously. Would the ladies be so kind as to come with me?" said the Gestapo agent in civilian clothing. "My comrade will accompany you at a discrete distance," he added glaring at Herbert.

Any further opposition would have been pointless. That had been made clear to us all. Herbert buckled on his belt and without another word, picked up his hat. He then helped me into my coat and whispered to me not to be frightened, to have faith. The smile on his face lacked humour, but I was grateful to him for his last-ditch effort to comfort me.

The black and red brick building at Ritterstrasse 21, had been the 'House of Soldiers' before the war. It used to be the modern, well appointed quarters of the Polish army. The Gestapo had the use of it now. Lights still shone from every window and two sentries stood guarding the entrance.

We were expected. As soon as we entered the room, one of many in a corridor with many doors, two uniformed men positioned themselves on either side of us. A third man in a fashionably tailored, double breasted, flannel suit, issued instructions for us to be separated from each other and I was escorted alone to a bare room with white walls. A single lamp on the ceiling emitted a cold light. There was no chair, only an empty space. I stood for about an hour before the 'flannel suit' entered, followed by the agent who had arrested us. Again they tried to persuade me to admit my real name, but I denied and challenged all charges against me. I had rehearsed the answers endlessly whilst waiting. Even when my Polish name was mentioned, I did not respond and stuck to the lie that I was a German national and had married my husband as such.

The 'flannel suit' smiled a knowing and self-satisfied smile that hit my shredded confidence with great force. He then gestured to his companion;

a signal for him to open the door. There... framed in the doorway, stood an elegantly dressed young woman with glasses.

She too was smiling, the same brand of smile as the one on the face of the 'flannel suit'. I must have been a trade mark among these people.

"You!" I gasped. It all fell into place. I could hear a voice inside my head, 'You have nurtured your hatred all these years? Is this your belated revenge on me for being the first to call you the 'Pill'? (It had been during a French lesson, when she had looked even paler than usual; white as a sheet in fact.) Did you resent so much that I excluded you when we climbed the school tower? (We used to play 'Three minutes truth' up there, Tuta the 'Lady' and myself; a game where one had to answer truthfully – by the Holy Mother Mary – any questions asked within the three-minute time limit.) Have you forgotten the kind face of Sister Bonaventure and the morning mist in the meadow when we walked to chapel for communion? Have you forgotten Father Sylvester who taught us to love one another? Do you remember how we used to sit, shivering on the school benches, reading the bible: 'before the cock crows three times'...?

The 'flannel suit' was holding a small case in his hand. A pigskin case! "Do you by any chance recognise this case?" He threw it at my feet. I kept my silence.

"You know where the bird has flown! The bird... Franck Jankowski, my little pigeon! You also know what was in the case... and you will tell us. You will tell us about that and all the other things that you know. Your neat little Hauptman will be of no help to you now. He is in trouble himself, right up to his pretty eyebrows! Speak up!" He was still smiling. "Answer me!" His smile vanished. Someone picked me up by the hair and threw me against the wall. I felt no pain.

The elegant woman with the glasses turned away, still smiling – and left.

As I was being led away down the corridor, I met Herbert. He looked years older, with wrinkles on his face where I had never noticed wrinkles before. The agent in civilian clothes was with me and Herbert asked his permission to speak to me. The civilian 'arranged' it with a smile. He had not been long enough in the job it seemed to have hardened completely. There were still traces of humanity left.

Herbert looked at me, his eyes brimming with everything that could not be said. When he spoke, his voice was fractured with stifled emotion.

"I am free, Maria. I have to report back to my unit in Berlin. I have no idea what happens then... but, you know that my life has no meaning without you. I shall use every hour to work for your freedom, Maria. Believe me girl – I shall get you out. Remember Glowna? Your Herbert will get you out."

I put my arms around him, knowing in my heart that this would be our last embrace for a long, long time. I smothered his words with kisses, fearful that his promises could not be fulfilled. They could well be the last kisses I would give him; the last ever.

Glowna! There would not be a car waiting for us at the gate this time. I knew, with wretched certainty... I knew!

30

I was taken down to the basement. Of mother, there was no sign and I was roughly pushed into a small cell for the night. I had seen the bare, brick walls by the light of the guard's torch as he opened the door. The door had slammed shut behind me and I heard the bolt being pushed home then and I had listened to the sound of hobnailed boots as they receded down the vaulted stone passage.

I leant against the wall and strained my ears long after the footsteps had faded. There was not a sound, only deafening silence. The darkness that surrounded me was complete. I could see nothing. I was totally alone and very frightened. My arms hung by my sides seemingly immovable, as though paralysed. My brain could only manage the same thoughts – over and over again. They chased each other in circles, round and round without pause, never varying. 'Grischna,' 'apartment in Berlin,' 'moving trains,' 'Jankowski in his workshop,' 'the hotel room,' 'the smiling 'Pill',' 'Herbert,' 'our sad embrace,' 'the slapped face,' 'the cell,' 'the brick wall at my back' and 'the pitch darkness that surrounded me.' No other thoughts – nothing else! Again and again... the same pictures, the same sequence, only faster and faster – lapping ever closer together. 'Grischna – apartment in Berlin – moving trains...' They chased through my mind on a roundabout, like an eddy of speeding film with neither beginning nor end.

I cannot guess how long I stood and when I could stand no longer and slithered down the wall, how long I crouched on the floor. I pulled my fur coat around me and must have slept. I did not hear the approaching footsteps and was jolted back to reality when the dazzling glare from a large torch suddenly woke me. I rose stiffly to my feet and obediently followed the voice behind the torch.

Dawn had not broken when we emerged into the yard. The lorry was waiting. It looked remarkably like the one that had taken me to Glowna more than three years earlier. Mother was already on the back with a group of women and girls. She pushed her way through them towards the running board when I appeared and after I had managed to clamber up, she threw her arms around me, moaning softly. We huddled together in a corner of the lorry and whispered together.

She had been up most of the night. They had interrogated her for hours, but had been unable to persuade her to admit anything. They had tried to deceive her, saying that I had made a full confession and that her denials were pointless. She was aware of the dangers of separate interrogations and, not knowing what I might have said, she professed to be confused; that she had been unable to remember things properly since being caught in a bomb blast. To add credence to this claim, she had produced some odd behaviour that would suggest that she was mentally unstable when stressed. It had occurred to her from the start that if she could cause considerable strain on time with her play acting, her inquisitors would hopefully desist when they appreciated that she was unable to tell them what they wanted to know. In that respect, she had been right. But her hope for a second miraculous rescue was a forlorn hope indeed.

The town was still asleep; not a soul was abroad. We drove by the Adelbert church, through Wilhelm Street and past the broad stone steps of the Sacré Coeur. How differently the sight of the building affected me now. Rather than the warm tinge of a dear memory, it elicited a stabbing twinge of betrayal that added to my misery.

Posen was surrounded by fortresses and strongholds. Our destination that morning was Fort VII. The lorry drove past some massive concrete bunkers and through an entrance into the hill. It rumbled on down a steep slope and between brick-lined walls, lit by powerful overhead lamps. The passage led into a broad gallery where the vehicle shuddered to a halt. A horde of ruffians in SS uniforms gave us a raucous reception. They jeered at us and made sarcastic comments as they bundled us off the lorry and lined us up in rows, three deep.

"The Commandant! Attention!" An authoritative voice rang out, bouncing echoes from the vaulted brick ceiling above our heads. The men came smartly to attention, their fingers pointing down the seam line of their trouser. All turned to face the same direction.

The SS officer who approached us was barely thirty. He carried a long-haired dachshund under his arm and from his wrist dangled a beige coloured riding crop. He was tall, slim and arrogantly handsome. As he neared, he muttered "Stand at ease!" and proceeded to stroll along the ranks of prisoners, closely inspecting each one of us in turn. His men watched with anticipation, as if some sort of performance was about to take place.

His inspection over, the commandant casually walked away, fondling his dog. Almost as an afterthought, he said, "Take their things!" and put his dog down on the floor, where it immediately rolled on to its back.

The SS men needed no further encouragement. The 'horde' swooped on us, as one. A lanky boy with a pock-marked, spotty face pulled my fur coat roughly from my back. He then proceeded to search my body with his coarse, disgusting hands. He took the bracelet off my arm, the rings from my fingers and rummaged in my handbag before tossing it aside.

Mother was manhandled in the same way. She was robbed of nearly everything. They found the cloth bag full of jewellery which she kept hidden under her clothes and only a pair of valuable rings that she had hidden in her hair during the night, remained undetected. The commandant and his assisting officer had started to call out names and occupations. When they came to mine, the entry 'dancer' caused them to exchange meaningful glances.

The confiscated belongings were bundled into blankets and we were led into a narrow passageway. There we were forced to stand facing the wall. Behind us were posted soldiers armed with sub-machine guns.

A dim glow from the central gallery was the only light that filtered along the passage. The wall in front of me was built of rough brickwork. The footfall of the guards behind me sounded hollow and ominous; their guns clanking on belts and buckles, threatening.

My thoughts had slowed to the pace of a snail. What did they intend to do with us? They had helped themselves to everything worth taking. All we had left were the clothes that we stood in. Were we facing the wall instead of being blindfolded in readiness for execution? Were they at this minute taking aim at us? I began to panic. 'Any moment,' I thought, 'Any moment, shots will be fired.'

What actually happened was that a guard touched the back of my leg with the toe of his boot. I glanced over my shoulder and saw that he wanted me to follow him. Mother too was called away from the wall and we were escorted to the same cell.

The heavy metal door closed with a clang behind us and it took a moment to adjust to the gloom. At first, I thought we were alone, but gradually I could make out the pale shapes of faces. There were between fifty and sixty of them, all women, sitting or lying on the stone floor. There were no beds or bunks, only a little straw in the corners where the oldest prisoners huddled for the small comfort it gave.

I was surprised that nobody wanted to know our 'where froms' and 'whys'. At the time, I did not know that the Gestapo planted spies in the larger cells to report every word. I also did not realise that people became completely indifferent after a long term of imprisonment. I still had many things to learn.

We eventually found a small space to sit and it was we who had to ask the questions. Most of the women, it seemed, came from a small Polish town, called Mosina where the German commandant had been found dead one morning. There were thirty-five of them connected with the 'Mosina Case' in that cell. One of them was a doctor. She sat most of the time facing the wall, her head tilted back as though in a trance. Marja Gorska had become interested in the treatment of tuberculosis while still a student. She had been an assistant to well known specialists and had eventually opened her own research clinic in Mosina. She had spent many years of hard work on her research, determined to help the sufferers of the insidious disease. She told me that she had even gone so far as to inject herself with the tuberculosis bacilli to test the results of the therapy that she had developed. Even she had to be a victim of the German reprisal.

That day, she talked in a monotone about the days and nights spent working in her little laboratory. Her voice was expressionless and lacked any sign of enthusiasm, her sentences punctuated by long pauses, which she sometimes absentmindedly prolonged indefinitely. Her tone remained unchanged when she answered my questions about conditions in the prison.

Fort VII apparently was only temporary accommodation. Each day, prisoners were taken out in trucks to build a vast new camp, full of newly constructed barracks.

We remained undisturbed within the four stone walls of the cell; six days and six nights of near darkness. The distribution of bread and soup, twice a day, were the only interruptions to our silent, agonizing wait. I kept telling myself that any moment, the door would open and I would be escorted to a waiting car and would escape the living limbo. Herbert would have done everything in his power in Berlin to affect my release.

On the morning of the sixth day, the slim commandant entered the cell. He called my name and waved his riding crop at me, indicating that I should follow him. There was a grey limousine waiting for me, but not to give me back my freedom. I was so blinded by the bright light of normal day that I had to grope for the door handle. Days in the dimness of the cell had rendered my eyes temporarily useless.

We drove to Posen. The commandant sat beside me in silence. Occasionally I caught him staring at me as though trying to make up his mind about something. The rest of the time, he continually stroked the dachshund which lay in his lap.

The car stopped in the yard of the Gestapo house in Ritterstrasse. Again, I was escorted down to the cellar. An hour or so later, my cell door opened. I had felt almost safe during the time on my own and the sudden interruption brought fear racing back.

I felt myself recede from reality and followed the guard as though hypnotised.

The main staircase was built of white marble; the stairs themselves, covered with luxurious red carpet. As I climbed them, I became conscious of my dirty crumpled clothes and my tousled hair. I had not washed in six days and felt disgusted with myself, especially with all the splendour around me.

I was escorted to an elegantly furnished room, also thickly carpeted, where the sunshine streamed through the tall window. Behind the heavily carved bureau sat the commandant, smoke from his cigarette drifting in thin wisps across the room. He looked up as I entered and a leer spread across his face. There was no mirth in his expression. His eyes were cold as he pointed to the wall behind me.

"Please, help yourself my gracious lady. You have the privilege of choosing; of selecting your own preference."

My eyes followed his finger. Against the wall, on a long narrow table, lay a collection of different sized whips and truncheons, the handles wrapped in strips of towelling.

I could not open my mouth. I could not move. Only my eyes and what they could see sent an involuntary shiver down my spine. The creep got up from his chair, placed his dog carefully on the desk and came towards me; his eyes, hot and greedy, the eyes of an animal fixating on its prey.

"Tell me my dear! Are you a spy or are you not, a spy?" 'Dear God,' I pleaded. 'Is he really going to take one of those whips and beat me with it? Can he be human... a human, created by you Heavenly Father?'

"Are you a spy, my pretty little princess?" The voice was close to me now. I felt his breath on my face.

"Speak! Yes or no!"

'Holy Mother of God – his hand – his right hand!' On each finger of the right hand, was a wide, shiny, spiked ring.

"Yes or no?" he repeated, his face inches from mine. "No!" I screamed back at him.

He pulled away and swung his fist into my face with such force that it made me stagger back. I tripped and fell to the floor.

He grabbed me by my hair and yanked me to my feet.

"Yes or no?"

"No!" I whimpered.

Grabbing one of the truncheons, he viciously beat me to the floor again. He pulled me to my feet and hit me again… and again. His dog leapt up at me, barking hysterically.

The 'flannel suit' materialised by the desk, like a ghost. I had not seen him enter the room. But, suddenly there he was, part of the mirage that spun in front of my eyes, receding further and further along an endless tunnel.

"Yes or no?" the words echoed from a great distance. I no longer cared what they meant as blessed oblivion had come to my rescue.

31

I regained consciousness, lying on the hard floor of the cell. My hands were tied behind me and I could not open my right eye; it burned fiercely with the heat of red hot iron. My mouth was dry and I could feel with my tongue that one of my molar teeth was missing.

Two buxom women stared down at me, their make-up thick on their faces. They seemed amused by what they saw. With them were two officers. They too, appeared to take pleasure in the scene. I had provided them with a little fun, it seemed.

The fire in my right eye blotted out all other pain. I threw myself from one side to the other, half mad with the agony. The stone floor felt like a bed of moss in comparison.

Somebody lifted me up and carried me out to the grey limousine. When they set me down on my feet, my stomach revolted and I was violently sick, casting up stinking bile. I had eaten nothing solid for over a week.

In the car, the commander sat next to me again, watching. The dog was on his knees as before, smugly absorbing the attentions of its master who softly stroked its long coat with the ringed fingers of his right hand.

Had he destroyed my eye? It surely felt like it. The pain etched deep into my temple... a searing, throbbing torment.

The car drew up at a building site, fenced by three rows of barbed wire. Men and women, some in civilian clothes, some in overalls, carried beams, pushed carts loaded with stones or stood in deep trenches, digging in the sandy soil. They worked without the assistance of horses, tractors or earth-moving equipment. Among them moved the distinctive black uniform of guards, their machine guns slung on their backs and wolf-like dogs that strained aggressively on their leashes.

The same officer that gave the order on our arrival at Fort Seven, shouted: "Attention!"

The prisoners stopped whatever they were doing and stood up straight to face towards the car as the commandant alighted. Immobile, they stood on top of the heaps of sand, in the ditches, behind the carts and on the scaffolding of the barracks under construction.

'Lange', the officer in charge, was indeed the second in command at Fort VII. This I had learned from my cell companions. A fleshy nose dominated his broad, sallow face and his forehead was short, with the prominent brows similar to that of an ape. As he approached us, he gave another order. The work continued. His voice did not reach the extremities of the site and the command was relayed from group to group. Each in turn, bent to their tasks like a ripple of wind in a field of wheat.

In front of the nearest barrack, he stopped and bawled a woman's name. A fat, wilting female of about fifty stepped forward, her hair drooping in lank strands on either side of her face.

"Come here, Liska!"

The old woman smiled a creepy, sly smile. She did not look at me.

"Tell me! Is this the one?"

The commandant pushed me forward and the woman raised her eyes and squinted at me with unsteady, evasive eyes. She nodded her head.

"Yes!" she said.

"What did she say?" the commandant persisted.

The woman had very few teeth. Her mouth was a dark hole that gaped open closing only to form words when she spoke

"She wanted to know what the barracks are made of, how far away the camp is from Posen, what the camp is called; how many hours the prisoners had to work per day and what kind of work the women had to do."

'Dear God!' I thought. 'Those are the questions I asked in the cell. Is this a crime? Is it not understandable that a new prisoner might be curious about such things?' I was learning first hand about the spies in our midst who were willing to cooperate with our tormentors.

In spite of the pain in my head, for a second, I felt pangs of indignation. They soon faded. How I wished the inferno in my eye would not burn so fiercely; that I could at least touch it. But my hands were still tied behind my back.

With no warning, I was shoved hard in the small of my back and fell, face down into the sand.

"Napieralski, bring the rats!"

I staggered to my feet, whereupon I received another sharp blow between my shoulder blades and I stumbled forward into a hole no more than a metre deep.

The commander shouted at me to kneel down and two soldiers laid the board of a trestle table on top of me. I ducked as they lowered it and felt one of them step on it, the weight forcing me deeper into the hole. I expected to be crushed and curled up tight to cope with the dreadful pressure, The man was replaced by a rock or something equally heavy, for however hard I tried, I could not shift the wooden cover on my back. My arms grew numb tied as they were behind me. They seemed to be no longer part of my body and I could barely breathe because my chest was so compressed by the sharp angle of my position.

A voice above, possibly belonging to Napieralski, whined, "I cannot find the rats. They must have escaped!" A curse followed; the sound of a blow and the thud of fallen body. Someone called for cold water and seconds later it was poured over the board lying on top of me. It started to flow over me, but gradually reduced in volume until only a few heavy drops fell through the gaps onto the back of my head and neck.

'This is death! This must be my death!' I lost consciousness.

It was evening. The prisoners stood waiting in long columns when I returned to my senses. I was lying in the sand some distance from them, my hands free at last. Awareness crept through my body.

Limb by limb, I came back to life and as the numbness ebbed away and feeling awoke, so did the pain… the screaming aftermath of torture.

I was lifted onto the back of one of the trucks that had come to transport the prisoners back to the Fort. I was in excruciating agony. My hands clenched the cloth of my dress in desperation, and I tasted fresh blood in my mouth when I bit through my lip. When they bore me into the cell, Mother sank down by my side with a cry of horror. I felt her hand on my forehead, caressing the bare patches where my hair had been torn from my scalp. I felt her tenderly touch the bruises on my arms, thighs and back.

I felt her tears on my swollen face and, opening my left eye, I saw her stricken face above me.

The daily ration included a weak 'coffee' in the evening. That day, Dr Gorska collected some from every prisoner in the cell to wash the sores and cool the swellings on my face. She worked in silence, the touch of her hand, gentle and sensitive. A chemistry student made room for me in her corner and there I lay on a handful of straw, Mother keeping vigil beside me, my hands in hers.

No one, not even Mother had asked me what had happened or how I had come by my injuries. They had seen them before. Everyone was punished in this fashion at some time. If today it is someone else's turn to suffer, tomorrow, it could be you. The injuries were similar and with no clean water available, the 'coffee' was all there was to ease the pain.

Mother bent down to me and spoke quietly into my ear. "They will not leave us alone... not until we 'confess'. I found a piece of glass today, when I was sweeping the corridor. It is sharp, razor sharp. They will torture you again tomorrow... and the day after that. They want our lives, but they will take them, bit by painful bit. The piece of glass can put an end to our lives... and their pleasure... We can choose!"

During the sleepless hours of that night, I confided to her the information that Grischa had given me; that Father, Grandfather, Grandmother, my aunts and my cousins were already dead. It would have been so simple to exit this world to join them. I felt the glass in my hand and was tempted to make the short, sharp incision that would free me forever. I tried to look at my mother in the darkness, but could only feel the warm comfort of her hand.

'Dear God. There are people all over the world, at this moment, enjoying themselves at the theatre or cinema, drinking and eating, sleeping in white bed linen with the quilt pulled up to their ears. Millions and millions of happy, contented people, looking forward to tomorrow, without fear! Why is Mother not one of these millions? Why can't I be one of them? Almighty and all-knowing Creator and Lord of this world, why can I not be one of them? Speak to me. Give me a sign, as you once gave a sign to Moses. I am nineteen. I have not lived long enough to doubt the fairness of your justice. Please explain to me... Why?'

I felt that God had turned away from me. He was not listening. He was as far away from me as Herbert.

Even so, the instinct to live survived. That night, I did not try to use the piece of glass that nestled in the palm of my hand.

32

All the women in Cell 17 were classified as 'dangerous political criminals' and therefore were not taken out as part of the work gangs to build a new camp.

I seemed to be the exception.

Early the next morning, at the hour when the trucks arrived and the work assignments were sorted out, footsteps were heard in the passage outside the cell. The bolt was drawn back and the door opened, screeching on its hinges. The noise caused all the inmates to stir. Two guards entered and I heard my name being called out.

I had not slept at all during the night. My hand still lay in that of my mother although her fingers had relaxed as she slept. I still clutched the piece of glass. Perhaps Mother had been right. I should have used it.

I tried to get up, but could not. My whole body was rigid and refused to answer the commands from my brain. I closed my good eye, trying to shut out the inevitable.

The inevitable happened. A guard grabbed me by the arm and hauled me to my feet. The sudden movement triggered every muscle to register agonizing complaint. My legs barely held me upright. I had lain on my side all night and the pain had died to a dull ache. Now it blasted into life and every bruise throbbed vengefully; the fire in my head and on my back blazing without remorse.

Mother saw the pain on my face and screamed. She threw herself at the guard, imploring him in a mixture of German and Polish, to leave me alone. When he ignored her completely, she started to shout insults at him. She got kicked in the stomach and thrown against the wall for her trouble.

I was taken to what I assumed must have been the clothes depot. There, I was given a pair of blue overalls, similar to those I had seen on the building site. I was also given a man's torn shirt and a pair of wooden clogs. The two guards watched me as I took off my dress and pulled on the new outfit of coarse linen. All my movements were clumsy and I had to concentrate hard to make each limb function. The simple task of changing clothes was very difficult with arms and legs that had a mind of their own. At last, I was ready and stood up in my new uniform, the letter 'P' painted on the front and a large yellow square on the back. My dress and underwear were rolled up in a bundle and taken away. The clogs on my feet were made of solid blocks of wood with thick, hobnailed soles. Walking in them was difficult. It was only possible to shuffle. A flat shapeless cap completed the ensemble and this last item, the guard presented to me with a grin. He had an oval almost girl-like face with large, dark, intelligent eyes.

In the lorry, his thick-set companion sat with his back to us as we drove out of Fort VII and I became aware that the young man beside me was nervous or embarrassed.

"What have you done to deserve the special interest of the commandant?" he asked in a bemused tone He doesn't normally order 'hard labour' for political prisoners."

I was unable to answer and cradled my head in my hands. Inside my skull, a voice repeated again and again, like a cracked gramophone record,

'It isn't over yet. It goes on. It goes on. It goes on.'

The gang leader had been notified in advance to expect our arrival.

Stavosta, was a Pole who had been detained for theft of army equipment. He was an informer and a creep, who had become a willing tool for the commandant. The latter used him freely, when a job was too dirty for himself or his horde of SS men. This animal, Stavosta, was more feared by the prisoners then the German enemy itself. He was broad and stocky in stature, with a tangle of red hair that grew straight out of his scalp, like grass stubble at hay-time. His head was large and round and twitched constantly in quick feverish movements. He only kept it still when listening or when watching something. His neck would stretch forward and his attention focus through his thick, steel-rimmed spectacles like a bird eyeing a worm for breakfast.

He always carried a thick wooden stick in his left hand, rapping it in the cup of his right hand when he gave instructions to any of his work gang. A slow reaction and the stick would descend with great force on the unfortunate worker.

Today, bricks had to be distributed to various buildings on the site. Twelve bricks at a time were to be carried in wooden hods. These we loaded and unloaded ourselves and the gang to which I was allocated, had to run with them across the site to a building by the gate.

"Faster my darling! And don't break one of those precious little bricks or I shall break every bone in your pretty little body!" Stavosta stood just behind me as I prepared to make a start.

I was the only woman. I loaded the first lot of bricks into my hod as it lay on the ground, but it took all my strength to lift the thing up and the sores on my back begged for mercy. The straps over my shoulders cut into me like knives and the clogs were already causing my feet to ache. We ran in single file, the distances between members of the work gang determined by the loading and unloading times. I kept my place in the line with great difficulty. The ill-fitting clogs did not help. Watching the others, I noticed that they took up their loads and set them down again with the handles on their ends and the carrier at shoulder level. I tried it. It was easier.

My feet started to blister inside the heavy clogs and my pace slowed. The prisoner behind me panted past at a steady lope, his legs moving like a machine. 'So that is what becomes of people condemned to 'hard labour' week in, week out... a mechanical automaton!' I thought.

Stavosta shouted at me and hit my back and legs with his stick. I hurried to load my bricks and asked him if I could take my clogs off.

"You could catch cold, my darling! And nothing is more important to the camp leader than your health!" He grinned, expecting approval from my two guards. The younger of the two, backed away and strolled towards the gate.

I managed to carry the bricks four times from the stack to the gate, but on the fifth journey, when I tried to put my loaded hod down, my legs crumpled and the bricks fell on top of me. I lay on the ground, my eyes closed. I waited for the shout, the beating, for someone to haul me back on to my feet. Nothing happened. For half an hour, maybe more, I lay in the cradling arms of mother earth. When at last, I did open my eyes I could see a pair of boots. They were not moving. Slowly I lifted my head and met the gaze of large, intelligent eyes. There was no hatred in those eyes, only anxiety. The owner spoke.

"You must get up ... It is better if you get up...", and I could! I picked up the bricks, stacked them and as I ran back with my empty hod, a jubilant voice inside me whispered:

'A human being! A human being! Amongst all these animals, I've found a human being!'

By the time I had completed two more trips, however, the inspiration that my new discovery had given me succumbed and exhaustion took over. My throat was dry, my tongue felt swollen and rough like that of a calf. My feet were now bleeding in the clogs and the sores on my shoulders and back had opened. I could barely drag myself along. Stavosta's voice came from a long, long way off as he ran towards me. I only felt the first blow.

I came round, as someone lifted me up from the ground. The commandant stood before me and with disdain in his voice, he enquired, "How is the gracious lady? Everything to her liking?"

I was only semi-conscious and far too pathetic to make any response to his acrid sarcasm.

"Water, please could I have some water!" I begged. "A little water would help!"

The commander picked up his dachshund and told me to follow him. I shuffled behind him to the shack that housed the temporary kitchen. There he ordered me to wait outside the door. When he returned, he actually carried a glass of water and handed it to me. It was boiling hot! I gave it back to him and, ignoring his expression of devilish amusement, turned away. I should have thrown it in his face. Why not? All he could have done was to kill me and that would have been a blessed release.

Persisting somewhere on the periphery of my thoughts, I still hoped to be rescued. Even then – with my body beaten and torn and my brain already beginning to function in a resigned, non-resistant, robot-like fashion, something inside me, a core of obstinacy, would not accept defeat.

The beating during the interrogation affected me in other ways than the temporary damage to my body. It also altered the me, the being inside my body. During the days that followed, my face slowly healed and my sore back lost its stiffness. My vigorous attention to exercise had ensured that I was physically fit and I was young. Nature is kind to youth.

After the incident on the building site, I was not disturbed again, but the memory of what happened during the remaining weeks that we spent at Fort VII, lacks clarity. For most of the time that I spent in that miserable cell with the women from Mosina, I slept. When I was aroused by Mother or the doctor, I was never fully conscious. I seemed to be cocooned in a world of my own. I ate my daily ration of bread and drank the 'coffee', not because I felt hungry or thirsty, but because either Mother or Marja Gorska insisted that I consumed something. I did not feel the cold. Lying on the hard floor of the cell, I did not feel particularly uncomfortable. It was as though my body existed, but my soul, the 'me', was floating about, adrift, unable to relate to the physical conditions that surrounded us.

Marja Gorska would spend what seemed like hours in muffled discussion with my mother. Whenever I opened my eyes, they always seemed to be huddled together, deep in conversation, occasionally glancing in my direction. When I asked my mother what it was that they talked about for such long periods, she did not reply immediately.

"We are a little anxious about you, my darling," she had said. "They hurt you badly."

"Mother, I'm fine," I had assured her. "See! My eye is perfect now!" I had opened both eyes wide.

"Yes, my love! Of course, you are fine!" And she would lapse into silence.

When I stood up, however, to make my way to the bucket in one corner of the cell which served as the toilet, I was obliged to steady myself against the wall. Somehow my limbs were not co-ordinating. The light-headedness, I reasoned, was probably due to a lack of wholesome food. An ability to balance on my own two feet without support seemed an elusive skill that after my years of training as a dancer should have caused me some anxiety. It did not, however, worry me at all and for some reason… it did not ever occur to me to care.

33

Liska, the woman with the unkempt hair and the toothless mouth, the woman who had informed on me, became the guard officer in our cell. She had been in Cell 17 for almost six months and in those six months, she had reported every word that she had heard. Now, she received her reward for services rendered – Guard Officer Liska!

She was the most puzzling of them all. The other guards were brutal, cruel and sadistic. Their behaviour was always predictable. Liska was capable of being more heartless than all the others, but suddenly, she could change. At times she was like a mother. She brought us additional bread rations, straw and blankets. As soon as she had distributed them, however, her eyes would narrow into evil pinheads and she would grab one of us by the hair and start to slap her face.

I feared that she would pick on me and emulate her superior, the commandant, by treating me badly, but she left me in peace. The commandant too seemed to lose interest in me. He had perhaps had his fun, become bored with taunting me and now satisfied his peculiar lusts by victimising someone else. For eight days, I did not have to join the work gangs and I was able to recover in peace. The cuts and sores started to heal and the swelling over my eye subsided.

Liska loved to be unpredictable. She in fact treated me with particular kindness. I had so many privileges during my days of recuperation, it was almost embarrassing. She smuggled ointments and bandages into the cell. Marja had only to tell her what was needed in order to get me back on my feet and Liska provided. She invariably wore a new dress every day. Sometimes the clothes were recognised by the previous owner. It was apparently one of the privileges of her position that our clothes were available for her use.

I considered the idea of suggesting to her that she might smuggle a letter out of the camp for me, to Herbert. After the special considerations that she had shown me, I began to trust her a little. I did not realise when I first thought of this idea that Liska, even though she was a guard officer, was still a prisoner and was not allowed outside the confines of the Fort. I fortunately discovered my naivety in time to save myself further trouble.

Herbert was always in the background and I longed to be able to find some way to let him know what had happened to us. I would wonder about the possibilities. 'Would a letter be able to reach him or, had he too, been thrown into a prison? Surely, if he was still free, he would have somehow found a means of rescuing us by now. Where was he? Why had nothing happened?' I believed in Herbert. He had been my saviour once and, however minute the possibility, I hung on to the hope that he could perform a second miracle.

Even my mother was still optimistic and hoped that we would hear from him. We would console each other with such notions when we got the chance to whisper together in the gloom of Cell 17.

I became more attached to Dr Marja Gorska. It was she that I had to thank for my speedy recovery and our conversations helped to fill the interminable emptiness of our imprisonment. We all tried to fight the dreadful boredom by talking about books that we had read in the past, or films and plays that we had seen. Everyone contributed. It made the time pass a little faster and occupied our minds by escaping to another world.

The hours of discussion with Marja, however, made and even deeper impression on me. They led far beyond school lessons and lectures. She was extremely well educated and her opinions and experience were inspiring, indicating a courageous spirit, unbent by the circumstances of her present predicament Her rare combination of intelligence and instinct surprised and fascinated me and I would spend hours meditating on the ideas she gave me, my wandering thoughts like leaves, drifting on a river.

Building work at a new camp site had started in the middle of the winter and had progressed steadily, even during the coldest spells of weather. Besides the occupants of Fort VII, it was said that English and Russian prisoners of war had also been forced to help in its construction. Like the other 'political criminals', we lived in Cell 17 without ever emerging into daylight. I had not been required to join the work gangs since that horrendous day when I had succumbed in the pit. My sentence of 'hard labour' had been cancelled at the same time as the commandant lost interest in me.

The move to the new camp was imminent. As more prisoners from Fort VII were employed every day to complete the project, the inmates of Cell 17 were enlisted to replace them to do the domestic chores in the Fort. Hence, one morning, all the remaining prisoners, even the 'dangerous political ones', were lined up in the main gallery in front of the commandant's bunker. We waited for a long time, our eyes slowly adjusting to the bright lights. Liska had warned us of the planned change in routine and we were looking forward to the variation in our diet of utter boredom.

Camp Leader Lange was in charge of organising the work parties. Another officer checked off the names on a list as each prisoner was allocated to a gang. The guards led away between ten and fifteen women at a time. One group was sent to the laundry, another to clean the corridors. Mother and I stood at the end of the second row. Lange had dismissed all those in front of us and he stood, with legs apart, tapping his boot with his whip.

"You are the actress! Eh?" he said.

Nervously, I nodded my head in reply. He hit the side of his boot hard with the whip as though he had made a snap decision.

"Come here!" he ordered.

I stepped forward and waited. Lange continued to sort out the different work gangs. Mother was in the last one, assigned to clean cars. I could feel her eyes on me, even as she was being led away. For a moment, she hesitated as if she might try to rush back to me, but she obviously thought better of it and disappeared down the tunnel behind the other prisoners.

I was the only one left. As the sound of the retreating feet faded, Camp Leader Lange indicated that I should follow him.

We walked through seemingly endless, long corridors, up steps and along more corridors. The Fort was an underground maze. Lange shoved doors open with the toe of his boot and looked back at me each time, before marching on. Eventually, we entered a room with a bed, a wardrobe and a desk in it; his private quarters.

Lange shut the door behind me and sat down at his desk. He suddenly started to talk to me as though I were his equal and not, the lowliest of the low, a prisoner in his charge.

"Please! Take a seat!" He reached for a packet of cigarettes. "Do you smoke?"

I had smoked a lot in Berlin and how I had often wished for the pleasure of smoking a cigarette during the recent months. Just one cigarette! But now, I declined the offer. It would have been impossible to hold it to my lips for my hand was shaking too much.

'What had the man in mind for me? What mischief had he thought up?' I asked myself, fearing the answer.

"How long have you been with us now?" Lange asked, closing the packet of cigarettes and putting them down on the desk.

"Three, nearly four weeks" I replied.

"And tell, why are you here?" he asked. There was no aggression in his voice. His tone was that of one asking a simple question.

'Is this whole charade a new type of interrogation?' I thought. 'My papers are in the commandant's office. He must have seen them! Surely?'

I repeated my story, as I had done so many times before, but noticed that he did not seem to be paying much attention to what I said. His next question was on such a totally different subject, that he must have been thinking about it, whilst I was talking.

"Can you cook?"

"No!" I replied.

"Of course, yes! You were an actress!" he said, a knowing smirk spreading across his face. Had I seen an expression like that before? Did it remind me of a certain deanery?

"...but you can tidy up and keep a room clean, can't you?" he said. My suspicions were further aroused as to what he had in mind. "It would be to your advantage, if you looked after my things and kept the place tidy. The work is light and it has its benefits..."

'So that's what they call it here in the Fort, 'keeping the place tidy!' I thought. I had noticed the two women wearing heavy make-up, who would parade about in our best clothes and flirt openly with the guards. They were more than just prisoners.

Lange leant back in his chair and put his feet up on the desk. "You are married! To a German officer, I hear!"

"Yes," I said.

"Do you love your husband very much? I mean... do you still love him?"

I did not answer. I resolved, why should I talk to him about Herbert? It is none of his business!

"Do you really believe in love?" Lange took his feet off the desk and abruptly stood up. He started to pace up and down, then pausing with his back towards me, he spoke as though he was voicing his thoughts aloud.

"I should have thought... you are still fairly young... but then, you must have known many men, being a dancer. I mean... You are beyond the stage of believing in sentimental lies aren't you or that a man can be faithful forever... to you only? Do you still believe that he loves you and only you?"

Slowly, he turned to face me, the expression in his eyes mocking. "You don't think he has been in bed on his own all this time, do you... a celibate for all these weeks?"

I jumped to my feet in response to his crude inferences. I immediately realised that protest was pointless, but I was angry and hurt. They could beat us and kill us, but somewhere deep inside the most pitiable victim of their assaults, there should remain a piece of no-man's-land that could not be touched or stained by them. He was trespassing.

He was aware of his little tactical error and changed his tune. In a more practical and business-like manner, he asked me to set the table.

"You'll find everything over there, in the cupboard. Lay the table for two and if anyone comes to the door, don't answer it." With that, he left, slamming the door behind him.

I found the crockery and cutlery and also butter, cheese, bread, ham and a piece of cold, fried fish. I busied myself laying the table but in spite of my normal diet of dark, dry bread and gruel, I felt no temptation to taste any of the food. It was strange, for in the cell, we often discussed at length how nice it would be to have the luxury of a little margarine on the bread.

A quarter of an hour later, Lange returned. His arms were full of bed linen, which he dropped into an empty chair before taking off his uniform jacket.

"Will you dine with me?" It was not a question. It was an order. He smiled sardonically and once we were seated issued an invitation.

"Help yourself!"

I took my time preparing a slice of bread with some ham. I dreaded having to try to eat it as I felt it would probably choke me. When was the last time that I had used a plate, a knife or a fork? How was I supposed to indulge in the use of such things now, in the presence of one of those who had taken them away in the first place? I had become used to my soup arriving in a tin bowl and sharing a spoon with my mother.

Lange noticed that I had not touched my bread and laughed. "There's plenty of time. You'll get used to your new diet soon enough. While we're waiting, you could change the bed linen."

I started on the bed, my back towards him. Every sound made me jump; a cup being replaced on a saucer; the clink of his fork; the clatter of plates being stacked. I had spread the sheet on the bed and put fresh cases on the pillows and as I was smoothing the cover, I heard the click of his lighter. He had lit a cigarette. The silence that followed was intolerable. Something was about to happen and instinctively, I braced myself.

The chair moved, the boots creaked, one step, another. They came closer. I was mechanically smoothing the quilt on his bed, when he grabbed be from behind and pulled me upright. I felt his hands clutching at my breasts and his mouth on my neck. He threw me on to the bed and himself, on top of me. He panted and gasped, his face centimetres from mine. His eyes were wide open and his fleshy nose, which I found particularly repugnant, snuffled against my cheek. His hands pinned my arms in a vicious grip, but I fought him. I fought him with my whole body, with every ounce of strength that I could find.

"Don't be a silly girl," he gasped, and tried again to put his face on my neck and between my breasts. I struggled to escape. He could not let go of my arms, so he tried to tear my blouse with his teeth. I was desperate that he would not succeed! If he managed to do that, all would be lost, even the little bit of decency that they had left me so far.

'Holy Maria, Mother of God, help me! You must help me!' I begged.

I heaved with all my strength and managed to roll his body to one side. I slipped out of his grasp and slid to the floor. I had hardly got to my feet, when he came at me again. He seemed to find my resistance exciting. His eyes were glowing. His mouth was half open and that nose of his, that broad ugly nose, was snuffling in for the victory.

I was not able to control myself any longer. I hit him, punching my fist into his face with all the strength, hatred and rage that I could muster.

Then I froze, stunned by what I had just done and expecting any moment to be on the receiving end of a lead bullet. I had retaliated. The unthinkable had happened. I could expect to receive only the ultimate punishment.

But Lange, shirt open and his hair tousled, picked up his jacket from the back of his chair and slipped his arms into the sleeves.

"Stuck up bitch!" was all he said before wrenching open the door and yelling for the guard. When the guard arrived, Lange kept his back to the door and gave orders for me to be taken back to the cell. Was his nose a touch broader, a touch fleshier? He did not look at me again and slammed the door shut behind me.

All day and all the following night, I waited, expecting a summons.

They had beaten me and hounded me for no apparent reason. What would be the punishment for hitting an officer in the face? Nothing it seemed... absolutely nothing at all. The monstrous ogre had raised its paw, but decided to ignore me and walk away. I could breathe again... until the next time.

34

The transfer to the Poggenburg, the new camp, started in May. The 'dangerous political criminals' were left at Fort VII until all other prisoners had been moved out. Mother and I were admitted to Poggenburg nearly a month later, on 1st June, 1943. The building site, as I had seen it only weeks earlier, had now become a small village of huts. They were still laying road surfaces when we arrived and finishing the odds and ends, but it was surprising how, in such a short space of time, they had managed to erect the camp. I reminded myself that it had been achieved without any assistance whatsoever from mechanical equipment. I wondered how many litres of sweat and blood the ground had soaked up before the authorities on high were notified:

"Poggenburg completed."

The camp lay in a man-made hole, with high banks on all sides. The original crater had possibly been a disused pit or earth works, now it had been modified to conceal Poggenburg. The camp could certainly not be seen from the road, which passed some two hundred metres to the north of the perimeter fence. The whole area was surrounded by three parallel fences of barbed wire and we were warned on arrival, that one of them was charged with high voltage electricity. The observation towers at each corner were armed with machine guns. Two guards were on duty in each, night and day. At night, extra guards with tracker dogs, patrolled the perimeter. Entertaining ideas of escape was pointless, unless one wanted to commit certain suicide.

The commandant's large hut stood near the gate with a small open space in front of it. On one side of the little square, in the spot to which I had been obliged to convey bricks, stood a windowless building. We learned later that this housed the torture chambers, the so-called 'death station', where prisoners were subjected to horrible physical punishment until no life was left in them. In front of the awful building, was a small lamp which glowed red whenever any of the cells were occupied. The light shone all too often.

The other huts at the front of the camp were used for new arrivals and prisoners about to be 'released'. One of them was the de-lousing department; others included workshops for shoemakers, tailors, needleworkers and various depots for camp necessities. There too, the laundry could be found. It was only the 'light cases' that were permitted to live and work in these huts; people who had been arrested for minor offences and who were sentenced to one or two months in the prison.

The longer term prisoners lived in barracks which bordered the big exercising ground in the centre of the camp. The exercise compound itself was surrounded by yet another barbed wire fence.

Barbed wire also encircled the barracks of the Jews, Jehovah's witnesses and political prisoners. We had our own special guards and dogs to patrol the huts.

The darkness, damp and cold of the cellars at the Fort were now replaced by the guards, dogs, guns and barbed wire of the new prison camp. There was little to chose between them and the conditions in Poggenburg could hardly have been called an improvement on those in Fort VII.

On the plus side, was the fact that we were no longer isolated from other prisoners. We were no longer forty women segregated from the rest of humanity, but a small group in many hundreds of all ages and nationalities. The discovery that there were so many, was a boost to the morale. It was somehow easier to cope with the situation with the knowledge that others, many others, had been obliged to travel the same road of endurance and suffering. Despair and frustration seemed to lose their potency and dissipate in the face of many thousands asking the same questions of the Almighty: "Is this fair? Why me?" We began to realise that there were probably many more thousands in many more similar camps – perhaps hundreds of thousands.

The number '17' denoted our status and all the 'dangerous political prisoners' were duly assembled in our new Cell 17. The barrack room was smaller than the cellar had been, but there were two barred windows, providing natural light and from which we could observe part of the camp outside. This in itself was a heaven-sent luxury. To be able to see the sun and the stars again after so long living like a mole and to be able to witness the world beyond made me feel that perhaps I was still a part of the human race.

The 'dangerous political criminals' were not taken out of the camp to work, but we did have to appear for roll call every morning and evening. For this exercise, all prisoners of every category were herded into the exercise compound. 'Roll call' was the polite term used for what rapidly developed into an endurance test. There were too many of us in the camp, for 'special treatment' to be administered to individual offenders. Instead, 'special treatment' was handed out indiscriminately to those who showed signs of weakness during the roll call.

We were woken at 4.00.a.m. Half an hour later, we had to be ready for the first roll call, standing in dead straight lines stretching across the compound. The endurance test was the ability to stand there, totally immobile and sometimes for hours. The commandant was in no hurry. The hotter, the colder or the wetter the weather, the later he would appear. While we were waiting, the guards strolled silently through the columns and used the butts of their rifles on anyone who talked, moved or could not stand upright. This was bad enough for the fit, but the sick were also dragged out each time for the ordeal. They were beaten in the ranks and then pulled over one of the wooden blocks which had been firmly embedded in the ground. Their overalls were removed and they would be thrashed, in front of everyone.

This sad harvest varied in content, depending on whether it was morning or evening. It was usually more plentiful in the latter. In the wake of a long, hard day, labouring with a work gang, only the very strong could stand upright for long periods.

I still vividly remember one particular winter evening, when the sleet stung our faces with the sharpness of a thousand needles. We were insufficiently clad in our overalls and were freezing. The entire guard unit, dressed in thick fur coats, had taken steps to overcome the severe cold by consuming brandy. Quite a few were drunk and looking for some amusing entertainment. They stalked their victims and 'discovered' many offenders. There was a queue at the wooden blocks. The commandant joined in and in spite of the cold, took off his coat so that he could try his hand at whipping the half-frozen bodies personally. He laughed and joked with his men, who seemed to have all gone mad, perspiring heavily from the frenzied exertion of beating the prisoners. Unconscious victims were left lying in the snow, still half naked and were eventually doused with water. This turned to ice within minutes and the ensuing screams are indescribable and unforgettable.

It was a rich harvest. There were twenty-eight 'discharges' in that one evening. The next morning, the bodies of the twenty-eight men and women still lay on and around the wooden blocks, their nakedness covered with a mantle of snow.

Poggenburg!

An architect, by the name of Tieke, had been transferred from Dachau. He said, Rather ten years there, than one year in this hell! I would kiss the ground at Dachau, if I could get back there."

Poggenburg must have held approximately a thousand prisoners although it could well have been more, it could have been less. It must have been one of the smallest camps in existence. Isolated and far from the international inspection controls, hidden away from the German authorities, the commandant was the absolute ruler. His horde of SS guards was answerable to no one else but him. They had never heard of a 'code of conduct' or guidelines of any sort. All newly admitted prisoners had to sign a form, but the text was covered. We never discovered what it was that we had signed. It might well have been our own death warrant for all we knew. Whatever it was, it was a frivolous concession to convention that could not have had any significant meaning.

If someone had come to me in my home in Posen and told me what was happening in the countryside outside the town, at a place called Poggenburg, I would not have believed it was possible. I would have assumed that they had become deranged. What went on there, day after day, week after week, made me wonder how God could allow that these blood-thirsty, soul-less animals could hide behind masks that suggested they might belong to the human race. Whatever the commandant might have been, it was not human. Camp Leader Lange, Stavoska, Liska and all officers and guards also showed little sign that they belonged to the species of homo sapiens. Giving them a human-like exterior had been nature's way of playing a hideous and terrible joke.

Every day that I spent in Poggenburg is etched clearly into my brain. Every person that I met will remain with me forever... unforgotten. As I recall details of that period of my imprisonment, I feel as though I am living through it all a second time, so vivid is the picture in my mind of the horror, of the misery and of the perpetual cold and hunger.

Mother was the first of the 'dangerous political criminals' to be taken out to work. It was a good sign. Good because, she was considered to be harmless.

She had continued to act the part of a slightly mentally disturbed person during the months of our internment. Even our fellow cell mates were unaware of her true state of mind. They were so concerned that they felt sorry for her and often expressed their sympathy to me. Sometimes when I watched her grin inanely at a guard, I would begin to worry about her myself. Her act was so convincing. When we lay beside each other at night, she would talk to me quietly, coherently and totally sensibly and I would thankfully confirm to myself that she was constantly playing a dangerous game of charades. She was clever enough though, not to carry her 'madness' too far. The safest route was to play the benign, good-natured fool. If she had proved cussed, awkward or silly, she would have been removed to the 'sick room'. The only treatment they administered there was a deadly injection, often administered by the commandant himself.

Mother was assigned to the vegetable section and was commended for her diligence. She had never been able to sit still when there was work to be done and the barbed wire made no difference to her instinctive enthusiasm. She was rapidly promoted to the manageress of the vegetable department, thanks to her eagerness and the fact that she was also good at keeping the accounts. Her 'mental condition' did not apparently affect her ability to juggle numbers. Her job included the checking of vegetable quantities and the sorting and distribution of the goods to the numerous kitchens around the camp. She was even allocated a number of prisoners to work under her personal supervision.

She was happy. She could move about and go out in the fresh air. On her visits to the kitchens, she sometimes received extra meals or bread rations. These treasures, she hid in her overalls, to be shared with me at night.

It had been Liska, the spying, informing Liska that had recommended Mother for the work duty. She was still disposed to be friendly towards Mother and me and one evening before supper, she drew me to one side, looking around to make sure that no one was listening.

"Take the ring out of your hair, at once!" she said in a harsh whisper.

I was horrified! How did she know that I had a ring hidden in my hair? Mother had given me one of the two rings that she had managed to conceal, thinking that it was better that we should have one each, in case we became separated. Somehow, Liska had come to know about it. What was she going to do?

She signalled for me to hurry. I had no alternative, but to extract the ring and give it to Guard Officer Liska. She slipped it into her pocket and left the cell without a word of explanation.

Returning almost immediately, she shouted orders to get ready for a roll call. Her behaviour had again reverted. She slapped a harmless old lady called Stepanska on the head for coming too close!

All prisoners assembled for roll call. Outwardly, everything seemed to be normal, but something was afoot. We had become used to listening to our instincts and could sense a subtle change. Something special was in store that night and although we were lined up at 7.00pm, we were still standing there long after sunset. It was the 1st of September. Beyond the barbed wire and the hill, farmers would have been bringing in the harvest; driving tall wagons loaded with golden sheaves, they would be rumbling along the road towards the barn.

"Attention!"

We stood to attention and guards ran up and down to check whether the columns were straight. Then the commandant appeared, surrounded by a crowd of officers and 'Scharfuhrer' (group leaders). The long-haired dachshund leapt about between their legs, yapping excitedly. We had named him 'Seppl'. It was forbidden to walk anywhere in the camp. Everything was accomplished at the run and the dog was trained to nip the laggards. The one good thing about Seppl was that he always gave us warning that the commandant was in the vicinity.

Our instincts had been right. Something always happened when the whole gang came out together. Camp Leader Lange stepped forward and started to read names from a list. They were all women and all from Cell 17. As each name was called, the prisoner joined the line at the front. Marja Gorska's name came first. Among those that followed were:

"Barbara Morawaka!" A small, slim woman stepped forward. She had been standing next to me and shot me a look full of puzzlement and fear as she stepped forward to join Marja. "Stefa Kuczowska!" She was a writer. We had learned her poems in school. They praised Poland, my fatherland. That was her sin.

"Krysis Verbanska!" who was not yet nineteen, was a medical student, imprisoned in connection with the 'Mosina' case.

"Maria Weychanowna!" I was the last to be summonsed forward. Lange was folding his list as I joined the line.

There were still forty women in Cell 17. Thirty nine of them were now standing to attention in that line. The fortieth, my mother, remained in the ranks behind us.

I had convinced myself that the whole rigmarole had something to do with pending transfer. Prisoners were quite frequently sent to other camps. Liska must have known about it and the ring would have been beyond her reach in the event of my moving out.

I became disconcerted, when ten prisoners brought out ten stools and placed them in a neat row in front of the commandant.

Lange signalled with his arm and the guards in the watch towers turned their spotlights directly on to the stools. Suddenly, radio music from the open windows of the SS canteen, could be heard, booming loudly across the square.

This was not a transfer exercise, but I had no other ideas. The group of waiting women was getting anxious. The tension ran up and down the line like an electrical current. Sidelong glances were exchanged silently relaying the message "What is it all about?"

The commandant smiled and ordered the first ten women to sit on the stools. They obeyed, sitting with their backs toward us. Ten inmates appeared with hair clippers. Marja cried out when her hair was touched. Lange slashed her in the face with his whip. She was silent after that and so were all the others.

The hair was shaved from the heads of all thirty nine of us. The commandant seemed to think it was amusing and laughed. He patted the naked scalp of the woman in front of him and obligingly produced a pocket mirror so that she could admire herself! When it had been my turn to sit on a stool, I had shaken uncontrollably. It was a psychological torture, worse than being beaten and kicked. A piercing scream had cut through the night when the first strands of my hair fell to the ground. Mother had not been able to keep silent. She loved my hair almost more than I did and, while the clippers were doing their job, I remembered how she had taken me to the hairdresser to have my hair trimmed and permed at quite an early age. How proud I had been of my new hair styles when I had returned to school after the holidays!

When I returned to the cell, Liska was waiting for me. Having first ascertained that no one was watching, she took my hand in hers. I felt something cold and knobbly nestle into my palm. She had returned my ring.

"Sew it into your knickers. That's the best place," she said and was gone. Liska! Fiend one minute and inexplicably a trusted friend the next!

35

We had been shorn like sheep because we were to be sent out of the camp to work. They seemed to think that we would have less chance of escaping with bald heads. The next day, as we climbed aboard the lorry, they confiscated our caps, adding further to our humiliation. Shaven like convicts, we were driven through the centre of Posen, in full view of everyone. I felt so ashamed and shed bitter tears in my misery. People stopped on the pavement to gape at us. They stared at us from windows and doors as if we were apparitions from some alien world. They probably thought that we were dangerous maniacs. If only they had known the truth!

Our destination was a munitions factory, where a civilian escorted us to the factory floor and conversed on equal terms with our guards. The reintroduction to a normal world was a shock. It seemed so unreal. English prisoners of war mingled with Polish artisans, working shoulder to shoulder, suitably dressed and adequately fed. The work was accomplished without the thrashing whip and bullying kicks and blows.

The job that we were given was, needless to say, dirty and unhealthy and assigned only to prisoners like ourselves. We had to dip iron plated and rusty grenade shells into a caustic liquid to clean them. My hands turned deep green from the acid in the water and it penetrated and roughened my skin within minutes. The opportunity to escape from the four walls of the cell, however, was more than welcome. We looked forward to our days in the factory in spite of the grim tasks we had to do there.

The canteen food was much better than the monotonous gruels that we devoured in camp. We also made contact with the Polish workers and received bread and even clothes from them. They frequently left small parcels for us, hidden in the toilets and there, unobserved, we could conceal their gifts under our overalls.

The head of the department in charge of our floor was a young fair-haired man, called Blum. He was always dressed in a blue suit, one arm of which was flat and fastened securely into his pocket. He often checked our work and soon, I became aware that he was watching me. One day, I heard him discussing me with one of the guards. He must have assumed that I spoke only Polish, for they did not try to lower their voices. Later that same day, I was called away from the acid bath and the guard took me to Herr Blum's office. I found him sitting behind his desk. A second man in the room, introduced himself as an interpreter. He proved to be superfluous, for to the first questioned that I was asked, I replied in German.

"Can you do office work?"

"Yes," I replied. "I have worked for two firms in Germany, as a junior shorthand typist!" I added boldly, not thinking for a minute that my dubious qualifications for those jobs were of current relevance.

But, from that day forward, I worked in the office. I was even promoted to 'supervisor'. My new German boss explained the move to my guards as 'making up statistics'! In reality, I was given milk, apples and sometimes cigarettes, in the privacy of the office.

The fact that Herr Blum had come from Hamburg had been a common link from the start. He admitted that he had noticed me when I arrived on the first day. He had felt particularly sorry for me. He was surprisingly well informed about the conditions in Poggenburg and confessed quite openly that he was ashamed of what was happening there in the name of Germany. He had lost his arm in the invasion of Poland, which led to his release from active service with the army. Instead the government had posted him back to Posen to manage the munitions factory.

I found myself sympathising with him, especially when he added that he felt that Hitler was aiming at impossible goals. He was the first German that I had spoken to, who did not believe that his country could win the war.

Herr Blum was happily married with two lovely fair-haired children. I met the whole family in the office one day. They had brought cigarettes and a slice of roast meat for me, which I gratefully accepted. I tied their presents under my shirt so that I could share them with Mother during the night. Before they left, Frau Blum offered to post a letter for me and I was permitted to sit at the desk and write to Herbert.

Herbert! To begin with, I was at a loss as to what to write. Should I tell him about what was happening to me? Would the letter reach him at all? In the end, I addressed it to his mother in Hamburg, saying simply, that I was in Poggenburg and was waiting for him – no more.

I thanked the Blum family sincerely. It had been a very long time since anyone had shown such kindness and consideration to me. They, in their turn, expressed their delight to be of some assistance and promised to let me know when an answer arrived at their home and I was looking forward to telling Mother the good news and sharing the meat with her. Meat was an unheard of luxury in the camp.

When the lorry arrived back in Poggenburg, however, we were ordered to line up in front of the camp office. A host of armed guards swarmed around us, marshalling us into position, two metres apart from each other. It was too late to get rid of anything hidden under our clothes and nearly all of us were hiding something.

A body search! It had to be a body search.

A woman that had joined the work gang the previous day, was summonsed into the office. With sinking hearts, we realised that she was probably a spy that had been planted in our midst.

The 'Iron Maidens' were dragged into view.

These much feared torture devices, consisted of hollow cones of barbed wire. We had to kneel down for a cone to be placed over each of us. It was not possible to hold one's head erect; the Iron maiden was not high enough. They fitted snugly over one's body. The slightest movement caused the barbs to scratch the skin. It was impossible to shift one's legs and the pain in the thighs gradually became a screaming agony. Again and again, the women would cry out – some fainted and slumped, rolling over in their cages and lying on their bed of barbs. The guards that were off duty, would watched us from the windows of their quarters, placing bets with each other as to which of us would collapse next.

An hour or so later, the first prisoner was led away to the 'discharge' building. When she returned, she whispered "Search!" before the cone was replaced over her.

The piece of meat did not worry me as much as the cigarettes and matches. Above all, it was strictly forbidden to carry matches. A suspicion of planned arson would be severely punished. I pretended to feel cold and rubbed my arms and sides as best I could within the restrictions of the cage and after a while, I managed to get the matches out of my overall pocket. I tried to slip them between my knees, before pushing them down into the sand to bury them. I almost succeeded.

Suddenly, I heard a shout from behind me... and Stavosta appeared! He grabbed the matches through the wire and holding them aloft in triumph, strutted off to the office.

I jumped the queue. My cage was removed and I was chased into the 'discharge' hut. It all happened so quickly that I was unable to 'lose' anything else on the way. Liska was waiting there to search me. She found the meat, five cigarettes and the apple with no difficulty and put them into the bowl bearing my name which stood on the table.

"Away with you and get back under your cone, you animal," she growled and I scurried back to my cage.

Only the commandant had the authority to make the decision as to what to do with us, but he was not in camp. We waited, kneeling with the cones over our heads, for his return.

Night fell and so did the rain. In the beam of the search light that was directed at us, I watched the water come down in glittering cascades. When it eventually stopped, a cold wind swept across the square and the sodden linen clothes clung to our bodies. The tufts of newly grown hair stuck to our faces. The guards inspected us, grinned, unbuttoned their trousers and urinated over us. Their dogs jumped excitedly at the cages and the wire cut deep into flesh.

The clock on the office struck three before we heard the sound of an approaching car. The camp gate rattled open and the commandant was back. The guards removed the cages, but we were unable to stand. Prolonged squatting in an awkward position had cut off the blood circulation and legs were lifeless.

Slowly and painfully, we recovered and the commandant ordered us all into his office. There, he tried to trick us into betraying each other. He wanted to know where our supplies had come from. And he wanted to know names. He was shouting at me in particular; that I had tried to smuggle out a letter – the others had told him so.

'Had the others told him?' I asked myself. 'How could they have done? They did not know about my letter to Herbert, so therefore, neither could he. He was bluffing, It was a trap...' I said nothing.

All denied knowledge. All kept silent. The commandant became impatient and prescribed fifteen strokes with the truncheon and a further dose of the cone treatment. Another rainstorm burst overhead. Again we were soaked to the skin.

The commandant stood there, glaring down at us, until dawn broke. We knelt until the sun rose.

Old Stepanska is singing hymns. Suddenly she sinks down with a cry. She does not lift her head again and the cry fades away to a gurgling mumble.

The sun is climbing now. The cages are removed and again, we cannot stand or walk. We recover and are sent to the de-lousing hut. The commandant stands at the door, his feet apart. He orders us to get undressed and to lie naked on the floor. He tells the guard to fetch the hosepipe that is used to clean the floor. He turns on the tap and enjoys the fun of dousing us with a jet of ice cold water. Then he departs, wishing us a "pleasant rest".

Seconds later, he returns. He has forgotten his little dachshund. The dog had whimpered for him and scratched frantically at the closed door. The man picks the dog up and sooths it, stroking its long ears. Tucking the animal under his arm, he walks calmly out of the door, the dog's tail wagging back and forth with delight.

Poggenburg!

36

We received neither food nor water for three days after the encounter with the 'Iron Maidens' and were forced to work in the 'coal gang'. The coal was distributed in wheelbarrows to the huts which housed the workshops. The guards had frequent opportunity to use their truncheons.

We had to run, of course, from morning until night – there were no rest periods. Not that there would have been any point in stopping, there was nothing to eat and activity helped one to forget an empty stomach.

By the third night, thirst was the greater problem. We begged Liska for water and finally she agreed. But there was no container in which it could be fetched, except the cell toilet bucket. This she took, emptied and refilled with water. We slaked our thirst from that stinking can. We had no choice.

The following day, we returned to work in the munitions factory. Everything resumed the old patterns until the morning of October 21st. That morning, as I climbed aboard the lorry, I was immediately ordered to climb down again by one of the guards. He escorted me to a car and we drove to Posen; to the tall, brick building in Ritterstrasse, the headquarters of the Gestapo. It had been some time since I had been there, but not long enough to forget the smallest detail. There was the marble staircase, covered with the same thick red carpet. Only the cell into which they put me was different. This cell had an iron hook fitted to the ceiling. A leather sling was looped around my ankles and they hung me upside down from the hook, not very different from a pig or calf in a slaughter house.

As I write about that day in Ritterstrasse, I turn cold. It was painful, yes, but somehow... it was someone else's body. My mind, my will, my sense of awareness, seemed to be a separate entity that existed on another sphere. It was as though my soul, the me inside my body was split into two levels of consciousness; the one half occupying the body and undergoing the punishment, the other half, observing the proceedings in an objective and almost critical fashion.

The initial approach that they took for the interrogation was that the present situation was, quite naturally, my own fault. Why did I tell them the same old story? They were bored with that version. No one likes to hear the same thing umpteen times. To see a good film twice is enough, but over and over again. I should understand that it was absolutely my fault and mine alone, that I was hanging upside down from the ceiling. I was far too boring! Why did I not tell them where the shoemaker, Jankowski was?

After all these months, they were still looking for him. Why did I not tell them where the little pigskin case had come from?

Poland was finished, non-existent according to my tormentors. The spirit in my body did not change its story, the detached half of my soul which seemed to be objectively observing the scene from somewhere outside that body, wondered whether Grischa or my fatherland would ever thank me.

"Very well, as you wish my dear!" And I hung there, by my feet, swinging to and fro, like a sack of turnips suspended from a beam in the barn. They beat my body with whips and occasionally enquired, "Well, what about Jankowski, my little pigeon?" "Where did you get this dear little suitcase, my love?"

My body was beyond pain! The free part of my mind, hovered close, eventually that too got bored and switched off.

I was still unconscious when they brought me back to camp. When I did wake up, Mother was with me, her face wet with tears. My mind was alert enough to want to comfort her; to tell her that all was well, that her Maria was back and safe with her.

But my body would not respond and I drifted in a twilight zone. Many of the problems that I experienced after the interrogation when I was first arrested, seemed to return for a while. I felt clumsy and found that I needed support to keep my balance. Fortunately, the symptoms lasted for a much shorter time.

But what was the meaning of this renewed interrogation? What was the sense in it all? What was so special about us – Mother and I? Any information that we gave now would be months out of date, would it not?

The vilest characteristic of the Gestapo was that it left its victims in a constant state of uncertainty – halfway between hope of life and the threat of death. No one knew what was going to happen to them nor did they know the true definition of the accusations made against them. There was no logic or justice, no sentence and certainly, no defence. Only in the death cells of the windowless building in the camp could you be sure that you had but a few hours of life left to you. They would bathe you as though you were about to go on holiday. But this washing was because it was easier to clean a living body than a dead one. They required your skin and any fat that loitered in your body for the manufacture of soap. They needed soap because they had a fetish about cleanliness! And they prepared the soap in the laundry house... the hut with the tall chimneys. Once you were dead, it really should not matter to you whether they disposed of your bones with or without your skin.

37

Nothing happened for a few days. I was not ordered onto the lorry and I assisted Mother with her camp tasks which permitted me to regain my strength after my latest confrontation with the Gestapo. But the respite did not last for long. One morning towards the conclusion of roll call, I heard my name being called. Ominously, it was only my name that received attention.

I was escorted by the commandant and two of his henchmen to the infamous E-block. Here, surrounded by their own security fence of triple barbed wire, only the most serious political offenders were housed.

The commandant appeared to be in a magnanimous mood and informed me that he had received orders from his superiors to move me to a more secure block. It seemed almost laughable. The security of the whole camp was such that I was hardly likely to disappear anywhere. Summoning up my courage, I dared to enquire whether my case was under further investigation and for what reason I needed to be put into more intensive confinement. He laughed and struck me with his whip across my back, not hard enough to hurt, more in the manner of a jovial slap on the shoulders.

"You will know soon enough, my dear!" he said and opened the heavy wooden door of my new cell.

There were three bunks in the narrow room, two of which were already occupied. As we entered, the two elderly women leapt to their feet and stood to attention. The yellow 'P' on their overalls indicated that they were both Polish.

"New arrival!" said the commandant dismissively and turning on his heel, left the room. The two women, hardly sparing me a glance, lay down on their bunks again and stared at the ceiling. Under normal circumstances, their behaviour could have been seen as extremely rude and hurtful, but in Poggenburg, I knew only too well, that a new acquaintance had to be treated with caution. From their point of view, I could so easily be a spy. Alternatively, they may have resented the arrival of a new cell mate. They may well have been used to the company of each other and found the arrival of a youngster, a disagreeable intrusion.

I sat on the vacant bunk to assess my new quarters. Apart from the luxury of the bunks, the little room was empty and the single window was secured by thicker bars than the windows of the communal cell.

Guard officer Liska brought my food bowl. My transfer was complete! She had hesitated by the door, with a quizzical look on her face and said, "I will tell your mother that you are here if you like?" It was evident that she too, was confused by the new arrangement.

I thanked her and asked her to tell Mother not to worry. Then I too, lay down on my bunk, to think. 'What should I make of this sudden change? Had they found new evidence, damaging evidence? My case was closed, was it not? Was there still a file with my name on it, passing from hand to hand, from office to office? Where was Herbert? What had happened to him?'

He felt very close to me as I lay on my back in the stillness of that cell. I closed my eyes and concentrated hard on his face until I could see it in every detail. Many times in the following months, I sought refuge in 'looking' at his picture behind closed eyelids. I imagined holding him in my arms as I had done at our farewell in the corridor of Gestapo headquarters in Ritterstrasse.

For the first time since my arrival in Poggenburg, I was not in a state of constant exhaustion and I had the time to think and reminisce. There was nothing much else to do in the E-block. I would lie on my bunk for hours on end, gazing at the ceiling and locked away in my own world of memories. The occupants of E-block never went out with the work gangs and they were exempt from roll call. Every second day, we were allowed to exercise in the small compound for an hour, walking around in circles with our hands behind our backs under the watchful eyes of the guards and their dogs.

My two cell companions belonged to Mother's generation. Had their skulls not been shaven, they would have had white hair. Stef Kuczowska was a Jehovah's Witness. She had been arrested in the prayer hall and accused of using religious services for political agitation. In addition, she had been held responsible for the derailment of a German troop train. Blame was laid at her door for having inspired the act of terrorism or at the very least, for not using her influence to prevent the disaster.

Countess Stefanie Warnka was the wife of a polish major general. She had been arrested during the first days of the occupation. Her two young daughters had been taken away from her and sent to a children's camp somewhere. She still had a locket, containing pictures of her husband and her children, which she concealed under her tongue during searches. She spent many hours, gazing nostalgically at that open locket. She had known my grandfather and her initial reserve receded more and more as she discovered who I was. We finally became good friends when she revealed that her eldest daughter had been a pupil at the Ursuline convent where I had been at school.

Having discovered common ground with the countess, it was not long before Kuczowska also came to accept and trust me. To pass the time, we scratched the pattern of a chess board on the stone floor with a spoon handle. For chess men, we sacrificed some of our meagre bread ration. It took nearly a month to save enough dough to shape the tiny figures. It was quite a ceremony when we 'tossed' for the first players. The countess and myself won!

Thereafter, we played every day, twelve games each day, the winner recording her victory by making a notch in the woodwork of her bunk. I had once read in the German news that pilots made a similar mark on the tail plane of their aircraft to record the number of enemy planes they had shot down.

We were totally cut off from the daily events in the camp. The guards that let us out for exercise, did not talk to us and the camp was empty during the day. Everyone was away working, besides which we were far too heavily guarded to be able to make contact with anyone, even to wave a hand in acknowledgement.

We did witness an incoming transport of Jews one day. They had been kited out in prison clothes with the yellow 'P' on their overalls surrounded by a circle. The Jewish star was painted on their foreheads. But apart from this one incident, we rarely saw another prisoner.

It was also strictly forbidden to look out of the window and we had to rely on our ears to tell us what was going on outside the four walls of our cell. We became quite expert at interpreting noises. We could, for example, identify which guard passed the door by the way his boots squeaked and could make fairly accurate guesses as to what was happening on the parade ground. The orders, the shouting and the loud speakers, all belonged to a world beyond the confines of our peaceful oasis. Time was the enemy. It plodded by in a pedestrian fashion and all we could do, was to tolerate and endure it.

I remember one night particularly and I would remind the reader that as I write, I am experiencing again the emotions of the moment – I can see it all so vividly.

The moon is full. It casts long, hard shadows on the cell walls and floor. A noise had woken us, a new undefined noise... and we are curious. We cannot stay in our bunk.

Stefa Kuczowska is the first to get up. She tiptoes cautiously along the wall to the window and there she stands, spellbound. The countess and I join her and stare out through the bars. We can see a small area of the parade ground from the window. It looks ghostly in the moonlight, the shadows of the fencing forming curious patterns on the scuffed and pitted sand. We can see now what is causing the dragging, creaking noise. Five guards, one of them the stockily built Stavosta, are pushing a cart over the sand. They stop at a point some ten metres from our window. They disappear out of our range of vision and reappear carrying a heavy wooden beam. As they stand the beam on its end, we can see that it is a gallows. It stands tall and black against the sky. The stillness is shattered by a series of hammer blows that echo with a booming sound across the empty compound; then silence again. We watch as the men climb up and down like cats. We hear the chink of chains and see a chair being placed under the structure. It is like a chilling, horror movie. I am more frightened for the victim than I have ever been for my own life.

We hear approaching footsteps and the commandant, two guards and a tall, slim civilian appear in frame. The commandant is turning towards the man and he is taking off his jacket. The prisoner's white shirt catches the moonlight. The profile of his face reveals a thick, untidy beard as though he had not shaved for many weeks. His silhouette is erect and suggests pride and dignity. They had hunted him down, relentlessly tracking from one hiding place to the next, but they have not tamed his spirit. They tie his hands behind his back and invite him to stand on the chair. Stavosta is placing the loop around the man's neck then raises his arm like a station master, signalling to a train that is ready to leave. Stavosta jumps to the ground. The prisoner stands on the chair, erect and motionless, the moon shines on his face and suddenly, suddenly I realise that I know the face. I recognise the man.

Stanislaus Sobieski! The thick beard has altered his appearance, but I can see his distinctive features clearly now. I cannot see the fire in his eyes, but I remember it well from our meeting at the bar in Warsaw. I recall the bright, checked jacket that he wore and how he talked in his deep, mellow voice, of the goodness of mankind and the importance of freedom.

You have fought your fight, Stanislaus Sobieski, with your drummer boy, Mario, at your side. I wonder what has become of him? They pulled his medallion from my neck in Fort VII. And you, brave partisan leader, would you still say that men are good, as you stand on your chair with a noose about your neck?

The commandant stands beneath the gallows, only a pace away from the condemned man. He signals with a nod of his head. Stavosta snatches the chair aside. The other guards heave on the rope. Sobieski's body lifts upwards in the first instant. Now we can see only the lower half of the dying man from our little window. His legs stretch briefly and then tread air wildly until they finally dangle, like the limbs of a limp rag doll.

The commandant looks up. He peers at his watch now and again. Is he timing how long it takes to die by hanging? Stavosta and his mates disappear from view again and this time reappear with a 'meat box'. As they place it down on the sand beneath the gallows, the Countess, Kuczowski and I turn away from the window. We are all wrapped in our own thoughts and move silently back to our bunks.

Poggenburg!

38

Autumn 1943 stepped aside for winter. It became colder and colder. Our diet was meagre, but as we did not have to labour all day, we could preserve our energy by lying on our backs with closed eyelids, experts at hibernating in total inactivity. We had decided to tot up the notches on our bunks to find the chess champion only when one of us was obliged to leave the cell. Christmas had passed, the Christian holiday earning us no respite from the monotonous boredom of the isolation cell.

A few days later and it was me, the last to come, who was the first to go. A new guard arrived and told me to pack my things. Stafanie Warnka, the countess, had turned out to be the over-all winner. I was second ahead of Stefa. The competition had been good for all of us and it was satisfying to record a result, so little in those days had a logical conclusion.

It took seconds to gather my 'things', but I waited an hour before someone came to fetch me. We spent the time discussing what might be happening to me this time. A transfer to another camp possibly? I hoped so. Or perhaps, I would return to Cell 17 and I would see Mother again? According to Liska, she was thankfully, still alive and well.

Our guesses did not prove to show much foresight. When the guard eventually collected me, we headed for the de-lousing hut. I handed in my blanket, my towel, food bowl and wooden clogs. Having done this, I then had, what I must admit, was a very big surprise... A fur coat was given to me; not any old fur coat, but my own fur coat and my shoes with my stockings still rolled up inside them. The shoes now barely fitted my feet. Nearly nine months of wearing clogs had encouraged lumps where lumps ought not to be. I was ordered to put the coat on over my prison clothes and I must have looked truly comical, with my bald head topping the spectacle.

'What could all this be about?' I wondered. The uncertainty was immensely frustrating. My destination was certainly not Cell 17. That much I did know.

A black limousine drew up and I was ordered get in. One of the guards climbed in behind me and settled himself on the back seat beside me. As the car moved off, he propped his rifle against the door and placed the leather briefcase that he had been holding on the floor between his feet. As he leant back in the seat, I recognised him. It was the same young man that had protected me when I lost consciousness during the brick shifting exercise, the boy with the girlish face and the big, dark eyes.

I guessed again. It was to be another interrogation, Gestapo house, marble staircase, red carpets, the cell, more beating, slapping and hitting. I knew what it would be like. I knew! But the car failed to turn into Ritterstrasse. It drove across Wilhelm Square to the main railway station where my guard told me to get out and follow him. From the questions he asked at the information desk, I understood that we were on our way to Marienburg. 'Marienburg?' I thought. 'I've not heard of a camp there.'

Strange?' I felt both excited and curious. Sitting opposite my young guard in the waiting room, I ventured to ask him whether he was permitted to tell me where he was taking me. He had shown sympathy and not hit me when he had an excusable opportunity and I hoped that he would sympathise now and give me a constructive answer. He did not give the impression that he really belonged to the masochistic SS guard's unit in Poggenburg. If anything, he seemed naive and I could not help but wonder how old he might be. Twenty maybe, I guessed. 'Too young to have forgotten what his mother had taught him about love and strong enough to withstand the influence of his uncivilised compatriots in the camp.'

He removed his cap and laid it on the bench beside him. Without it, he looked even younger, a boy who had been dressed up in a uniform. He smiled at me, shyly, as though slightly embarrassed and addressed me with the formal 'sie' as if it was the most natural thing to do.

"We are travelling to Königsburg! Your presence is required there to give evidence at a court martial." He said no more. Perhaps, he knew no more. Perhaps those that took orders from the German authority were kept as ignorant as those that were in their charge.

Aboard the train, my personal guard made his way to the dining car. I trotted along demurely in his wake. The waiter took his order and the required coupons from his ration card. I felt very self-conscious. Everyone was staring at me; whispering pointing and gossiping. A voice inside my head tried to excuse them.

'They don't know... oh, how much they don't know! Poggenburg lies in a shallow valley. It cannot be seen from the road. It is well hidden. Many things are well hidden.'

The aromas of sauerkraut, dumplings and pork invaded my nostrils. The waiter had arrived with his dinner and my eyes feasted on the plate that was placed on the table. A glass of beer too, descended from the waiter's tray. 'If I could only nibble taste just one of those dumplings,' I thought forlornly. 'And a sip of that beer! Dear God – I've had nothing but thin soup for what seemed like a lifetime.'

The guard must have seen the look of yearning on my face. He smiled as though apologising, recalled the waiter and retrieved his ration card from his wallet. Unbelievably, he was ordering another plate for me. For me!

I felt the excitement build within me until it glowed, a burning fire of anticipation. The prospect of the chance to hold a knife and fork and to attack a plateful of real food. The very idea made me almost sick. The bliss! I ate and ate... and ate.

My guard could not help but smile at my vain attempts to keep my ravenous hunger in check. How I warmed to that young man. When I began to slow down, he took a packet of cigarettes from his briefcase, extracted a single cigarette from the packet and lit up. The packet was new. There were twenty-four cigarettes in it and I wondered if he would leave me an end that I could reclaim from the ashtray. But again, he observed my interest in what he was doing and pushed the packet towards me. The curious stares of the people around us caused him some embarrassment, but he offered me a light and I inhaled, once, twice, three times. A wonderful intoxication swept through my whole body.

'This young man is wearing the black uniform of the demons,' I mused. 'He is one of "them". He has probably shouted and punished when he is with the others. But, when it comes to the "Day of Judgement", then young man, I shall stand before the Almighty Judge and put in a good word for you.'

We reached Marienburg at one o'clock in the morning. My bald head had caused quite a sensation on the train and my escort solved the problem by somehow acquiring a silk scarf. It was as much relief for me and as it was possibly for him, to become a little less conspicuous. People did not stare as much.

We travelled on to Königsburg in the staff compartment. The ticket inspector was absent most of the time and we were able to stretch out on the wooden benches. We did not talk in the presence of the inspector and the packet of cigarettes was soon finished. But once we were alone, my companion produced an envelope containing loose tobacco with some cigarette papers and proceeded to manufacture his own brand. He also produced some sandwiches from his briefcase and inviting me to help myself first, he ate what I left!

"You know that in Königsburg, they may well decide your destiny?" he had stated out of the blue. After a moment's thought, he asked me why I had been imprisoned and what did I have to do with a court martial. In reply to his first question, I gave a short account of my usual story, but I could not answer his query about the court martial. I did not really know what a court martial entailed, so what I had to do with one, was a mystery to me.

"I was court martialled once in Fulda. I was eighteen," he said. He offered me one of his rolled cigarettes as he continued to elucidate. "I went straight from High School to the army, a year before the final exams. Maths was not my best subject," he confided, "but I'd have managed. My dream was to become a pianist, although that was probably a bit ambitious. But, instead of entering the School of Music, I ended up in the front line of the Druezbasin; close range fighting, flame throwers, tanks, Stalin organs (multiple rocket launchers). It was six weeks training, then in at the deep end." He paused. "I'm not a coward, but everything happened so quickly. One day, I ran in the wrong direction, towards the Russians – quite by mistake, I assure you. Anyway, one of my unit stopped me by shooting at me. Fortunately, he only winged me and that's how I know about a court martial."

I had not interrupted him while he was talking. He seemed to need to explain himself. I no longer thought of him as my guard. He was just a troubled young man who possibly for the first time was pouring his heart out to someone. I would have done him good. A prisoner made an excellent 'wall' to talk to. There was no danger that an echo would reverberate.

"I was transferred to the Dirndlwanger Brigade. Have you heard of it?" There was resignation in his voice. "It's a probation unit. They couldn't shoot me, I was too young. I arrived in the Dirndlwanger and put into an SS uniform because I was too young to be shot. Ironic isn't it? We were dispatched to wherever hell had broken loose. When whole villages had been burned down, the Dirndlwanger Brigade was brought forward to exterminate the survivors. When I was shot in the lung and became useless for front-line duty, they sent me to the backwaters. They gave me the Iron Cross, first class and transferred me once again, this time to the guard unit, Poggenburg."

A wistful expression came into his eyes. "I wonder whether I shall be too old to go to the School of Music when all this is over?" The train was slowing down by the time he had concluded his story and we chugged past houses on the outskirts of a town.

Another day was dawning. He got to his feet and buckled on his belt.

"Get ready, we're nearly there," he said with some impatience, perhaps regretting that he had been so open with me. He checked his rifle. A café near the station was just opening up. The chairs were still on the tables, but we had plenty of time. I was not due to appear in court until eleven o'clock. My guard ordered coffee and crisp, fresh rolls for breakfast for us both. Afterwards, he asked me to wait, while he went to the barber for a shave!

As soon as I was left alone, my situation rapidly became clear to me. 'I could escape!', I realised. 'I could get up from the table and walk away and no one would stop me. This boy, this big soft boy, had gone off with his rifle, as if it were a walking stick, leaving me on my own, unguarded, unfettered and free to run. What did I care about him? Did he think he could buy my loyalty with a few cigarettes and a full stomach? He was a pleasant enough lad and the first thing they would do with him when he returned without me, would be to change his uniform for prison dress. Did that really concern me?'

'Königsburg!' I pondered. 'I have never been here before, but there must be a hole here somewhere into which I can crawl.' I was not fussy any more. Camp life had somewhat reduced the expectancies and standards that I had been used to before the Germans had taken charge of my homeland. The blue prison trousers would not necessarily give me away. People in Germany itself were not as well dressed as they had been before the war. But, another thought hit me.

Had this sentimental fellow given me the chance to escape on purpose? Would he be surprised to find me waiting for him when he got back? Then the voice of caution chipped in.

'Perhaps the whole thing was a trap? Had my guard been specially chosen for the job, with his soft hands, slim wrists and innocent, dreamy eyes? Could he be concealed in a doorway perhaps... watching me... ready to shoot at me as soon as I emerged on to the street? Would he be triumphant at the success of his mission?' They were sobering thoughts. As I sat there, a lone woman, sipping her morning coffee, I remembered my mother, still in the camp at Poggenburg. Even if I was successful in my bid to escape, to what perils would I expose her? They would 'interrogate' her mercilessly. They would take their revenge and she would pay the price of my freedom. She was still in their control and a hostage for my cooperation. I knew, she would have told me to run, to grab this God-given chance. But I knew too that I would be condemning her to death and the price was too high.

No daughter has the right to expect her mother to forfeit so much.

Hence, I was still there when my guard returned from the barber. It was apparent that the thought that I could have escaped in his absence, had not entered his head.

"What do you think of these?" he asked triumphantly, and pointed at his sparkling boots. A shoeshine boy attending to his footwear, it seemed, was more important to him than worrying about whether his charge had taken advantage of his carelessness and absconded.

It was time to leave.

39

We were directed to the side entrance of the imposing courthouse in Königsburg. I waited, while my guard reported our arrival. The door to the office was left ajar and I overheard a voice saying, "Weychanowna?" There was a pause and a rustle of paper. "Yes here it is. Kurzke versus Weychanowna. You'll have to wait. The case against the paymaster hasn't finished yet. Go to the waiting room next to the courtroom on the first floor. You will be called when they're ready."

As I climbed the stairs and walked down the long white corridor, I could hear only 'Kurzke versus Weychanowna' tumbling over and over in my brain. 'The hearing is 'Kurzke versus Weychanowna'. Of course...Herbert!' Why on earth had I not made the connection before? I was apprehensive and at the same time hopeful. How stupid I had been, a court martial could only have applied to Herbert if I was to stand as a witness. My hopes soared, as I realised that he must be in the building. But I was fearful that he would not recognise me with my shaven head and battered features and that he might turn his back on me. He would disown me.

Suddenly he was there, standing by the tall double doors that led to the courtroom. I could not manage to suppress a cry of recognition. He turned. He had heard my voice and immediately he strode purposefully towards me. My guard clicked his heels and stood to attention. Herbert still wore the uniform of a Hauptmann.

He took my hands in his. He gave no greeting; offered no embrace, but just stood in front of me with a look of bewilderment on his face.

"Who hit you?" The scars on my cheek were obvious. "...and where is your hair?" he added with incredulity in his voice.

'How little you know, you dear, dear, ignorant man!' I thought. 'How very little you know.'

I saw the door open. I saw the tears in his eyes. I touched his sleeve. My hand was shaking.

"Don't admit anything, Herbert. You can trust me. Don't confess to anything." I said quickly.

A voice bellowed out across the room.

"Hauptmann Kurzke!" He turned away. I found a bench by the wall and sank forlornly on to it. The room seemed to have become misty; the forms in it, obscure and distant. Like a child in innocence I began to pray to God and the Holy Mother Mary. I needed so much to know that they were with me... that they were supporting me.

"Weychanowna, Maria Theresa!" again the voice rang out.

I heard my name called and my body rose obediently and went through the double doors, but I did not see the courtroom. My eyes would not focus properly. It swam away, everything and everybody in it was blurred and undefined. Only with concentrated effort could I see the belt and pistol which lay on the table in front of the judge. Were they Herbert's? I tried to find him among the rows of anonymous pink faces and eventually, I found the chair of the accused. There he was, sitting alone, behind a latticed screen.

"Come forward!" The command was uttered by the man with grey sideboards and many wrinkles; the man with plaited epaulettes and horn-rimmed spectacles. A thick file lay open on the table in front of him.

"Your name, please!"

"Kurzke, Maria Theresa!"

"I mean your real name!" The eyes behind the spectacles looked up sharply and glared at me. I returned the stare. I would not be cowed so easily. I knew that I had to stand firm. I felt my wits sharpen and the instinctive impulse to fight, to defy the inevitable.

"Who I am and what my name is, must already be known to you," I retorted. "There is therefore no sense in denying that my name is Maria Theresa Weychanowna."

"Born?"

"January 4th, 1922!" I replied. I answered those initial questions honestly. We soon got to the more complicated part of my 'story'.

"How long had you been living in Germany? "

"Since February, 1940."

The gentleman seated beside the judge put his elbows on the table and rested his chin on his hands. With raised eyebrows he peered at me expectantly and asked, "And what was your occupation there?" An ironic smile played about his mouth.

The directions in which the questions were leading filled me with dread. It was one that I needed to avoid at all costs. I tried to divert his attention by offering the information in my own way.

"May I be allowed to briefly tell you the story of my life, because I fear, that you may have been misinformed."

The judge smiled behind his glasses, exchanged an amused look with one of his associates and nodded his head.

"Please, be my guest!" he invited. His manner suggested that he really meant 'Let's see what you are going to serve up for us, we are curious'.

I did not get side-tracked. I had been in a Gestapo prison for eight months. I had been beaten and tortured and no reason or explanation had been given. Now I was standing in a court room. It was a real courtroom with a dock, witness box, judge and public prosecutor, exactly as I had seen in films. I was going to make them listen to my point of view by speaking up for myself. "My mother was born in Germany," I began. This was actually true although her parents were polish citizens from Posen. "During the Great War she returned to Poland and married a man in Posen, but she made sure that I studied German as a child and was brought up in the German tradition." My training in the theatre was suddenly becoming extremely useful. I concentrated hard to develop my new role.

"Like all German nationals, living in Poland, we were obliged to become Polish citizens. Since there were no German schools, I attended a Polish boarding school. Admittedly, my father was a Polish patriot, but this caused my parents to separate. My mother's heart has always beaten for Germany. I paused for good effect and, reminding myself to speak slowly and clearly continued, "My mother used to write to me in German while I was at the boarding school and quite early on, I was given the name 'Schwab'. The name stayed with me and I was still referred to as 'Schwab' when I appeared on the stage. Feelings became so strong, that I was once openly accused of collaborating with the Germans and was nearly arrested in Gotenhafen. I managed to escape, thanks to a Pole with fascist sympathies." I was now in full flow, blending half-truths with blatant untruths and altering the sequence of events to suit my purpose.

"When my Mother and I returned to Posen from Warsaw after the blitz, we found that our home had been destroyed and looted by Poles who were aware of our political loyalties. We immediately applied for German identification papers and received notice to wait." It was time to mention Herbert, which had to be done in such a way that no blame could be laid on his head.

"At about this time, I met Herbert Kurzke." I said as innocently as I could. "I knew that it was forbidden for Germans to associated with Poles, so I pretended to be a German national. In December 1939, I met a Pole who supplied my mother and me with forged German documents. At the time it was our only option. The German offices had not been established and I wanted to follow Herbert, who had been transferred back to Germany. We travelled without difficulty to Hamburg in February 1940 and received identification papers on the strength of our travel documents." With all the references to different papers and documents, it would be very difficult to check back on the accuracy of this part of my statement, however, the next piece of my evidence would have been recorded.

"I was a member of the NSV and volunteered for the women's force." It's amazing how one can twist a meaning in the translation! "I was rejected by them because I was already employed in an essential occupation with an industrial firm. When Herbert was posted to Berlin, my mother and I followed him and I worked at the AEG." I paused and noted that the courtroom was hushed. I had their attention.

"Then Herbert received notice that he had to go to the front and we got married!" At this point, the Judge interrupted and the questions began.

"I am informed that you worked at the UFA film Company. How did this come about?"

In reply, I described how I had been approached by a producer on a train.

"Didn't you have to produce your Aryan certificate before signing your contract?" queried the judge.

"I had a letter from the Gausippenamt in Posen, saying that my application was still being processed." I replied. The judge nodded studiously and signalled for me to continue.

I told him about the new ruling from the headquarters in Berlin, which meant that all Germans who had been living in Poland in 1937, had to produce papers from the appropriate Polish authority. How we had thought it best to return to Poland ourselves to sort things out once and for all, but during that visit, we had been arrested.

"Did you have any contact with Poland while you were in Berlin? Displaced persons in work camps and such like? For instance... the people who gave you the suitcase?" We had arrived at the crucial point. It had in fact been my mother who had been in contact with these people and she had not involved me in any way. The eyes behind the spectacles were cold and expressionless.

Looking him boldly in the eye I replied. "An elderly lady spoke to me, just as I approached the ticket barrier to board the train to Posen. She told me that she wanted to send some things to her severely disabled son who had lost everything in Posen. She begged me to help her as she could not find any other way to get the suitcase to him. I agreed to help, but I can see today that I should not have taken pity on her."

I had rehearsed my story ever since I had first been arrested, grooming it until all anomalies had been removed. I was confidently word perfect and not even the piercing gaze of the judge could cause me to falter.

"If you were as sympathetic as you profess to the German cause, why did you not belong to a secret organisation?" He was still probing. I reminded him that I had been seventeen when the war broke out and that my interests and ambitions had been in the direction of a dancing career.

"Can you swear that Herbert Kurzke knew nothing about your forged papers?" The judge had suddenly changed his line of questioning.

"Yes!" I answered trying to be as emphatic as I could.

"Why didn't you tell him about it?" he snapped.

"I loved him too much and was frightened of losing him." I reasoned.

"Why?" the Judge spat at me.

I took a deep breath before replying. "The Herbert Kurzke that I knew was an upright officer. He would have acted against his personal feelings, had he known everything." There was absolute silence in the court room. The judge, his chin still cupped in his hands, was gazing at the top of his desk. He looked up and directly at me. He seemed to be deep in thought. My story had impressed him. The expression on his face had lost all suggestion of mirth or derision. I decided to play one last card and asked him politely whether I could be granted a final request. He nodded his head.

Unaware of the irregularity of my actions, I stepped closer to the tall desk. It was an audacious thing to do, but 'I' was no longer in control; I was part of a courtroom drama, playing a role in a film which must roll on to its celluloid conclusion.

Looking up at the judge I said, "I am not concerned about your verdict with regard to myself. I realise now that I have become guilty because of my great love for Herbert. Maybe I am the only one..." I could not go on. The immensity of the situation caused me to faulter. Old and half forgotten childhood dreams stirred; Napoleon, Alexander, Koszuski and the Maid of Orleans. I sensed her standing beside me, her flag flying high above me in the wind. Blown away, was the stale air of the courtroom. "...maybe I am the only person who knows that no officer could serve his country with more enthusiasm and sincerity than Herbert. If all soldiers were as dedicated to their duties as he is, Germany would win the war." The judge remained silent. I became aware of his eyes, watching me, critically assessing my performance. Abruptly, he gathered his papers and stood up. His eyes still held me in a steady gaze and I boldly returned his challenge. I would not admit defeat and pleaded silently for my cause.

The court rose.

40

I had tried. While the Judge was out of the courtroom, I waited in a state of mental exhaustion. I had given everything. I could do no more.

I am slowly realising that everyone is standing; the recording clerks; the officers behind me; my guard and over there... over there, behind the grill... Herbert. They all seem to be moving in slow motion as though the air has become like water and is impeding their movements.

The judge is returning through the door at the side of the courtroom. He is followed by his assistants looking like marionettes in their neat, tailored uniforms. He waits until everyone is seated again and an expectant stillness settles on the courtroom. I wonder whether the gentleman with the grey sideboards and owlish spectacles had to translate Heroditus in his school days. Maybe since then, he has had to read many papers, regulations and statute books and has forgotten most of the classical literature of his youth. But I remember that Xerxes ordered the skin of the bad judge to be stretched across the seat of judgement.

"Please God! Let this be a wise judge!" I beg of my maker.

The man on the seat of judgement, turning the pages of the file in front of him, was a human being just like you and me. He cleaned his teeth, occasionally got his fingernails dirty, wore slippers and probably appreciated a hot-water bottle on cold nights. He was in short, a man like any other, with little weaknesses and odd habits. By the law of the land, often incomprehensible to the ordinary person, he had been given the powers to decide whether Herbert was to be a free man or whether he or I or perhaps both of us should die.

The spectacles peered at me again and I heard his voice say, "I do not know, Maria Theresa Weychanowna, whether you are aware of the fact, but you have already been sentenced to death by the Secret State Police for aiding espionage. I now confirm this verdict and sentence. They will be informed in Posen."

The arm belonging to the plaited epaulette, waved dismissively in the air, my guard tapped me on my shoulder and led me from the room.

At last, I had heard what was in store for me. The uncertainty was over. I did not scream. I did not faint. I was neither worried nor frightened, for as I left the courtroom I had seen that they were giving the belt and pistol back to Herbert.

I had succeeded. He was free!

As I walked down the corridor with my guard, I heard hurrying footsteps behind us.

"Excuse me, madam!" said a deep voice.

'Was he addressing me?' I wondered doubtfully. 'Was someone making fun of me now that I was condemned? Who could be so unkind?' I turned my head and recognised the wing commander who had sat beside the judge in the courtroom.

"My name is Dr Strohmeier." He glanced up and down the corridor and looked my guard straight in the eye. He must have approved of what he saw in the 'doe-eyes' for he continued, "Herbert is a good friend of mine. We were at school together. I would like to give you the chance to have a few words with him, but we must be discrete. Wait by the ticket office at the station." More to the guard than to me, he said, "You cannot leave before tonight anyway." The young head under the SS cap nodded.

As we walked along the road on our way to the station, 'doe-eyes' remarked, apparently with genuine enthusiasm, "A great guy, that wing commander!"

We loitered as bidden by the waiting room. When the car drew up, I could see Herbert and Dr Strohmeier in the back seat.

Rudi, the ever cheerful chap from Cologne was behind the wheel. The doctor and Herbert climbed out as soon as the car slid to a halt and making no sign of recognition, they walked away together. Rudi waited for a few minutes, then, casually signalled to us to approach and get into the car. We drove to Dr Strohmeier's house and there Rudi ushered us into a comfortably furnished lounge. He then disappeared to retrieve Herbert and his good friend.

Dr Strohmeier arranged that Rudi and my guard should go to town together until the evening. Before leaving Herbert and me alone, he promised me that he would do all he could for me. He would delay the posting of my file for as long as possible and suggested that I gave my false name and addresses at any further hearings which would take time to check out. In his opinion, the present stage of the war was such, that a delay could be enough to give me back my freedom in the near future. Even the army lawyers, it seemed, did not comprehend the true state of their law as practised in Poggenburg. I hoped his delay in returning my file would be sufficiently long. I did not have much faith in the 'hearings' ever happening.

He shook my hand to confirm his good intentions, offering a firm grasp full of sincerity and sympathy. He then excused himself, leaving Herbert and me alone.

After so many months of dreaming of how life could be and living in sub-primitive conditions, the pleasant room, the flowers, the wallpaper and curtains seemed almost obscene luxury. It seemed that I had dreamt of this moment for as long as I could remember.

I sat on the soft, upholstered sofa, holding his hands in mine and broke down. I wept uncontrollably. Herbert wept unashamedly with me. If tears are the symbol of deepest grief and greatest love, then both were shed together in that room.

Most importantly, he was free, absolved from all blame. The few words that I whispered to him before the hearing had helped him to decide his plea. He had stated that he did not know that I had no claim to German papers and denied having given me false papers. Our testimonies had coincided sufficiently to convince the court. Illustrating the true spirit of the man, he was still caring for Vera. Despite all the anxiety concerning his pending trial, he had continued to shelter an unregistered foreigner with his sister.

Frau Strohmeier served us a meal; the best that she could find was on the table. Afterwards, she tactfully withdrew and left us alone for a few precious hours.

The tears had been shed. Herbert took me in his arms, our lips met and we became as one. Later, I was content just to hold his hand as his fingers tenderly traced the scars of torture on my body.

Rudi and 'doe eyes' returned in the evening, bearing a vast treasure of goods. Herbert had given them all his ration tokens! Frau Strohmeier made parcels of the food for our journey back to Posen and we drove to the station. Herbert bought two first class tickets and a pile of magazines "to keep you occupied while you're locked up," he said.

It did not seem to enter his head that I should not go back. I had left him in ignorance about Poggenburg. There did not seem much point in worrying him unnecessarily, for he would surely have disgraced his uniform by doing something unforgivable, ending up in the same position as myself.

'No, my dear husband, my beloved, it is for the best that you know nothing.'

I thought to myself. 'You have taken my hairless head in your hands and kissed my ugly scars with the same tenderness that you kissed your eighteen year old bride. You could not know how fearful I have been of our meeting again. It could have been so different and the hopes and dreams that have inspired me for so long, could so easily have been shattered if you were not the wonderful man that you are. But now, our love has passed the last great test and now, now I am very happy.'

Poggenburg seemed a very long way away. A final embrace in the corridor of the train; a last memory of him as he stood on the station platform, his arms dangling limp by his sides, a picture of dejection as his tall, slim figure became smaller and smaller and then disappeared from sight as the track swung away from the platform.

You had been acquitted, but had received orders to report for duty on the eastern front in the morning. You no longer believed in victory and my innermost feelings told me that you would be looking for death and find it. The tide was turning. It is still difficult for me to understand you. As a German male, you were brought up very differently. False ideals of honour and duty, how they hammered them into you! You still felt guilty, which you should not! It is the idols that were held aloft for you to venerate in your boyhood that carry immeasurable guilt for trampling on the dignity of men and preventing real justice.

I regret now that I did not tell you about Poggenburg, the commandant, the barbed wire cones, Liska, Stavosta and the rest of them.

You did not recognise the devil, Herbert, yet you lived in his shadow.

41

My fur coat had been hung back on its peg in the barracks next to the de-lousing house, where all the civilian clothes of the surviving prisoners were hung and I was back in E-block, in cell number 1, lying on my back. Like my companions the countess and the Jehovah's Witness, I gazed at the ceiling as though nothing had happened.

I did not attempt to bring in the magazines, but I had managed to smuggle a packet of cigarettes and some matches into the cell and we smoked during the night. I still had five left. In a fashion, we had celebrated a belated Christmas. Little else had caused my two cell companions any diversion. But the next day, I was to bid farewell to them both once more. I never saw them again.

That same day, I once again joined my old friends from Cell 17 on the truck and went back to work in the munitions factory. Everything resumed the old pattern and I once more supervised the prisoners on my floor. Snow was back with us again and the temperature had dropped well below freezing. Herr Blum gave me some warm clothes; a scarf and a pullover that I would give to my mother. For the moment, I had carefully wrapped both the woollen scarf and the pullover around my body under my shirt. We had to be very careful to conceal the extra layer of warmth from everyone. In the camp, the same clothes were worn, summer and winter alike. There was no concession to the seasonal changes.

It was a relief to slip back into the old routine among people that I had come to love and trust. The deprivations of the prison removed all protection from the soul, yet far from weakening our resolve, the group of women that had lived together in that cell for so long, formed an increasingly profound bond of understanding. All levels of society were represented in the group, but each one supported her neighbour.

Old Stepanska was nearly seventy. She was a kind generous soul who was the only woman in Cell 17 who had actually been aggressively active against the Germans. Most of the others were there either because their husbands were

Polish officers or patriots, or because they were caught up in the wave of arrests at Mosina.

Old Stepanska had been an orphan. She had no family. She had never known her mother or father and had never been married. She grew up amongst Romany gypsies and had learned from them how to tell fortunes from cards. She also learned to value her freedom and when the Germans came and dragged the gypsy folk from their caravans and put them to work in factories, she revolted, escaped and joined the partisans. The partisans fought for freedom and with them, she lived much as she had done before, in the open beneath the stars or under canvas. Again she told fortunes with the help of her cards, this time to the men before they went off to fight.

Old Stepanska is telling my fortune with the 'cards' that she has made out of scraps of paper on which she has drawn various designs in pencil. There is no official light source in the cell. We are not permitted lamps, but Mother has brought a sliver of wood from the kitchen. The wood has been soaked in a liquid which causes it to glow with as much light as a candle.

Old Stepanska squats beside me in the light of the make shift torch. She tells me to shuffle the pieces of paper and lift them to my heart, three times.

'If only I could believe you, Old Stepanska! You are predicting freedom. Freedom... in a year's time. You are predicting happiness and a dark-haired man that I will marry. You see water... I will travel across water. But you don't talk of Herbert. You cannot see him! But you do predict enjoyment for the near future; a surprise re-union with a woman who is dear to me.'

Suddenly the door was flung open. Liska's high pitched voice screamed; "Attention!" It was too late to extinguish and hide the 'torch'; too late to clear away the 'cards'. The long haired dachshund bustled around the corner, followed closely by its master.

He neither shouted at us nor remarked on the light. He walked towards Stepanska and pointed at the cards with the toe of his boot.

"Do they belong to you?" he asked.

Old Stepanska, standing to attention, nodded her head. "Yes Commandant, sir!"

The commandant strolled casually across the cell to the window. Looking out through the bars into the night, he asked; "Can you guarantee what you read in the cards?"

"I do, with my life, sir!" she replied, her eyes bright with conviction.

"I want you to tell my fortune!" said the commandant, the suggestion of a smile creasing his face as he turned towards her.

He did exactly what I had done. He shuffled the cards then lifted them to his heart, three times. Old Stepanska carefully placed each card down in front of her; each card important in its role of spelling out the truth of fate. Her expression became serious, then hard. Her eyes narrowed to slits. The light from the burning wood flickered over the wrinkles on her hands and the features of the commandant's face. Abruptly, she swept up the cards and stuffed them into her pocket. Her face was expressionless and she stared vacantly into the distance.

The commandant prodded her with his boot. He commanded her to say something, but Old Stepanska did not move nor even try to open her mouth. He pulled her to her feet.

"Will you tell me! What is it? Are you afraid that I might believe you?" There was a note of anxiety in his voice.

"It is better for me to keep quiet, Commandant sir."

The man, in his immaculately tailored uniform jacket and elegant breeches, bowed and laid his hand gently on the old woman's shoulder.

"Tell me the truth! I am not made of marzipan. Don't hesitate. Tell me what you saw. Good fortune is not predicted in your cards, eh?"

"You won't grow old, Commandant sir!"

He seemed slightly amused and smiling, he bent down to pick up his dog before asking; "I am to die... well... and when may I ask? When old woman?"

"Within the year, Commandant sir!"

His smile remained, but it had lost its confidence. The muscles in his jaw tightened.

"And how? Have you any idea , how?"

"I saw...I saw a rope, Commandant sir!"

The rest of us listened with bated breath. Any minute now, I thought, he would knock her to the ground and kick her mercilessly. He would kick her for as long as he kicked the young Russian last week... until she was dead.

But, nothing happened. The commandant looked up at us and on seeing the fear on our faces and in our eyes, smiled his normal smug, self-satisfied smile.

"Liska," he said. The guard officer snapped upright to attention.

"Stepanska is to be given meals from the officers canteen, for one week." With these astounding words still echoing in our ears, he marched out of the cell, the dog under his arm, wagging its tail as though in ridiculous comment.

42

Shots are fired. Dogs bark and shouts echo through the night. All is fairly quiet for a moment... only distant footsteps and muffled voices... until the bell rings.

The bell wakes everybody. It means that we have to get up and go outside to line up in the exercise square. The time is 1.30am "Attempted escape!"

The message whispers its way from the columns of men. Another prisoner has thought that he could take no more. To attempt escape from Poggenburg was a futile exercise for the simple reason that there was absolutely no hope of succeeding. The camp, situated where it was, was completely secure.

We did not think very highly of these 'suicide candidates'. As soon as their absence was noticed, the whole camp had to assemble for a roll call. This would be the initial move on the part of our captors. The next orders would oblige all the prisoners to stand in ranks, without rations, until the escapee had been recaptured. It usually took a few hours, but there had been occasions when we had stood for two days. They always found them in the end. Hunted by dogs, their clothes torn and covered in blood from the beatings they received from the triumphant guards, they would be hauled back to the camp. The unfortunate deserter, if he was still alive, would then be dragged onto the parade ground, where he would be beaten and kicked to death in front of us all.

The prisoner that had tried to escape on this particular night, had succeeded in climbing two of the three fences, behind the Jews' quarters, where the grass grew long. He had managed to get past the electrified central fence, but at the third, the search light had picked him out and he was gunned down in a hail of flying lead.

Two prisoners carried his body into the compound. The face was covered with blood and it was impossible to tell whether he was old or young. We had stood for three hours that chilly night on his account. When I saw his bullet ridden body surrounded by the milling dogs, I could not help but feel sympathy for him and a solidarity with the other inmates. He had been a human being, one of us.

They carried out one of their wooden coffins – they called them 'meat boxes' – and the dead man was bundled into it, naked. We all had to report for work immediately after that. There was no time for washing or breakfast. Besides, they had a third treat for us that morning.

The 'meat box' and its contents were placed across the narrow gateway that led to the little square in front of the commandant's hut. We were then herded with flailing whips and truncheons down the passageway and through the narrow opening. Some stumbled and fell on top of the corpse in the scramble. Attached to the genitals of the dead man was a note for all to read. "You escape. You are dead."

It was a relief to get back to the munitions factory and sit once more opposite Herr Blum in his little office. There was always a bunch of flowers on his desk, even in winter. I often suspected that he put them there for my sake, to cheer me up and to remind me that roses and carnations could still bloom. Even the grass and buttercups had given up within the confines of the camp.

I had said nothing about the incidents of the previous night, but he must have guessed from my sombre expression, that the beast of gruesome experience had once again been on the prowl. He was particularly thoughtful and kind that morning, but his eyes revealed great sadness, concern and sympathy for my mood. He had some news for me too that morning, which under normal circumstances would have made me overjoyed. It was a contact with the life I had led seemingly a hundred years ago. Herr Blum told me that he had managed to get in touch with Vera's sister and that he had invited her to come to the office on the following day so that I could meet her. I should have been ecstatic, instead I wondered at the generosity of the man. He was not satisfied with handing out charity. He had dared to actually 'do' something for me, confirming that there were some very good Germans that had not lowered their human values.

Vera's sister, Pelagia, was in the office next morning as promised. Herr Blum left us alone and stood watch outside the door. Intelligence is not always shared equally amongst the children in a family and compared to Vera, her sister was not as clever. She was certainly rather vague in her knowledge of important things. Vera apparently, was now staying with Herbert's sister at Bad Kreuznach, where she was still in hiding. It had become too dangerous for her to remain at his mother's house where she had sought refuge after the arrest of Mother and I. Of Herbert, she had no news. I was desperately disappointed and paid little attention as she rambled on about times past, how when Vera had taken me home to their house, she had carried me in her arms. I became a little more interested when she turned to the subject of the farm, the fields and my stallion. He was still at the stables at Stiruzki and had been ridden by nobody else since I had left for Warsaw. How long ago it seemed.

She promised to write to Vera on my behalf and… all too soon, we had no more time. Herr Blum re-entered the office. He apologised and said, "Someone will become suspicious if I stay away from the office too long." He was right of course and a few minutes later, a woman in a plain woollen dress and white head scarf left the factory.

The cards did not lie. 'Your first prediction has come true, Old Stepanska.' I thought triumphantly. Although I had not learned much, I was glad to have had some contact with a friend from the past. Maybe I would eventually get a reply to my letter to Herbert. Herr Blum had said that he would post it and now, I trusted him implicitly. What I did not realise was that this was to be my last day at the munitions factory.

When we returned to Poggenburg that evening, my name and my name only was called out and I was escorted to the camp office.

'What do they want of me this time?' I thought. 'Dear God… is it possible? Has confirmation of the death sentence arrived? No! Another interrogation? Has someone spied on me and reported? Do they know about my letter? Have they been watching Blum?' The questions raced through my brain.

I was delivered to the room of the officer in charge. He was waiting for me with two of the SS guards and Liska.

"Get undressed!" the guard officer of our cell hissed.

She felt the woollen scarf as soon as I had unbuttoned my shirt. She grabbed it and pulled it off me.

"Who gave you this?" she wanted to know.

I admitted that it had been given to me by a Polish worker.

From beneath the table, she drew a pullover and flapped it in my face. It was Mother's. With the approach of another winter, Herr Blum had given me the clothing to provide some warmth against the colder weather.

"Have you seen this before?" she screeched.

"Yes!" I replied.

"Who gave it to you?"

I told her that it had been in the same parcel as the scarf and that I had given it to my mother. The senior SS officer proceeded to roll the clothes up in a ball as though the episode was closed. He had accepted my explanation and for him the matter was resolved.

"So you have no idea, where these clothes came from?" he said in conclusion.

At this juncture, the commandant walked in. He asked whether I had confessed to which Liska, the unpredictable Liska, replied to the negative. The commandant observed me for a minute without speaking, tapping the toe of his boot pensively with his whip.

"OK! I'm sorry, but you are asking for trouble." He prodded me in the chest with the end of his whip. "Take her to the ice-cellar."

We processed across the yard. High on the bank, a number of prisoners bearing heavy wooden beams on their backs were being chased around in a never ending circle by their guards, like horses on a carousel.

I barely noticed them, I was too frightened for myself. I knew what the 'ice-cellar' meant. The little medical student had been there only last week and I had seen her when she had been brought back to the cell. We entered the low barn behind the windowless building that housed the death cells. The wire-mesh carts for transporting corpses were kept here and in the concrete floor, at the back of the shed, was a metal trap door. The guards opened it and pushed me down into the gaping black hole.

I hear the trapdoor being closed above me. I hear the commandant's voice call down to me, "Perhaps this will teach you a lesson, young lady. Let us see what your friends can do for you now."

I feel pain from the fall and then I feel the icy cold air creeping over me.

In the pitchy darkness, a terrible fear paralyses me. I sense that I am not. I do not exist... perhaps I was stunned for a moment, by the fall. I cannot tell. In total darkness, it is difficult to know about time. Without light, there is nothing... only the ability to touch and hear remains.

Gradually, I realise that I am lying in water. The icy chill starts to freeze my legs and arms. I try to move and my overall clings like wet chamois leather to my body. I push myself up from the floor and slowly, carefully stand erect.

I can hear the tracker dogs in their kennels and I start to examine my inky black prison with arms outstretched. The walls feel wet and slimy. The water covers my ankles and makes slight splashing noises as I shuffle forward, slowly drawing breath in the dank, lifeless air. The cell would seem to be little more than two metres square and empty; no bunk, or chair, or bench. But as I move about carefully, my fingers groping over the joints and knobbles of the wall, my leg knocks against something solid. I bend down to investigate the object with my hands and feel a face, a face that is cold, clammy and belonging to a very dead body.

'So this is the little shock treatment that the gentlemen in the commandants office have rigged up for me.' I thought. 'What they have forgotten is that I have got quite used to death and corpses during my sojourn in Poggenburg. One dead prisoner means much the same as a living one. The one could perhaps be envied. He was beyond further suffering. My feelings on the matter had become dulled to indifference. That indifference to the presence of the corpse was my saviour. My next thoughts involved my own survival.

"The only way to get my feet out of the water, comrade, is to sit on your legs. I'm sure you won't mind. You'll understand," I reasoned with him, talking aloud, as though he could hear me. "After all, you are one of us and who knows what they did to you before you decided to quit. I cannot see your bruises and sores. I don't know whether you are young or old. But I do know that your suffering is over. You cannot feel anything now, not even indignation that they use your corpse to scare me out of my wits." Is it necessary to say that they left me with my silent companion all night? The following day, they pulled me out, soaking wet, frozen and exhausted.

The first beating is always the most painful. Those that follow are only fractionally worse. You, the reader, may be alarmed or shocked by the first account of an atrocity. Further horrors do not have the same impact. The mind just cannot comprehend more and more of the same. It becomes dulled by repetition and cannot grasp any enlargement.

The commandant was eating his breakfast when they hauled me before him. He was feeding his little dog bread rolls with thick butter on them. He told me that he knew about Blum, that the unfortunate man had made a full confession.

"As to your affair with him... How often did you oblige him in his tidy little office?" He did not look at me or make any attempt to observe my reaction to his accusations. It was clear to me that he paid only casual notice of me as he attended diligently to the requirements of his dog.

I had eaten nothing for over twenty-four hours. The butter looked so yellow and the bread rolls must have been freshly baked for they made that lovely crunching sound in the hands of that monster.

If he had identified Blum and was able to put a name to him, he must have known something about Blum's help. How much had the spy discovered and how much Blum himself had really 'confessed', I could only guess.

I remained silent. For my insolence, I was thrown back into the ice-cellar with my dead friend for a further two days and nights.

When they finally took me out, I was semi-delirious. The presence of my dead companion had been one thing. He had not been exactly talkative and his inertness had been a constant reminder that I was still alive. It was the utter darkness that had affected me badly. I had become totally disoriented without visible clues and my mental and physical state had suffered as a consequence.

I was put to work in the 'Russian' gang. The work that they had to do seemed to me to be non-sensical. I was the only woman amongst a host of men. We had to carry boxes of wet sand, at the run of course, over a distance of about three hundred metres to another heap of sand. As I remember, when I got to the second heap, I emptied my box and in my confused state tried to refill it again before running back. I did not have the strength to lift the box. My companion, a young man from the Caucasus mountains tried to help me, but I was beyond caring and could not be bothered to cooperate.

Liska appeared on the scene and started to shout at me. It eventually dawned on me that she wanted me to follow her. I remember the guard laughing, but cannot remember why. Nevertheless, he allowed me to go with Liska. She led me back to the barracks and unlocked the door to Cell 17.

"Take a rest, you stupid woman! And don't you dare say anything about this to the commandant!" She spoke like a teacher, admonishing a wayward child... Liska, the unfathomable.

The door slammed and I was left alone in the cell. This one, however, contained no corpse and daylight filtered through the dirty window.

43

I do not remember much about the next couple of days – only fleeting moments and impressions. Sometimes, when I was lucid, my mother was beside me but, often, I was alone. I had survived for over eight months with a death sentence lost in the post somewhere. I had learnt to live each day with the threat that tomorrow my life could be abruptly ended by a bullet. I had adjusted to this possibility and was resigned to the fate that destiny had ordained for me. But now destiny was threatening to change its mind. I was in real trouble. For a while, it looked as though the ice-cellar had destroyed me.

I only came to know what actually happened by what Mother told me afterwards. Apparently, death was beckoning when she first found me. Liska had sent her a message that I had been returned to the cell and Mother had managed to find an excuse to absent herself from the vegetable garden for a short while. She was horrified by the crumpled heap that she found curled in the corner of the cell. I was burning with fever one minute and shivering violently the next. My lips were white and my face flushed. She had tried to make me as comfortable as she could before returning to her duties. When she came back to the cell that evening, I had been sick, throwing up bile and was complaining of severe stomach cramp. Dr Gorska and Mother between them had virtually carried me out to the parade ground for roll call that evening. I do not remember them doing so. A bitterly cold wind had been blowing across the square and that, I do vaguely recall. Thankfully they had not inspected the ranks.

The following day an extraordinary event took place. For the first time ever, roll call was cancelled. Further, all the lorries that normally transported the prisoners to external work sites, failed to collect their daily cargoes.

Liska, the chameleon that she was, once again changed her colours and was looking after me, almost mothering me. When they carried me back to the cell on that first day of my illness, she had brought me hot tea and warm blankets. And in spite of the fact that it was forbidden to stay in the cells during the day, she made no attempt to move me out.

Old Stepanska fell ill that evening.

She had worked all day with the gang clearing the first of the winter snow and because the guard was not satisfied with her efforts, she had been forced to remove her shirt, exposing her frail body to the chill temperature with only a worn vest for protection. Stavosta had decreed that if she worked harder, she would keep warm!

Two patients in one cell was too much for Liska. 'Patients' should have been reported to the sick room, where the lethal injection would cure all ills – permanently. The inhabitants of the cell closed ranks. They helped us both out to the evening roll call, Mother and Marja Gorska again holding me erect while other woman supported Stepanska in the back row. She was trembling from head to foot and fell down twice, but again fortune was with us and the guards did not notice.

Dr Gorska could not help us without medicine. By the following morning, my mouth was so swollen that I could not swallow or open my lips and my legs would not bear my body weight. I remember the feeling of light-headedness – I no longer cared whether I held on to life or slipped gently away to drift forever beyond pain.

It was decided that it was pointless to try to get me out to the parade ground for roll call and it was hoped, as so often was now the case, that the guards had become bored with the mundane repetition of the exercise and would skimp the count so that they could get back into the warm as soon as possible. Fortune was on my side.

Stepanska's condition deteriorated during the night. By morning, she was delirious and shouting noisily. "Go on! Shoot them down, the dogs!" she yelled out repeatedly as though she were leading a group of partisans into battle. She too missed the roll call. I remember feeling very low spirited, lying there, waiting for the other women to return. Stepanska was ranting on in crazy delirium, oblivious of the danger, but I was very aware, that at any moment, the guards could come in and carry us both away for ever. It was a great relief when Mother returned and assured me that the morning assembly had been uneventful and that Liska had again concealed our absence.

And there she was again, peering over Mother's shoulder – Guard Officer Liska; Liska, the unpredictable. In one hand she held a tin of hot tea, in the other a little bottle of medicine with 'Goldwasser' inscribed on its label.

"Keep your mouth shut about this!" she had snapped at Mother. "I got it from the SS barracks! It wasn't easy!"

She had counted out some drops for me and a similar dose for Stepanska. The old woman had asked for more and received another ten drops. I had great difficulty forcing even a few drops down my swollen throat and declined a second helping. Mother was left in charge of the bottle and Liska had told her to repeat the dose at midday. But by midday, Stepanska had looked a lot worse. She was frothing at the mouth and her breathing was shallow and noisy and she thrashed about in great pain. I was not as feverish as I had been, but I was aware that my stomach hurt and that it felt heavy as though I had feasted on lead.

Mother had become very anxious about us both. She did not like our bright red faces and the way our eyes seemed to be popping out of our heads. She had fetched Marja from the coal bunkers during the midday break, to hear her opinion.

Dr Gorska had taken one sniff of the medicine bottle and promptly poured the contents out of the window. She had wanted to know how much we had taken and shaken her head despairingly.

"It was poison!" she said. "Undiluted poison!"

That evening, guard officer Liska came into the cell to enquire about the progress of the 'patients'.

"Better!" was Mother's response. "Thank you for the medicine." I could hear the heavy sarcasm in her voice. Liska, however, was not capable of playing the gruesome comedy to its conclusion.

"What! They aren't dead yet?" she squawked and, grabbing the empty bottle, ran.

Poor Stepanska died an hour later. Mother stroked down the lids over her staring eyes and afterwards remained by my side filled with remorse. She had so nearly killed her own daughter. I felt nauseous and wretched. Later that night, the pain in my stomach eased and I managed to drink some cold coffee and nibble a piece of bread.

By the morning, I could once again stand unassisted and was steady enough on my feet to attend the roll call. I also had to go to work, as the death cart was expected to visit the cell to collect Stepanska's body. I would almost certainly have been discovered and removed to where all 'patients' should be. Liska must have decided that it was not my destiny to die yet awhile and if that was the case, perhaps she would be more helpful in assisting me to live. She transferred me to the laundry gang where at least it was warm.

I must admit, that until that day, I had never washed anything for myself in my whole life, not even a handkerchief. There had always been a flotilla of maids to deal with such things before the war and Vera had coped when my style of living had been reduced in the Warsaw apartment. Now I was ordered to wash one hundred towels, fifty shirts, five overalls and ten blankets in one day... and all by hand! I was not worried about fulfilling the quota. Not knowing anything about it, I was undaunted by the task, but I did find that the revolting stench in the hot, steamy laundry filled me with disgust. Each prisoner was issued with one small, coarse, linen towel which was changed every six weeks. Overalls and underwear had to last for three months! The evil odour that was emitted by the boiling washing was indescribable. The towels invariably emerged from the boiler as dirty as they had gone in and by the time the huge tub was filled a second time, my fingers were already sore. There was no soap, only some ineffective soap powder. Most of the shirts were stained with blood which had to be rubbed off first and we had to scrape the lice and their eggs out of the seams with the aid of a spoon.

As soon as the guard left, the elderly woman next to me pushed a brush towards me. Brushes were forbidden. They wore through the fabric too quickly. But she told me not to worry and to throw it into the tub with the clothes, should the guard return. Everything had to be scrubbed at least three times before being boiled again. Those with experience could recognise the clothes that had been worn by prisoners locked away in solitary confinement. A Jehovah's Witness showed me the shirt of a high-ranking Polish officer. They must have attacked him with axes, judging from the chunks of dry, crusty skin that stuck to the cloth.

Laundry workers received double rations, but that first day, I could eat nothing. Gradually, I began to feel better despite the obvious drawback of my inexperience at the wash tub. The warmth of the laundry was a bonus and my strength steadily returned. It was apparent to me that there were distinct advantages to be gained by working there and I tried hard to create a good impression on the supervisors in the hope that I would be able to continue washing those filthy rags.

I had been in the smelly hot house for about a week, when I felt something hard sewn into the jacket of a civilian suit. I tore the lining and found a piece of a cigarette box. The pencilled message read;

"I Stanislaus Napiorkowski, solicitor, born 12.6.12 in Buszikow, shall tomorrow, 2nd January, 1944, be executed by firing squad."

I still possess this piece of cardboard and although I have not found any of the family to date, perhaps his message will find its destination through these pages. The same afternoon, new prisoners arrived. Among them was a man with one sleeve dangling empty from his shoulder. Blum!

They had dragged him out of his tidy little office to serve a sentence of fifty-nine days. Fifty-nine days in Poggenburg for a few apples, a little milk, a letter, a shawl and a pullover, was an expensive price to pay. Herr Blum was a human being amongst a host of evil monsters yet they had to degrade and humiliate him.

44

Every day, I stood in line on the parade ground for the roll calls and every day I worked in the laundry. At night, I told the women about my trip to Königsburg and the news that even the Germans were talking of an early end to the war. Over and over again, I tell them.

Everyone was gladdened to hear news about life outside. Another world still existed beyond the barbed fences. It seemed to have so little relevance to the circumstances in which we were forced to live.

Throughout the summer, the rumours had reached us of the Russian advance. Germany was losing. Germany was retreating. My mother was able to pick up a lot of the gossip during her visits to the various camp kitchens. When the others fell asleep, I would lie close to her and we whispered. I still wondered what had become of Herbert and it was a relief to tell someone. Mother was a good listener.

We discovered the reason for the cancelled roll call and lorry transports from Mother when she returned to the cell one evening. She had overheard Stavosta talking to an officer.

The commandant, who always carried his whip so elegantly, who wore boots of the finest shining leather, breeches of the latest cut with his fashionably tailored jacket; our noble commandant had hanged himself during the night in the privacy of his room, boots, breeches, jacket and all.

Your cards predicted well old Stepanska.

The news that the Russians were in Lublin reached us as Christmas approached. "The Russians are in Lublin!" The message rustled through the hut like a dried leaves stirring in a soft breeze. It was the best and most handsome Christmas present that we could receive. We turned the gift this way and that before we began to unwrap the meaning of it. It meant that a good part of our beloved Poland was already free. It meant that our German guards would have to flee; that we would soon be rid of our tormentors.

A packet with five cigarettes has been smuggled into the camp and they passed from mouth to mouth on Christmas Eve. We were not permitted to make a noise, but we hummed the old tunes. The familiar melodies winged their way softly through the cell, a gentle reminder of Christmas days long ago, when we had no idea that a place like Poggenburg, its horrors and its barbed wire, could exist. There were no candles, no Christmas pastries, no glass baubles, but it was Christmas just the same; perhaps our happiest, most beautiful Christmas ever.

We were not required to work on the two days over Christmas. It was not a holiday for our benefit. Oh no! We were informed that the guards needed time off for the festival and that there were not enough of them left on duty to watch the different work gangs.

But the guards never returned at all. Instead, we saw more and more elderly men, apparently German nationals, who had been put into uniform overnight. The front line was throwing its shadow over Poggenburg. The younger men had been ordered forward to the weakening defence. Hitler had started to use his last reserves in a desperate effort to stall the progress of the Russians.

On New Years Eve, they started to burn files outside the office.

Mountains of paper were consumed by roaring flames.

The prisoners had not been out of their barracks for a week. We saw fewer and fewer guards on duty. The officers were now distributing the bread and gruel themselves. Everyone was packing and carrying boxes. Guard officer Liska was trying to transfer her purloined assets, the coats and dresses, to Posen. She was becoming stupid with fear and seemed to spend all day knitting.

She was looking after us like a mother hen, hoping that we would forget the evil past.

The Russian advance also, however, endangered the prisoners themselves. Anxiety grew. Would we be handed over to them alive? All the staff in the commandant's barracks knew that their future was in jeopardy. Would they, when the time came, take everyone down with them, as criminals are prone to do when every escape route is closed?

On my twenty-third birthday, the 4th of January 1945, Liska told me and my mother to gather up our few belongings and go with her. She locked us in the 'discharge' barrack for the night, together with five men. Was it transportation... another camp? Many of the prisoners had been transferred during the past few weeks. But, early the following day, we were driven in the 'black maria' to Gestapo House, Ritterstrasse in Posen. There, we were all locked inside a single cell. I had been here before, hanging upside down from the hook in the ceiling.

Another interrogation? Had they received my file from Königsburg? Perhaps the wing commander could not prolong the delay any longer!

No one paid any attention to us all day, or during the following night. It was as though our presence in the building had been forgotten. We had tired of discussing our situation and fallen silent, when we heard a key turn in the lock and the cell door was flung open by a civilian. His hair was tousled, his shirt was torn and his face was alive with excitement as he stood, legs apart in the doorway.

"Raus! Raus!" he shouted.

Can we believe what he is saying? Mother tried to ask him what was happening. "Get out, fast!" he muttered in Polish. "I am here to release members of the resistance! You're lucky!" Mother froze. We all stared in disbelief.

He hardly looked like the angel of peace. Was this another trap; another kind of torment, they had conjured up? Did they want us to run so that they could shoot us in the back? Where were the machine guns? Why, comrade, are they using you?

We go, for we must go, but we go slowly. Why should we please them by running if they intend to shoot us anyway?

The lights are ablaze. The white marble entrance hall, with its red carpet, stairs and corridors, are filled with feverish activity. Everyone is hurrying about with boxes, suitcases and back packs, in shirt sleeves, their jackets awry. They have shed their arrogance. It has blown away like chaff in the wind. They are the quarry now. They are on the run and do not waste time looking back over their shoulder.

In stunned silence at the crazy activity surrounding us, we troop in single file past the marble staircase with its plush red carpet and shuffle demurely out through the front door. No one accosts us, though they brush past, hastening in the opposite direction, their arms laden.

We rush around the corner and fall into each other's arms. Incredibly, we are free! Fortune has lead us out of hell... It was so simple!

But, caution! It would be too conspicuous to sing and dance, we must behave like shadows. We disperse and Mother and I seek a private house for shelter. We are lucky, the family welcomes us and gives us clothes to replace the prison overalls. We thank them earnestly and leave to find more permanent refuge with one of our friends.

It was not until we were safely installed in the home of one of Vera's sisters, that we stopped to think of the momentous events of the day. We preferred to remain in the bedroom, where the smallness of the room made us feel more secure. Every knock at the door or ring on the bell made us tremble. Like mice we hid, quivering in a hole, fearing the prowling cat outside. We still could not believe that we were truly free.

The next day, we ventured out again and could see with our own eyes that our fears were unfounded. They were not looking for us any more. They had no time left to concern themselves with such trivia. They were too busy abandoning the town in their cars, running for their lives.

Mother decided that before the final collapse, we too must get to Germany; to Hamburg or Berlin. Our few belongings and jewellery were there; we had nothing left in Posen. There too, we would find Vera and possibly Herbert.

I could hear shooting, somewhere to my left. The Russians were closing in and fear of the Russian and his disregard for life and property added wings to my feet. On my way to the police station, the sporadic gun fire reminded me of the first days of fighting in Warsaw. We had to get out fast – before everything caved in. I knew the danger. I had had enough time to study it. I was now making use of that knowledge.

At the police station, I told the official that I was a secret agent and my department had left in a hurry. The Poles, I assured him, were after me and my mother like wolves and we needed to get back to Germany at once.

He did not argue or procrastinate but filled in his forms with accomplished ease.

Mother and I duly received certificates stating that we, 'German nationals', must travel to Berlin, where we must report to Gestapo HQ. We were even entitled to army rations. The little piece of paper entitling us to food represented a small but very satisfying revenge. It was not much, but we were as pleased as successful pickpockets.

The streets near the railway station were packed with people, adults and children. Everyone seemed to want to get out while there was still time. They had been queuing all night, camping in the road, between the tram lines and on the pavement. Undeterred, Mother found a policeman and he escorted us through the crowd to the ticket office, our piece of paper and the fact that we had no luggage, helped. A solid wall of people was waiting at the ticket office. Our way was blocked. But our bodies, lean from a prison diet, flexible from practise in the wire cones and hurdling over 'meat boxes', slithered through, round and over the two meter high barricade of human flesh. The platform on the other side of the gate was also packed tight with a seething mass of people. The wailing of lost children and bawling parents added to the din.

Only goods trains waited in the station. But suddenly an SS train came hissing past the platform and disappeared behind clouds of steam as it stopped.

"Stand back there. Stand back! Army transport only! No one is allowed to get on the train," shouted the station master.

Railway officials pushed the crowd back. But I squirmed forward. A policeman grabbed me, but he did not have the firm grip necessary to detain a 'dangerous political criminal' and I slipped easily from his precarious hold and dashed for a door. The crowd roared in protest, but before the policeman could catch up with me and before the station master in his red cap could reach me, I had given my piece of paper to one of the SS man who was guarding the door. I briefly told him my fairy story about being hounded by Poles and he allowed me to board the train, ordering the policeman to clear a path for my mother.

My coat was torn and I had nearly lost the head scarf that I had wound around my head, turban fashion to cover my short hair, but... we were both safely aboard.

The train was so crowded with soldiers that we had to stand on the iron platform between the carriages. Snow blew in through the gaps in the canvas, concertina roof, but after the Poggenburg parade ground, it was heaven. Besides, we were rolling towards Berlin.

The SS officer who had let me on board is offering me a cigarette, a very good cigarette out of a blue packet, of the kind that I have not seen since the beginning of the war. We buy our first newspaper at the Schleisischer Bahnhof in Berlin and read that the army is admitting in print that, last night, Posen was attacked by the Russians.

As we travel in the suburban train to Alexander Platz and walk towards our apartment through streets ruined by bombing, I am profoundly aware that people are fighting and dying at this very moment in Königsburg, Breslau, Gdansk, Kostrzyn, Cologne, Mannheim and other towns and villages of the Luneburger Heath.

War had raised its ugly head in a last desperate madness, like a mortally wounded monster that is bleeding profusely. It had reared up its head for the last time, wildly attacking and destroying everything within reach, before sinking down to die on earth, soaked with the blood of its final orgy.

Berlin knows of the two thundering tidal waves that are speeding towards it from east and west, threatening to bury its very existence. The swell is getting stronger, the roar louder. Bombers and hunters attack continuously from cloudless skies. They appear like seagulls before the incoming tide. Roads are ripped up and barricades of bricks, iron girders, wrecked cars and broken furniture grow across the highways. Bridges are destroyed and everyone is digging trenches and holes in the parks and along the avenues. Women, children, old men and invalids are all at work. There is no exception.

"Hannibal ante Portas!"

From the Latin teacher at school, I had learnt, a million years ago, the crippling effect of those words. Today, it is not ancient Rome that trembles before the aggressor bent on revenge. Today it is a modern city with wireless sets, telephone exchanges, high power cables, cinemas and water closets. But the panic is similar. We find our apartment had been closed down after our arrest.

The furniture and all our possessions had been removed in a lorry. In the whole of this enormous city, there is not a thing that we can call our own, not a bed, nor a chair, nor a tube of toothpaste.

Food is a problem. There is none! I have found a bicycle and early in the morning, I travel in the luggage van of the local train to Potsdam. From there, I can cycle into the country with my rucksack on my back. I usually manage to bring home some bread and vegetables from my trips. Cycling along the lanes, beside green meadows or in the shade of flowering trees, I begin to comprehend the meaning of freedom; at long, long last, I really am totally and absolutely, free.

Everything had happened in such a matter of course fashion since the escape from Ritterstrasse. The doors of opportunity had opened in timely succession with such ease. It was not a dream, but events had followed each other in such quick, neat order, as though the hand of destiny had control. There had been no time to think; to appreciate and realise the import of our actions.

The most unbelievable, long nurtured ambition of freedom had suddenly become a reality. No more tears, cells or barbed wire. No Poggenburg! Our nightmare had vanished and with it our fear. We had not hugged each other. We had not cried, nor shouted for joy. We had accepted it in the same way that we would have done had Liska sent us off to another work gang or as the gas man would call to record the meter readings.

Alone with my bicycle, riding down a country lane, I am becoming aware of the wonderful fact that freedom is mine. Death has retreated into the far distance; I am free. During the past two years, Mother and I had been able to speak to each other only in whispers, with hand over mouth, but now, now as I'm cycling along, I sing! I sing and shout, bursting with joy, the wind caressing my face.

The full realisation of my happiness is racing through my veins to fingertips and toes. I cycle faster and faster and sing louder and louder, with neither sense in the words nor melody. It is a passionate, rousing song. I feel like pulling the trees out by the roots, just to test the strength of my power. I believe I could do it!

Even when the tidal waves finally met over Berlin with the thunder of bombs and buildings crashing to the ground, even then, the joy remains within me. I am not afraid for my life. Heaven has not given me back my freedom so that I should be crushed by falling masonry. Life had been given back to me for living, not for ending abruptly with these foreign people in their dying city.

Unbeknown to me at the time, Herbert's life did come to an end during the final assaults on Berlin. I like to think that he died on the night that I went outside after an air raid and looked up at the stars, bright in the sky; that perhaps those twinkling stars, shining so innocently down on the crumbling city, were the last things that he had seen.

Vera is with us again. It was she who brought the news of Herbert's death. She had heard that a teacher had been with him in a trench on the outskirts of Berlin and I managed to find him to speak with him. When he saw me, he put down the hammer and took up his coat. He and some of his pupils were trying to repair a classroom, ravaged by a bomb. He told me that he thought Herbert had been hit by machine gun fire. He had not seen it happen, but he had been found dying in the bottom of the trench.

Those that survived the tornado that split the earth, taking so many lives, those human beings are indeed the chosen ones. They received the most precious gift, a gift that was denied many thousands who passed through the hands of the fiends of Fort VII and camp Poggenburg. When the Russians neared Posen, the few German guards that had remained in the camp, poured fuel over the wooden huts and set them alight. The prisoners inside perished. Anyone who tried to escape from the burning buildings was gunned down.

A chauffeur, a man who in peacetime had ferried diplomats for the Polish Embassy in Berlin, told us what had happened. He lost his wife in the flames of Poggenburg. When he finished his story, we could not speak. Mother took my hand and squeezed it hard. I understood and was filled with a profound gratitude and relief.

Dear, beloved Life!

END

POSTSCRIPT 2022

War in the 21st century is a terrifying prospect. The weapons that have been developed since WWII have the potential of killing hundreds of thousands of the world's population in one strike and destroying the atmosphere for millions more. Today, the human race has the capacity to annihilate itself.

"Never again" is a cry that blows away in the wind as another autocratic despot rises from the ranks to beat the drum of war.

While national, political and religious 'tribes' continue to attempt to impose their will by force and fire power, wars will continue.

Russia was not called to answer for her war crimes after WWII for she was allied to the victors. Stalin should have been in the dock alongside the accused Germans. His persecution of the Slavic tribes in Poland and the Ukraine had not been as methodical as that of the Germans, but it had been as destructive. It was not until 1989, when Communism imploded, that the west began to access information about what really happened in Eastern Europe.

When the 'Wall' came down that year, the USSR lost its influence over the vast tracts of Eastern Europe that she had occupied since 1945. During the last months of WWII, Russian troops had swept through Poland. Hungary and East Germany, destroying everything in their path. Cities, towns and villages were flattened by heavy bombardments. Machinery was smashed or removed, homes were pillaged and set ablaze and anything in skirts was raped. The Nuremberg Trials ignored these crimes. Poland, the country that had suffered most, was not permitted to give evidence.

Concealing the truth by laying blame on others seems to be a Russian tradition. For example, Stalin lied about who was responsible for the Katyn grave. Red Cross representatives were present when the Germans disinterred the site in 1943 and reported back to their HQ in Switzerland that the decaying corpses had been buried for more than two years. The authorities in Western Europe knew the truth, yet the myth persisted until 1990 when Russia admitted guilt and disclosed the existence of two previously unknown mass graves of Polish civilians that between them, held over 14,000 victims. Russia was never called to account.

Today, modern technology has moved the goal posts. Drones spy from the sky and western television broadcasts daily visual evidence of the Russian tactics. They have changed little since 1945.

The communist system, imprisoned their occupied territories behind a political and cultural wall of non-communication during the so-called Cold War. Individuals that crossed that barrier into the Russian zone of influence were usually arrested and 'disappeared'. It was as though the Russian State could be contaminated by Western ideas and as such, they threatened its security. 'Prawda', the State newspaper, was carefully groomed to present the Truth according to the Kremlin; a truth that denied criticism and moulded opinion with distortions and deceit.

The Internet has made it harder for Russian leaders to hide the truth.

The nursery tale of the Emperor's New Clothes takes on new significance. Today's emperor is clothed in a fabric that has been carefully designed by his courtiers; a fabric that is woven from a web of lies and disinformation. How long will it be before the Russian population realises the elaborate regalia worn by their trusted leader, is fake?

Index for key names and places

Abwehr – the German Intelligence.
AK – (Arme Krajova) the National Underground army, led from London.
Canaris, Admiral Wilhelm – Head of Abwehr and Abwehr IV (foreign division).
Davies, Norman – Britain's leading historian about Poland.
Königsberg – now Chojne.
Krakow – Cracow.
Lange – gas bunker operator in Fort VII.
Lichtmanstadt– now Łódz.
Piekenbrock – head of Abwehr I (military division).
Poggenberg High Security camp – now Zabikowo.
Posen – Poźnan.
Pospieszalski – Polish historian.
Siatka 'A' – (Network 'A') German anti-Nazi resistance group in Poland.
SS/SD – (Sicherheitsdienst) German security divisions.
Szymanski, Halina – Abwehr agent in Switzerland.
Walter, Heinz – Poggenberg Commandant.
Wiebek – Inspector of prison camps, member of Siatka 'A'.

Population of Poland on 1st September, 1939............35,000,000
Population of Poland on 1st February, 1946............14,800,000

This book is printed on paper from sustainable sources managed under the Forest Stewardship Council (FSC) scheme.

It has been printed in the UK to reduce transportation miles and their impact upon the environment.

For every new title that Matador publishes, we plant a tree to offset CO_2, partnering with the More Trees scheme.

▲ MORE TREES
LET'S PLANT A BILLION TREES

For more about how Matador offsets its environmental impact, see www.troubador.co.uk/about/